ENCYCLOPEDIA OF INDIAN PHILOSOPHIES

ENCYCLOPEDIA OF INDIAN PHILOSOPHIES
General Editor: Karl H. Potter

I. **Bibliography [Sections I and II] (1995)**—Ed. *Karl H. Potter*

II. **Indian Metaphysics and Epistemology:** The Tradition of Nyāya Vaiśeṣika up to Gaṅgeśa (1977)—Ed. *Karl H. Potter*

III. **Advaita Vedānta up to Śaṁkara and His Pupils (1981)** —Ed. *Karl H. Potter*

IV. **Sāṁkhya:** A Dualist Tradition in Indian Philosophy (1987) —Eds. *Gerald James Larson & Ram Shankar Bhattacharyya*

V. **The Philosophy of the Grammarians (1990)**—Eds. *H.G. Coward & K. Kunjunni Raja*

VI. **Indian Philosophical Analysis:** Nyāya-Vaiśeṣika from Gaṅgeśa to Raghunātha
Śiromaṇi (1993)—Eds. *Karl H. Potter & Sibjiban Bhattacharyya*

VII. **Abhidharma Buddhism with to 150 A.D. (1996)**—Eds. *Karl H. Potter,* with *Robert E. Buswell Jr., Padmanabh S. Jaini & Noble Ross Reat*

VIII. **Buddhist Philosophy from 100 to 350 A.D. (1999)** —Ed. *Karl H. Potter*

IX. **Buddhist Philosophy from 350 to 600 A.D. (2003)** —Ed. *Karl H. Potter*

X. **Jain Philosophy [Part I] (2007)**—Eds. *Dalsukh Malvania & Jayendra Soni*

XI. **Advaita Vedānta from 800 to 1200 A.D. (2006)**—Ed. *Karl H. Potter*

XII. **Yoga: India's Philosophy of Meditation (2008)**—Eds. *Gerald J. Larson & Rama Shankar Bhattacharyya*

XIII. **Nyāya-Vaiśeṣika Philosophy from 1515 to 1660 A.D. (2010)** —Eds. *Sibjiban Bhattacharyya & Karl H. Potter*

XIV. **Jain Philosophy [Part II] (2012)**—Eds. *Karl H. Potter & Piotr Balcerowicz*

XV. **Bhedābheda and Dvaitādvaita Systems (2013)**—Eds. *M.M. Agrawal & Karl H. Potter*

XVI. **Pūrvamīmāṁsā Philosophy (2014)**—Eds. *K.T. Pandurangi & Karl H. Potter*

XVII. **Jain Philosophy [Part III]**—Eds. *Karl H. Potter & Piotr Balcerowicz*

XVIII. **Dvaita Vedānta Philosophy**—Ed. *Karl H. Potter*

XIX. **Acintyabhedābheda Philosophy**—Ed. *Karl H. Potter*

XX. **Viśiṣṭādvaita Vedānta Philosophy**–Eds. *Stephen A. Phillips & Karl H. Potter*

XXI. **Buddhist Philosophy from 600 to 750 A.D.**—Ed. *Karl H. Potter* with an introduction by *Eli Franco* and *Karen Lang*

VOLUMES UNDER PREPARATION

Buddhist Philosophy from 750 to 1300 A.D.—Ed. *Karl H. Potter*

Kaśmīr Śaiva Philosophy—Ed. *Navjivan Rastogi*

Advaita Vedānta from 1200 A.D. to the present—Ed. *Godavarisa Misra*

Cārvāka Philosophy—Ed. *Eli Franco*

Śuddhādvaita Vedānta Philosophy—Eds. *Sharad Aniruddha Goswami & Shyam Manoharaji Goswami*

Vīraśaiva Philosophy—Eds. *N.G. Mahadevappa*

Collective Glossary-Index—Ed. *Karl H. Potter*

ENCYCLOPEDIA OF INDIAN PHILOSOPHIES

Volume XIX

Acintyabhedhābheda
Vaiṣṇava Philosophy

Edited by
KARL H. POTTER

MOTILAL BANARSIDASS
SINCE 1903 IN INDOLOGY

MOTILAL BANARSIDASS PUBLISHERS
PRIVATE LIMITED • DELHI

First Edition: Delhi, 2015

ISBN: 978-81-208-3997-7

Also Available at:
MOTILAL BANARSIDASS
41 U.A. Bungalow Road, Jawahar Nagar, Delhi 110 007
8 Mahalaxmi Chamber, 22 Bhulabhai Desai Road, Mumbai 400 026
203 Royapettah High Road, Mylapore, Chennai 600 004
236, 9th Main III Block, Jayanagar, Bengaluru 560 011
8 Camac Street, Kolkata 700 017
Ashok Rajpath, Patna 800 004
Chowk, Varanasi 221 001

MLBD Cataloging-in-Publication Data
Encyclopedia of Indian Philosophy Vol. XIX
Acintyabhedhābheda Vaiṣṇava Philosophy by Karl H.Potter
Includes bibliography and index
ISBN : 978-81-208-000-0
I. Philosophy II. Acintyabhedhābheda Vaiṣṇava
III. Potter H. Karl IV. Encyclopedia V. Indian Philosophy

Printed in India
by RP Jain at NAB Printing Unit,
A-44, Naraina Industrial Area, Phase I, New Delhi–110028
and published by JP Jain for Motilal Banarsidass Publishers (P) Ltd,
41 U.A. Bungalow Road, Jawahar Nagar, Delhi-110007

CONTRIBUTORS

Arthur Avalon (Sir John Woodroffe)
Umesh Chandra Bhattacharji
Narasimha Brahmachari
Ramakanta Chakravarti
Chinmayi Chatterjee
Surendra NathDasgupta
Susil Kumar De
Edward C. Dimock
Stuart Elkman
Krishnagopal Goswami
David L. Haberman
Isvaradasa
Klaus Klostermaier
Bruce Martin
Bhaktivedanta Narayana Maharaja
Joseph T. O'Connell

PART ONE

INTRODUCTION

INTRODUCTION

Gauḍīya Vaiṣṇavism in Bengal*

By Ramakanta Chakravarti

"Epigraphic evidence of the worship of Viṣṇu or Kṛṣṇa in ancient Bengal is meager and often rendered complicated by contradictory interpretations. It is also quite difficult to identify any definite cult or sect in them.[1]

"Vaiṣṇavism in Bengal assumed a tangible form only during the century of the Sena dynasty (A.D.1100-1206) which was of Kānārese origin. The pristine *bhakti* movement of the Deccan had already been set on a firm basis by Ācārya Rāmānuja. The influence of the *Śrī-Vaiṣṇava* doctrine might have percolated into Bengal at this time.[2] In the twelfth century A.D. Jayadeva composed the *Gītāgovinda* in which *Śrī-Vaiṣṇava* influence and that of the *Brahmavaivartapurāṇa* (composed in the seventh century A.D.) may be discernible.[3] The songs of the *Gītāgovinda* attach a greater importance to Rādhā than to Kṛṣṇa. The extant modes of rendering the verses of this work into songs are of Kānārese origins.[4] These facts may be regarded as an indication of the influence of the Deccanese *bhakti* movement. But the philosophical aspects of the Vaiṣṇava faith of the time are not definitely identifiable. A synthesis of the ancient *Vyūha* and *Avatāra* doctrines might have taken place.[5] But yet the fact was that Jayadeva had put considerable emphasis on the erotic aspects of Rādhā-Kṛṣṇa worship. Stray verses had been composed on this particular theme in the past.[6] But what were the forces which led to the composition of a whole, ornate *Kāvya* on this motif? According to Suniti Kumar Chaṭṭerjee,

---

*Ramakanta Chakravarti, "Gauḍīya Vaiṣṇavism in Bengal", Journal of Indian Philosophy 5.1-2, 1977, 107-149. Reprinted with the permission of the publisher.

Jayadeva, who was probably not a Vaiṣṇava, derived his theme from a pre-existent 'vernacular lyric drama'.[7] But the origins of erotic devotionalism may be found in the Kṛṣṇa legends of the *Padma,* the *Bhāgavata,* and the *Brahmavaivarta Purāṇas.*[8] The sculptures on the basement of the Pāhārour temple which depict the main events of the life of Kṛṣṇa indicate the popularity of the Kṛṣṇa cult in Bengal during the Pāla period, from the middle of the eighth century to the beginning of the twelfth.[9] It is quite reasonable to suppose that Jayadeva's motif was not unknown to contemporary Bengal. Poor pilgrims sang the songs of Rādhā and 'Mādhava'.

"The Bengali poet named Dimboka composed the following verse on this theme:

> The pilgrims in the street have warded off the painful cold with
> their broad quilts sewn of a hundred rags;
> and now with voices clear and sweet
> they break the morning slumber of the city folk
> with the songs of the secret love of Mādhava and Rādhā.[10]

The earlier epigraphic records hardly mention the lives of Rādhā and Kṛṣṇa. Suddenly, in the twelfth century Kṛṣṇa appears in the ornate poetry of eastern India as a supernatural lover of the milk maids. Jayadeva might have set the pattern which was followed by the poets of the contemporary anthologies. Ācārya Govardhana, a contemporary of Jayadeva, wrote a good number of verses on the loves and the supernatural achievements of Kṛṣṇa.[11] Both Aniruddha Bhaṭṭa and Halāyudha, two eminent compilers and interpreters of the *Dharmaśāstra* wrote short but significant manuals on Vaiṣṇava rituals. The importance of the Vaiṣṇava religion is emphasized in the contemporary *Bṛhaddharmapurāṇa*; Vaiṣṇavism was used to bolster up non-vedic or puranic faiths. According to one authority some *paṇḍitas* of Mithilā went to Assam (Kāmarūpa) and 'tried to aryanise the country by means of Vaiṣṇavism.'[12]

"But the aspects of the Kṛṣṇa cult of the twelfth and the thirteenth centuries are not very distinct. The Kṛṣṇa worshipers had to wage a long war against the Tāntric Buddhists and the votaries of Śiva-Śakti.[13] Tāntric Buddhism was decadent; its dying traditions were somehow kept up by a number of secret societies which practiced the worst forms of licentiousness.[14] The main opponents of Vaiṣṇavism were the devotees of Śiva-Śakti.[15] According to D.D. Kosambi the Śiva-Śakti cult was patronized by the rich landowners while Vaiṣṇavism was popular among the peasantry.[16]

The Pāikpāḍā-Vetkā-Vāsudeva image inscription of the time of Govindacandra and the Maḍanapāḍā and Madhyapāḍā Copper Plate inscriptions of Viśvarūpasena 'show that the merchant community as a whole (including betel-growers) showed their inclination to Vaiṣṇavism'.[17] But the social affiliations of these sects are not always definitely identifiable. The Vaiṣṇavas had, however, clearly neutralized the Buddhists by accepting the Buddha as an incarnation of Viṣṇu.[18] The legend of the Vaiṣṇava incarnations of the Buddha was current even in the fourteenth century. With the beginning of the powerful Caitanya movement the Buddha, at least in Bengal, was finally consigned to limbo.[19] The Vaiṣṇava emphasis on the idea that Rādhā was Śakti *par excellence* of Kṛṣṇa might have stemmed from the *Śakti* theory of Tāntric Buddhism. The Vaiṣṇavas also accepted the Śakti-Śaiva idea in a modified form. But while the worshipers of Śakti believed in the predominance of the female Śakti over the male gods, the Vaiṣṇavas regarded Śakti as the most essential attribute of Viṣṇu-Kṛṣṇa, the Supreme God.

"The growing strength of Vaiṣṇavism in Tirhut-Mithilā and Bengal is seen best in the development of vernacular Vaiṣṇava poetry. Early in the fifteenth century, Vidyāpati, the Court Poet of Mithilā, wrote in Vajrabulī language a large number of excellent verses on the loves of Rādhā and Kṛṣṇa. These verses provided the model of Vaiṣṇava love poetry which was followed even by Rabindranath Tagore.[20] Vidyāpati, too, was a *Smārta-pañcopāsaka*, and not a Vaiṣṇava.[21] He created different concepts of Rādhā as heroine of different moods and erotic situations. Perhaps the model for him was one of the adolescent and beautiful wives of a medieval *hārem*. Vidyāpati also composed a number of verses on Hara (Śiva) and Pārvatī. At least in two verses of Vidyāpati Rādhā describes Kṛṣṇa as her *Pati* and *Svāmini* (husband).[22] Perhaps the idea that Rādhā was a *parakīya* (another man's wife) was not acceptable to him. Yet he was definitely influenced by the Kṛṣṇa legend of the *Brahmavaivarta-Purāṇa* and the *Bhāgavata-Purāṇa*.[23]

"A remarkable product of pre-Caitanya Vaiṣṇavism was the *Śrīkṛṣṇakīrtana* of Vaḍu Caṇḍīdāsa. There are many valid reasons for regarding him as a poet of the late fourteenth and the early fifteenth centuries.[24] Vaḍu Caṇḍīdāsa seems to be fully conversant with the mythical legends of Kṛṣṇa and Rādhā. But his language is rather archaic. He lacks the refinement of Vidyāpati.

"The Rādhā of *Śrīkṛṣṇakīrtana* is a young village girl, chased and teased by Kṛṣṇa, who is but a cowboy with divine pretensions. The work was neglected by the Gauḍīya Vaiṣṇavas and it lay forgotten for centuries.[25] But it focuses a good deal of light on the pre-Caitanya Kṛṣṇa cult in Bengal. The poet worshiped a minor goddess named Vāsulī whose cult was popular in some regions of Bengal even in the sixteenth century.[26] The poet asserts that he had composed the work at the orders of the said Goddess. It may, therefore, be reasonably presumed that the singing of Rādhā-Kṛṣṇa songs was an essential ritual of Vāsulī worship. In this work Kṛṣṇa is depicted as a youth who is always trying to seduce Rādhā. Much is made of the inevitable sex act.[27] These facts certainly indicate the probability of the association of this cult of Rādhā-Kṛṣṇa with an unknown fertility cult, indications of which may be discernible in some types of folk songs of North Bengal.[28] In *Śrīkṛṣṇakīrtana* the divinity of Kṛṣṇa has always been invoked to justify his unjustifiable conduct. Rādhā is at first very much unwilling to fall in love with him. But once she is won over, her dedication becomes absolute. She grows almost insane when Kṛṣṇa forsakes her. The songs on *Rādhā-Viraha* or Rādhā's agony caused by her separation from Kṛṣṇa clearly adumbrate the *Māthura* concept of later *Padāvalī* literature.[29] Vaḍu Caṇḍīdāsa shows in some verses his knowledge of the *bhakti* doctrine; yet he has depicted Rādhā as a girl of real flesh and blood. This unmistakably human element in *Śrīkṛṣṇakīrtana* might have rendered it unattractive to the devotees of the Caitanya sect.

"The *Bhāgavatapurāṇa* concept was first rendered into vernacular poetry by Mālādhara Basu, a Bengali poet of the fifteenth century, in *Śrīkṛṣṇavijaya*. This work was an indication of the growing popularity of the legend of Kṛṣṇa as narrated in the *Bhāgavatapurāṇa*. Towards the beginning of the fifteenth century Śūlapāṇi, an exponent of the *Dharmaśāstra*, wrote at least three ritualistic works on the subject of Kṛṣṇa worship.[30] Vaiṣṇavism was definitely gaining a foothold even among the orthodox Brāhmaṇas.

"Literary evidence, therefore, indicates that the Caitanya movement of the fifteenth century was not altogether a new movement in Bengal. Caitanya's contemporary and fellow citizen was Kṛṣṇānanda Āgamavāgīśa, who edited the famous *Tantrasāra*, a compendium still in use. The *Śaktisaṃgama Tantra*, (*Kālī and Tārā Khaṇḍas*) describes the contemporary Tāntric orders. Vṛndāvana Dāsa, the composer of *Caitanyabhāgavata*, the earliest Bengali biography of the great religious leader, mentions the popularity of the Tāntric forms in the town of Navadvīpa.[31] But the Rādhā-Kṛṣṇa cult was fast growing popular. Both Jayadeva and Vidyāpati were influenced by the *Brahmavaivartapurāṇa*, and, to some extent, by the *Padmapurāṇa*. But it was probably in the fifteenth century that the *Bhāgavata* legend of Kṛṣṇa gained a foothold in Bengal. It was the vital source from which the Bengali Vaiṣṇavas later on derived the basic ideas and approaches.

"According to the biographers of Caitanya, the religious and the cultural condition of Navadvipā at the time of his advent was very complex. The Śākta sects and Brāhmaṇical orthodoxy were particularly strong. While the Tāntric 'leftists' were deliberately undermining the moral foundations of the Hindu society by the practice of '*pañcamakāra*',[32] the 'rightists' represented by the *Smārta-Brāhmaṇas* were deliberately strengthening the forces of conservatism and reaction.[33] The suggestion of the biographers is that Caitanya's advent as a Vaiṣṇava religious leader was absolutely necessary. Some historians have seen a link between the advent of Caitanya and the religious and social tyranny of the Muhammadan rulers of the time. It is said that one of the undeclared purposes of the Caitanya movement was too save the Hindus of the low castes from Muhammadan proselytization. But this suggestion is not based on any sound historical evidence.[34]

"Being centrally located between West Bengal and North-East Bengal, Navadvīpa was an important intellectual center where, at the time of Caitanya's advent, the study of Navyanyāya or New Logic was very popular. The early biographers of Caitanya, however, regarded Navyanyāya as a philosophical system which had no connection with *bhakti*, and which, therefore, made the intellectual atmosphere of Navadvīpa arid, rough and heartless.

"There were some men in Navadvīpa who considered the old concept of *bhakti* as a panacea for the current ills and evils.[35] According to Gauḍīya Vaiṣṇava tradition these men were led by the savant Advaita Ācārya, who was born in the middle of the fifteenth century, and who had come to Navadvīpa from Śrīhaṭṭa or Sylhet, now an eastern district of Bangladesh. Advaita was a disciple of an ascetic named Mādhavendra Purī, who was a powerful preacher of *bhakti* emotionalism. Jagannātha Miśra, Caitanya's father, and Viśvarūpa, Caitanya's elder brother, who later renounced the world and was heard of no more, had Vaiṣṇava sympathies. In fact the Vaiṣṇava milieu at Navadvīpa was constituted by men most of whom had come to that town from Sylhet. Only one native of West Bengal, who was well-known as a prominent Vaiṣṇava, was Īśvara Purī, a disciple of Mādhavendra Purī.[36] From the larger number of Śrīhaṭṭiyās (natives of Sylhet) who professed the Vaiṣṇava faith in Navadvīpa it may be said that the Vaiṣṇava *bhakti* movement was brought to Navadvīpa from Śrīhaṭṭa. But no reliable data on the Vaiṣṇavism of contemporary Śrīhaṭṭa are available.[37]

"The Vaiṣṇavas of Navadvīpa, led by Advaita, conformed to the Brāhmaṇical way of life.[38] But they were not at all happy with the predominance of sects and philosophies which militated against Vaiṣṇavism. They certainly wanted a change. It is interesting to note that the Caitanya movement was sponsored mainly by the Brāhmaṇas.[39]

"No history of the Caitanya movement can, however, afford to be oblivious of Mādhavendra Purī, of whom almost nothing is known.[40] He was the *guru* of Advaita Ācārya, Īśvara Purī, and, probably of Rāmānanda Rāya and Nityānanda Avadhūta. These were the men who helped Caitanya build up the movement. It was Īśvara Purī who converted Caitanya into Vaiṣṇavism at Gaya. It was Advaita who gave him unflinching support when both Brāhmaṇical and Muhammadan opposition against him was strong. It should also be noted that at the time of Caitanya's advent (A.D. 1486) Śrīdhara Svāmin's commentary on the *Bhāgavatapurāṇa* was steadily gaining popularity in many regions of India.[41] Śrīdhara Svāmin was mainly responsible for the revision of the theory of *māyā* or illusion as propounded by Śaṃkara in his celebrated commentary on the *Brahmasūtra.* Śrīdhara equated Kṛṣṇa with Brahman in his commentary on the *Gītā*. He interpreted *māyā* as an attribute of Brahman. He did not believe in Śaṃkara's theory of release as a state of cease-work. He believed that *bhakti* as a form of work that is 'disinterested' shall continue even after the final liberation. He is believed to have stressed the importance of hymns and the singing of hymns.[42] Some of the basic formulations of Gauḍīya Vaiṣṇavism were taken from Śrīdhara's commentaries. Caitanya himself is reported to have regarded him as a *jagadguru* or Universal Mentor.[43]

"Īśvara Purī had some contact with the Vaiṣṇavas of Navadvīpa.[44] Caitanya's conversion at Gayā was not entirely fortuitous. It is reasonable to suppose that the milieu of the Caitanya movement was gradually built up with th help and cooperation of the disciples of Mādhavendra Purī. There is an idea that the Sufi mystics of the time cast their influence on the development of Vaiṣṇava emotionalism. But no evidence in support of this idea is available.[45] The Sufis, however, exerted considerable influence on the development of religion and the rituals of the Bāuls of Bengal, who were popular even in the days of Caitanya.[46]

"The vagaries of the tyrannical rule of Sultān Ālā-ud-din Hussain Shah (1493/1519), the social atrophy caused by Brāhmanical conservatism, the licentiousness of the 'Sexo-Yogic' cults, the aridness of New Logic – these 'evils' required reform. It is now generally admitted that the Caitanya movement assumed the shape of a religious movement with a pronounced social purpose. 'With Caitanya and his followers', writes D.D. Kosambi, 'a way was found through *bhakti* music, ecstasy and dance to make the rich surrender a part at least of their prerogatives, for we are told that whole villages would dance to the next settlement in joy. People dance on that scale only when some new form of life has developed that bears a vision of hope; one may see this for himself in New China.'[47] 'Caitanyadeva', writes Bhupendranāth Datta, 'brought about a new age.'[48]

"Śrī Gaurāṅga or Śrī Caitanya was born at Navadvīpa in A.D. 1486, and died in mysterious circumstances in Purī in A.D. 1533.[49] He went to Purī after his initiation as an ascetic. His wife, Viṣṇupriyā Devī, and his widowed mother, Śacī Devī, remained at Navadvīpa. Caitanya traveled extensively in the

Deccan and North India. He visited Allahabad, Vāraṇāsī and Vṛndāvana.[50] It is interesting to note that at least four tribes of Orissa (Korapur District) regard one 'Mahāprabhu' (Great Lord) as their supreme God. 'Mahāprabhu' was the honorific title of Caitanya.[51]

"Five men played a vital role in the development of the Caitanya movement. The foremost of them was Advaita Ācārya, who really moulded Caitanya as a religious leader. He was also the first important man to attribute divinity to the young and very handsome saint.[52] The other four were Nityānanda Avadhūta, Rāya Rāmānanda, Sanātana Gosvāmin, and his brother Rūpa Gosvāmin. Nityānanda, an itinerant ascetic of the Advadhūta order, and probably a Tāntrika, was older than Caitanya by some eight years.[53] He infused into the movement a great passion. He and 'Yavana' Haridāsa, a Muhammadan Vaiṣṇava, converted two notorious scoundrels of Navadvīpa into the new faith. These men were brothers Jagai and Mādhai, of respectable Brāhmaṇa lineage.[54] Rāmānanda Rāya was the Governor of Vidyānagar (Rājmahendry) on the Godāvarī, under Pratāpa Rudradeva, King of Purī (A.D. 1497-1540). Caitanya met him at Vidyānagar on his way to the Deccan. According to Rādhāgovinda Nāth, Caitanya got the idea of the Rādhā-Kṛṣṇa cult from him, and transmitted it to Rūpa Gosvāmin at Allahabad and to Sanātana at Benares.[55] But it is doubtful whether the fundamental tenets were formulated by Rāmānanda, who has been described by Kavi Karṇapūra, contemporary biographer of Caitanya, as a Sahajavaiṣṇava, or a Vaiṣṇava who believed in the Sahajiyā doctrine.[56] Sanātana and his brother Rūpa were high bureaucrats under Sultān Ālā-ud-din Hussain Shāh at Gauḍa, the capital city. They lived like Muhammadan grandees,[57] but were devout Vaiṣṇavas even before their meeting with Caitanya at Rāmakeli village, which was then a noted center of Sanskrit learning. Caitanya easily persuaded the two talented brothers to renounce the world and depart for Vṛndāvana as ascetics. Their nephew, Jīva Gosvāmin, who later on became the chief theological interpreter or the sect, was then a mere boy.

"As long as Caitanya lived he was (despite his frequent and debilitating emotional tantrums) the main driving force behind the powerful movement. Both S.K. De and J.N. Farqhar have attributed the great success of this movement to his unique personality.[58] But they have not given him any credit for organising the movement. S.K. De, however, admits that 'on the main lines of its growth and expansion the movement was directly inspired by the example of his life and experience, even if he did not actually persevere at the task."[59] This view does not seem to be entirely correct. It was Caitanya who transformed *saṃkīrtana* singing into a powerful mass medium. In fact, his fearless activities in Navadvīpa seriously disturbed the social and intellectual balance; he was threatened by some '*paḍukās*' or students who probably criticized his way of life and told him either to renounce the world and quit the town or to face the untold misery of social ostracism. He opted for the first suggestion and became a mendicant, perhaps to save his family from the consequences of social ostracism. The threatening attitude of the Pāṣaṇḍas has been described by Vṛndāvana Dasa.[60] Merely 'a unique religious personality' might not have roused the wrath off the conservative elements. They surely grew afraid of the revolutionary possibilities of the movement, the heart and soul of which was the young saint. Secondly, the early biographers of Caitanya mention the fact that he transmitted the basic ideas to Rāmānanda Rāya, Sanātana and Rūpa. This he did with a view to building up his bases in the important religious centers in Northern India. Thirdly, his pilgrimage and travels might be construed as conscious effort on his part to spread the movement far and wide. Unlike the other mystic *sādhus* Caitanya did not live in a hide-out in far Himālayas or in the jungles of Madhya Pradeśa. He was a social saint with numerous social connections. His sojourn in a great pilgrim center like Purī, where pilgrims came from all parts of

India, had, no doubt, a significant bearing on the propagationof his faith. Wherever he went, thousands followed him, singing the hymns and dancing in ecstasy.

"Caitanya's whole life was a tremendous experiment with the theory and practice of devotion. He pursued *bhakti* with a monomaniacal fixity of purpose and faith. Fear, force, and violence had no place in his faith. It was in the context of the contemporary society, the most humane faith. Caitanya was a devotee of abstract beauty. He did not care for the terrible *avatāras* of Viṣṇu. The Kṛṣṇa whom he worshiped was the most beautiful god who played on his flute, and played the love game with the most beautiful girls in the most beautiful of heavens. Such a religion had a special appeal in a caste-ridden society. By intense *bhakti* for such a nice god, the people could forget the iniquities of life.

"Caitanya's premature death created a cleavage within the movement just when it was gathering momentum. Kṛṣṇadāsa Kavirāja tries to hide this fact in a remarkable legend. He describes how Caitanya, the Gardener (*Caitanyamālī)* sowed the seeds of the *bhakti* tree; how, thanks to his constant care, the tree grew up as a veritable giant with main branches, side branches, sub-branches and branches of sub-branches; and how thereafter millions and millions of people began to enjoy its delicious fruits and fragrant flowers.[61] But the fact was that Navadvīpa and Vṛndāvana began to look at the movement from quite different angles. In Bengal Caitanya was deified; he was regarded as the human combination of Rādhā and Kṛṣṇa. It was said that Kṛṣṇa, the Supreme God, wanted to relish his sports with Rādhā, his *hlādinīśakti*, by sharing in an equal measure her joys and sorrows. And so Caitanya, the human combination of Kṛṣṇa and Rādhā, was born.[62] At Vṛndāvana, however, Kṛṣṇa, minus his Caitanya embodiment, reigned supreme, while Caitanya, minus his Kṛṣṇa identity, was regarded by the Gosvāmins as the supreme saint and *guru*.[63] In Bengal the mantle of leadership fell on Nityānanda who was bigamous.[64]

Nityānanda became almost *persona non grata* in the Vaiṣṇava theology formulated by the Vṛndāvana-Gosvāmins. The *pañcatattva* doctrine, which recognizes the primacy of both Advaita and Nityānanda in the Gauḍīya Vaiṣṇava hierarchy or saints was not accepted by the scholastic philosophers of Vṛndāvana.[65]

"The celebrated 'six Gosvāmins' (*ṣaḍgosvāmi*) of Vṛndāvana were six ascetics who were Caitanya's contemporaries and who lived and died in Vṛndāvana. They rescued the holy city from creeping wilderness, and made it a great center of Vaiṣṇava pilgrimage. These men were Sanātana, his younger brother Rūpa, their nephew Jīva, Raghunātha Bhaṭṭa, Gopāla Bhaṭṭa, and Ragunātha Dāsa.[66] All of them were great scholars and remarkably sophisticated men who had once enjoyed affluence in urban centers. They emulated the conduct of the Deccanese Vaiṣṇava Ācāryas by fastening on the essentially simple faith of Caitanya a philosophical system, a theological system, a hagiographical system, a peculiarly Vaiṣṇava version of poetics, grammar aned aesthetics, an elaborate ritual and lots of unoriginal and ornate poetry They really sanskritized *bhakti* in such a manner that it lost its original emotional effusion.

"The form and content of Gauḍīya Vaiṣṇavism evolved in urban-intellectual centers like Navadvīpa, Purī, Benares and Vṛndāvana. The form was fashioned out of ancient myths. The rationale of the movement was sought in a novel interpretation of *pramāṇa* or evidence of the myths. The full exposition of the theory of *pramāṇa* is found in Jīva Gosvāmin's *Tattvasandarbha* and Baladeva Vidyābhūṣaṇa's commentary on it. According to Jīva Gosvāmin, the most perfect evidence is the oral authority as revealed in the *śruti* which, unfortunately, grew incomprehensible in Kaliyuga, the age of decadence. The *Purāṇas* and the *Itihāsas* were, therefore, written for the interpretation of the *śruti*, in a manner which might render it comprehensible to the men of the Kaliyuga. But then the *Purāṇas* describe the methods of worshiping a multitude of divinities. The mortals may not, therefore, know which divinity they should worship. Each myth is supposed to fulfil the spiritual need of a particular age. Jīva Gosvāmin says that the *Purāṇas* are of three types, and of them the best, and the most pertinent to the needs of Kaliyuga is the *Bhāgavatapurāṇa* which, according to him, provides the best explanation of the *śruti*. It is also the most reliable commentary on the *Brahmasūtra* of Vyāsadeva. The best commentary on the *Bhāgavatapurāṇa* is the commentary of Śrīdharasvāmin. According to the *Bhāgavata Purāṇa* Kṛṣṇa is the best and highest of the gods. He and no other god should therefore be worshiped in Kaliyuga. 'The introduction of the mystic formula of incomprehensibility seems to discharge the Vaiṣṇavas of this school from all responsibility of logically explaining their dogmas and creeds, and, thus uncontrolled, they descend from the domain of reason to the domain of Puranic faith of a mythological character.'[67]

Initially the movement removed the barriers between town and village, between castes, between the intellectual and the illiterate. But the Gosvāmins of Vṛndāvana transformed it into an elite movement. They assiduously worked for the establishment of a link between Caitanya's simple *bhakti* for Kṛṣṇa and Brāhmanical Hinduism. The urge for sanskritizing the movement might have come from their ineradicable aristocracy and scholarship. It might also have stemmed from the non-Bengali atmosphere and environment of Vṛndāvana.[68] But their attempt to formulate the aforesaid systems was tantamount to sacrilege, for the fundamental idea of Caitanya was that the genuine devotee of Kṛṣṇa realizes Him not by Learning and Logic, but by simple faith and devotion. It is devotion, recollected in emotion, that brought Vāsudeva Sārvabhauma, the great Vedāntic scholar of Purī, to Caitanya's feet.[69] Even today a Bāul-Vaiṣṇava mystic, a poor man, considers the Caitanya movement an irresistible Train hauled by an Engine of immense power. He says the following in a song:

> Look! Caitanya's train has arrived at the golden city of Nadiā. Caitanya Himself is the Driver of the Engine. The coaches belong to Rādhā & Co. The yard of Śrīṇivāsa's abode is the Railway Junction. Ragāi and Mādhāi are its passengers. Nityānanda is the Ticket-Master (the official who sells tickets for the journey). What a great advantage for poor men! The rich may not claim all the benefits! Only the poor believe in *bhakti*, they are given the Ticket! So says poor Sarat Bhāul (the author of the song); Let me, too, travel by this train; those who have acquired permits from our Queen, Rādhā, may very well travel to sacred Vrajadhāma in First Class coaches.[70] (translated)

But it must also be said that the great labors of the Gosvāmins saved the nascent cult from the aggressions of the caste-conscious Brāhmaṇas and Tāntric 'leftism'. But yet the original effusion of *bhakti* was considerably, if not wholly, plugged by their unrelenting scholasticism.

"Bengal was not at first aware of the development of scholasticism in Vṛndāvana. Advaita built up a subsect at Śāntipur. Nityānanda gathered his flock at Pāṇihāti, near Calcutta. In 1600, or thereabouts, three men named Śrīnivāsa, Narottama Dāsa and Śyāmānanda brought over to Bengal cartloads of manuscripts prepared by the Vṛndāvana Gosvāmins. 'It was through Śrīnivāsa', writes one authority, 'that the works of the Goswāmins of Vṛindavana received publicity in Bengal and the neighboring provinces'.[71] The most important of these manuscripts were the following:

Rūpa Gosvāmin	*Bhaktirasāmṛtasindhu*
	Ujjvalanīlamaṇi
Jīva Gosvāmin	*Ṣaṭsaṃdarbha*
	Gopālacampū
	Commentary on the *Bhāgavatapurāṇa (?)*

Sanātana Gosvāmin	Commentary on the Tenth *Skandha* of the *Bhāgavatapurāṇa*
Gopāla Bhaṭṭa Gosvāmin	*Haribhaktivilāsa*
Kṛṣṇadāsa Kavirāja	*Caitanyacaritāmṛta*
	Govindalīlāmṛtaṃ

The fundamental philosophical, theological, ritualistic and aesthetic concepts of Gauḍīya Vaiṣṇavism are explained in these basic works. Kṛṣṇadāsa Kavirāja's *Caitanyacaritāmṛta* soon became the Bible of this sect. Written in brilliant Bengali, aglow with the fervor of lifelong devotion and asceticism, this biography of Caitanya was the first complete masterpiece which immediately attracted the attention of the Vaiṣṇava devotees. Its authority and popularity are still very great. The other very popular and reliable source book of Gauḍīya Vaiṣṇavism is Vṛndāvana Dāsa's *Caitanyabhāgavata.*[72]

II

"The Gosvāmins of Vṛndāvana must be given high credit for producing in a short time a vast and intricate philosophical and ritualistic literature. The basic texts and the commentaries fill up several large and thick volumes. Kṛṣṇadāsa Kavirāja's achievement was that he summarized them in his biographical work. The following account of the philosophy and theology of the Caitanya movement is based mainly on Kṛṣṇadāsa's interpretations.[73]

"The cardinal point of Caitanya's religion or Gauḍīya Vaiṣṇavism is *bhakti* or devotion, which is the source of many other philosophical principles. *Bhakti* is the intensification of devotion to a degree where the *bhakta* or devotee feels a personal relation between God and himself. A mystic link is established, through devotion, between God and man. The nature of the link is mystic, and hence indescribable. The Gauḍīya Vaiṣṇavas believe in the superiority of insight over reason and analysis. They consider plurality illusory. To them, physical reality is an illusion created by God, and both good and evil are illusion.

"Kṛṣṇa, *Bhagavān*, God, is conceived of as the Supreme Being.[74] But he has a human form, an abode, everything a human being has, or should have. But everything that belongs to Kṛṣṇa is made of unalloyed Bliss. He is the embodiment of the Upaniṣadic *rasa, ānanda,* or Bliss. He, therefore, eternally indulges in sports in his own abode in the sweet company of certain male and female divinities who are but the manifestations of his own bliss-consciousness attribute.

"The theory that Yoga signifies the fusion of the individual soul with *paramātman*, the supreme soul or God, is not acceptable to the Gauḍīya Vaiṣṇavas. They have not the slightest desire to be a part of God, or even to be equal to God Himself. Hācān Rāja, the famous Mohammadan Bāul mystic of Sylhet once said: 'I have been asking people for the identity of Kānāi (Kṛṣṇa). I have been elaborating on this point for a long time. And now I have come to the conclusion that I myself am Kānāi.'[75] This conclusion militates against [the] Gauḍīya Vaiṣṇava concept of the relation between *jīva* and God. Their only and humble aim is to raise their respective stations to a level wherefrom they may be able to contribute their mite to the eternal bliss of Kṛṣṇa. The devotees's love of Kṛṣṇa admits of no conditions or pre-conditions, qualifications or ambiguity. Its effusion should be natural and spontaneous. This love is beyond injunctions, sanctions and extraneous impulse. This love is self-manifest. The theory is that a deep current of love flows down from Vṛndāvana, the highest of heavens. The flow reaches the soul of the devotee through an intangible medium, which is normally stationed in Vṛndāvana, and which sometimes comes down to earth out of great compassion for mortals lost in worldly bondage.[76]

"There are six well-defined stages of devotional love. In the beginning the humble devotee is lost in the infinite ocean of Kṛṣṇa's supernatural luster. This is the early stage of

Brahmānanda, the stage when the devotee experiences the ineffable joy of being drowned in Brahman's supernatural luster. The second stage is that of the realization of Brahman in the form of Narāyaṇa. This stage is technically known as that of *Śāntarati* or *Paramārthasphurti.* The third and the next higher stage is that of *Premabhakti* or *Dāsyarati,* at which the devotee feels that there is a definite personal relationship between God and himself. He regards God as the Supreme Master, and thinks of himself as His humblest servant. At this stage Kṛṣṇa is conceived of as the source of innumerable incarnations, the creator of numberless universes, the lord and protector of whole worlds, the limitless ocean of benevolence and benediction. The devotee regards Him with *sambhrama* (veneration) which implies total effacement of self, a feeling of being inferior even to straw, a feeling that the devotee is caressing God. These are also the indications of a *dāsabhakta* or 'servant-devotee'.[77]

"But the feeling of extreme inferiority consequent to the contemplation of divine splendor impedes the flow of such devotion as may contribute to God's joy or *ānanda*. Hence the next higher stage of *Sakhyarati* is conceived. The term means Love born of Friendship. *Sakhya,* friendship, is the friendship between two persons of the same complexion, dress, qualifications, rank and status. Such friendship is never inhibited by diffidence and rules of etiquette. Kṛṣṇa has some friends in Vṛndāvana who are not inferior to him in any respect. But so great is their friendship for him that some of them even ply a fan while he sleeps on a flower-bed in the close embrace of a milkmaid.[78]

"Yet friendly love may have certain limitations. On *vatsalyarati* or parental love no limitations are put. A devotee may consider Kṛṣṇa as his son. The spiritual significance of such relationship is that it considerably diminishes the unbearable luster of God. When Kṛṣṇa, the beloved baby of Yaśodā, shows her the entire universe and the heavens in the tiny cavity of His mouth simply by the ruse of a yawn, she merely considers the exhibition the symptom of a disease caused by the evil eye.[79] The same exhibition nearly stunned a great hero like Arjuna in the *Gītā*.

"The highest stage of devotional love is that of *Madhurati*, the blissful love of lovers. But love for Kṛṣṇa is unsullied by sex and sensuousness. The *Upaniṣads* affirm that God is *rasa*. When *jīva*, life-entity, realizes *rasa*, it realizes something too deep for words. God and *rasa* are inalienable. The *Bhāgavatapurāṇa* is but the elaboration of the *rasa*-concept. This *Purāṇa* describes the sports of Kṛṣṇa, who is the transcendental *rāsika* (the possessor of bliss).

"The sports of Kṛṣṇa, and the sense of relish born of them, are mostly similar to those of the phenomenal world. Kṛṣṇa has to dim the blaze of his luster while he sports, and relishes the sports. This fact makes him different from his other incarnations, some of which are horrible, and also make him look like a mortal, a beautiful mortal, whose blooming adolescence never ends. These things cannot be understood by reason. Kṛṣṇa's love sports are characterized by seemingly sexual but really asexual conjugality. This is enjoyed by him in the eternal company of his own bliss-attributes who assume the semblance of pretty, eternally adolescent cowgirls. Libido drives material beings towards egotistical hankering for the pleasure of orgasm. But the Love that pleases Kṛṣṇa, God, is absolutely free of dirt and smut, and is an absolute negation of sexuality.[80]

"*Bhaktirasa*, a basic concept of Gauḍīya Vaiṣṇavism, means the pleasure-giving 'juice' that real devotion yields.[81] There is also the 'juice' of poetry or *kāvyarasa*. The 'juice' of devotion oozes out of the intuition of God and His eternal sports. The 'juice' of poetry flows from something mortal, something transitory, something blemished by humanity. The first *rasa* is, therefore, immeasurably superior to the second one.

"There is some difference of opinion about the exact location of *rasa*. According to aesthetics *rasa* is located in the reader, the spectator, the audience, or, in other words, in the *sāmājika*. The human enjoyment of *rasa* is rendered possible only through its grace. When, however, a human being is fortunate enough to enjoy what a Vaiṣṇava poet has termed *śyāmarasa*, he enjoys *bhaktirasa* in the best and the truest sense of the term. Since the bliss potency of God constantly throbs in the soul of the genuine devotee, the state of relish of the divine bliss is quite natural to that soul.[81]

"The Gauḍīya Vaiṣṇavas ascribe the same potency to *rasa* as they do to *priti* or love. The real devotee does not see any difference between *rasa* and *prīti* which are commingled by the factor of devotion. The permanent mood or *sthāyībhāva* in a devotee's soul is the *prīti* or love of Kṛṣṇa. *Rasa* is born out of this love.[82]

"*Rasa*, too, has types which correspond to those of *prīti*. The best *rasa* is, no doubt, *madhurarasa* or *ujjvalarasa*. Its main feature is the intuitive realization of Kṛṣṇa as the embodiment of transcendental love. *Madhurarati* is blended with *madhurasa*. The blending of *rati* and *rasa* takes place in eight sequences, namely, *rati* (mental delight), *premabhakti* (devotion in the form of nascent love), *sneha* (when love becomes soft and oily), *praṇaya* (deepening of love), *māna* (enhancement of love by chagrin, jealousy, anger), *anurāga* (when Kṛṣṇa, the object of love appears eternally fresh), and *mahābhāva* (maddening by the wonder of great ecstacy). In *mahābhāva* the physical sensations grow dull. The devotee feels the highest pleasure and the acutest pain. At this state Caitanya himself looked pale; he wept, trembled, rolled on the ground. Rādhā herself often experienced *mahābhāva*.

"The highest sequence of *madhurasa* is *divyonmāda*, a sequence contemplated for Rādhā only. The Rāsa festival of the autumnal season is considered as the expression of both *mahābhāva* and *divyonmāda*.

"The Gauḍīya Vaiṣṇavas have interpreted *mukti* or liberation in a novel manner. According to them final release may mean *sālokya* (presence in God's abode), *sārṣṭya* (attainment of divine power), *sāmīpya* (proximity to God), *sārūpya* (attainment of divine form), *sāyujya* (fusion with God). The third category or proximity to God is the desirable form of liberation. In proximity to Kṛṣṇa the humble devotee finds his station elevated to a level wherefrom he can contribute his mite to Kṛṣṇa's pleasure. But any of the aforementioned stages the devotee escapes the cycle of birth and rebirth. The main feature of *sāyujya* liberation is the immersion of the *jīva* soul in the timeless bliss of Brahman. But such immersion of the soul in Brahman is considered undesirable. A particular *tattva* or theory is applied to explain this point. This is known as the *acintyabhedābhedatattva* (incomprehensible dualistic monism).[84] This theory is enunciated by Jivā Gosvāmin in his *Sarvasaṃvādinī*. The relation between *jīva* and Kṛṣṇa (*Bhagavān*) 'incomprehensible' because it is a relation of both (*bheda*) and (*abheda*) non-difference. Inasmuch as *jīva* is a part of *Bhagavān* with the characteristic features of *Bhagavān*, the relation is one of *abheda* or non-difference. But while the attributes of *Bhagavān* are superlative, those of the *jīva* are qualitatively inferior to them. There is, therefore, a difference (*bheda*) between God and *jīva*. The sub-ordination of *jīva* to God is eternal, for while the *jīva* is controlled by *māyāśakti* (power of illusion), God remains far above illusion or its power. *Māyāśakti*, no doubt, emanates from God, but cannot effect Him. Being a part of God, the *jīva* can approach Him. But being different from God, it cannot be equal to Him. So, proximity to God is considered the best and the most desirable stage of release. Moreover, the blending of the *jīva* soul with Brahman does not really help it contribute its mite to God's *ānanda* or joy. It should also be noted that liberation at any stage does not signify a state of cease-work. The practice of devotion must continue in any stage of release.

"Gauḍīya Vaiṣṇava theology does not see any difference between Supreme Brahman and the eternally adolescent Kṛṣṇa, who possesses and infinite number of supranatural powers and attributes. Other gods like Vāsudeva, Viṣṇu and Śiva are only the manifestations of Kṛṣṇa. As his manifestations they are also eternal, infinite, omnipresent and omnipotent. But they exist, because Kṛṣṇa exists. The followers of Caitanya skillfully used this idea to show that their brand of Vaiṣṇavism was not based upon the negation of other cults. But the Śaiva *tāntrikas* did not appreciate the idea. In one of their works they describe Caitanya, Nityānanda and Advaita as demons and *asuras* who were reborn to destroy the worship of Śiva.[85] The Gauḍīya Vaiṣṇavas hardly say anything about the Buddha whose worship was no longer fashionable in Bengal.

"Kṛṣṇa has a human form, because his *līlā* in human form is considered the best of all of his *līlās* (sports) in other incarnations. But Kṛṣṇa's humanity is eternal, perfect, and non-material. He cannot be realized by pondering upon time, space and relativity. He is *sat* (existence absolute), *cit* (consciousness absolute) and *ānanda* (bliss absolute). *Ānanda* is the essence of Kṛṣṇa-Brahman; *sat* and *cit* are His attributes. As He is bliss, He is relishable. As He is relishable, He is love. As he is love, He also possesses love's *mādhurya* or sweetness.

"Kṛṣṇa's playmates, both male and female, are his attributes who are bliss-conscious. They dwell in Vṛndāvana, Kṛṣṇa's abode. His playmates and associates are also considered both different and non-different from him. Vṛndāvana is the geographical expression of something infinite, all-pervading, and blissful. The material body of a true Vaiṣṇava is also the mystic Vṛndāvana. Rām Ṭhākur, a Bengali mystic, once described Vṛndāvana in the following manner:

> Vraja has an area of eighty-four *krośas*. Vṛndāvana is centrally located in Vraja. It is eternally restless, and the restlessness is attributable to Yogamāyā. She is a female force capable of producing illusions. In Vraja love reigns supreme. If one comes to this place, one never returns back to earth. But the only access to Vraja lies through the constant contemplation of the sports of Kṛṣṇa...*This body is vraja.* It has a dimension of eighty-

> four finger spans. Here, right at the center, is located the *Nidhuvana*-bower of Kṛṣṇa. Here everything is eternally restless. The predominant moods here are those of a servant, a friend, a parent, a lover. Here, in the *vraja*-body Śrī Rādhā is the fountain of all moods. Here nobody is a master. Even Rādhā is not a mistress. Here even Kṛṣṇa is not a master. Everything here is controlled by Yogamāyā. But still everything here is natural...Nobody can come to this place with a soul corrupted by egoism. This is a place which is absolutely free of libido...[86]

"Rām Ṭhakur's emphasis on the function of Yogamāyā was likely to be contradicted by the orthodox Vaiṣṇavas; but his account is based on mystic experience which is beyond logic.

"Kṛṣṇa loves the *gopinīs* or milkmaids of Vṛndāvana. The love is mutual, and is never sullied by carnality.[87] The Gauḍīya Vaiṣṇavas distinguish between the Vṛndāvana sports which are manifest, and the Vṛndāvana sports which are not. They believe that it was Caitanya who made these sports manifest for the spiritual benefit of the devotees.

"In unmanifest sports the milkmaids are Kṛṣṇa's wives. But in sports manifest they are *seemingly* the wives of other persons. Rūpa Gosvāmin justifies Kṛṣṇa's manifest sports in the following manner:

> According to *Bhaktirasāmṛtasindhu* even though Kṛṣṇa is *ātmārāma* (self-complacent) He divides Himself into as many Kṛṣṇas as there are milkmaids, and plays with them. In this way He shows His appreciation of the devotional love the milkmaids feel for Him.
>
> But what God does a mere mortal cannot do. The *Bhāgavata* has strictly forbidden the emulation of the sports of Kṛṣṇa as a mortal. God, as Rudra drank off the poison churned out of the primeval ocean. Would not an ordinary man give up his ghost if he drinks that poison?
>
> But then why should God, the Fountain of Knowledge, the Source of Intelligence, the Friend of all living beings, do anything which is ordinarily done by inconsiderate and indisciplined persons? The answer to this question is that God sports with the milkmaids only to satisfy the genuine desire of

the real devotees to witness, or better, hear of, such beatific sports, which are not to be described in the presence of people who do not understand or support the concept of God as Love.

Kṛṣṇa really does not sport with other mens' wives. The milkmaids are, no doubt, married; but they have no physical relation with their spouses. The saint Śukadeva reveals the fact that the so-called husbands of Vṛndāvana are so hoodwinked by Yogamāyā, the female embodiment of Kṛṣṇa's power to generate a spell, that they never know that their so-called wives are merely shadows without substance, merely simulacra.[88]

"The description of the mystic Vṛndāvana in Gauḍīya Vaiṣṇava literature conforms to that of a semi-feudal kingdom, where the prince is surrounded by a hierarchical retinue.[89] A particular duty is assigned to each of the prince's servants and friends. It is interesting to note that a Brāhmaṇa youth named Madhumangala functions as the court jester. King Nanda's household is very much like that of a small king. But Vṛndāvana is a beautiful place, where the meadows are green and the woods are green, and where the beautiful river Kālindī flows like a river of bliss. The verdent woods have bowers wherein Kṛṣṇa plays with his milkmaids and their maidservants. The *yogamāyā* makes each of the seasons eternally manifest in each particular sector of the wood, so that Kṛṣṇa may enjoy the seasonal sports.[90]

"Kṛṣṇa, as *Bhagavān*, has three powers, namely, *svarūpaśakti* (sentient power), *māyāśakti* (non-sentient power), and *jīva-śakti* (marginal power). His first power makes his *līlā* sports possible. His second power brings the material world into existence. His third power makes life possible. The Vaiṣṇavas naturally place a good deal of stress on the first power, which is a the root of their theological speculations. The aid of this power is invoked to justify Kṛṣṇa's sports with the wives of other persons.[91] The hierarchical principle is applied to the description of the categories of male friends and milkmaids who are regarded as the bliss attributes of Kṛṣṇa. Nimvārka (thirteenth century A.D.) had exalted Rādhā as the eternal consort of Kṛṣṇa, and relegated Rukmiṇī to the background. According to Śaśībhuṣan Dāsgupta, Caitanya's tress on the importance of Rādhā was a consequence of his wanderings in South India and his association with Rāmānanda Rāya.[92] But the philosophical basis of Rādhā worship by the Gauḍīya Vaiṣṇavas was laid by Jīva Gosvāmin. Rādhā is conceived of as the *hlādinīśakti* (the power which makes God capable of relishing His own sports) of Kṛṣṇa. The *hlādinīśakti* is an emanation from God's *svarūpaśakti* or sentient power. In God *svarūpaśakti* resides in the semblance of *rasa*, and makes God the transcendental *rasika*. In the devotee, this power resides in the semblance of *bhakti*. Rādhā is not only the personification of eternal love, but also that of the abstract idea of the eternal lover. She is the *summum bonum* of love divine, and far superior to the other milkmaids. She is also the greatest devotee of Kṛṣṇa. Caitanya was born to acquaint the world with the glory of Rādhā.[93]

"The concept of Kṛṣṇa as a God-Hero who sports with Rādhā and the other innumerable milkmaids was the basis of Gauḍīya Vaiṣṇava aesthetics, or *rasaśāstra*, the earliest and the most notable exponent of which was Rūpa Gosvāmin. He 'gave a new turn to the old *Rāsa* theory of conventional poetics (and) also to the religious emotion underlying the older Vaiṣṇava faith.'[94] He elaborately expounded the sentiment of love as the sublimation of conventional erotics achieved through the medium of devotion or *bhakti*. The two concepts are very closely interlinked. *Ujjvalanīlamaṇi*, which contains the aesthetic propositions and formulations of Rūpa Gosvāmin, is the counterpart of the *Bhaktirasāmṛtasindhu*, which contains the theories of *bhakti*. The schemes of these two important products of the Caitanya movement are, however, too elaborate and complicated to be elucidated in this short survey.[95] But the main features of the *Ujjvalanīlamāṇi* may be stated. The work deals with *madhurasa*.But the model of the exposition of this *rasa* is the secular exposition of *śṛṅgārarasa* which is found in standard Sanskrit works on poetics and aesthetics. The basics of *madhurasa* have been elaborated from Kṛṣṇa's point of view. The traditional preference for categorization is another feature of this work. The hero all moods and emotions is Kṛṣṇa. The greatest heroine is, of course, Rādhā. The classification of sentiments, moods, and situations and types are exceptionally detailed and intricate. Each of these sentiments, moods, situations and types is judged and explained in the background of *bhakti*. Rūpa Gosvāmin's choice of explanatory verses is invariably apt. But he very careful about possible digression into secular erotics.[96] The work greatly influenced the composers of the Bengali *Padāvalīs*.

III

"The reasons behind the ascendancy of Kṛṣṇa over the ancient Viṣṇu-Vāsudeva and Nārāyaṇa are not far to seek. The heroic mood and the martial spirit gradually disappeared from the Hindu world. The frequent rise and fall of transient empires, the consequent 'Balkanization' of India, the deep shadows of religiosity lengthening northwards from the Deccan, the Muhammadan conquest of India, the unending dynastic aggressions and wars–these, no doubt, caused an ennui, a fatigue, which was aggravated by the retrogressive orthodoxy of the Brahmanas. Sex cults, dimly seen in ancient texts, began to develop all over India in the tenth century. The sculpture of coitus began to appear in large numbers on the panels of the temples.[97] Even orthodox religious concepts were interpreted in the so-called 'Sexo-Yogic' terms. The Vajrayāna-Tantrayāna apostasy and Hindu Tantric 'leftism' grew strong.[98] It was, therefore, natural for the old Vāsudeva cult to be slowly transferred into the Kṛṣṇa cult. The Vṛndāvana legend was incipient in the *Bhāgavatapurāṇa*. The followers of Caitanya gave it an attractive color and made it popular.

"The Caitanya movement had, of course, many merits. It was a non-violent assault on Tāntric perversion, *Smārta* conservatism, and Navyanyāya hair-splitting. It was doubtless a mystic movement, but it was never entirely devoid of human values. The Vaiṣṇavas were required to practice self-control, compassion, humility, generosity and patience. Egoism, selfishness, and lust were deprecated. [99] The rules of casteism were initially ignored.[100] Caitanya, a Vaidika Brāhmaṇa, did not always conform to the rules of caste-ism. He deliberately shunned the company of the rich. He lived like a mendicant. Tāntric Bohemianism was severely denounced, and celibacy was very strictly insisted upon. Gauḍīya Vaiṣṇa puritanism and conservatism were as real as the eroticism of the Gauḍīya Vaiṣṇava concept of the sports of Kṛṣṇa. Vaiṣṇava puritanism stemmed from the theory that a Vaiṣṇava's one and only concern was Kṛṣṇa. A devotee was not permitted to deviate from his devotion for Kṛṣṇa. The ḍevotee's life had to be very simple and austere. He had to beg. He could possess only a homespun rug (*kānthā*) and a wooden bowl (*kaḍanka*). Vaiṣṇava humanity was tantamount to self-effacement. The life or poverty brought the Vaiṣṇava down to the level of the poor millions. The practice of poverty and humility was one of the reasons behind the transformation of the movement into a mass movement. People of the lower castes were attracted by it. S.K. De opines that the Vaiṣṇava movement was not primarily concerned with ethics.[101] But a close study of Gopāla Bhaṭṭa Gosvāmin's *Haribhaktivilāsa* leads to the conclusion that in this authoritative work many ethical ideas were ritualized.[102] Vaiṣṇava puritanism certainly weakened the Tāntric stress on *bhoga* or enjoyment. The admission of the people of the lower castes into the Gauḍīya Vaiṣṇava order certainly generated a liberal view of the caste rules at least in Bengal.[103]

"The Caitanya movement attached a great importance to vernacular literature. According to Jadunāth Sarkār, [104] it revived the study of Sanskrit among all castes. Vaiṣṇava vocabulary considerably enriched and sweetened the Bengali language and made it the most powerful and expressive language of Eastern India. At the same time it provided the essential stimulus for the further development of Oriya and Assamese languages.[105] The cultural relation between Bengal, Orissa, and Assam was strengthened by the Vaiṣṇava movement.

"In the wake of the Caitanya movement appeared the rich and rhythmic *Padāvalī* which, despite certain limitations, indicated the beginning of a literary renaissance. Man was not neglected in Vaiṣṇava literature. "Indeed", wrote Benoy Kumar Sarkar,

> in the Caṇḍīdāsa-Vidyāpati complex...it is the masses that speak. We encounter here the direct delineations of the diverse incidents in the life that is actually lived by the folk.,-...the milkmen, the cowherds, the traders, the boatmen, the cultivators. Bengali poetry is nothing if it is not democratic. It is life's urges, the *elan de la vie* in its thousand and one forms, that furnish the Bengali poets with the sunshine of Bengal's villages and towns.[106]

Man has a distinct place in the tradition of Vaiṣṇava worship in Bengal. Caṇḍīdāsa, a talented composer of Vaiṣṇava lyrics, wrote: 'Listen, O Brother Man! The only Truth that is above everything is Man!'[107] In Vaiṣṇava theology even God is made to shed off some of his luster so that He may be close to man. The system of beginning a series of verses on the subject of Kṛṣṇa's life in Vṛndāvana with *Gauracandrikā* which dealt with particular aspects of Caitanya's life in Navadvīpa, introduced in Bengali poetry a human element which has a great bearing on the further development of that poetry. In the *Padāvalī* songs Kṛṣṇa, Rādhā and her numerous maids and companions are given human semblance, which enhances their charm. The mildness of Vaiṣṇava poetry influenced Kaviranjana Rāmaprasāda Sen, one of the leading Śākta poets of the eighteenth century.[108]

"The Caitanya cult gave rise to biographical literature which was indeed a revolutionary development in contemporary Bengali literature.[109] The models were provided by Vṛndāvana Dāsa and Kṛṣṇadāsa Kavirāja, whose biographies of Caitanya are still regarded as masterpieces. The Rādhā-Kṛṣṇa legend inspired Biharīlāl Caube (1600-1650) to compose seven hundred verses in Hindi, the anthology of which is known as *Bharīsatsai*. These verses deal mainly with Rādhā-Kṛṣṇa love, and they are said to have lent to medieval Hindi poetry a new, dynamic quality.

"Vṛndāvana became the center of the Caitanya cult. Here the Gosvāmins rescued the city from desolation. Vṛndāvana radiated the impulses which led to an artistic renaissance in Western and North-Western India. The traditional Western Indian Art was mainly Jaina Art. A pictorial version of the *Gītāgovinda*was produced in Western Indian in about 1450.[110] At the end of the sixteenth century a new type of painting dealing with the events of Kṛṣṇa's life came into vogue. The Kṛṣṇa theme brought an element of sophistication. The artistic efflorescence in the Rājput state of Udaipur (1628-1681) was a direct result of the growing popularity of the Kṛṣṇa cult. Archer writes:

> Such pictures have a lyrical splendor, a certain wild elation quite distinct from the previous Indian painting and we can explain these new stylistic qualities by reference to the cult of Krishna himself. The realization that Krishna was adorable, that his practice of romantic love was a sublime revelation of Godhead, and that in his worship lay release it the motive force behind these pictures and the result is a new style transcending in its rhythmical assurance and growing ardor all previous achievements.[111]

The Kṛṣṇa cult was a musical cult. It led to the development of new modes of classical songs like *Dhrupa, Dhūmār, Horī, Thumri* and *Tappā*.[112] The unique gift of Vaiṣṇavism to Bengal, Orissa and Assam was a very effective medium of mass communication called *kīrtana*, in which the wonderful lyricism of *Padāvalī* poetry found eloquent expression. Caitanya's biographies often refer to *kīrtana* singing, but its modes are not described in them. Later on at least three different styles of *kīrtana* developed in Bengal.[113]

"An important result of the Caitanya movement was the enrichment of Bengali, Assamese and Bihari folk literatures. Thousands of folk songs on Rādhā-Kṛṣṇa, *bhakti*, Caitanya, Nityānanda and the Vaiṣṇava way of life were composed by he unknown folk poets.[114] The Vaiṣṇava concept of the pangs of separation from the beloved was a very popular theme of the folks songs. On this idea grew up the *Bāramāsya* literature in the regional languages of Eastern India.[115] Even one hundred and two Muhammadan poets of Bengal composed songs on the loves of Rādhā and Kṛṣṇa.[116]

"The Bengali terracotta art was very much influenced by Vaiṣṇavism. The art was developed mainly in the Bānkurā district of WestBengal. Towards the close of the sixteenth century, Vīra Hāmvīra, the Malla king of Viṣṇupur, now a subdivisional town of the Bānkurā district, was converted into the faith probably by Śrīnivāsa Ācārya, who had brought cartloads of Vaiṣṇava manuscripts from Vṛndāvana. Vaiṣṇavism became the state religion of Viṣṇupur. The royal patronage of the Vaiṣṇava religion led to the building of numerous Vaiṣṇava temples in Viṣṇupur and Bānkurā. Thus a distinct style of architecture, known as the Bengali style, and different f rom the Nāgara, the Vesara, and the Drāviḍa styles, developed in West Bengal. The sculptural ornamentation was done on terracotta, and the variegation was indeed remarkable. The temples which were built towards the close of the sixteenth and the beginning of the seventeenth centuries were decorated with the sculpture of *līlās* of Kṛṣṇa and Rādhā as delineated in the Vaiṣṇava *Padāvalī* literature. The builders and patrons of these Vaiṣṇava temples were the Rājās, big and small. Later on the temples were built even by carpenters and ironsmiths.[117]

IV

"The turning point in the history of the Vaiṣṇava movement came when its most effective leader, Caitanya, went away to Purī, where he lived a life of devotional ecstasy till his death in 1533. After his death three main subsects grew up at Śantipur, Khaḍadaha and Vṛndāvana. Later on another subsect deveoped in the Śrīkhaṇḍa in the district of Burdwān.

"Though ascetics, and unquestionably celibate, the Gosvāmins of Vṛndāvana spent their lives in seeking philosophical and theological justification for the theory of the sportiveness of Kṛṣṇa. Their explanation of the afore-mentioned asexual conjugality looked strange when some of them began to write verses which were unmistakably erotic. The *Ujjvalanīlamaṇi* of Rūpa Gosvāmin is a big anthology of erotic verses. His *Dānakelikaumudī*, a *Bhaṇikā*, has scenes which are, to say the least, extremely improper. Many of its verses are highly suggestive *double entendres*. In one scene of this play Nāndīmukhī, a young nun of Vṛndāvana, shows Kṛṣṇa her bosom.[118] Raghunātha Gosvāmin (Dāsa), famous for his long and painful penance, wrote the *Muktācaritra* which records some speeches of Kṛṣṇa which are rather offensive.[119] The Gosvāmins emphasized the necessity of contemplation, remembrance, and constant analysis (*manana, smaraṇa, nididhyāsana*) of the sports of Kṛṣṇa. So, the *smaraṇamaṅgala* formulae were enunciated by Rūpa Gosvāmin, according to which well-defined periods are assigned to any particular day from dawn to dawn. During each of these periods Kṛṣṇa was supposed to have sported with Rādhā and her principal companions and their maidservants. More than thirty Sanskrit *Kāvyas* and innumerable vernacular verses were composed on these unending sports.[120]

"A strange dualism is seen in the lives and works of the Gosvāmins. They lived in great poverty; they were celibate. Their dedication to the cause was undoubtedly great. But their works are deeply tinged with libido. It is extremely difficult to establish a logical link between what they practiced and preached and what they produced, between their poor, austere, pure, unambitious lives and their outcrop of erotic literature. Toward the end of the nineteenth century Bankimchandra Chatterjee bitterly criticized the idea of God as a womanizer and beau. Towards the beginning of the nineteenth century Rammohun Ray poohpoohed the idea of ascribing divinity to Śrī Caitanya.[121]

"Caitanya was depicted as a god in the biographies. Later on he was given the mantle of a Nāgar or clandestine lover of the women of Navadvīpa.[122] But the Vṛndāvana Gosvāmins refused to recognize the validity of this idea. Yet its creators began to write highly erotic songs on the subject of the lover conceived by the ladies of Navadvīpa for handsome Gaurāṅga. It should, however, noted that in *Gaurāṅga* songs, Gaurāṅga (Caitanya) is more sinned against than sinning. The poets never say that he committed adultery with the women of Navadvīpa, who are depicted as the sinners. According to Vaiṣṇava theory, proximity to God (*samīpya*) was the most desirable stage that was to be attained by a real devotee. The Vaiṣṇavas thought that the best way of reaching that stage was to worship Rādhā-Kṛṣṇa as a *mañjarī* or adolescent maidservant. This type of worship gradually degenerated into transvestism. This form of worship, being sullied by libido, had not the simplicity and the wonderful spiritual uplift so beautifully described by Anatole France in *Our Lady's Juggler*, where the humble juggler tried to worship Mary simply by his jugglery with his balls. The *mañjarī* worship became so important that the Vaiṣṇavas believed that the establishment of a personal relation between God and the devotee was directly dependent on the intermediacy of a *mañjarī*. Even a talented poet like Rayā Śekhara regarded himself as a *mañjarī* of Rādhā.[123] Raghunātha Dāsa Gosvāmin wept and prayed so that he might be granted the *mañjarī* status. Rūpa Gosvāmin was regarded as Rūpamañjarī, who was the most important of all the maids of Rādhā.[124]

"The 'sexo-yogic' *sahajiyā* cult was popular in Bengal even before the advent of Caitanya. But, according to Dimock, the cult later on derived a good deal of inspiration from the Caitanya movement.[125] The *Sahajiyās* did not keep 'divine erotics' confined within the limits of contemplation, remembrance and analysis.[126] They did not believe in the celibacy of Caitanya and the seven Gosvāmins of Vṛndāvana.[127]

"It has been claimed by Sukumar Sen that the Caitanya movement did not really enfeeble the Bengali race.[126] But the point is a debatable one."'*Bhakti*', says J.N. Farqhar, '...is a surging emotion which chokes the speech, makes the tears flow and the hair thrill with pleasurable excitement, and often leads to hysterical laughing and weeping by turns, to sudden fainting fits and to long trances of unconsciousness.'[129] The *kīrtana* was designed to take the devotee to the farthest limits of ecstacy. The following is an eye-witness account of a *kirtana*, the main figure of which was Vijayakṛṣṇa Gosvāmin, a famous religious and social leader and reformer of nineteenth century Bengal:

> The Bāuls and the Vaiṣṇava saw the trembling figure of the Gosvāmin (Vijayakṛṣṇa) and began to sing the *kīrtana*. Many drums and cymbals were being simultaneously played upon. The tremendous sound made one 's hair thrill. The Gosvāmin at first danced to the tune. But suddenly he jumped up, and caught hold of Lāl, a young boy. Both of them danced, and the boy Lāl grew more and more ecstatic. He somehow came out of the Gosvāmin's embrace, and just danced a jig. The Gosvāmin cast a fierce look at him and like a veritable wrestler began to beat upon his own arms. Keeping watch on the Gosvāmin the boy went on dancing. The Gosvāmin let out a terrific roar, closed his left fist, stretched it towards the boy, and imitated the efforts of a bowman about to draw up his bow. He took a few steps towards the boy and then came back to his original position. Once again he roared and advanced towards the boy who, too, spread out his left arm in the form of a shield and tried hard to evade the Gosvāmin. He danced back to a spot that was 25-30 yards off from the position of the Gosvāmin. Then the boy also gave out a roar...and jumped forward and ran towards the

> Gosvāmin, who at once retreated 25-30 yards back. The Gosvāmin now yelled...and came forward in a menacing manner. The boy at once jumped back to his original position. This advance and retreat went one for a pretty long time. Śrīdhara (a disciple of the Gosvāmin,, and slightly mad) now took up the big, hot, smoking incense burner, and began to dance like a mad man. He suddenly advanced towards the Gosvāmin carrying the incense burner aloft...but the Gosvāmin ran. This scene caused a veritable pandemonium. People began to fall down in fainting fits.[130] (translated)

"For the practice of *bhakti* the Vaiṣṇavas sequestrated themselves in *ākhḍās* (monasteries). The *ākhḍās* created a gulf between Vaiṣṇavism and the common people, and the religion grew exclusive. A time came when even the *Padāvali* poems were secreted inside the inaccessible *ākhḍās* by jealous monks. Towards the close of the nineteenth century eminent scholars like Haraprasad Śāstrī, Saradācharan Mitra, Akṣayakumar Sarkār, Jagatbandhu Bhadra, Śiśirkumar Ghosh, Rajkrishna Mukherjee, Rāmagati Nyāyaratna, and Dīnesh Chandra Sen and others had to work very hard to discover them.[131]

"Vaiṣṇava exclusiveness and the conformity to the aesthetic rules enunciated by Rūpa Gosvāmin made the *Padāvalīs* ornate and artificial. Sukumar Sen writes:

> I admit that there is no variety in the story of Rādhā-Kṛṣṇa love as told by the Vaiṣṇava poets. I admit that it lacks depth and breadth, and that its social implications are not faultless. But when I consider that the love is symbolic, I forget the limitations of time and place.[132] (translated)

"The same was the view of Rabindranath Tagore. But it was also Rabindranath Tagore who expressed in strong terms his dislike of the tricks of amorous Kṛṣṇa on which the *Kabiyāl* poets of nineteenth century Bengal had composed numerous songs.[133]

"According to one authority Caitanya was able to establish the supremacy of the spiritual man over the carnal man, the economic man, and the man of might.[134] But his contention is rejected by S.K. De, who considers eroticism the bane of the faith.[135]

NOTES

1 The extent and nature of epigraphic evidence has been discussed by S.C. Mukherjee in *A Study of Vaisnavism in Ancient and Medieval Bengal.* According to Suniti Kumar Chatterjee, 'there is a hiatus in the history of the Vaishnava sect in North-Eastern India from the twelfth to the fifteenth century, to fill up which iconography can supply no materials". Jayadeva, pp. 63-64.

2 Raṃānuja (d. 1137 A.D.), author of *Śrībhāṣya,* organized a party of seventy-four spiritual leaders who preached Viśiṣṭādvaitavāda.

3The opening verse of *Gītāgovinda* refers to an incident described in the *Brahmavaivartapurāṇa,* II, 4, 15.

4 Nihar Ranjan Ray, *Bāngālīr Itihās,* p. 401. See Āychiyār Kauryāi, *Gītāgovinda and its Abhinaya,* ed. Vāsudeva Śāstrī, Tanjore, Sarasvati Mahal Library, 1963; also, Svāmī Prajñānanda, *Padāvalī Kīrtaner Itihās,* Vol. I, Ch. 10 and 11. Jayadeva has been claimed for Orissa; iconographic evidence has been adduced to prove the Orissan origin of Jayadeva's religious concepts. *A Descriptive Catalogue of Sanskrit Manuscripts of Orissa, in the collection of the Orissa State Museum, Bhuvaneswara,* ed. Kedarnath Brahapatra, Bhuvaneswara, Orissa Sāhitya Akademi, 1960, pp. xxxvi-lxi.

5 S.C. Mukherjee, op. cit., pp. 25-26.

6 Hāla, *Gāthāsaptaśatī,* with the commentary of Mathurānāth Śāstrī, Bombay: Nirnaya Sagara Press, 3d ed. 1933. I: verse 89; II: verse 14; V: verse 47.

7 B.B. Majumdar (Bimānbiharī Majumdār) *Kṛṣṇa in History and Legend,* pp. 192-193; S.K. Chatterjee, *Jayadeva,* p. 13.

8 B.B. Majumdar, op. cit. Ch. I, Appendix I: Chs. III, IV.

9 S.C. Mukherjee, op. cit., pp. 23-24.

10 Daniel H.H. Ingalls, *Sanskrit Poetry from Vidyākara's 'Treasury',* Cambridge, Mass. Harvard University Press, 1968, p. 208, translation of verse 980.

11 Govardhanācārya, Jayadeva's contemporary, composed a good number of *ślokas* on Krsna's divine achievements and love. *Āryāsaptaśatī,* ed. with the commentary of Ananta Paṇdita, Kāvyamālā-I, Bombay, Nirnayasagar Press, 3d ed., 1934. Some of

these verses are: 104, 286, 310, 379, 431, 437, 488, 508, 509, 530. Numerous other poets composed verses on the Rādhā-Kṛṣṇa theme in the twelfth and thirteenth centuries. These verses are collected in *Subhāṣitaratnakośa,* Śrīdhara Dāsa's *Saduktikarṇāmṛta* (ed. S.C. Banerjee, Calcutta: Firma K.L. Mukhopadhyay, 1965), Vallabhadeva's *Subhāṣitāvalī* (ed. P. Peterson, and Durgāprasād, Bombay: 1886), etc. Nearly 200 verses on Rādhā-Kṛṣṇa have been collected from different anthologies and sources by Nārāyaṇa Rām Achārya, Kāvyatīrtha, in *Subhāṣitaratnabhaṇḍāgāram*, Bombay, Nirnaya Sagar Press, eighth ed. 1952, pp. 22-26. According to Sukumar Sen (*Bāngālā Sāhityer Itihās,* Vol. I, Part I, p. 99) the *Bhāgavatapurāṇa* was unknown to the Bengalis before the fifteen century A.D. But this view has been challenged by Jāṇhavīkumār Chakravarti in *Āryāsaptatī o Gauḍavanga,* Calcutta; Sanyal & Co. B.E. 1378 (19710, pp. 84-91. Jāṇhavīkumār shows that some of the verses of Govardhanācārya bear unmistakable evidence of the influence of the *Bhāgavatapurāṇa.*

12 Jayadev Gaṇguly, "The social and religious background of the study of *smṛti* in Mithila", *Our Heritage*. Sanskrit College, Calcutta, January-June, 1962, Vol. X, Part I, p. 51: "There can be little doubt that those Mithila settlers tried to aryanise the country by means of Vaiṣṇavism."

13 *Subhāṣitaratnakośa,* pp. li-lvi.

14 *Ekallavīracaṇḍamahāroṣaṇa Tantra*, for instance, advises the practice of incest and other perversions. "One can go hopelessly astray", writes D.L. Snellgrove, "if one attempts to make deductions oneself from literal interpretations of the *tantras*. Such procedure may throw light upon their origins, but by no means does it explain their significance for Buddhist tradition." *The Hevajra Tantra: A Critical Study* (in two parts) London: Oxford University Press, 1959, Preface, VIII. Alex Wayman (*The Buddhist Tantras*, London: Routledge and Kegan Paul, 1974) also supports this view. Should we, then, rely on the interpretations of the commentators? If we are rely on them, we will find that even some of the commentators prefer a literal interpretation of the Buddhist *tantras*. The *Yogaratnamālā* commentary on verse 13, part II, Chapter XI of the *Hevajratantra* is the following: "*dolāyetyādineti caturṇāṃ sekānāṃ svabhāvakalakṣaṇopadeśakāraṇāny āha. doleva lolā. aupariṣṭakam / atra strī kartrī.*"

Then it goes on quoting verses describing coital postures. Snellgrove, op. cit., part II, p. 98; 158.

15 *Subhāṣitaratnakośa* pp. lvi ff.

16 Ibid.

17 Pramode Lal Paul, *The Early History of Bengal, from the Earliest Times to the Muslim Conquest,* 2 vols. Calcutta: Indian Research Publications no. 2 and 3, 1939-40. Vol. 2, Ch. XI, pp. 90-94; S.C. Mukherjee, op. cit. p. 38. Nalinīkānta Bhaṭṭaśālī discussed the prevalence of Vaiṣṇavism in two articles published in monthly journal *Vikrampura* (ed. Jogendranāth Gupta, Dacca), Kārika, 1320 B.E. (1913) and Māgha, 1320 B.E. (1913). In the second article published in Māgha, 1913 he mentions the following villages of Vikrampura where images of Viṣṇu had been discovered: Rāmapāla, Pāikpāḍā, Vajrayoginī, Cuḍāin, Munsīganja, Ābdullāpur, Sonārang, Tāngībāḍī, Vetkā, Mahākālī, Bāheraka, Kāmārkhāḍā, Pālang, Kuḍāsī, Ṇāgara, Nadiyā, Nasankara, Hānsāil, Śīyāldi, Bāghra, Lauhajang, Brāmanġāon, Korhati, Rikābibāzār, Āutsahī, Bharākair, Kalmā, Chhayagāon, Keoar, Duāllī, Kukudiyā. "Vikrarpurer Prācīna Bhāskarakīrti", p. 184.

18 *Gītāgovinda,* I, verse 9.

19 Vaḍu Caṇḍīdāsa, *Śrīkṛṣṇakīrtana,* p. 235, verse 4; *Bhaktirasāmṛtasindhu* 2:5:119, regards Mīna (Fish) Incarnation of Viṣṇu as the incarnation of *Bibhatasarasa.* But Jīva Gosvāmin, in his commentary, opines that for *Mīna,* Buddha should be read: *Mīnasthāne Buddho vā paṭhaniyāḥ. Taccestāyā arocakatvāt, / Mīnasya Saccidāndnadvigrahatvāt. // Durghatasamāsagamani,* 2.5.119.

20 Govindadāsa, one of the major composers of Vaiṣṇava *Padāvalīs*, was deeply influenced by the Vrajabulī language used by Vidyāpati. Rabindranath Tagore composed *Bhāṇusiṃha Ṭhākurer Padāvalī* (Calcutta, 1884) in that language. Sukumar Sen, *Vicitra Nibandha,* Calcutta: Śatāvdī Granthabhavan, 1961, pp. 72-137.

21 Vidyāpati, *Kīrtilatā*, ed. Haraprasād Śāstrī, Calcutta: 1924, p.19.

22 Vidyāpati, *Padāvalī, padas* 498, 499.

23 Vidyāpati puts a great stress on Rādhā. Here the influence of the *Brahmavaivartapurāṇa* is discernible. But his description of Kṛṣṇa as the supreme lord in many *padas* is an evidence of the influence of *Bhāgavatapurāṇa.*

24 Sukumar Sen, *Bāngālā Sāhityer Itihās*, Vol. I, Part I, pp. 136-182 Satyakinkar Sādhanā, *Caṇḍīdāsa Prasaṅga*, and Jogesh Chandra Rāy's introduction to Kṛṣṇaprasāda Sen's *Caṇḍīdāsacarita*.

25 The Gauḍīya Vaiṣṇavas neglected it presumably because Vāḍu Caṇḍīdāsa's idea of Rādhā and Kṛṣṇa was different from their concept. According to B.B. Majumdar, "Nowhere else in the whole range of Indian literature has Kṛṣṇa been vilified so much as in this poem." *Kṛṣṇa in History and Legend*, p. 201. But Sukumar Sen (op. cit. p. 181) describes Vaḍu Caṇḍīdāsa as a 'great poet'.

26 *Vāśulīmaṅgala*, ed. Subal Chandra Bandhopādhyāy and Subhendusundar Sinharāy, Calcutta: Gangīya Sāhitya Pariṣat, B.E. 1364 (1957). This work was written towards the beginning of the fifteenth century. According to Maheśvar Dās, Vāsulī was not a folk goddess, but was identifiable with Vāgīśvarī. But this view is not based upon sufficient data. See *Suvarṇalekhā*, Calcutta: Published by the Department of Bengali, University of Calcutta, 1974, on the completion of the fifty years. "Mangalakāvyer Deva Devī", p. 629. Vṛndāvana Dāsa refers to the worship of Vāśulī in Navadvīpa at the time of Caitanya's advent: *Vāsulī Pūjaye Keha Nānā Upahāre / Madya Māṃsa Diyā Keha Yakṣa Pūjā Kare //*. (Some people worship Vāsulī with many presents; some worship the *Yakṣa* with wine and meat.) *Caitanyabhāgavata*, p. 12.

27 *Śrīkṛṣṇākīrtana, Bālakāṇḍa*, pp. 289-292.

28 These folk songs are known as *Kṛṣṇa Dhāmalī*. Dinesh Chandra Sen, *Bṛhat Banga* Vol. II, pp. 970, 972, 1006. The influence of these song lingers in the *Bhāoyāyiyā* and *Catkā* folk songs of North Bengal, many of which are collected in *Uttar Banger Pallīgīti*, ed. Hariśchandra Pāl, Calcutta: Sāyal & Co. 2 Vols. 1973-1974. The erotic aspects of the career of Kṛṣṇa in Vṛndāvana is the subject of Bhavānanda's *Harivaṃsa* ed. Satīś Chandra Rāy, Dacca; University of Decca, 1932. The episodes are described in this curious work in a manner which is designed to titillate the erotic fancies of the reader. The manuscripts of this work were discovered in Mymensing, Comilla, and Western Tripura districts of Bangladesh. Some of the songs of this work greatly influenced the love poems composed by the Muhammadan poets of Sylhet. Sukumar Sen thinks that the work was modeled on an undiscovered Sanskrit Kāvya titled *Harivaṃsa* in which he erotic sports of Kṛṣṇa were narrated. The *Harivaṃsa* of

Bhavānanda is undoubtedly a work like Vaḍu Caṇḍīdāsa's *Śrīkṛṣṇakīrtana*. Sukumar Sen, *Bāṅgālā Sāhityer Itihās,* Vol. I, Part II, pp. 70-82. He analyzes the folk elements in this work. The continuing influence of the Rādhā-Kṛṣṇa legend on the folk songs of Bengal deserves a separate study.

29 *Śrīkṛṣṇakīrtana*, pp. 332-39. The milkmaids of Vṛndāvana experienced great agony when Kṛṣṇa went away to Mathurā. In later Padāvalī songs this development is styled *Māthura.*

30 *Ekādaśīviveka, Dolayātraviveka, Rāsayātraviveka,* etc.

31 Note 26, and the quotation from *Caitanyabhāgavata.* Kṛṣṇānanda Āgamavāgīśā, author of *Tantrasāra*, is said to have been a classmate of Caitanya. Kānticandra Rāḍi, (*Navadvīpa Mahimā*, pp. 68-86), gives an account of the Buddhist influence in Navadvīpa, and discusses the influence and popularity of *Tantrasāra,* (op. cit. 203, 209). Kānticandra Rāḍi discusses mainly the traditions and legends.

32 *Pañcamakāra* means the Tantric ritual use of *madya* (wine), *māṃsa* (meat), *matsya* (fish), *mudrā* (food that is taken with wine),and *maithuna* (coitus). *Śaktisaṃgama Tantra* (*Tārā Khaṇḍa*) describes many of the orgiastic rituals in enigmatic language which has been severely bowdlerized by B. Bhattacharyya.

33 Ramesh Chandra Majumdar, *Bāṅgladeśer Itihās,* Vol. II, pp. 260-268; Harekṛṣṇa Mukhopādhyāy, *Padāvalī Paricaya,* Calcutta: Gurudas Chattopadhyay & Sons, B.E. 1366 (1959), pp. 39-40. According to Bāṇī Chakravartī, Raghunandana, the celebrated writer of *Smṛti* tracts was a '*samājasaṃskāraka*' (social reformer)(Bāṇī Chakravartī, *Samājakasaṃskāraka Raghunandana,* Calcutta: Navagranthana, 1964). Benoy Kumar Sarkar describes Raghunandana as a 'rationalist' in regard to Hindu image and worship". B.K. Sarkar, *The Positive Background of Hindu Sociology,* Allahabad, 1937, p. 615. But, according to Jayadev Gāṅgulī, the trend in the *smṛti* writings of Mithilā, Gauḍa and Orissa was definitely conservative and, in some respects, even reactionary. According to him, there were two groups of *smṛti* writers from the end of the fourteenth century towards the middle of the fifteenth. The first group consisted of conservative and traditional *smṛti* writers like Indrapati and Udayasiṃha. The second group was constituted by liberal *Smṛti* writers who tried to introduce reformatory measures 'by

introducing extra-vedic texts in view of the changed conditions in the society.' *Our Heritage*, July-December, 1962, Vol. X, part II, p. 107.

34 Jayānanda, in *Caitanyamaṅgala*, gives some details about the tyranny of the Muhammadans: Nadīya-4,pp. 13-14. The importance of the Muslim conquest of Bengal considered as the background of the 'liberal' movement of Caitanya is explained by Devajyoti Burman in *Indo-Muslim Relations: A Study in Historical Background*, Calcutta: Jugabāṇī Sāhitya Chakra, 28 Kabir Road, n. d. pp. 48-52, 83-95. Janārdan Chakravartī, however, opines that the Muslim rulers of Bengal tolerated the Caitanya movement and thus showed their liberalism. Janārdan Chakravartī, *Śrī Rādhātattva O Śrī Caitanyasaṃskṛti*, Kamalā Lectures, Calcutta: University of Calcutta, 1972, pp. 176-193.

35 The necessity of adopting *bhakti* as a panacea is explained by Vṛndāvana Dāsa, *Caitanyabhāgavata*, Ādi Khaṇḍa, pp. 9-18. Kavi Kamṇapūra explains it in the *Caitanyacandrodaya*, Acts I and II. The themes of these two Acts seem to have been borrowed from Kṛṣṇa Miśra Yati's *Prabodhacandrodaya*.

36 Īśvara Purī was born in Kumārahaṭṭa (Hālisahar), near Calcutta. Bimānbiharī Majumdār, *Śrīcaitanyacariter Upādān*, p. 625.

37 A detailed account (which is mainly based on local legends and traditions) of Vaisṇavism in Śrīhaṭṭa occurs in Acyutaraṇ Chaudhurī and Baidyanāth De's *Śrīhatter Itivṛtta*, Parts I-IV, Silchar, B.E. 1324 (1927).

38 The *Gaurapadataraṅginī*, ed. Jagadbandhu Bhadra, has a collection of songs which describe the various ceremonies and rituals performed by Jagannātha Miśra, Caitanya's father, and his friends. See *Dvitīyaraṅga*. See also Vṛndāvana Dāsa, op. cit. Ādi Khaṇḍam Chapters 3-9.

39 According to Bimānbiharī Majumdār, of 490 followers of Caitanya, as many as 239 followers were Brāhmaṇas, 29 Kāyasthas, 37 Vaidyas, 2 Muhammadans,and 16 'women'. *Śrīcaitanyacarite Upādān*, p. 567.

40 Gītā Chattopadhyay, *Bhāgavata O Banglāsāhitya*, pp 159-172; Bimanbiharī Majumdār, op. cit., pp. 540-543; Sukumar Sen, *Bāngālā Sāhityer Itihās*, Vol. I Part I, pp. 129-131; Kṛṣṇadāsa Kavirāja, in *Caitanyacaritāmṛta*, pp. 41-42, attaches great importance to

Mādhavendra Purī, who is regarded as the principal figure in the Vaiṣṇava revival by Cūḍāmaṇi Dāsa, in *Gaurāṅgavijaya*, pp. 6-15.

41 According to Dinesh Chandra Bhattāchāryya, Srīdharasvāmin was a Bengali.'Śrīdhara Svāmir Kulaparicaya o Kālanirmaya', *Pravaśī* (Bengali Monthly Journal), Calcutta: Māgha, B.E. 1358 (1951), pp. 411-414. See P.K. Gode, "Date of Śrīdharasvāmin, author of the Commentaries on the Bhāgavatapurāṇa", Annals of the Bhandarkar Oriental Research Institute, Vol. XXX, Parts III, IV, pp. 277-283. The theory and practice of *bhakti* were enunciated in *Bhaktisūtras of Nārada and Śāṇḍīlya Sūtraṃ* (translated by Nandalal Sinha, Oriental Publishers, Delhi, n.d.) and *The Bhaktiratnāvalī* (translated by A.B., Allahabad, The Panini Office, 1918) with the commentary of Viṣṇu Purī.

42 Sundarananda Vidyāvinoda, *Gauḍīya Darśaner Itihās O Vaiśiṣṭa*, pp. 120-124; Rūpa Gosvāmin, *Padyāvalī*, verses 15, 28, 43; S.K. De, *Vaiṣṇava Faith and Movement*, pp. 17-18; Kṛṣṇadāsa Kavirāja, op. cit. p. 512.

43 Kṛṇadāsa Kavirāja, p. cit. p. 512; *Śrīdhara Avāmī Prasāde Bhāgavata Jāni / Jagatguru Śrīdhara Svāmī Guru Kari Māni //* (I know the *Bhāgavata* through the commentary of Śrīdharasvāmin. He is the Preceptor of the World; that is why I regard him as my Preceptor, too.)

44 Sukumar Sen, op. cit. Vol. I, Part I, p. 288.

45 Sukumar Sen suggests that Sufi influence might have come from 'Yavana' Haridāsa.

46 This has been discussed in detail by Upandranāth Bhattāchāryya in *Bānglār Bāul O Bāul Gān*, Part I; see Dimock, *The Place of the Hidden Moon*, pp. 251-270. The influence of the Rādhā-Kṛṣṇa legend is faintly seen in a story of the Arabian Nights. See 'The Tender Tale of Prince Jasmine and Princess Almond', in *The Book of the Thousand Nights and One Night*, Powys Mathers, London: Routledge and Kegan Paul, 1956, Vol. IV.

47 *Subhāṣitaratnakośa*, pp. liv-lv.

48 Bhupendranath Datta, *Vaiṣṇave Sāhitye Samājatattva*, intro. p. 6.

49 The early biographers of Caitanya, including Kṛṣṇādāsa Kavirāja, are silent about Caitanya's death. Locana, in *Caitanya-maṅgala*, Śeṣakhaṇḍa, pp. 116-117 gives a legendary account of his

fusion with the idol of Jagannātha. Only Jayānanda describes an accident that caused Caitanya's death. According to him Caitanya's left foot was wounded while he was dancing. On the sixth day after the accident he felt a great pain on his foot. On the following day he died of the wound. See *Caitanyamaṅgala* (Asiatic Society ed.), Uttarakhaṇḍa, verses 144-151, p. 234. According to Sukumar Sen Jayānanda's account may be 'partly true'; op. cit., Vol. I, Part I, p. 383. But even a highly reliable Vaiṣṇava scholar like Rādhāgovinda Nāth believes that Caitanya simply 'disappeared'. *Śrī Śrī Caitanyacaritāmṛter Bhūmikā*, 4th ed. p. 63.

50 The true history of his travels is lost in a maze of conflicting legends. Bimānbiharī Majumdāra, *Śrīcaitanyacariter Bhūmikā*, pp. 15-21, 215-221,241-256, 354-365, 396-404, 518.

51 Verrier Elwin, *The Tribal Myths of Orissa*; the tribes are Beinjhwar, Bondo Highlanders, Gadāba, Parnenga. But the tribal 'Mahāprabhu' was certainly not a Vaiṣṇava.

52 Vṛndāvana Dāsa, Madhyakhaṇḍa, Ch. 14; Sukumar Sen, op. cit., Vol. I, Part I, pp. 293-294.

53 R.G. Bhandarkar wrongly refers to him as the elder brother of Caitanya. *Vaiṣṇavism, Saivism,* etc. p. 119.

54 Vṛndāvana Dāsa describes how Nityānanda and 'Yavana' Haridāsa were chased by Jagāi and Mādhāi through the narrow streets of Navadvīpa when the former proposed conversion. *Caitanyabhāgavata,* Madhya Khāṇda, Ch. 13. Jagāi and Mādhāi were Brāhmaṇas.

55 *The Cultural Heritage of India,* Vol. II, p. 153.

56 Kavi Karṇapūra, op. cit. Act VII, p. 262: "'*Mahārāja, Sa khalu sahajavaiṣṇava bhavati. Pūrvam ayam asmākamupahāsapātram āsīt...*" (O King! He is but a 'Sahaja' (simple) Vaiṣṇava. Formerly he was the butt of our ridicule.) S.K. De, *Vaiṣṇava Faith and Movement*, pp. 92-94.

57 Ramesh Chandra Majumdār, *Bānglā Deśer Itihās*, Vol. II, pp. 87-95; Bimanbiharī Majumdār, op. cit. Ch. 5; Govardhana Dāsa, *Śrī ŚrīVrajadhāma O Gosvāmīgaṇa* Vol. II, Chapter 4-6.

58 S.K. De, op. cit. p. 103; J.N. Farqhar, *An Outline of the Religious Literature,* pp. 229-230.

59 S.K. De, op. cit. p. 104. The views of S.K. De and J.N. Farqhar have been challenged by Girijaśankar Rāychaudhurī in *Bānglā Carita*

Granthe Śrīcaitanya, pp. 302-303. According to Kṛṣṇadāsa Kavirāja, *Caitanyacaritāmṛta*, p. 35, Caitanya himself directed Rūpa and Sanātana to spread the cult in Mathurā and Vṛndāvana regions. The later development of the Bengali Vaiṣṇava colonies in these areas and in the Uttar Pradesh province is described by Jñānendramohan Dās in *Banger Bāhire Bāngālī*, Calcutta: Anāth Nāth Mukhopādhyāy, 1915.

60 Vṛndāvana Dāsa, *Caitanyabhāgavata*, p. 275: They even decided to report to the Muhammadan 'Kāzi' (Magistrate) of Navadvīpa what they considered Caitanya's misconduct. Kṛṣṇadāsa Kavirāja, in *Caitanyacaritāmṛta*, pp. 93-94, refers to four or five '*Pāṣaṇḍī*'s (infidels) who regarded Caitanya's 'Kīrtana' songs highly dangerous to the *Dharma* of the Hindus. Obviously the conservative elements of Navadvīpa were not impressed by the 'unique' religious personality of Caitanya who fearlessly preached his faith specially among the lower castes. As to Caitanya's quarrel with the students who were prepared to form a '*samavāya*' (Union) against him, see Vṛndāvana Dāsa, op. cit., pp. 291-292.

61 *Caitanyacaritāmṛta*, pp. 41-54.

62 Ibid., p. 13:

Rādhā Kṛṣṇa Eka Ātmā Dui Deha Dhāre /
Anyonye Vilase Rasa Āsvādana Kare //
Sei Dui Eka Eve Caitanyagosāiṇ /
Rasa Āsvādite Donhe Haila Eka Thāin //

(Rādhā and Kṛṣṇa have one soul but two separate bodies. Each of them luxuriates in mutual enjoyment of love's bliss. These two entities are now unified in Caitanya Gosvāmin. They have combined in him to taste bliss.

Vāsudeva Ghoṣa, one of the intimate companions of Caitanya at Navadvīpa, wrote the following song on the subject of Rādhā-Kṛṣṇa combination in the body of Caitanya:

Gaurānga Nahita Ki Mene Haita
Kemane Dharita De /
Rādhāra Mahimā Premarasasīmā
Jagate Jānata Ke //

(Were Gauranga (Caitanya) not born, what would have happened? How could have I lived? Who would have preached in this world the sublime significance of Rāḍhā, and the very limits of love's benediction?) See *Vāsu Ghoṣer Padāvalī*, ed. Mālavikā Chākī, Cacutta: Bangīya Sāhitya Pariṣat, B.E. 1368 (1961), pp. 160-161. The exposition of the embodiment of Rādhā-Kṛṣṇa conjugality in Caitanya seems to be one of the primary purposes of Kṛṣṇadāsa Kavirāja, who begins his great work with its formulation. Dimock analyses the mystic significance of this idea and its impact on the development of the Sahajiyā doctrine, op. cit. pp. 146-152.

63 The idea of the Raḍhā-Kṛṣṇa combination in Caitanya is not emphasized in Sanātana Gosvāmin's *Bṛhatbhagavatāmṛta*. According to him, Caitanya's primary objective was to preach *prema* and *bhakti*. Vide, the first three verses of *Bṛhatbhagavatāmṛta* and the commentary on them. Rūpa Gosvāmin in *Caitanyāṣṭakaṃ* describes Caitanya as God; but the opening verses in his *Haṃsadūtaṃ* does not contain any reference to Caitanya. Jīva Gosvāmin has not described any of the *līlās* (sports) of Caitanya, nor has he composed a *Sandarbha* on him. But in the terminating verse of *Kṛṣṇasandarbha* he has equated Caitanya with Kṛṣṇa. In *Sarvasaṃvādinī* he has tried to establish the theory of Caitanya's divinity. Prabodhānanda Sarasvatī was the first among Caitanya's biographers to stress perhaps the beginning of the theory of *Gaurapāramyavāda*. In verse 132 Prabodhānanda also described Caitanya or Gaurāṅga as *Gaurāṅganāgarararaḥ*. Prabodhānanda's method or worship was very similar to that of Narahari Sarkar and Locana Dāsa. But the Gosvāmins of Vṛndāvana do not refer to *Gaurapāramyavāda* or *Gauranāgaravāda* in their works. They wrote far more works on Kṛṣṇa and his worship than on Caitanya. The differences between the Gauḍīya and the Vṛndāvana schools are explained by S.K. De, op. cit., pp. 421-447.

64 Sukumar Sen, op. cit. Vol. I, Part I, pp. 294-295; 441: the following doggerel was current in Bengal:

Māgur Mācher Jhol,
Bharā Yuvatīr Kol,
Bol Hari Bol

(To the people who shout the name of Hari, religion means the curry of Māgur fish, and the lap of a full-blooded wench) This doggerel is a banter on the unorthodox ways of Nityānanda.

65 The *Pañcatattva* doctrine was first enunciated by Kṛṣṇadāsa Kavirāja, in *Caitanyacaritāmṛta*, pp. 97-98. It recognized Gaurāṅga,

Nityānanda, and Advaita as the cardinals of the faith. Later on Śrīnivāsa and Gadādhara Paṇḍita were regarded as two other cardinals. The history of this theory is discussed by Bimānbihārī Majumdār, op. cit. pp. 260-261; p. 575.

Recently Kṣudirām Dās has challenged the idea of a split among the Vaiṣṇavas. But his approach seems to be emotional. ('Gaura-Kṛṣṇa Upāsanāya Navadvīpa-Vṛndāvana', in *Ācaryya Rādhagovinda Nāth Smārakagrantha,* ed. Janārdana Chakravarti, p. 49ff.) Śiśir Kumār Ghosh, the founder of the *Amrita Bazar Patrika* of Calcutta, and an orthodox Gauḍīya Vaiṣṇava, laid much stress on the differences between the methods adopted by Nityānanda and the Gosvāmins of Vṛndāvana for the propagation of the faith. In his opinion Nityānanda's approach was basically emotional, while that of the Gosvāmins was intellectual. He considers Nityānanda's methods much more efficacious than those of the Gosvāmins. Śiśir Kumār Ghosh, *Śrī Amiya Nimāicarita,* vol. 5, 3rd ed. Calcutta, Amritabazar Patrika Office, 1917, pp. 173-174.

66 S.K. De, op. cit. Ch. III. Sundarānanda Vidyāvinoda analyzes their philosophical views in *Gauḍīya Darśaner Itihās O Vaiśiṣṭya,* pp. 327-393.

67 S.N. Dasgupta, *A History of Indian Philosophy,* Cambridge, Cambridge University Press, 1955, Vol. IV, pp. 17-18. Jīva Gosvāmin's emphasis on Purāṇic evidence resulted in practical circumscription of evidence within the limits of a few Vaiṣṇava Purāṇas. Non-Vaiṣṇava texts are considered untruthful.

68 Sukumar Sen, op. cit. Vol. I, Part I, p. 324. Tapan Raychaudhuri, *Bengal under Akbar and Jahangir,* pp. 125-128. According to Max Weber (*From Max Weber, Essays in Sociology,* ed. H.H. Gerth and C. Wright Mills, London, Routledge and Kegan Paul, 1957, pp. 283-284) the religion of the "mystagogues in Asia...the cult of Krishna as well as the cult of Christ have been more firmly rooted among civic strata than among any other." By 'civic strata' Weber means 'artisans, traders, enterprizers, engaged in cottage industry and their derivatives existing only in the modern Occident". It is only in the account of Vṛndāvana Dāsa that we find a clear reference to Caitanya's association with the various trading communities of Navadvīpa. He is said to have visited their shops and establishments. Obviously Caitanya tried to spead the faith among the affluent but

lowly traders. *Caitanyabhāgavata*, Ch. 2, pp. 9-18; Ch. 10, p. 66. According to Jadunāth Sarkār, "the new life breathed into Bengal Hinduism by Chaitanya's creed burst forth in another direction. The Vaiṣṇava Gosains set themselves to converting aboriginal tribes and thus brought a new light into their lives after ages of neglect, contumely and superstition." *History of Bengal*, II, pp. 221-222.

69 Dinesh Chandra Bhattāchāryya quotes the opening verse of Vāsudeva Sārvabhauma's *Hetvābhāsaprakaraṇa* to prove that he was a devout Vaiṣṇava even before he came into contact with Caitanya at Purī. The following is that important *śloka*"

Hṛdvyomakamalāsīnaṃ Tattvasādhakamadbhutaṃ /
Anābhāsaṃ Paraṃ Dhāma Ghanaśyāmanaṃ Aham Bhaje //

Dinesh Chandra Bhattāchāryya, *Bāngalīr Sārasvat Avadān*, Vol. 1, Calcutta: Bangīya Sāhitya Pariṣat, 1st ed. B.E. 1358 (1951), p. 38. Rūpa Gosvāmin quotes the following verses of Sārvabhauma:

Jñātaṃ Kāṇabhujaṃ Mataṃ Paricitaivānvīkṣikī, Śikṣitā,
Mīmāṃsā, Viditaiva Sāṃkhyasaraṇir Yoge Vitīrṇā Matiḥ /
Vedāntāḥ Pariśīlītāḥ Sarabhasam, Kintu Sphuranmādhurī,
Dhārā Kācana Nandasūnumuralī Maccittamākarṣati //

Rūpa Gosvāmin, *Padyāvalī*, verse 99. (I have learnt the theories of Kāṇabhuja (Kanāda). I am acquainted with the intricacies of *Ānvikṣikī*-Logic. I have cultivated Mīmāṃsā. I have learnt the ways of Sāṃkhya philosophy. My intellect has been drowned in the philosophy of Yoga. Quite furiously have I cultivated Vedānta. But not one of these subjects has attracted my mind so much as the flow of pure bliss that comes out of the flute of one Kṛṣṇa, son of Nanda.)

70 Chittaranjan Dev, *Bānglār Palīgīti*, Calcutta: National Book Agency, 1966, pp. 403-404.

71 *The Cultural Heritage of India*, II, p. 154. The Śrīnivāsa legend is given in Narahari Chakravarti's *Bhaktiratnākara, Taraṅga*, 6-7.

72 Vṛndāvana Dāsa was a direct disciple of Nityānanda. In this biography Caitanya is depicted as a God-intoxicated young man who felt very little concern for scholasticism. Scholars felt a great dread in his presence.

73 Kṛṣṇadāsa Kavirāja, *Caitanyacaritāmṛta*, ed. Sukumar Sen, Sāhitya Akademi, New Delhi, 1963. Vide, *Ādilīlā*: Ch. I, pp. 2-4; III, pp. 6-10; IV, pp. 11-18;VII, pp. 26-35; IX, pp. 41-44; XVII, pp. 83-84; 97-98. *Madhyalīlā*: Ch. I, pp. 112-121; VI, 156-158; 161-164; VII, the

whole Chapter; IX, 208-214; XIII, 264-266; XV, 284; XVII, 321-324; XVIII, 336, 340-341; XIX, 374-379; XXII, 379-387; XXIII,387-391; XXIV, 392-405. *Antyalīlā*: I, pp. 430-432; III, 449-451; VII, 505-506; 510-512; XV, 578-583; XVI, 589-592; XX, 613-617.

74 *Iśvaraḥ Paramaḥ Kṛṣṇaḥ Saccidānandavigrahaḥ* /
Anādir Āsi Govindaḥ Sarvakāraṇakāraṇaṃ //
Brahmasaṃhitā, 5: I.

75 Dīnendra Chaudhurī, *Pūrvabaṅglār Lokasangīta*, Calcutta: B.E. 1375 (1968), p. 147.

76 Girīndranārayan Mallik, *The Philosophy of Vaisnava Religion*, Vol. I, pp. 267-268. Kṛṣṇadāsa Kavirāja states that Kṛṣṇa is realized in Love and not in the cultivation of Knowledge or Yoga, op. cit. p. 87. Kṛṣṇa is said to have assumed the form of Caitanya, the *bhakta*, in order to enjoy his own bliss, op. cit. p. 27. Caitanya was the embodiment of devotion.

77 The various categories of devotional love are explained in the Fifth Wave of Rūpa Gosvāmin's *Bhaktirasāmṛtasindhu*. Kṛṣṇadāsa Kavirāja, p. 354.

78 Rūpa Gosvāmin, *Ujjvalanīlamaṇi*, (Haridās Dās, ed.,) p. 16: The *Priyanarmasakhā* category of Kṛṣṇa's bosom friends.

79 The scene is vividly painted in Kavi Karṇapūra's *Ānandavṛndāvana Campū*, Ch. 5, p. 105.

80 Says Kṛṣṇadāsa Kavirāja (p. 17)

Kāma Preme Dohākāra Vibhinna Lakṣaṇa /
Lauha Āra Heme Yaiche Svarūpa Vilakṣaṇa //
Ātmendriya Prīti Icchā Tāre Vali Kāma /
Kṛṣṇendriya Prīti Icchā Dhare Prema Nāma. //
Kāmera Tātparya Nija Sambhoga Kevala //
Kṛṣṇa Sukha Tātparya Prema Haya Mahāvala //
Ataeva Kāma Preme Vahuta Antra /
Kāma Andhatama Prema Nirmala Bhāsvara, //

(*Kāma* (libido) and *Prema* (love) have quite different characteristics. *Kāma* is as much different from *Prema* as iron from gold. The desire to cultivate the love of Kṛṣṇa to such an extent that only the will to please Kṛṣṇa's sense-organs becomes predominant over all other desires. The significance of *Kāma* lies in self-satisfying enjoyments. The significance of *Prema* lies in the all-absorbing will to cause happiness to Kṛṣṇa..There is, therefore, great difference between

Kāma and *Prema*. *Kāma* is blind darkness; *Prema* is pure and effulgent.)

81 Vijayakṛṣṇa Gosvami, a famous ascetic of nineteenth-century Bengal, offered a physiological interpretation of *Bhaktirasa*. "Intense *Bhakti*", he said, "generates a sort of intoxicating juice in the human body. This juice is called Nectar (*Amṛta*). If one drinks this juice, one escapes rebirth. The juice accumulates in the brain-cells. Gradually it flows into the cavity of the mouth. If one drinks two or three drops of that juice, one gets so much intoxicated that one may easily pass 5/7 days without taking any food. The moment one drinks this juice, one becomes unconscious...The taste of *bhakti* juice differs according to feeling, *Bhāva*. Sometimes the taste is that of salt. Sometimes it is sweet. Sometimes it is both sweet and salty. If regularly drunk, the juice keeps the body very fit." Kuladānanda Brahmacārī, *Śrī Śrī Sadguruprasanga,* Vol. II, pp. 80-81.

82 Jīva Gosvāmin, *Prītisaṃdarbha,* sections 67-69. Kṛṣṇadāsa Kavirāja: p. 353:

Śuddhabhakti Haite Haya Premera Udgama /
Ataeva Śuddhabhaktira Kahiye Lakṣaṇa /
Anya Vānchā Anya Pūjā Chāḍi Jajñakarma. /
Ānukūlye Sarvendriya Kṛṣṇanuśīlana. //

(Love is born of pure devotion. I, therefore, state the characteristics of pure devotion. It means the cultivation of Kṛṣṇa with all sense-organs to the exclusion of all other desires, worships and sacrificial activities.)

83 Kṛṣṇadāsa Kavirāja, op. cit. p. 189-190; *Ujjvalanīlamaṇi,* Ch. 14 and 15.

84 The theory of Acintyabhedabheda was first enunciated by Svarūpa Dāmodāra and later on explained by Kṛṣṇadāsa Kavirāja in the following verses :

Rādhā Pūrṇaśakti Kṛṣṇa Pūrṇaśaktimān /
Dui Vastu Bheda Nāhi Śāstra Paramān /
Mṛgamada Tāra Gandha Yaiche Aviccheda /
Agni Jvālate Yaiche Kabhu Nahe Bheda /
Rādhā Kṛṣṇa Aiche Sadā Ekai Svarūpa /
Līlārasa Āśvādite Dhare Dui Rūpa //

The following is the meaning of these verses: Kṛṣṇa is absolutely powerful. Rādhā is the embodiment of absolute power. They constitute duality in unity, and unity in duality. Power, and the state of being powerful cannot be two different and separate entities. But while Kṛṣṇa is the subject, Rādhā is the object. Kṛṣṇa is noun; Rādhā is adjective. Thus between Kṛṣṇa and Rādhā there is both non-difference and difference. The musk and its aroma are inseparable, and so are fire and its power to burn. But the aroma is not musk nor simple power to burn, fire. The non-duality of Kṛṣṇa and Rādhā becomes duality when they desire to enjoy bliss.

85 Rājā Rāmmohun Rāy criticized the Gauḍīya Vaiṣṇava practice deriving evidence from Vaiṣṇava and pro-Vaiṣṇava Purāṇas. In order to show the basic defect of their practice he quoted some verses from the *Nirvāṇa Tantra* according to which Kṛṣṇa could become the king of Vaikuntha only through the grace of Kālī. He also quoted some verses from *Tantraratnākara* to the effect that Caitanya and his companions were demons reborn through black magic to destroy the Śaiva religion. See *Rammohana Rāya Granthāvalī*, ed. Brajendranāth Bandypādhyāy and Sajanīkānta Dās. Calcutta: Bangīya Sāhitya Pariṣat, n.d. Vol. II, p. 19, Vol. VI, pp. 113-114.

86 Gopīnātha Kavirāja, *Sādhudarśana O Saṭprasanga*, Vol. I, pp. 140-141.

87 Kṛṣṇadās Kavirāja: op. cit. p. 17:

Kāmabandhahīna Svābhāvika Gopīprema /
Nirmala Ujjvala Śuddha Yena Dagdhahema. //

(The love of the milkmaids is without the smell of libido, natural, unblemished, bright, and pure as molten gold.)

88 *Ujjvalanīlamaṇi*, Ch. 3, *prakaraṇa* 27-32: translated with the commentary of Viṣṇudāsa Gosvāmin. The Gosvāmins of Vṛndāvana preached the theory that the maidens of Gokula were married to Kṛṣṇa, and hence his wives (*svakīyā*). Rūpa Gosvāmin (*Ujjvalanīlamaṇi*, Ch. I, *prakaraṇa* 16) quotes a text titled *Mūlamādhava* to prove his contention that the Gokula maidens were really *svakīyā*. Later on Jīva Gosvāmin described Kṛṣṇa's marriage with Rādhā in the *Uttarārdha* (Part II) of *Gopāla Campū* (Chapters 32-36). This was one of the reasons behind the cleavage between the Gosvāmins of Vṛndāvana and the Vaiṣṇavas of Bengal. Recently interpreters like Haridās Dās have tried to minimize the difference. According to them Rādhā's marriage with Kṛṣṇa took place in some

state of the 'unmanifest' sports of Kṛṣṇa. Haridās Dās, *Gauḍīya Vaiṣṇava Sāhitya*, Ch. IV, pp. 155-157.

89 The hierarchical order of friends and lovers is defined and described in *Ujjvalanīlamaṇi*, Chapters 2, 3, 6.

90 Vivid description of Kṛṣṇa's seasonal sports in the woods of Vṛndāvana in Kṛṣṇadāsa Kavirāja's *Govindalīlāmṛtam (Madhyalīlā*, canto 12); Viśvanātha Cakravartī's *Śrī Kṛṣṇabhāvanāmṛtaṃ*, Canto 10.

91 Caitanya himself expounded this theory to Vāsudeva Sārvabhauma: *Caitanyacaritāmṛta*, pp. 161-163.

92 Śāśībhuṣaṇ Dāsgupta, *Śrī Rādhāra Kramavikās*, p. 197.

93 The nature and predominance of Rādhā are expounded in Jīva Gosvāmin's *Śrī Kṛṣṇadandarbha. Caitanyacaritāmṛta*, pp. 13-14; see note 62.

94 S.K. De, op. cit. p. 166, 203-204.

95 Very lucid summary of this important and delicate work by S.K. De, op. cit. Ch. IV.

96 It is claimed by Satyendranath Basu that a deep knowledge of Vātsyāyana's *Kāmasūtra* is really necessary for an understanding of the manifest sports of Kṛṣṇa, as delineated in *Ujjvalanīlamaṇi*. (Satyendranāth Basu, *Vātsyāyaner Kāmasutra*, Text and Bengali Translation, Calcutta: Oriental Agency, n.d., Preface). The author has translated into Bengali Rūpa Gosvāmin's *Lalitamādhava* and *Vidagdhamādhava* (Calcutta: Basumati Sahitya Madir, n.d.).

97 Mulk Raj Anand, *Kamakala*, Geneva, Nagelzpublishers, 1958, Text.

98 See notes 14 and 32.

99 Kṛṣṇadāsa Kavirāja gives a long list of the duties and responsibilities of a true Vaiṣṇava: op. cit. pp. 384-386, 49-499. He places a good deal of emphasis on the central refinement of the faithful. S.K. De, however, describes Caitanya's Vaiṣṇavism as something 'unmoral', op. cit. p. 548. His judgment seems to have been influenced by the puritanical views of the Gauḍīya Vaiṣṇava religion. But whether eroticism means the negation of all virtues is debatable.

100 There are two conflicting views about the caste system. The Gauḍīya Vaiṣṇavas are not supposed to pay any attention to the caste of a devotee. Caitanya is reported to have said:

Nicajāti Haile Nahe Bhajane Ayogya /
Satkule Vipra Nahe Bhajanera Yogya //
Kṛṣṇabhajane Nāhi Jātikulādivicāra //

(Those who belong to the low castes should not be considered unfit to worship Kṛṣṇa. Those who are Brāhmaṇas and belong to good families may not be fit to worship Him. In the worship of Kṛṣṇa there should not be any consideration of caste and family.) *Caitanyacaritāmṛta*, p. 466. See note 68. The movement resulted in a definite relaxation of the caste rules. In the *Bhaktiratnākara* of Narahari Cakravarti (*Prathama Taraṅga*, p. 11) there is an account of Vaiṣṇava intercaste marriage. One Ciranjīva Sena married the daughter of Dāmodara Vipra. But later on the numerous Gosvāmins and Gurus of the Caitanya Order adopted a rigid attitude with regard to caste rules. The very first *Vilāsa* of *Haribhaktivilāsa* prohibited initiation of Brāhmaṇas by Śudra Gurus. "Thus", writes S.K. De, "Anuloma initiation is permitted, but Pratiloma initiation is expressly prohibited." S.K. De, op. cit. p.412. Rādhāgovinda Nāth suggests that the Vaiṣṇava's duty was to abjure *varṇāśramadharma* after he had developed *śraddhā* (respect) for Kṛṣṇa. *Śrī Śrī Caitanyacaritāmṛter Bhūmikā,* pp. 322-323. But this point is not explained or elaborated. According to Sukumar Sen,Caitanya could live in Navadvīpa and Purī only because he strictly conformed to social and scriptural norms. Op. cit. Vol. I, Part II, p. 38. But then it would mean that Caitanya did not conform to what he publicly preached with regard to caste.

Recently Dulāl Chandra Bāg has expressed the opinion that originally the Caitanya movement was, sociologically speaking, a 'puritanical' movement in which people of all castes were involved. But later on it assumed the form of a 'vertical' movement confined within the elite sections of the society which represented the higher castes. Socialist Perspective (A Quarterly Journal of the Social Sciences published by the Council of Political Studies, Calcutta) Vol. 1, No. 2, September 1973, pp. 62-70: 'Religious Organizations in India'. Professor Bhāg has not tried to base his thesis on the evidence of data. But the development of powerful and conservative sections inside the Vaiṣṇava community of Bengal is narrated in an obscure but very important work titled *Gauḍīya Vaiṣṇava Itihāsa: Vaiṣṇava Vivṛti* (English subtitle: *A Short History of Vaishnavas in Bengal)* by

Madhusudana Tattvavacaspati (2nd ed. B.E. 1333: 1926, printed and published in Hooghly). This work is referred to in S.K. De's *Vaiṣṇava Faith sand Movement*, p. 20, fn.)

101 S.K. De, op. cit. pp. 542-555. He accuses Caitanya of ignoring humanity, "with the result that the larger humanity in its turn has practically ignored it" (p. 555). S.K. De merely repeats what Sylvain Levi wrote in his Foreword to D.C. Sen's *Chaitanya and His Age* (Calcutta: The University of Calcutta, 1922, p. XXIII): Levi wrote: "Chaitanya maybe one of the greatest seers of India. Humanity does not, however, recognize him as one of its great men. He did not recognize mankind. So mankind does not recognize him."

102 *Haribhaktivilāsa, Vilāsa* IX and X.

103 Sukumar Sen, op. cit. Vol. I, Part II, pp. 3-4. Describing the effect of the Caitanya movement on Tantric worship Jadunath Sarkar writes: "It has all but extinguished...the worship of the Divine Creative Energy in its female form (Shakti) which used to prevail all over Bengal before the advent of Chaitanya...We owe to it...the almost total abolition of the ritualistic sacrifice of animals and the drinking of strong wine...as a religious duty." *History of Bengal*, Vol. II, p. 221. The same was the view of Bholanath Chunder, *The Travels of a Hindoo, to Various Parts of Bengal and Upper India*, 2 vols., London: N. Trubner & Co., 1896, Vol. I, pp. 30-31.

104 *History of Bengal*, II, pp. 221-222.

105 See Haridās Dās, *Gauḍīya Vaiṣṇava Abhidhāna*, Vol. I, which is the largest lexicon of Vaiṣṇava terms.

106 B.K. Sarkar, *The Positive Background of Hindu Sociology*, p. 486.

107 Literal translation of the following verse: *Sunaha Mānuṣa Bhāi / Sabāra Upare Mānuṣa Satya Tāhara Upare Nāi //* But *Mānusa* (man) has a technical meaning; he is a '*sahajiyā*' man.

108 Sukumar Sen, op. cit., Vol. I, Part II, pp. 494-495.

109 Vaiṣṇava influence on the development of biographical literature in Bengali has been assessed by Devīpada Bhaṭṭācārya in *Bānglā Caritasāhitya*, Calcutta: Suprakāśa, 1964, pp. 23-29.

110 W.G. Archer, *The Loves of Kṛṣṇa*, p. 96.

111 Ibid., p. 101.

112 Kṛṣṇānanda Vyās, *Saṃgītarāgakalpadruma: Rengīna Gaur*, Calcutta1846. It is the oldest printed anthology of the varieties of

Vaiṣṇava songs current in Northern India nearly two hundred years ago. See Haridāsa Dās, *Gauḍīya Vaiṣṇava Abhidhāna*, Vol. II, pp. 1069-1143, and Harekṛṣṇa Mukhopadhyāya, *Bānglār Kīrtan O Kīrtanīyā*.

113 Harekrṣṇa Mukhopadhāya, op. cit., Intro. 12-17, Text, pp. 61-126.

114 Śāśībhuṣaṇ Dāsgupta, *Śrī Rādhār Kramavikās*, pp. 329-400; Jatīndramohan Bhaṭṭācārya, *Bānglār Vaiṣṇava Bhāvāpanna MusalmanKavi,* Calcutta: University of Calcutta, 1962; Aśutosh Bhaṭṭācārya, *Bānglār Lokasāhitya,* Calcutta: Calcutta Book House, 1965, Vol. III; Gurusadaya Datta and Nimalendu Bhowmik, eds., *Śrīhaṭṭer Lokasaṃgīta,* Calcutta: University of Calcutta, 1966.

115 M. S. Randhwa, *Kangra Paintings on Love,* New Delhi, National Museum, 1962, Ch. X.

116 See the works of Jatindramohan Bhattacharyya, Asutosh Bhattacharyya, Gurusadaya Datta and Nirmalendu Bhowmik mentioned in note 114.

117 Amiya Kumar Bandyopadhyay, *Bānkura Jelār Purākīrti,* Calcutta: Government of West Bengal, Pūrta Bibhāg, B.E 1377 (1970).

118 Rūpa Gosvāmin, *Dānakelikaumudī*, p. 20, verse 34; p. 26, verse 47; p. 37, verse 65; p. 83, verse 141, etc.; also, p. 130.

119 The legend given in *Muktācaritra* is really fantastic. Once Kṛṣṇa planted a creeper which bore gems and pearls. When the milkmaids, including Rādhā, wanted to buy them, Kṛṣṇa said that the only price which would be satisfactory to him was that each of them must be prepared to embrace him and allow him to take liberties. He himself determined the price of each of them.

120 A Vaiṣṇava ascetic named Siddha Kṛṣṇadāsa prepared an anthology of nearly forty *Smaraṇamaṅgala Kāvyas* written in Sanskrit. The anthology, titled *Bhāvanāsārasaṃgraha,* was edited and published by Haridās Dās (Navadvīpa, Haribol Kutir, 1950).

121 See note 85. Also, Ramakanta Chakravarti, "Vaiṣṇavism, the Caitanya movement, and the renaissance in Bengal (1800-1900)' in Jadavpur Journal of Comparative Literature, Jadavpur University, Calcutta, Vol. 13, 1975.

122 Songs on *Gauranāgara* are collected in Jagadbandhu Bhadra's *Gaurapadataraṅginī*. Songs on the subject composed by

Narahari Cakravarti are collected in *Gauracaritracintāmaṇi*, ed. Haridās Dās.

123 Harekṛṣṇa Mukhopadhyay, *Vaiṣṇava Padāvalī*, p. 332; *Rohinī Sahite Ranghana Karite Basilā Rājara Jhi / Saba Sakhīgaṇa Jogāya Jogāna Śekhara Jogāya Ghis* // (The king's daughter (Rādhā) sat down to cook the meal with Rohinī (Bālarāma's mother). The female companions acted as the helpers; Śekhara, the poet, supplied *ghī*.

124 *Stavāvalī*, pp. 37-42.

125 Dimock, *The Place of the Hidden Moon*, pp. 146-152.

126 Ibid., translation of *Nāyika-Sādhanā-Ṭīkā*, pp. 235-245.

127 *Vivartavilāsagrantha* by Akiñcana Dāsa, pp. 106-107: Each of the Gosvāmis of Vṛndāvana was said to have performed *sādhanā* with a female companion. Almost similar verses have been quoted by Sukumar Sen (op. cit. Vol. 1, Part II, pp. 45-46) from another Sahajiyā work.

128 In *Madhyayuger Bāṅgāla O Bāṅgālī*, Viśvavidyāsaṃgraha 44, Visvabharati 1962, pp. 22-23. Sukumar Sen writes that the Caitanya movement had undoubtedly enfeebled the Bengalis. But a quite different opinion is found in his *Bāṅgāla Sāhityer Itihās*, Vol. I, Part I, pp. 321-322.

129 J. N. Farqhar, op. cit., p. 230.

130 Kuladānanda Brahmacarī, *Śrī Śrī Sadguruprasaṅga*, Vol. I, pp. 70-71. The five volumes contain similar accounts of ecstasy.

131 See Sunitikumar Chatterjee's introduction to Harekṛṣṇa Mukhopādhyay's *Padāvalīparicaya*.

132 Sukumar Sen, op. cit. Vol. I, Part I, p. 405.

133 Rabindranath Tagore, *Lokasāhitya*, Viśvabhāratī, 1965, pp. 82-83, 85. The orthodox Vaiṣṇavas have often criticized Tagore for his views on Vaiṣṇava poetry and songs. He has been violently attacked by Sundarānanda Vidyāvinoda in *Gauḍīya Sāhitya*, Calcutta: Gauḍīya Math, B.E. 1336 (1929), pp. 27-37.

134 Janārdan Chakravarti, *Śrī Rādhā Tattva O Śrī Caitanyasaṃskṛti*, pp. 176-193, 194.

135 S. K. De, p. cit., pp. 542-555.

REFERENCES

Sanskrit Texts

Āgamavāgīśa, Kṛṣṇānanda, *Tantrasāra,* ed. Pancānana Tarkaratna with Bengali translation by Vīreśanātha Vidyāsāgara. Calcutta: Bangabāsī Press, B.E. 1344 (1937).

Bhaktiratnākara, Sanskrit Text and English Translation, A.B.; Allahabad: Panini Office, 1918

Brahmasaṃhitā, with the commentary of Jīva Gosvāmin and Bengali translation by Bhaktivinoda Ṭhakkura, Calcutta: Gauḍīya Math, 1928.

Brahvaivartapurāṇa, Text and translation into Bengali, ed. Pancānana Tarkaratna, Calcutta: Bangabāsī Press, B.E. 1332 (1925)

Bhāgavatapurāṇa, with the commentary of Śrīdhara Svāmin, d. Pancānana Tarkaratna, Calcutta: Bangabāsī Press, B.E. 1309 (1902)

Ekallavīracaṇḍamahāroṣaṇa Tantra, Calcutta: Asiatic Society: MS N. 9089.

Gosvāmin, Jīva, *Bhaktirasāmṛtasindhu Durgatasamāsagamanī,* Purīdāsa Gosvāmi, Vṛndāvana, 1951.

Gosvāmin, Jīva, *Bhagavatasaṃdarbha,* Purīdāsa Gosvāmin, Vṛndāvana, 1951.

Gosvāmin, Jīva, *Bhaktisaṃdarbha,* Purīdāsa Gosvāmin, Vṛndāvana, 1951

Gosvāmin, Jīva, *Kramasaṃdarbha,* ed. Purīdāsa Gosvāmin, Vṛndāvana 1952.

Gosvāmin, Jīva, *Paramātmasaṃdarbha,* ed. Purīdāsa Gosvāmin, Vṛndāvana, 1951

Gosvāmin, Jīva, *Prītisaṃdarbha,* ed. Purīdāsa Gosvāmin, Vṛndāvana, 1951.

Gosvāmin, Jīva, *Sarvasaṃvādinī,* ed. Purīdāsa Gosvāmin, Vṛndāvana, 1953

Gosvāmin, Jīva, *Tattvasaṃdarbha,* ed. Purīdāsa Gosvāmin, Vṛndāvana, 1951.

Gosvāmin, Raghunātha Dāsa, *Muktācaritra,* ed. with translation into Bengali, Nityasvarūpa Brahmacārī, Vṛndāvana, 1908.

Gosvāmin, Raghunātha Dāsa, *Stavāvalī*, ed. Rāmadeva Miśra, with translation into Bengali, Murshidabad, Baharampur Rādhāramaṇa Press, B.E. 1329 (1922)

Gosvāmin, Rūpa, *Bhaktirasāmṛtasindhu,* with the *Durgatasamāsagamaṇī* commentary of Jīva Gosvāmin, ed. Haridāsa Dās, Navadvīpa: Haribol Kutir, 1955. Also published with the *Locanarocanī* commentary of Jīva Gosvāmin, and the *Ānandacandrikā* commentary of Viśvanātha Cakravartī, Kāvyamālā-95: Bombay: Nirnayasagar Press. Second ed., 1932; first ed. 1913.

Gosvāmin, Rūpa, *Ujjvalanīlamaṇi, with the Svātmapramodinī commentary of Viṣṇudāsa Gosvāmin,* ed. Vrajanātha Miśra, Murshidabad: Baharampura Rādhāramaṇa Press, third ed. B.E. 1339 (1932); first ed. (ed. Rāmanārāyaṇa Vidyāratna), 1287 (1880).

Gosvāmin, Rūpa, *Padyāvalī*, ed. with introduction, S.K. De, Dacca: University of Dacca, 1934

Gosvāmin, Sanātana, *Bṛhadbhāgavatāmṛtam, with the Digdarśanī commentary, Parts I and II,* ed. with Bengali translation, Bhaktiratna Gosvāmin and Bhaktiśāstrī Gosvāmin, Sauri, Midnapur, B.E. 1362 (1955).

Gupta, Murāri, *Śrīkṛṣṇacaitanyacaritāmta,* ed. Mṛnāl Kānti Ghosh, Calcutta: Amritabazar Patrika Office, 1931.

Jayadeva, *Gītāgovinda, with the commentary Rasikpriyā of King Kumbha and Rasamañjarī of Mahāmadhopādhyāya Śankara Miśra,* ed. with various readings, Mangesa Ramkrishna Telang and Wāsudeva Laxman Śāstrī Paṇśīkar, seventh ed. Bombay: Nirṇaya Sāgara Press, 1929; first ed. 1869.

Kavi, Karṇapūra, *Alaṃkārakaustubha, Parts I and II,* ed. Śivaprasāda Bhattāchāryya, with an old commentary. Rājshāhi: Varendra Research Society, 1926.

Kavi, Karṇapūra, *Ānandavṛndāvana Campū,* ed. with commentary in Sanskrit, Mukundadeva Śāstrī, Bombay: Mitra Press, 1869.

Kavi, Karṇapūra, *Caitanyacandrodaya,* ed. and translated into Bengali, Rāmanārāyaṇa Vidyāratna, Murshidabad: Baharampura Rādhāramaṇa Press, B.E. 1305 (1898). Also 24-Paraganas, B.E. 1378 (1971).

Kavi, Karṇapūra, *Gauragaṇoddeśadīpikā,* ed. Rāmadeva Miśra, Murshidābad: Baharampura Rādhāramana Press, B.E. 1329 (1922).

Kavirāja, Kṛṣṇadāsa, *Govindalīlāmṛta,* ed. Sacinandana Gosvāmin, with Bengali translation and a commentary in Sanskrit, Vṛndāvana, 1908.

Kavirāja, Viśvanātha, *Śrīkṛṣṇabhāvanāmṛtamahākāvya,* with Sanskrit commentary and Bengali translation, ed. Rādhikānātha Gosvāmin, Vṛndāvana, 1904.

Saduktikarṇāmṛta of Śrīdharadāsa, ed. S.C. Banerjee, Calcutta: Firma K.L. Mukhopadhyay, 1965

Śaktisaṃgamatantra: Kālī Khaṇḍa and Tārākhaṇḍa, ed. B. Bhattacharyya, Baroda: Gaekwad's Oriental Series, Nos. 61 and 91, 1932-1941

Sarasvatī, Prabodhānanda, *Caitanyacandrāmṛta,* published by the Gauḍīya Math, Calcutta: 1926.

Śrībhāṣya (of Rāmānujācārya), ed. Durgācaraṇa Sāṃkhya-Vedāntatīrtha, Calcutta: Bangīya Sāhitya Pariṣad, B.E. 1322 (1915).

Subhāṣitaratnakośa of Vidyākara, ed. D.D. Kosambi and V.V. Gokhale, Harvard Oriental Series 42: Cambridge, Mass. 1957.

Bengali Texts

Bāsu, Mālādhara, *Śrīkṛṣṇavijaya,* ed. Khagendranāth Mitra, Calcutta: Universityof Calcutta, 1944

Basu, Manīndramohan, *Sahajiyā Sāhitya,* Calcutta: University of Calcutta, 1932.

Bhadra, Jagatbandhu, *Gaurapadataraṅgiṇī,* Calcutta: ed. Mṛnāl Kānti Ghosh, Calcutta:Amritabazar Patrika Office, 1935. First ed. Calcutta: Bangīya Sāhitya Pariṣad, 1902.

Bhattachāryya, Upendranāth, *Bānglār Bāul Gān,* Calcutta:Oriental Book Company, 1364 B.E. (1957). Part I: Introduction; Part II, collection of Bāul songs.

Brahmacaṛī, Kuladānanda, *Śrī Śrī Sadguruprasaṅga,* 5 vols. Puri: Thākurbāḍī Āśram, fourth ed. B.E. 1370 (1963); first ed. 1928

Cakravarti, Narahari, *Gauracaritracintāmaṇi,* Vol. I, ed. Haridāsa Dās, Navadīpa, Haribol Mission, second ed. 1960, first ed. 1940

Cakravarti, Narahari, *Bhaktiratnākara*, ed. Nandalāl Vidyasāgar, Calcutta: Gauḍīya Mission, second ed. 1960; first ed. 1940

Caṇḍīdāsa, Vaḍu, *Śrīkṛṣṇakīrtana*, ed. Basanta Ranjan Ray, Calcutta: Bangīya Sāhitya Pariṣad, 1916

Chattopādhyāya, Bankimchandra, *Bankim Racanāvalī*, 2 vols. Calcutta: Sāhitya Saṃsad, 1954.

Chattopādhyāya, Gītā, *Bhāgavata O Bānglā Sāhitya*, Calcutta: Kavi O Kavitā, B.E. 1379 (1972)

Chaudhuri, Bāsantī, *Bānglār Vaiṣṇava Samāj, Sangīt O Sāhitya, Aṣṭada; Satābdir Pūrvārdha*, Calcutta: Bookland, 1968

Dāsa, Akincana, *Vivartavilāsagrantha*, Tārāchānd Das & Sons. Calcutta, 1957.

Dāsa, Cūḍāmaṇi, *Gauraṅgavijaya*, Calcutta: Asiatic Society, 1957.

Dāsa, Govardhana, *Śrī Śrī Vrajadhāma O Gosvāmīgaṇa*, 4 vols. Vṛndāvana: Gopīnāth Bāg, Giridārī Kunja, 1961-1965.

Dās, Haridās. *Śrī Śrī Gauḍīya Vaiṣṇava Abhidhāna*, 2 vols. Navadvīpa, Haribol Kutir, 1957.

Dāsa,, Locana, *Caitanyamaṅgala*, ed. Mṛnāl Kānti Ghosh, Calcutta: Amritabazar Partika Office, 1930.

Dāsa, Paritoṣ, *Caitanyottar Prathama Cāriti Sahajiyā Punthi*, Calcutta: Bhārati Book Stall, 1972 (with an introduction from Gopīnāth Kavirāja).

Dāsgupta, Śaśhibhuṣan, *Śrī Rādhār Kramavikāś, Darśane O Sāhitye*, Calcutta: A. Mukherjee, 1952.

Datta, Akṣayakumār, *Bhāratavarṣīya Upāsaka Sampradāya*, ed. Benoy Ghosh, Calcutta: Pāthabhavana, 1969. (The first edition of this famous work was published in Calcutta in two volumes between 1870 and 1883.)

Datta, Bhupendranath, *Vaiṣṇava Sāhitye Samājatattva*, Calcutta: Bhārat Sāhtya Bhavan, 1944

Jayānanda, *Caitanyamaṅgala*, ed. Bimānbihārī Majumdār and Sukhamaya Mukhopādhyāya, Calcutta: Asiatic Society, 1971.

Kavirāja, Gopināthа, *Bhāratīya Sādhanār Dhāra*, Calcutta: Sanskrit College (Government of West Bengal), 1955

Kavirāja, Gopīnātha, *Sādhudarśana O Satprasanga*, Vol. I. Calcutta: Śrīprakāsana, 1962 (B.E. 1369).

Majumdār, Bimānbihārī, *Śrīcatanyacariter Upādan*, Calcutta: University of Calcutta, second ed, 1959; first ed. 1939.

Majumdār, Ramesh Chandra, *Bānglādeśer Itihās, vol. ii*, Calcutta: General Printers and Publishers, B.E. 1373 (1966).

Mukhopādhyāya, Harekṛṣṇa, *Kavi Jayadeva O Śrīgītagovinda*, Calcutta: Gurudās Chattopādhyaya and Sons, B.E. 1362 (1957).

Mukhopādhyāya, Harekṛṣṇa, *Vaiṣṇava Padāvalī*, Calcutta: Sāhitya Saṃsad, 1961

Mukhopādhyāya, Harekṛṣṇa, *Bānglār Kīrtan O Kīrtanīya*, Calctta: Sāhitya Samsad,1971.

Nāth, Rādhāgovinda, *Śrī Śrī Caitanyacaritāmṛter Bhūmikā*, Calcutta:: Prācyavāṇī 1958 (4th ed.) 1st ed. 1949.

(Ācārya) Rādhāgovinda Nāth Smāraka Grantha, ed. Janārdana Cakravarti, Calcutta: Sādhanā Prakāsanī, 1973

Rāḍī, Kānticandra, *Navadvīpa Mahimā*, Calcutta Book Company, second ed. 1937; first ed. B.E. 1298 (1891).

Ray, Nihārranjan, *Bangālīr Itihās, Saṃkṣepita Saṃskaraṇa*, Calcutta: Lekhaka Samavāya Samiti, 1966.

Rāychaudhurī, Girijaśankar, *Bānglacaritagranthe Śrī Caitanya*, Calcutta University 1949.

Sāhānā, Satyakinkar, *Caṇḍīdāsa Prasaṅga*, Calcutta: Jijṇāsa, 1959.

Sen, Dinesh Chandra, *Bṛhat Baṅga, vol. ii*, Calcutta: University of Calcutta, 1935 (2 vols.).

Sen, Kṛṣṇaprasāda, *Caṇḍīdāsacarita*, ed. Jogesh Chandra Rāy Vidyānidhi, Calcutta: Pravāsī Press, B.E. 1344 (1937).

Sen, Sukumar, *Bāngāla Sāhityer Itihās, Vol. I, Parts I and II*, Calcutta: Eastern Publishers, fifth ed. 1970; first ed. in one volume, 1940.

Svāmī, Prajñānanda, *Padāvalīkīrtaner Itihās*, Vol. I, Calcutta: Rāmakrishna Vedānta Math, 1970.

Tarkabhuṣaṇa, Pramathānanda, *Bānglār Vaiṣṇava Darśana*, Calcutta: Śrīguru Library, 1963.

Vyās, Kṛṣṇānanda, *Saṃgītarāgakalpadruma,, Raṅgīna Gāna*, Calcutta: 1846 (publshed with the financial assistance of many *zamindars* of Calcutta).

Vidyāpati, *Padāvalī*, ed. Khagendranāth Mitra and Bimānbihar Majumdār, Calcutta: Sanatkumār Mitra. B.E. 1359 (1952).

Vidyāvinoda, Sundarānanda, *Gauḍīya Darśaner Itrihās O Vaiśiṣṭya*, Calcutta: Gauḍīya Mission, 1953.

English Texts

Archer, W. G., *The Loves of Krishna.* London: George Allen and Unwin, 1957.

Bhandarkar, R. G., *Vaisnavism, Saivism, and Minor Religious Systems,* Poona: Bhandarkar Oriental Religious Institute, 1928

Chatterjee, Suniti Kumar, *Jayadeva,* New Delhi: Sahitya Akademi, 1973

Cultural Heritage of India, The Vol. II, Calcutta: Sri Ramakrishna Centenary Committee, Belur Math, n.d. (four vols.)

Dasgupta, Sasibhusan, *Obscure Religious Cults as a Background to Bengali Literature,* Calcutta: Firma K. L. Mukhopadhyay, second ed. 1962, first ed. University of Calcutta, 1946.

De, S. K., *Early History of the Vaisnava Faith and Movement in Bengal from Sanskrit and Bengali Sources,* Calcutta: Firma K. L. Mukhopadhyay, second ed. 1961; first ed. Calcutta: University of Calcutta, 1946.

De, S. K., *Bengal's contribution to Sanskrit Literature and Studies in Bengal Vaisnavism,* Calcutta: Religious Studies Past and Present, 1960.

Dimock, Jr. Edward C., *The Place of the Hidden Moon,* Chicago: The University of Chicago Press, 1966.

Elwin, Verrier, *The Tribal Myths of Orissa,* Calcutta: The Oxford University Press, 1954.

Farqhar, J. N., *An Outline of the Religious Literature of India,* Delhi: Motilal Banarsidas, second ed. 1967; first ed. Oxford University Press, 1920.

Gonda, J., *Aspects of Early Visnuism,* Utrecht: N. V. A. Oosthoek's Uitgevers Mij, 1954.

Kennedy, Melvillle, *The Chaitanya Movement, A Study of Vaisnavism of Bengal,* Calcutta: Association Press, 1925.

Majumdar, Bimanbihari, *Kṛṣṇa in History and Legend,* Calcutta: University of Calcutta, 1969.

Mallik, Girindranarayan, *The Philosophy of Vaisnava Religion,* 2 vols. Lahore: Motilall Banarsidas, 1927.

Mukherjee, S. C., *A Study of Vaisnavism in Ancient and Medieval Bengal up to the advent of Caitanya, based on Archaeological and Literary Data,* Calcutta: Punthi Pustak, 1966.

Ray, Benal Gopal, *Religious Movements in Modern Bengal,* Santiniketan,Visvabharati, 1965.

Raychaudhuri, Tapan, *Bengal under Akbar and Jahangir: An Introductory Study in Social History,* Delhi: Munsiram Manoharlal, second ed. 1969; first ed. 1953.

Sarkar, Jadunath, *History of Bengal*, Vol. II Dacca: University of Dacca, 1948.

Sen, Dinesh Chandra, *History of Bengal Language and Literature,* second ed. Calcutta: University of Calcutta, 1954; first ed. 1911.

Sen, Kshitimohan, *Mediaeval Mysticism of India* (with an Introduction from Rabindranath Tagore), London: Luzac and Co.

Wilson, H. H., *Religious Sects of the Hindus*, Calcutta: Sushil Gupta, 1958; first ed. London: Trubner and Co., 1861

PART TWO

SUMMARIES OF WORKS
(Arranged Chronologically)

1 CAITANYA (1520)

The following account of Caitanya's life is taken from Edward C. Dimock's Introduction to Dimock 1999, pp. 10-22 (reproduced for the most part without the author's footnotes).

"Although Caitanya was not the founder of the Vaiṣṇava movement in Bengal, he was its revivalist. Evidence that the movement existed well before his time is ample...the lyrics of such poets as Caṇḍidāsa and Vidyāpati, it is said in the *Caitanyacaritāmṛta*, were 'read with pleasure' by Caitanya. Although there is a good deal of controversy centering around the actual persons of these poets, there is no doubt that poets by those two names lived well before Caitanya's time. The *Gītāgovinda* of Jayadeva, court poet to Lakṣmaṇa Sena of Bengal in the late twelfth century, celebrates the love affair between Rādha and Kṛṣṇa, and there is still earlier evidence in the poetry of Ḍimboka and others of the currency of the story. What is less certain is the extent and power of the *bhakti* movement in Bengal before Caitanya appeared on the scene. The texts...would have us believe that there was little Kṛṣṇa-*bhakti*, and this is in fact given as the reason for the coming of Caitanya. But it is certain that there were some *bhaktas* around. There is no reason to doubt the statement that Caitanya's own family was Vaiṣṇava (CC1.13.71), and it seems likely that Śrīnivāsa and others among his early followers were already persuaded people when Caitanya took over leadership. On the other hand, certain forms of Tantrism and Śaktism were evidently in vogue. Brahmanical forms of Hinduism and of social stricture do seem to have been rigid. Possibly this was in reaction to the advent of Islam, especially Sufi Islam with its highly emotional and humanistic orientation. The point is that the land of Bengal was not wholly unprepared for the advent of the man who was perhaps its greatest religious leader, though to what extent the preparation was negative and to what extent positive is largely a matter of speculation.

"Caitanya was born on the night of an eclipse of the full moon of the month of Phalguna in A.D. 1486 in the city of Navadvīpa. His father was Jagannātha Miśra, a learned and pious Vaiṣṇava *brāhmaṇa* whose family had migrated to Nadīyā from a village in Sylhet district in the east; his mother was named Śacī. Despite protestations from many of his biographers, very little is known about Caitanya's early life; incidents are so mingled with stories of the child Kṛṣṇa as told in the *Bhagavata Puraṇa* that it is hard to separate fact from fancy. Some deductions can be made. It seems for example that the boy studied Sanskrit grammar at the *ṭola*, the traditional school, run by Gaṅgadāsa, and this would not have been unusual for a *brāhmaṇa* boy of the time. His biographers are understandably anxious to make him out to be a great philosopher, rhetorician, and poet, but there is no reliable evidence to suggest that he was any of these things, or that he had any significant amount of education in them. There are many stories, including some in Kṛṣṇadāsa's text, of how with his learning, skill, and power in argument, together with his vast understanding of the human kind, he vanquished the greatest scholars of the day, including Vāsudeva Sārvabhauma, a logician famed all over India. It was significant that most learning, then as now in India, is a characteristic which great men cannot be without. The fact is that Caitanya has left almost no writing. There are eight *ślokas*, called the *śikṣāṣṭaka*, which Kṛṣṇadāsa, quoting them from the *Padyāvalī* of Rūpa Gosvāmin, gives in the last chapter of his work (CC 3.20.7-38. *śl.* 3-10). But Amūlyacandra Sen[1], in his iconoclastic but often thought-provoking *Itihāsera śrīcaitanya,* calls the authenticity even of these into question. He asks when the verses might have been written; they could not have been composed during the last

---

[1]Amūlyacandra Sena, *Itihāsera śrīcaitanya* (Calcutta: Kiraṇa Kumāra Rāya through Sārasvata Lāibreri, 1965), 195-196, hereafter cited as ISC.

years of Caitanya's life, for in those years he was totally absorbed by the madness of his separation from Kṛṣṇa, and the verses are careful Sanskrit. Madness, says Dr. Sen, who is a trained physician, is not a condition appropriate to the composition of Sanskrit verse; further he adds acerbically, there is no suggestion anywhere that he could compose Sanskrit verse even when lucid. In any case, it is true that nothing is really known of Caitanya's intellectual power; even if the *śikṣāṣṭaka* verses are his, they are verses of devotion, not of logic or learning.

"All of the biographers, especially Vṛndāvana Dāsa in his *Caitanya Bhāgavata*, are clear on the fact that Caitanya, whether or not intellectually precocious, was a boy full of fun and mischief; he was constantly playing pranks on groups of his peers, and sometimes, perhaps a little cruelly, making fun of others and mocking their peculiarities of speech. It also seems that he had a temper. Murāri Gupta's *Kṛṣṇacaitanyacaritāmṛta*[1] records an incident, left out by the other biographers, of Caitanya's throwing a brick at his mother in his rage (KCC 1.5.11-31). And there are stories of how he took after fellow students (CC 1.17.248-50), and even his young wife, to beat them.

"In any case, the young Caitanya was sent to school, though with some trepidation on his parents' part, for they feared that education would lead him to the ascetic life. In his childhood his elder and only brother Viśvarūpa had become an ascetic, taking on the occasion of his *saṃnyāsa* the name Śaṅkarāraṇya. It was an incident which broke his mother Śacī's heart, and one which was to have a great deal of bearing on Caitanya's later life and on the history of the movement. While Caitanya was

---

[1]*Kṛṣṇacaitanyacaritāmṛta* of Murāri Gupta, ed. Mṛṇālakānti Ghoṣa, with Bengali trans. by Haridāsa Dāsa. 4th ed. (Calcutta: by the editor, 459 GA [=1945 A.D.], hereafter cited as KCC. Citation will be to book (*prakrama*), chapter (*sarga*), and verse(s).

still a student, his father died, and the burden of the support of his mother fell upon the boy. It was about this time also that he married a girl named Lakṣmīpriyā, the daughter of one Vallabhācārya (not the founder of the Vaiṣṇava sect by that name), with whom he had fallen in love when they first met by the riverbank.

"Caitanya's (or Viśvambhara's, for he was not at this time yet known by the name Kṛṣṇa Caitanya, which he took on entering *saṃnyāsa*) youthful relations with other women and girls of the town are also of some significance for what comes later. Although some writers such as Narahari Sarakāra and his disciple Locana Dāsa were to paint Caitanya as a real Kṛṣṇa in his erotic attractiveness to women, none of the earlier biographers suggests that even before his *saṃnyāsa* he was anything but chaste. He seems to have been a very attractive youth both physically and because his nature had a gentle, perhaps even feminine side; and he became skilled in dance and song, women's arts which he must have learned through associations with them. But in his adolescence and maturity he seems to have turned away from women, and in fact to have been embarrassed and troubled by them. The fact that Caitanya had no children is not relevant, for Lakṣmīpriyā was probably very young when she died, and he took *saṃnyāsa* very soon after his second marriage.

"Because of his family responsibilities, Caitanya opened at about this time a *ṭola*, a Sanskrit school of his own, and while accounts of the vastness of the numbers of his students are probably exaggerated, it would seem that he had a living. Perhaps it was not enough of a living, however, for also about this time he took a trip to his father's ancestral village in the east...for the purpose of raising money, perhaps from relatives (KCC 1.11.5). While he was away on that trip, his young wife died of snakebite (CC 1.16.18-19). And shortly after his return to Navadvīpa, he married a second time, this time a girl named Viṣṇupriyā, the daughter of a local pandit named Sanātana

Miśra. Surprisingly little is known about this girl, especially considering that she occupied a place of special reverence in the later phases of the movement.

"When Viśvambhara was twenty-two, he went to the city of Gayā to perform *śrāddha*, funeral obsequies for his father, in that place. What happened there is a mystery. Even Caitanya himself does not enlighten us, for every time the name of the place is mentioned he breaks down into tears. It is certain that he met there one Īśvara Puri, whom S. K. De calls 'that emotional ascetic' [De 1961, p. 76], who initiated him and gave him the Kṛṣṇa-*mantra*, the formula with the name of Kṛṣṇa which he would repeat and on which he would meditate throughout his religious life. He returned to Navadvīpa God-maddened, and proceeded to have *kīrtana*, with dancing and singing of the names and praises of Kṛṣṇa, every night in the courtyard of his friend and neighbor Śrīnivāsa[1]. From an arrogant young householder-pandit he had suddenly been transformed into a devotee, and from that time even his teaching of grammar was shot through with Kṛṣṇa-*bhakti*. It was also at this time that Nityānanda, a Tāntric *avadhūta* who had early left his home and wandered the countryside, came into his life. Nityānanda was some years older than Caitanya, but was a kindred spirit, and was so like his departed brother Viśvarūpa that Ṣacī took him into her home and treated him as her own son.

"The *kīrtana* seems to have started out as a small and private affair. But very soon it grew in popularity and in size; it came out of the courtyard and into the street, taking the form of a *nāgara kīrtana*, a street procession. The rapid growth of the movement, of which this is an indication, seems to have aroused various kinds of hostilities. *Brāhmaṇas* were afraid of

---

[1]Sometimes Śrīvāṣa iṣ called Śrīṇivāsa, and is not to be confused with the important Vaiṣṇava of the same name who became prominent over a half century later.

its strength, for the emotionalism of it all seemed to them antagonistic to orthodox brahmanical Hinduism; the Śāktas were also opposed...and the Muslim government seems to have feared what they saw to be the political implications of so many people beyond normal social control. Jayānanda describes the situation this way:

> For many ages there had been controversy between the *brāhmaṇas* and the Muslims (*yavana*). Near Navadvīpa there was a village of hostile Piralyā *brāhmaṇas*, and they gave false evidence in the presence of the king of Gauḍa: 'The *brāhmaṇas* of Navadvīpa will cause you danger, for they believe that there will be a *brāhmaṇa* king of Gauḍa. Do not stay here without care, for danger is nigh. A *brāhmaṇa* will certainly be king in Navadvīpa; it is written by the Gandharvas that the king will be skilled with the bow.' These false words stuck in the mind of the king, and he gave the order: 'Destroy Nadīyā...'[1] (JCM 2.4.22-27)

But the fierce goddess Kālī appeared to him in a dream, with her bloodied sword and necklace of severed heads; the king relented, and Hindu life went on as before in Nadīya (JCM 2.4.31-50). It is of interest that Nīlambara Cakravartī, Caitanya's maternal grandfather, when he saw the infant Caitanya, remarked that 'he will become the *brāhmaṇa* king in Gauḍa'.

"It was perhaps because of such opposition that Caitanya's decision to enter the ascetic life was formed, for Kṛṣṇadāsa has him argue to himself that if people see him as a *saṃnyāsin* they will appreciate the seriousness of his purpose. The real reason, S. K. De suggests, was undoubtedly deeper, for the passionate devotionalism which had been aroused in him at Gayā was

[1]*Caitanya Maṅgala* of Jayānanda Miśra, ed. Bimenbehari Majumdar and Sukhamay Mukhopadhyay (Calcutta: The Asiatic Society, 1971); hereafter cited as JCM. Textual references are to series (*khaṇḍa*), chapter, and verse(s).

almost certainly not as abrupt as it might appear, and he had probably been toying for at least two years with the idea of dedicating himself completely to his deity and to the religious life.

"Regardless of the apparent precipitousness, he was soon initiated by one Keśava Bhāratī, a *saṃnyāsin* of Kāṭoyā on the other side of the river from Navadvīpa, and he became, nominally at least, a member of the Bhāratī *sampradāya* of the *daśanāmi* order of Śaṃkara-*advaitin saṃnyāsins*, taking the religious name Kṛṣṇa Caitanya. He was in name and in appearance a follower of the monistic philosophy, for Sārvabhauma Bhaṭṭācārya, the great *advaitin* or follower of the monistic school, recognized him when they first met as an *advaitin saṃnyāsin*. This did not at all hinder his intense devotionalism, and throughout his life he was taken to task for being a 'sentimentalist' (*bhāvaka*) rather than the philosopher more appropriate to his nominal persuasion.

"After he had taken his orders he returned to Śāntipura, near Navadvīpa, to the house of Advaitācārya, an old friend and confidant, where he met his mother; for having taken *saṃnyāsa*, he could not return to his own home for twelve years. Śacī, having lost her second son, was disconsolate. Caitanya wanted very much to go to Vṛndāvana in northern India, the place of his beloved Kṛṣṇa, but his mother's pleas made him change his mind and decide to go to live in Puri in Orissa, the place of the great temple of Jagannātha and a pilgrimage place for the Bengali Vaiṣṇavas of the time. There may have been another reason for this decision, for Kṛṣṇadāsa and other biographers hint that Caitanya's elder brother Viśvarūpa may also have gone to Puri to live. A search for his brother is also suggested as a possible reason for his long pilgrimage to the south and west after he had gone to Puri. In any case, Puri was accessible to Bengali Vaiṣṇavas, who were to go there every year for the annual Car Festival and in this way

Caitanya's link with the *bhaktas* of Bengal, and with his mother and wife, was maintained.

"According to the biographer Kavikarṇapūra,[1] Caitanya remained in Puri on this first trip only eighteen days (KCCM 12.94). At the end of that time he left to go on a long pilgrimage to the south and west of the sub-continent. Why he stayed in this first instance so short a time is a matter for speculation. A. C. Sena suggests reasonably that at this time Orissa was in an extremely dangerous situation, with Muslim invasions imminent from the north and a war with the Vijayanagara empire going on in the south. He even suggests that perhaps the image of Jagannātha had been removed to some secret place, in fear of the Muslims, and that if this was so there was little point in Caitanya staying in Puri.[2] But even in such a short time, Caitanya's presence had its impact, for it is said that during this stay both the great scholar Sārvabhauma Bhaṭṭācārya and the king Pratāparudra came under his influence.

"Sārvabhauma[3] was a famous scholar of Vedānta and Nyāya who had written several books on these subjects, including a commentary on Lakṣmīdhara's *Advaitamakaranda* and one on the *Tattvacintāmaṇi* of Gaṅgeśa, though De questions the latter ascription.[4] He had lived for a long time at

---

[1]*Kṛṣṇacaitanyacaritāmṛta Mahākāvya* of Kavikarṇapūra (Paramānanda Sena), ed. with intro. and Bengali trans. by Prāṇkiśora Gosvāmī (Calcutta: by the editor, n.d. [1377 BS]; hereafter cited as KCCM. Textual reference will be to chapter (*sarga*) and verse(s).

[2]Sena, ISC, 90, 101; see the section '*Śrīcaitanya yugena uḍisyā*', 98-107.

[3]This is Vāsudeva Sārvabhauma; see Volume VI of this Encyclopedia, pp. 489-490 for more information.

[4]De 1961, p. 85.

Navadvīpa and had known Caitanya's family, but had moved to Puri, perhaps because that place was under a Hindu king, and was a teacher of Advaita in the city. A. C. Sena,[1] casting doubt on the historicity of Sārvabhauma's conversion, points out that there are verses of devotional *bhakti* included in Rūpa's collection *Padyāvalī* which are ascribed to Sārvabhauma.[2] He says accurately that it is impossible to date those verses, and it may well be that Sārvabhauma had had leanings toward *bhakti* even before his meeting with Caitanya; and indeed it was possible in the context to be both philosopher and devotee, as Śaṃkara himself seems to have been. S. K. De does not doubt the conversion, but argues that it did not take place during Caitanya's first residence in Puri:

> '...at the time when Sārvabhauma wrote his commentary on *Advaitamakaranda,* which is distinctly Advaita-vedāntic, he could not have accepted Caitanya's dualistic faith. In this work he refers to the vanquishing of Kṛṣṇarāya of Karṇāṭa by his patron Gajapati Pratāparudra of Orissa, but Kṛṣṇarāya did not come to the throne until 1510 AD, and his expedition against Orissa did not begin until 1513, so that work could not have been composed before this date'.[3]

Caitanya arrived in Puri, according to calculations based on the biographies, in 1510. Neither argument of course suggests that Sārvabhauma did not in one way or another or at one time or another come under the influence of Caitanya's immensely powerful personality.

---

[1]Sena, ISC, 90-97.

[2]For the verses in question see *Padyāvaḷī* compiled by Rūpa Gosvāmin, ed. Sushil Kumar De, Oriental Publications Series no. 3 (Dacca: University of Dacca, 1934), vv. 72, 73, 90, 91, 99, 100, 133, and possibly 132 (under the name of Kavi Sārvabhauma).

[3]De 1961, p. 85, n. 1.

"The conversion of Pratāparudra (ca. 1597-1540 AD) is similarly questioned,[4] though the ancient intimate relationship between the family of the Mahārāja of Puri and the temple of Jagannātha might suggest grounds for mutual respect and interaction between Pratāparudra and Caitanya in much the way in which it is described by Kṛṣṇadāsa. Whether or not the Mahārāja was already a Vaiṣṇava when he met Caitanya, or whether he was converted at that time, or whether neither of these is true, there is no reason to discount Kṛṣṇadāsa's statements that Pratāparudra and his deputies not only did not obstruct Caitanya's activities, but actively assisted them. There is also a story, not recorded in the standard sources but told by the family of the Mahārāja of Mayūrabhañja, that on his way from Bengal to Puri Caitanya converted that Mahārāja, whose family is related to that of Puri. There are supposed to be letters from Caitanya himself proving this; but these have not to our knowledge been seen by scholars of the subject.

"After this brief stay in Puri, Caitanya left on a pilgrimage which, legend has it, took him all the way to Cape Cormorin, up the west coast of India to Gujarat, and across central India back to Orissa. It is regrettable that the details of this trip must still be categorized as legend for they could tell us much not only about the influence of Caitanya on other schools of Vaiṣṇavism, but about ways in which the mobility of *saṃnyāsins* might have affected exchange of religious ideas throughout the subcontinent. In fact, although it is unlikely that the early biographers would be mistaken about the trip itself, the true extent of it is unknown, for the list of sites seems heavily standardized and conforms with other such pilgrimages by famous *bhaktas* in the tradition.

---

[4]De 1961, p. 90.

"The *Kaḍacā* of Govindadāsa,[1] the authenticity of which text has been called into question, has Caitanya reaching Kanyākumāri, at the very southern tip of India, on the full moon (*pūrṇimā*) of Māgha, exactly one year after his *saṃnyāsa*, and then traveling all the way up the west coast to Dvāraka in Gujarat. As he neared Dvāraka, according to Govindadāsa (GDK, p. 63), he met two Bengalis and became homesick (GDK, p. 63). The language which he spoke on his pilgrimage is also a matter of speculation. Govindadāsa says that 'sometimes Gaurarāya spoke Tamil, sometimes Sanskrit' (GDK, p. 51); that he knew any Tamil is to be seriously doubted. Sanskrit however is a plausible medium, and if indeed Caitanya was only one of many *saṃnyāsins* wandering over the sub-continent at the time, the forces working towards cultural unity may have been greater than is sometimes suspected. It is also of some interest that songs about Caitanya, and even some songs in the Bengali language, are still sung in the *bhajana* rituals of the Tamil country.

"It would seem in any case that Caitanya was away from Puri for about two years, time enough for him to travel that great distance. But Caitanya, with the penchant for solitude which we shall see again and again, took only one companion on the pilgrimage, and there is even difference of opinion as to the identity of that one. Kṛṣṇadāsa Kavirāja claims it was one Kṛṣṇadāsa (CC 2.7.34-38), and in this he follows one of his critical sources, Kavikarṇapūra (KCCM 3.21-30). The 'diary' or 'notebook' (*kaḍacā*) mentioned above, however, is signed Govinda Karmakāra or Govindadāsa, who claims to be the companion of Caitanya on the southern trip. It is obviously, potentially an extremely valuable document; but doubt has been cast on its authenticity by the face that it suddenly

---

[1]*Kaḍacā* of Govindadāsa, ed. Dineśacandra Sena and Banoyārīlāla Gosvāmi, new ed. (Calcutta Calcutta University, 1926); hereafter cited as GDK.

appeared, without manuscript basis, in print in 1895, and by the fact that in its printed form it is undoubtedly fairly modern, including as it does some loan words from Portuguese and even English.[1] There is, furthermore, a feel to the text which is quite different from that of most texts of that period. The following, a description of Caitanya visiting the southern coast, sounds almost like a Christian mystic poet:

> 'Huge waves crashed upon the shore in that place, and their song made one aware of the greatness of God. As one gazed, in that condition, the mind became full of joy and the body thrilled with the rising of emotion. The sand was piled up in monuments like mountains, as if witnessing the greatness of God. The sea called its incessant affirmation. What can I say more than this? Everything in that place was beautiful; there was nothing which was not radiant, and his mind was purified, who gazed upon that beauty.' (GDK, p. 42)

S. K De's considered opinion, which always carries weight, is that although the text has been modernized and contains many interpolations, the basis of it is very likely valid. He also feels that part of the antagonism of some scholars toward the text is due to the fact that it paints a rather unorthodox, human picture of Caitanya. It is also difficult to overcome the nearly unquestioning faith most scholars have in Kṛṣṇadāsa Kavirāja, who is reckoned to be one of their own, that is, a trustworthy scholar of extraordinary talent. The *Kaḍaxā* says it was written by Govindadāsa. As Kṛṣṇadāsa disagrees, the veracity of it is seriously questioned. Until that controversy is settled, we are left in almost total ignorance of what happened to Caitanya on his long journey. We are even left in ignorance of his motive in going. A. C. Sena suggests two possible reasons: the imminent invasions mentioned before, and a further search for his lost

---

[1]De 1961, p. 62, n. 1.

brother, the latter proposed by Kṛṣṇadāsa Kavirāja himself (CC 2.7.10).[1]

"The texts agree, however, on one significant event which took place at the beginning of the trip, and that is the meeting with Rāmānanda Rāya on the banks of the Godāvarī River, in what is now northern Andhra Pradesh. Rāmānanda was a high official, as were other members of his family, in the administration ofthe kingdom of the Mahārāja Pratāparudra (CC 1.10. 129-132); he was also a great *bhakta*, whose profound devotion had been praised by Sārvabhauma to Caitanya...Certain of his practices as well as his reported conversation would seem to indicate that he was a Sahajiyā or Tāntric Vaiṣṇava, and his doctrinal position might well have influenced Caitanya's own attitudes. The significance of the meeting lay not only in the fact that because of it Rāmānanda 'became one of Caitanya's most intimate followers, taking leave from the service of the Mahārāja in order to remain with Caitanya until the end of the latter's life, but in the fact that it was Rāmānanda who revealed Caitanya's own Rādhā-*bhāva*, his personality as Rādhā, to Caitanya himself (CC 2.8). He saw Caitanya as both Rādhā and Kṛṣṇa: and from that time Rādhā manifested herself more and more in Caitanya's person, until in the anguish of his pain of separation from Kṛṣṇa she took him over completely, and he became irrevocably withdrawn from the world of ordinary men–mad, as it seemed to worldly human sight.

"After two years he returned to Puri, and his followers from Bengal began a series of annual excursions to visit him at the Car Festival of Jagannātha. This was a pattern which was broken only twice in the rest of his life, one when Caitanya was on another pilgrimage, and once when he sent word to his followers that he would that year visit them in Bengal. Caitanya had long cherished the idea of a pilgrimage to Vṛndāvana, the

---

[1]Sena, ISC pp. 108, 124-126.

place of his beloved Kṛṣṇa, and about two years after his return fro the south and west he set out for that place, choosing to go through Bengal, both because the way was better and because it would give him the opportunity to see old friends. According to the version of Kṛṣṇadāsa, it was on this trip that he first met Rūpa and Sanātana, two of his six Gosvāmins, those scholars and devotees who were to be credited by members of the community with 'reclaiming' Vṛndāvana and who wrote the texts which were to give the enthusiastic devotionalism of Caitanya a theological and orthodox shape....Rūpa and Sanātana...were high officials in the court of the Muslim Nawab of Bengal, Husain Shah (r. 1493-1518 AD). They were so passionately drawn to Caitanya that they left their high positions to become his disciples. Caitanya dispatched these two to join Lokanātha, whom he had sent earlier, in Vṛndāvana, to rescue the temple and pilgrimage sites which, according to the Bengali writers at least, had fallen into disuse. A. C. Sena questions the idea that the Bengalis were pioneers in rehabilitating these sites, saying that 'for a long time Nimbārka, and before Rūpa and Sanātana, Vallabha had established *āśramas* there, with many pupils' (Sena, ISC p. 148). This seems to be partially at least borne out by the fact that Rūpa and Sanātana did encounter stiff opposition from members of the Vallabha-*sampradāya*, who seems to resent what they felt to be the intrusion of the Bengalis on their territory.

"This first attempt of Caitanya to go to Vṛndāvana was abortive. While he was in Bengal, many people were constantly with him, and many obviously had the intention of accompanying him on his pilgrimage. It was, interestingly, his new follower Sanātana who suggested to him that it was inappropriate for a *saṃnyāsin* to go on a pilgrimage with great crowds of people in his retinue. So Caitanya, seeing the reason in that argument, retraced his steps to Puri. After a short time he again set out for Vṛndāvana, this time in relative secret and accompanied only by a *brāhmaṇa* and that *brahmaṇa* a servant. While he was in Vṛndāvana he was in constant ecstacy, and this so frightened his companions that they escorted him away from the place before, in his frenzy, an accident occurred. So they started back for Puri by way of Prayāga (Allahabad), in which place he was joined by Rūpa and Rūpa's younger brother Anupama or Vallabha. The latter, a devotee of Rāma, is important to the movement not so much because of his own contribution–he died young, in fact very shortly after this meeting–but for the fact that he was the father of the youngest and the greatest philosopher of the six Gosvāmins, Jīva by name. Caitanya then left for Vārāṇāsi, where he met Sanātana and instructed him; it was here that he purportedly performed another conversion, this time the convert being the scholar Prakāśānanda. There is less reason to believe in the historicity of this conversion than of the others. The biographies by Murāri, Vṛndāvana Dāsa, Kavikarṇapūra, Jayānanda, and Locana Dāsa do not mention the incident at all, and even Kṛṣṇadāsa is unusually vague on the matter. As De points out, Kṛṣṇanātha is far from amiable toward Prakāśānanda, despite the fact that he always has good words for converts to the faith. (De 1961, p. 100.n. 1).

"Finally returning to Puri, Caitanya settled down, at about the age of thirty, to a life of devotion, in fact ecstasy, which was to last until his death eighteen years later. Attacked increasingly by his divine madness, for the last twelve years of his life he was about entirely out of touch with the everyday world, and was on several occasions rescued from death only by the watchfulness and care of his to most intimate companions, Svarūpā Dāmodara and servant Govinda. Where he stayed during the last years is not known. A. C. Sena points out that it must have been in a large, brick-built house, for it is said that he stayed in a *gambhīrā,* the Oriya word for an inner chamber of such a large structure. Sena in fact feels that it is likely that the house was the present-day monastery known as the Rādhākānta Maṭha, near the main gate of the temple (Sena,

ISC, p. 155) and where, it is true, the visitor is shown the room in which Caitanya lived and, it is said, died. Kavikarṇapūra and Jayānanda feel that Caitanya stayed in the garden (*ṭoṭā*) of Kāśīśvara Miśra. Significantly, the great Vaiṣṇava scholar, Haridāsa Dāsa, perhaps conflating sacred geography, locates the *gambhīrā* in Kāśīśvara Miśra's compound as well.[1]

"The manner of Caitanya's death is a mystery: Murāri (KCC 1.2.14) mentions it only in passing, giving no details. Kṛṣṇadāsa (CC 1.13.7-8) says only that he died in 1455 *śaka* (1533 A.D.). Locana Dāsa records what is probably the popular legend, that Caitanya was absorbed into the great image of Jagannātha, since the two were identical, and simply disappeared (LCM 4.15; pp. 210-211). Jayānanda records the least orthodox, least acceptable, and probably the most accurate, in this case, account: that near the end of the Car Festival Caitanya injured his left foot while dancing, and after being in great pain for six days, died from an infection of the wound (JCM 9.119-156). A.C. Sena of course agrees with this, and adds that the chances would be very good that such a wound would become septic, the ground being covered with the droppings of cows and goats (Sena, ISC, pp. 196-199). There are other, conflicting accounts. Melville Kennedy, for example, records another tradition, that Caitanya drowned, a tradition which persists among certain Baul musicians today.[2] But this story is probably based on the incident reported by Kṛṣṇadāsa, in which Caitanya is rescued from drowning by a fisherman (CC 3.18.24-79), and in all, the Jayānanda account seems most reasonable. The tales show a remarkable structural unity in their narratives, which remains consistent with basic philosophical principles regarding the

---

[1]Haridāsa Dāsa, *Śrīśrī gauḍīya vaiṣṇava abhidhāna*, 2 vols. (Navadvīpa: by the editor at Haribola Kuṭīra, 471 GA), 2:1858.

[2]Tony K. Stewart, "When biographical narratives disagree; the death of Kṛṣṇa Caitanya", Numen 38, no. 2 (1991), p. 242.

nature of devotion and the devotee's place in this world.[1] Explaining Caitanya's death was not easy, but on the time of the death, there is general agreement: both Jayānanda (JCM 9.147-148) and Locana Dāsa (LCM 4.15; p. 210) report that it was on the twenty-first of Āśāṛha, 1533 A.D.

."The problem does not quite end there, for the question arises: what happened to the body? It was probably buried, as was the body of Haridāsa, on the seashore (CC 3.11.65), and as the bodies of perfected *bhaktas* usually are. But everyone is silent about it, which probably accounts for the stories of its simple disappearance. One popular story attributed to the eighteenth century Oriya *Pramatarangiṇī* of Sadānanda purports that the grave was 'in the *ṭoṭā* of Gopīnātha,' but there is some uncertainty as to what that means. How could it have been kept so quiet? For all the *bhaktas* of Bengal were in Puri for the Car Festival, as was the Mahārāja, Caitanya's devotee."

2 RAGHUNĀTHA GOSVAMĪ DĀSA (1495-1571)

(Excerpted from S.K. De, 1961, pp. 119-124) "Of Raghunātha-dāsa, who lived with Caitanya for many years at Puri, a great deal is known from Kṛṣṇadāsa Kavirāja, who was his intimate friend and disciple at Vṛndāvana...He was the son of a rich Kāyastha, named Govardhana, a zamindar of Saptagrāma in the district of Hooghly...On the occasion of Caitanya's visit to Śāntipur on is way to Rāmakeli, Raghunātha is said to have met Caitanya for the first time...After an arduous journey, he reached Caitanya at Puri, where he was handed over for spiritual training to Svarūpa Dāmodara. The extreme austerities which Raghunātha practiced was a thing of wonder even to the devout Vaiṣṇavas, and Caitanya himself is said to have acknowledged their depth and sincerity...After Caitanya's death he is said to have left Puri for Vṛndāvana, where he

[1]Ibid., pp. 249-255.

joined Rūpa and Sanātana and lived a self-imposed life of hard asceticism near Rādhā-kuṇḍa till his death...'

"His literary works, which deal in impassioned Sanskrit verse and prose with the mystic-erotic aspects of Rādhā-Kṛṣṇa worship, are not very extensive. They are mostly in the nature of fervent lyrical hymns, *stavas* or *stotras*, which have been collected together and published under the title **Stavāvalī*" (published Murshidabad: Radharaman Press, in Bengali characters with Bengali translation; also with a Sanskrit commentary by Vaṅgeśvara, De, p. 121, fn. 1)..." Most of them give an emotional treatment in highly erotic imagery of the various aspects of Kṛṣṇa-līlā. The total number of these hymns is twenty-nine...Raghunātha's only sustained composition, however, was his *Muktā-caritra*," (ed. Nityasvarup Brahmacari in Bengali characters with Bengali translation, Vrndavan 1908)"a Sanskrit Kāvya of the Campū type written in prose and occasional verse, but interspersed with witty dialogues. The theme is Kṛṣṇa's early sports at Vrndavana, its object being to show the superiority of his free love for Rādhā over his wedded love for Satyabhāmā..." (De goes on to mention one or two other works the ascription of which is perhaps not so clear.)

For a more complete assessment consult Steven Rosen at Rosen 1991, pp. 35-60.

3 SANĀTANA GOSVĀMIN (1488-1558)

(S.K. De, op. cit., pp. 146-149) "Of the two brothers, Sanātana and Rūpa, and their nephew Jīva...there exists a more detailed and reliable record. Jīva himself at the close of his abridgement (*Laghu-toṣaṇī*) of Sanātana's commentary on the *Bhāgavata,* gives us the genealogy of the family, as well as a list of the principal works of Sanātana and Rūpa. This list, which can be generally corroborated from other sources, is quoted with approval in the *Bhaktiratnākara*, which together with Kṛṣṇadāsa Kavirāja's biography and the *Prema-vilāsa*, supplies additional information about these three venerable Gosvāmins of Vṛndavana. From these accounts we learn that they were originally Karṇāta Brahmins, who had migrated at about the end of the 14th and beginning of the 15th century and settled in Bengal...The previous history of the family of Rūpa and Sanātana is thus given by Jīva. There was a prince of Karṇāta, named Sarvajña Jagadguru of the Bharadvāja-gotra of Brahmins, who is said to have added to his other princely qualities a knowledge of the three Vedas. His son Aniruddha, who succeeded him, was also a renowned prince, but he fancied only the Yajur-veda. Of Aniruddha's two sons, Rūpeśvara and Harihara, by his two wives, the first became an accomplished scholar, but the second took to evil ways and turned out his elder brother from his principality. Rūpeśvara, who fled to some country in the east, had a son, named Padmanābha, who was well-versed in the Yajur-veda and the Upaniṣads. Padmanābha settled on the banks of the Ganges at Navahaṭṭa (modern Nauhati, according to the *Bhakti-ratnākara*), performed a *yajña* (sacrifice) and had five sons, of whom Mukunda was the youngest. On account of a quarrel with his relations Mukunda left Navahaṭṭa and went to Vaṅga (East Bengal) settling, according to the *Bhaktratnākara*, at Fatoyabad, near Jessore, under the Bāktā Candradvīpa Pergunna. Mukunda had a son named Kumāra. Kumāra appears to have several sons of whom we are concerned here with three; to them Caitanya gave the names of Sanātana, Rūpa and Anupama.

"The eldest Sanātana appears to have learnt Sanskrit from (Ratnākara?) Vidyāvācaspati[1], a scholar of Navadvīpa, who is said to have been a younger brother of Vāsudeva Sārvabhauma and whom Sanātana reverentially mentions as his *guru* in the

---

[1]On Ratnākara Vidyāvācaspati, see Gopinath Kaviraj, *History and Bibliography of Nyāya-Vaiśeṣika* (Calcutta 1962), pp. 68-69. He is said to have written a commentary on the *Tattvacintāṃāṇyāloka* of Pakṣadhara.

opening verses of his *Vaiṣṇava-toṣaṇī.* He became a high official (a Mahāmantrin, we are told) at the Muhammadan court at Gauḍa, acquired considerable wealth and power and settled with his brothers at the village of Rāmakeli, near Gauḍa, where he met Caitanya for the first time. Rūpa also appears to have held some official position at the same court. Although Sanātana and Rūpa were widely known by their Muhammadan name or title of Sāker Malik and Dabir Khās respectively, before Caitanya gave them new names, there is no evidence to show that they actually adopted the Muhammadan faith. On the contrary, the *Bhaktiratnākara* tells us that they invited a colony of Karṇāta Brahmans to settle near Rātnakeli and apparently kept up their inherited social and religious practices, only considering themselves impure because of their contact with the Mlecchas. They kept themselves in touch with the Vaiṣṇavas of Navadvīpa, and had from the beginning an obviously Vaiṣṇava disposition...After some time Rūpa left home with his younger brother Anupama (alias Vallabha) and joined Caitanya at Allahabad on the latter's way back from Vṛndāvana. After ten days' stay Rūpa wanted to accompany Caitanyato Benares, but he was directed to go to Vṛndāvana. Sanātana came to Caitanya at Benares, and requested Caitanya's permission to accompany him to Puri; but he was also directed to go to Vṛndāvana first and then come to him at Puri and returned to Vṛndāvana. Caitanya is represented as giving him at Allahabad, as well as his brother Sanātana at Benares, detailed instructions regarding the composition of various Śāstric works for the sect. Soon after Rūpa left, Sanātana also visited Caitanya at Puri. After these short visits, Sanātana and Rūpa settled at Vṛndāvana till their death, carrying on with selfless devotion the laborious work which was entrusted to them by Caitanya and for which they were eminently fitted by their great learning and piety..."

More details of Sanātana's life are provided in Bhakti Vilas Tirtha's "Foreword" to the Second edition of the edition of the *Bṛhat-Bhāgavatāmṛta* cited below. See also Neal Delmonico,

"Rūpa Gosvāmin: his life, family, and early Vraja commentators", Journal of Vaisnava Studies 1.2, 1993, pp. 133-157. Delmonico's account puts dates on De's account (above), and adds some important details, disagreeing with De's dates, for example. Here is Delmonico's discussion of the determination of the dating of the deaths of the two brothers (p. 138):

"The exact dates their deaths are not known. One line of reasoning places Sanātana's death in 1554 or 1555. This is based on a verse in Jīva's *Mādhavamahotsava* which appears to refer to the death of Sanātana. This poem was written in 1555. As Sanātana's final work, the *Vaiṣṇava-toṣaṇī*, is dated to 1554, he is thought to have died between 1554 and 1555. Rūpa is said to have died a year or two afterwards. Sukhamaya Mukhopādhyāya has criticized this line of reasoning as a misreading of Jīva's verse, however, and argues that Sanātana and Rūpa died just before the arrival of Śrīnivāsa in Vṛndāvana in 1562. He therefore gives their final dates as 1560 and 1562.[1]

Cf. also Rosen 1991, pp. 117-142.

3.1 SANĀTANA GOSVĀMI, *Bṛhatvaiṣṇavatoṣaṇī* on the tenth section of the *Bhāgavatapurāṇa*

Outside of a 19th century edition, edited with Vrndavanacandra Tarkalamkarara's commentary by Ramanarayana Vidyaratna, from Murshidabad 1870, 1896, which is no longer

---

[1]Sukhamaya Mukhopāḍḥyāya, *Madhyayugera Bāṃlā Sāhītyera Tathya o Kalakrama* (Kalikātta: G. Bhāṛadvāja and Co., 1974, pp. 125-131). This supposition is based on the idea that all of the early texts say that Śrīṇivāsa arrived just after the deaths of Sanātana and Rūpa, or, more specifically, that they died while he was en route to Vṛndāvan. These texts say the same thing about Śrīnivāsa's attempt to see Caitanya, who died in 1533 in Puri. It is somewhat hard to believe that having missed Caitanya in Puri he would have waited twenty-five years to travel to see Rūpa and Sanātana in Vṛndāvāṇa.

listed as available anywhere, the other printed versions of this text are in Bengali or Oriya script (cf. Bib 3, #969).

3.2 SANĀTANA GOSVĀMIN, *Bṛhat Bhagavatāmṛta*

The work is translated into English by Sriman Bhakti Prajnan Yati Maharaj, published by the Sree Gaudiya Math: Madras, Second edition, Madras 1975. The brief summary given here is found on p. 10 of the Foreword by Bhakti Vilas Tirtha to that text. The text is not a work on philosophy, though doubtless it provides information pertinent to understanding the background from which Sanātana's philosophical understanding stems.

Summary by Bhakti Vilas Tirtha

"*Śrī Bṛhat Bhāgavatāmṛtam* deals with intricate questions and elaborations of the various incarnations of Krishna–Vishnu and His entourage, *bhakti, prema,* devotees and so on in its two volumes each of which consists of seven chapters.

"In the first Volume of *Bṛhat Bhāgavatāmṛtam* Śrī Sanātana Gosvāmi deals with Bhāgavata Kṛpānirdhāraṇa–ascertainment of gist of divine kindness and in the second volume deals with ascertainment of Glory of Śrī Golaka, the Kingdom of Kṛṣṇa. The seven chapters of the first Volume are named (1) Bhauma, (2) Divya), (3) Prapañcātīta, (4) Bhakta, (5) Priya, (6) Priyatama and (7) Purṇa Kṛpā Pātra. The seven chapters of the second volme are named as follows: (1) Vairāgya, (2) Jñāna, (3) Bhajana, (4) Vaikuntha, (5) Priya, (6) Abhistalāva and (7) Jagadānanda.

"In the second volume, Shri Sanātana Gosvāmi delineates the devotional process of a devotee starting from initiation by the *guru* into Kṛṣṇa Mantra as a first step to spiritual uplift passing through step by step ultimately attaining the highest step at the lotus feet of Sri Krishna experiencing devotional bliss intensified to superlative degree."

3.3 SANĀTANA GOSVĀMIN, *Haribhaktivilāsa*

As can be seen from the summary below, this is not a work on philosophy. However, since it is credited to Sanātana's authorship and deals with the practical aspects of participation in the practices of the school here under discussion, we provide a brief summary of its contents.

The summary below is found in *Śrī Hari-bhakti-vilāsa* by Śrīla Sanātana Gosvāmī, translated by Bhumipati Dasa, edited by Purnaprakma Dasa, Ras Bihari Lal & Sons: Vrndavan, Five Volumes 2005: Contents, Volume I, pp. v-vi.

Mans Broo says the work was written by Gopāla Bhatta Gosvamin (1501-1586), a *brāhmaṇa* from Sri Rangam, around 1534, perhaps with the assistance of Sanātana Gosvāmin.

First *Vilāsa*

In the first *vilāsa*, the following subjects are covered–the need for taking shelter at the lotus feet of a spiritual master, the characteristics of a bond-fide spiritual master, the symptoms of a genuine disciple, the spiritual master's and the disciple's tests of one another, the process for worshiping the spiritual master, the prayer of a disciple, the glories of the Supreme Lord, the glories of Vaiṣṇava *mantras*, the process of purification, and the processes for purifying *mantras*.

Second *Vilāsa*

In the second *vilāsa*, the process of initiation is described.

Third *Vilāsa*

In the third *vilāsa*, the following subjects are discussed–the proper code of conduct for a devotee, rising every day at the time of *brahma-muhūrta* (one hour and thirty-six minutes before sunrise) to chant the glories of Kṛṣṇa, washing the face, cleansing the teeth, wearing fresh cloth, hearing and chanting about the pastimes of Kṛṣṇa in the morning, waking up the Deity while playing musical instruments, removing flowers from the altar, offering *maṅgala-ārati,* the proper way to pass urine and stool; cleaning the body; rinsing the mouth; cleaning the teeth, which is to be performed right after getting up from bed; the morning bath; chanting *mantras*; and worshiping the Lord in the water.

Fourth *Vilāsa*

In the fourth *vilāsa,* the following subjects are discussed–cleansing the Lord's temple, drawing auspicious signs like the *svāstika,* picking *tulasī* leaves, collecting flowers, taking a mid-day bath at home with warm water if there is no holy river available nearby, wearing clothes, the proper sitting place, and decorating one's body with marks of *tilaka* made from *gopī-candana.* After putting on *tilaka,* one should decorate his body with various auspicious marks, wear *tulasī* beads, sit at home and chant the *gāyatrī mantra,* worship the spiritual master, and recited in praise of the spiritual master.

Fifth *Vilāsa*

In the fifth *vilāsa*, the following are discussed–the worship of the doors of the temple, the proper *āsana* for worshiping the Lord; placing pots of *arghya* and other substances in their proper places; putting the necessary ingredients in the pots, such as *pādya*; installing auspicious water pots; praying to the Lord for removing all obstacles; offering obeisance to the spiritual master; purifying oneself; the proper breathing process, the *nyāsas*, five kinds of *mudrās*, meditation on Kṛṣṇa, worshiping Kṛṣṇa in the mind, the proper place of worship, the Deity form of the Lord, the *śālagrāma-śīlās, Dvāraka-śīlā,* and purifying all of the ingredients for worship.

4 RŪPA GOSVĀMIN (1489-1564)

See above under 3 Sanātana Gosvāmin, his brother.

4.1 RŪPA GOSVĀMIN, *Bhaktirasāmṛtasindhu*

The literature on this work is extensive; cf. Bib. 3, #969.2. The summary below is drawn from Haberman, pp. xlix-lxv of Haberman 2003.

Summary by David L. Haberman

"The *Bhaktirasāmṛtasindhu* is conceived of as an ocean of *rasa,* and its overall aim is the articulation of a systematic aesthetics of loving devotion to Kṛṣṇa. In keeping with the oceanic image, the text is divided into four directional divisions (*vibhāgas*); each of these quadrants is further subdivided into chapters called waves (*laharīs*).[1] The first and Eastern Quadrant contains an explanation of the general characteristics of devotion (*bhakti*) as defined by Rūpa. Moving clockwise, the Southern Quadrant lays out devotional *rasa* in successive chapters in terms of the primary aesthetic components established by Bharata in the *Nāṭyaśāstra*: the Excitants (*vibhāvas*), Indications (*anubhāvas*), Responses (*sāttvikas*). Transitory Emotions (*vyabhicāra-bhāvas*), and the Foundational Emotions (*sthāyi-bhāvas*). The Western Quadrant outlines the major features of the five primary devotional *rasas*: the Peaceful (*śānta*), Respectful (*prīta*), Companionable (*preyas*), Parentally Affectionate (*vatsala*), and Amorous (*madhura*). The final and Northern Quadrant presents the major features of seven secondary devotional *rasas*: the Humorous (*hāsya*), Wonderful (*adbhūta*), Heroic (*vīra*), Compassionate (*karuṇa*), Furious (*raudra*), Dreadful (*bhayānaka*), and Abhorrent (*bībhatsa*); this division ends with a discussion of the compatibility and

[1]The numbering system I use to identify verses follows this format: the first number refers one of the four quadrants, the second number refers to the chapter, and the third number refers to the individual verse. Thus, 2.4.32, for example, refers to the thirty -second verse in the second verse of the Southern Quadrant. (DH)

incompatibility of *rasas*, and the semblance of *rasas*, or defective *rasas*.

"The format of presentation in the *Bhaktirasāmṛtasindhu* reveals the scholastic influence of the new logic known as Navya Nyāya–marked by a great concern for careful definitions and elaborate classification–that was prevalent during the time of Rūpa's education. In a manner very typical of the Vṛndāvana Gosvāmins, Rūpa supports his definitions and statements with quotations drawn from a wide range of texts. This not only suggests that scripture (*śabda*) is the most important source of authoritative knowledge (*pramāṇa*) for Rūpa, but also that he was well-educated in both Sanskrit aesthetics and Vaiṣṇava philosophy. His analysis and theoretical statements about *rasa* are supported with quotations from previous works on aesthetics, such as Bharata's *Nāṭyaśāstra*, Viśvanātha Kavirāja's *Sāhitya Darpaṇa*, and Siṃhabhūpāla's *Rasa Saduhākara*. His presentation of the various components of each type of *rasa* is often illustrated with quotations from Vaiṣṇava scriptures, such as the *Padma, Skanda* and *Nārada Purāṇas*, but especially from the *Bhāgavata Purāṇa*. In fact, in many ways the *Bhaktirasāmṛtasindhu* can be read as a commentary on the *Bhagavata Purāṇa*, at least from an aesthetic perspective. The *Bhāgavata* holds a particularly emanent position in the school of Gauḍīya Vaiṣṇavism, for whereas other Vedāntic schools produced commentaries on the *Vedānta Sūtra*, the Gauḍīyas consider the *Bhāgavata* as Vyāsa's own commentary on the *Vedānta Sūtra*. Accordingly, the *Bhāgavata* is the single most authoritative text for Gauḍīya Vaiṣṇavas....

"Rūpa's exploration of the ocean of devotional aesthetic begins with a definition of devotion or *bhakti* in the first chapter of the Eastern Quadrant, entitled 'The General Characteristics of Devotion". After praising his *gurus*, the saint Caitanya and his older brother Sanātana, Rūpa defines *bhakti* as 'dedicated service to Kṛṣṇa that is rendered pleasantly, is devoid of desire for anything else, and is unobstructed by intellectual knowledge (*jñāna*) or purposeful action (*karman)*' (I.1.11). This means that the true object of all devotion is Kṛṣṇa, understood as the highest reality. Rūpa follows the theology of the *Bhāgavata Purāna* in assuming that Kṛṣṇa is the supreme non-dual reality and the very source of all *avatāras*. Devotion itself is defined as 'dedicated service', which involves both emotional attitudes (*bhāva*) and physical actions (*ceṣṭā*). It is 'in service with the senses to the Lord of the Senses' (I.1.12). The devotion that Rūpa marks as the highest and most worthy of emulation is a means of focusing the mind and other senses on Kṛṣṇa through pleasant feelings, thus avoiding the negative emotional examples found in Vaiṣṇava scripture, such as Kaṃsa, who focused his mind on Kṛṣṇa with fear, and Śiśupāla, who focused his mind on Kṛṣṇa with hatred. The highest devotion is to be purely selfless, desiring nothing other than loving service itself. Specifically, this means avoiding the seduction of both worldly pleasures (*bhukti*) and spiritual liberation (*mukti*), which would result in either a selfish love or a state of absolute union wherein love becomes impossible. Rūpa identifies and explains six special qualities of *bhakti*: it destroys difficulties, bestows auspiciousness, trivializes *mokṣa*, is very difficult to attain, consists of a special concentrated joy, and attracts Śrī Kṛṣṇa (1.1.17 ff.).

"Rūpa's understanding of *rasa* differs greatly from those of other theoreticians who preceded him. Whereas previous writers normally restricted the *rasa* experience to the limited space of the theater, he extends it to all of life. *Rasa* is now not understood to be simply a temporary aesthetic experience, but rather as the culminating core of a genuine human life. For Rūpa there is only one true *rasa*, *bhakti-rasa*, which constitutes the highest religious experience. This one true *rasa* is to be distinguished from the ordinary (*laukika*) *rasas* of classical theory, for it is understood to be extraordinary (*alaukika*), even an aspect of divinity. The divinity of *bhakti-rasa* is expressed with the terms *śuddha sattva* ('pure and luminous quality,"

(1.3.1) and *mahāśakti* ('great power', 2.5.92). The first of these terms indicates the extraordinary nature of devotional *rasa*, for the pure and luminous quality of *śuddha sattva* is by definition beyond the ordinary qualities that make up the ordinary world (*tamas, rajas, sattva*). The second term indicates that it participates in that aspect of divinity known as *śakti*. Rūpa's nephew, Jīva Gosvāmin, identifies both of these terms with the joyful power (*hlādinī-śakti*) of Kṛṣṇa, which he marks as the highest dimension and essential nature (*svarūpa*) of divinity on the basis of the *Viṣṇu Purāṇa*.

"The special nature of devotional *rasa* for Rūpa, however, can best be seen by closely examining his understanding of its Foundational Emotion (*sthāyi-bhāva*); furthermore, an understanding of the uniqueness of this Foundational Emotion is the key to understanding Rūpa's entire system. Rūpa states: 'The Foundational Emotion here is declared to be that love (*rati*) which takes Śrī Kṛṣṇa as its object (*viṣaya*)' (2.5.2)...The classical *rasa* theory passed down from Bharata recognized eight Foundational Emotions; a ninth was added later. Although Rūpa will proceed to introduce variety into love, it is clear that *bhakti-rasa* has a single and very special Foundational Emotion. For him, then, all genuine *rasa* is based on some form of love, or more specifically, some form of love for Kṛṣṇa. This is a significant point of departure from previous *bhakti* theoreticians, such as Vopadeva, who recognized the traditional nine Foundational Emotions, although in many ways Rūpa is in agreement with the viewpoint of Bhoja, who reduced all *rasas* to one (called either *śṛṅgāra* or *prema*).

"Rūpa writes: '*Bhāva* is a special form of the pure and luminous quality, and it is like a beam of the sun of supreme love (*prema*)'. (1.3.1). Here the word '*bhāva*' means the Foundational Emotion of love, as is made explicit in 1.3.13. The word *prema*, which I have translated as 'supreme love', refers to the higher states of love, which in effect are *bhakti-rasa*. It is clear from a reading of 1.4.1 that *prema* or supreme love is an intensified form of love, *bhāva* or *rati*. Again, Rūpa is in agreement with Bhoja, who viewed *rasa* as an intensified form of the Foundational Emotion, and opposed to Abhinavagupta, who viewed the Foundational Emotions and *rasa* as being ultimately different. For Rūpa, *bhāva* is the first stage of *prema*; stated the other way around, *prema* is merely the intensified or fully manifest form of *bhāva*. Once the *bhāva* is present, *rasa* is sure to follow under the right conditions. Thus the importance of the presence of the *bhāva* or Foundational Emotion. Since Rūpa places so much emphasis on the Foundational Emotion, a major concern of his was to determine how it becomes present. He writes: 'This loving emotion (*bhāva*) is born in two ways: either from diligent dedication to spiritual practices (*sādhana*), or for the very fortunate, by the grace of Kṛṣṇa or His devotees. The first, however, is more common; the second is rare' (1.3.6). This being the case, and considering the immense importance Rūpa placed in the *sthāyi-bhāva*, he gives great attention to *sādhana*, a subject taken up in the lengthy second chapter of the first division of this text.

"Rūpa divides *sādhana bhakti* into two types: *vaidhī* and *rāgānugā*. *Vaidhī bhakti sādhana* is said to be a form of practice that is motivated by the injunctions of scripture (1.2.6), whereas *rājānugā bhakti sādhana* is a form of practice that is motivated by a desire to follow one of Kṛṣṇa's close companions (1.2.270). Rūpa enumerates sixty-four practices of *vaidhī*, supporting each with illustrations drawn from Vaiṣṇava scriptures. He declares the last five practices to be particularly powerful (1.2.238). These consist of lovingly serving an image of Kṛṣṇa, reading the *Bhāgavata Purāṇa*, associating with devotees of Kṛṣṇa, singing the names of Kṛṣṇa, and living in the region of Vraja. *Vaidhī* appears to be a preliminary state of practice, which culminates in the desire to identify with the emotional state of one of Kṛṣṇa's close companions. Once this desire has blossomed, one is ready for *rāgānugā sādhana*.

"*Rāgānugā sādhana* is defined as a form of devotion that imitates (*anusṛtā*) the devotion of the various residents of Vraja (1.2.270). The residents of Vraja are considered to be perfected beings, and as such function as paradigms for ideal devotion. Their devotion is called *rāgānugā bhakti*, which is defined as a passionate absorption in the beloved (1.2.272). Rūpa typically singles out the amorous relationship for special attention, and so therefore divides *rāgānugā bhakti* into two types: Amorous (*kāmarūpa*) and Relational (*sambandharūpa*), 1.2.263). Following this twofold division, *rāgānugā* is also divided into two types: Imitation of Amorous *bhakti* (*kāmānugā*) and Imitation of Relational *bhakti* (*sambandhānugā*), 1.2.290). The models for the first are the *gopīs* of Vraja; the models for the second are the friends and relatives of Kṛṣṇa. The desire for attaining the emotional state (*bhāva*) of one of the residents of Vraja is the sign of eligibility for this type of spiritual practice (1.2.291). The practice itself, which has a long developmental history, is best indicated by two verses in the text (1.2.294-295). Rūpa advises the *rāgānuga* practitioner to dwell continually in Vraja (mentally if not physically), and remain absorbed in the stories of Kṛṣṇa and his intimate companions. In this way, the practitioner comes to know intimately the script of Kṛṣṇa's divine play (*līlā*). The next move is to take an active role in that script by performing services (*sevā*) which imitate the residents of Vraja with both the practitioner's body (*sādhaka-rūpa*) and perfected body (*siddha-rūpa*).

"A great deal could be said about these terse instructional remarks, but briefly this practice begins with initiation by a qualified *guru*, who has the ability to discern the identity of an individual's character in the ultimate reality of Kṛṣṇa's divine play or *līlā*. According to Gauḍīya Vaiṣṇavism everyone has a spiritual double, called the 'perfected body', that defines one's true identity. Use of the term perfected body (*siddha-rūpa*) had a previous history among the Nātha and Haṭha *yogīs*, who employed the term to refer to the body that had become perfected through techniques of *yoga* and had achieved a deathless state. In the Gauḍīya Vaiṣṇava tradition, however, the perfected body refers to both a meditative body and one's eternal form. Jīva Gosvāmin glosses the term as 'an internal body suitable for one's desired services for Kṛṣṇa' (*antaś-cintitābhiṣṭa-tat-sevopayogi-deha*). The perfected body is revealed to the practitioner by a *guru* who has mastered a meditative technique known as *līlā-smaraṇa*. This practice involves visualizing in great detail particular dramatic scenes of Vraja. The culmination of this practice is a direct vision (*sākṣāt-darśana*) of Kṛṣṇa and his *līlā*. As a master of this meditative technique, the *guru* can discern the practitioner's true identity, whereas the practitioner employs this technique as a way of entering into the ultimate world of Kṛṣṇa's *līlā*. It is then with the meditative body of the *siddha-rūpa*–technically defined as a *gopī*–that much of the service to Kṛṣṇa is performed by the practitioner of *rāgānugā sādhana*. After the death of the current body, one takes to eternal residence in the perfected body.

"Although the perfected body is of greater importance for the higher acts of service, acts of service performed with the 'practitioner's body' are also held to be important and efficacious. In his commentary on 1.2.295 Jivā glosses the practitioner's body (*sādhaka-rūpa*) as the 'body as it presently is' (*yathāsthitadeha*). Although heated debates arose regarding the nature of the proper employment of the practitioner's body, the orthodox position is that the acts of service with the practitioner's body involve the standard acts of devotion, such as praising (*kīrtana*) Kṛṣṇa and worshiping him through images. In fact, the commentator Viśvanātha Cakravartin was to argue in his commentary on 1.2.295 that the two types of bodies are to imitate two different types of models. One is to imitate the perfected body; and one is to imitate Śrī Rūpa, Sanātana and the other Vṛndāvana Gosvāmins with the practitioner's body. Regardless of the particular interpretation, all agree that the purpose of the *rāgānugā sādhana* is the generation of a *bhāva*, specifically a love for Kṛṣṇa as exemplified by the residents of Vraja, the very Foundational Emotion of the ultimate devotional *rasa*...

"One of the major religious contributions of Rūpā's text is a sustained critique of *mokṣa*, understood here to be the Advaitin goal of unity or absolute identity with Brahman. Although this critique is assumed throughout the text, it is taken up most directly in the second chapter of the first quadrant in the context of a discussion regarding eligibility for the higher devotional life of *bhakti* (1.2.22-57). Those eligible for *bhakti* simply reject the quest for *mokṣa* as being ultimate. Most particularly it is *sāyujya mukti*, often glossed as complete union (*ekavat*), that is marked as most problematic, for achieving this state would end all possibility of relationship with Kṛṣṇa, and it is only in relationship that one can taste the bliss of *bhakti-rasa*. The *bhakti* theologians in pursuit of divine love are fond of saying that they desire to taste sugar, not become sugar. Rūpa quotes a verse from the mouth of Hanumān to make his point: 'I do not desire *mokṣa*, which cuts one's connection with the world and destroys the relationship expressed as: "You are the Lord and I am the servant"' (1.2.49). As an aesthetic experience, the bliss of *bhakti* is dependent upon some differentiation between the experiencing subject and the experienced object. In classical aesthetic terminology, this means that there has to be a split between the *āśraya* (here the lover or devotee) and the *viṣaya* (here the beloved, Kṛṣṇa) for love to occur. The highest reality, then, for the Vaiṣṇavas is not the unqualified absolute Brahman of the Advaitins, but rather the infinitely qualified Bhagavān. Consequently, the result is the detailed study of Kṛṣṇa's qualities we find in 2.1.17-271. Although from the philosophical perspective Kṛṣṇa is not different (*abheda*) from his close companions, from the aestetic perspective a difference (*bheda*) is necessary. Thus one arrives at the philosophical position of Gauḍīya Vaiṣṇavism, 'inconceivable difference in non-difference' (*acintyabhedābheda*).

This is commonly expressed in a popular poster form throughout Vraja called *ek prāṇa, do deha*, 'one essence, two bodies', in which Rādhā and Kṛṣṇa's bodies are so intertwined that it is difficult to distinguish the boundaries separating the two. Although ultimate reality is recognized as being non-dual, for the purpose [of] enjoying its own dialectical dynamic of love (*prema*) it splits into the duality of the lover (*āśraya*) and beloved (*viṣaya*). It is very important to remember, however, that according to the theology expressed in Rūpa's text all three of these interrelated aspects–beloved, lover, and love–are divine.

"Rupā introduces the reader to his particular application of the technical terminology of the classical aesthetic theory to the religious context of emotional Kṛṣṇa *bhakti* in the Southern Quadrant. In 2.1.12-13 he gives a brief introductory definition of four of the five aesthetic components, which he then expands in subsequent chapters. The Excitants (*vibhāvas*) are defined as the 'causes of love, such as Kṛṣṇa, his devotees, and the sound of the flute'. The Substantial Excitant is further divided into the 'object' (*viṣaya*) of love and the 'vessel' (*āśraya*) of the emotion (2.1.6). This is specifically what Rūpa means in the statement just quoted. Kṛṣṇa is declared to be the object of love, and his devotees are declared to be the vessels of love, the two aspects of the Substantial Excitant. That is, Kṛṣṇa is here understood to be both the agent who arouses love as well as the focus for the ensuing love. His devotees are those who experience the joy of that love. The sound of Kṛṣṇa's flute is identified as an example of an Enhancing Excitant. The Enhancing Excitants serve to promote further the love inspire by the Substantial Excitant of Kṛṣṇa himself. These include such things as Kṛṣṇa's actions and ornaments (2.1.301). The Substantial and Enhancing Excitants are explored in detail in the first chapter of the Southern Quadrant. Since the most important dimension of the Excitant is Kṛṣṇa himself, the greater portion of this chapter is devoted to a presentation of the qualities of Kṛṣṇa (2.1.17-271). In effect, this chapter is tantamount to a detailed theological treatise on Kṛṣṇa. Besides the fact that he is the supreme lover, some key tenets are that he is not simply a single incarnation (*avatāra*), but rather the very source of all incarnations (2.1.202), that he is a concentrated form of being (*sat*), consciousness (*cit*) and bliss (*ānanda*) (2.1.18), that he encompasses the entire universe (2.1.199), and that he is most full manifest in Vraja (2.1.223).

"Rūpa defines the Indications (*anubhāvas*) as the resulting physical expressions of love enacted by Kṛṣṇa's devotees (2.1.12-13). He gives the example of smiling, but clearly intends it to serve as a reference to the longer list of general external reactions explored in the second chapter of the Southern Quadrant. He defines the Responses (*sāttvikas*) as eight devotional reactions such as stupefaction. These are involuntary bodily reactions that are caused by certain mental states. A person can reproduce one of the Indications without necessarily experiencing an inner emotion, but the Responses cannot be produced unless one is imbued with a true emotional state (2.3.1). Besides stupefaction, the Responses include perspiration, goose-bumps, broken voice, trembling, change of color, tears, and loss of consciousness (2.3.16). The Transitory Emotions (*vyabhicāri-bhāvas*) are defined as assisting emotions, such as indifference. Thirty-three such emotions are examined in the fourth chapter of this division. Rūpa explains that the Transitory Emotions accompany the Foundational Emotion of love, thereby enhancing it and introducing the element of variety (2.4.1-2). In this way the thirty-three Transitory Emotions account for the different forms that love takes, even within a single *rasa*. Parental Affection, for example, may be either happy or alarming, depending upon which Transitory Emotion accompanies it.

"The Foundational Emotion (*sthāyi-bhāva*) is not mentioned in 2.1.12-13, since it is the core emotion upon which the other components act to raise it to the intense level of a *rasa*.

Rūpa states: 'Love for Kṛṣṇa is the Foundational Emotion that becomes the *rasa* or devotion. It is raised by means of the Excitants, Indicating, Responses, and Transitory Emotions to a relishable state in the heart of devotees engaged in such actions as listening to the stories of the Lord' (2.1.5). He explains that the Foundational Emotion is one which dominates all other emotions, just as a king dominates all other people (2.5.1). And in the next verse he declares that the Foundational Emotion of all true *rasas* are rooted in the single Foundational Emotion of love for Kṛṣṇa (*kṛṣṇa-rati*).

"Rupā has a keen awareness of the great differences found among the various kinds of devotees. In fact, he claims that the type of love experienced is dependent upon the type of 'vessel' (*pātra* or *āśraya*) experiencing it; thus he is able to develop a system that simultaneously recognizes the oneness and multiplicity of love. He writes: 'The particular form that love takes is determined by the specific nature of the individual experiencing it, just as a reflected image of the sun is determined by the nature of the jewel through which it is being reflected' (2.5.7). Though love is one, it is experienced as many because of the different types of people experiencing it. Concomitantly, the form in which Kṛṣṇa appears is determined by the perceptual disposition of the devotee; this means that divinity is also simultaneously one and multiple. This allows Rūpa to develop what amounts to a typology of religious experiences. Though he has declared devotional *rasa* to be one, a typology of religious experences (or *bhāvas* to use his Sanskrit term) enables him to correlate his theory to the previous theories which recognize a number of *rasas*, while at the same time maintaining that all *rasas* are rooted in the same foundational emotion of love for Kṛṣṇa.

"Rūpa divides the *rasas* into primary *rasas* and secondary *rasas*. The Primary *rasas* are five in number and are understood to be direct forms of *rati* or 'love' for Kṛṣṇa. The Secondary *rasas* are seven in number, and correspond to the remaining *rasas of classical* theory. The ninth *rasa* of classical theory, the Peaceful *rasa* of *śānta,* is included as the first of the Primary *rasas* by being defined as a particular type of love. What distinguishes a Primary *rasa* from a Secondary *rasa* is that the former are based on a Foundational Emotion that is 'self-supporting', whereas the Secondary *rasas* are based on Foundational Emotions that are supported by a Primary Foundational Emotion. In all cases, the Primary Foundational Emotion is a form of love (*rati*), defined as 'a special form of the pure and luminous quality' (2.5.3), the very same terminology used to define a true *bhāva* in 1.3.1 On their own, the Secondary Foundational Emotions lack this essential quality, but come to share in it through associations with a Primary form of love. Once again, we observe the centrality of love or *rati* in Rūpa's system. In effect, then the five Primary *rasas* are simply variant forms of what is called the *śṛṅgāra rasa* in the classical theory, since this is the *rasa* based on the Foundational Emotion of *rati.* Rūpa employs the terminology of all the aesthetic components to lay out his twelve-fold scheme of *rasa.* He does this in a generic way in the Southern Quadrant, devoting five respective chapters to a general discussion of the Excitants, Indications, Responses, Transitory Emotions, and Foundational Emotions. Having laid this foundation he proceeds to a detailed analysis of the five forms of Primary *rasa* in the Western Quadrant, and of the seven Secondary *rasas* in the final Northern Quadrant.

"The five forms of Primary *rasa*--Peaceful, Respectful, Companionable, Parentally Affectionate and Amorous–are presented in a hierarchical manner by Rūpa, with the last clearly being the highest. He devotes a sequel to the *Bhaktirasāmṛtasindhu*, the *Ujjvalanīlamaṇi,* entirely to this *rasa*. The criterion of hierarchical judgment employed is the intensity of emotional connectedness (*sambandha*), expressed in terms of several related concepts. One of these has to do with a particular understanding of the sense of 'myness' (*mamatā*), which signals personal attachment. Although this term is frequently assumed to have negative connotations in philosophical literature concerned with achieving absolute unity with Brahman, Rūpa uses it in a very positive fashion to indicate an important ingredient of a strong relationship with Kṛṣṇa. Gauḍī Vāiṣṇavism philosophy rejects the realization of absolute unity with Brahman in favor of an intimate relationship with Brahman as the infinitely qualified Bhagavān Kṛṣṇa. This requires personal attachment, which depends upon a sense of ownership and individuality. This is what is being expressed by the positive use of the term 'myness'. Rūpa employs this term to define the Foundational Emotion of the Peaceful *rasa*: 'Generally, Peaceful Love arises in tranquil people who comprehend Kṛṣṇa as the highest Self (*paramātman*) but are without even a trace of the sense of 'myness''' (2.5.18). Accordingly, he places the Peaceful *rasa* (*śānta*) on the bottom of his hierarchical list of the Primary *rasas*, for the others involve increasing amounts of this sense of myness (2.5.22), and the Amorous *rasa* identifies most intensely with this sentiment. It is also worth noting that the term *kāma* ('desire' or 'passion') is often marked with a high degree of negativity, whereas in Rūpa's text it is used to denote the perfected state of the highest lovers of Kṛṣṇa, the *gopīs* (1.2.273 and 28.3-84). Understanding the passionate nature of the divine emotions explored here will better prepare the reader for an understanding of the presence and positive use of such emotions as agitation, anger, and jealousy.

"Another related term that has a negative connotation in the ascetic schools which aim for absolute unity is *abhimāna*. In certain contexts this term is often translated as 'pride', but can also be translated more neutrally as a 'sense of individuality'. Although it is almost always an obstacle to be overcome in schools that aim toward the absolute unity of *mokṣa*, here where relationship is being sought it is considered to be something of great value. Rūpa uses the term to indicate a key aspect of any close relationship with Kṛṣṇa. He defines Relational *bhakti,* for example, as that which involves an identification (*abhimāna*) of oneself as one of Kṛṣṇa's relatives (1.2.228). Jīva Gosvāmin extends the use of this term to define the precise nature of each unique relationship with Kṛṣṇa that is the heart of the Primary *rasas*. One who experiences Parental Affection, for example, is one who has an identity of oneself as Kṛṣṇa's elder (*gurutva-abhimāna*). The Peaceful *rasa* is also rated the lowest among the Primary *rasas* since it lacks a particular identity (3.1.32), and therefore is not associated with a particular kind of relationship with Kṛṣṇa (2.5.21), whereas the other emotions–especially Amorousness- involve high degrees of both these.

"Rūpa employs a pair of terms to express yet another concept that allows him to delineate the hierarchical relationship of the *rasas*. While discussing the relationship of servitude within the Respectful *rasa*, for example, he remarks that the servants are predominantly aware of Kṛṣṇa's majesty (3.2.16). The Sanskrit term here being translated as 'majesty' is *prabhutā*. This term is synonymous with another term Rūpa uses to express the same concept, namely, *aiśvarya.* Both of these terms are in contrast to another, *mādhurya*, which means 'sweetness'. These are important theological terms for Gauḍīya theologians, expressing two very different perspectives by which the Lord is viewed. The majestically powerful form of the Lord inspires awe and fear, and causes the devotee to draw back in an attitude of respect, whereas the sweet form of the Lord attracts the devotee and inspire intimacy. Arjuna's encounter with Kṛṣṇa in the eleventh chapter of the *Bhagavadgītā* is frequently used to express this theological distinction. Kṛṣṇa reveals his majestic form (*aiśvarya-rūpa*) to Arjuna, who draws back with fright, and the close affection Arjuna feels for Kṛṣṇa leaves him immediately. When Kṛṣṇa returns to his gentle human form (*saumya-mānuṣa-rūpa*) Arjuna is once again able to relate to him as an intimate.

Perception of the majestic form is therefore an inhibiting factor in developing a close relationship with Kṛṣṇa, whereas perception of the sweet form is a factor that nurtures this development. Therefore, the Primary *rasas* are ranked according to the absence and presence of these two factors. The servants of Kṛṣṇa operate within a perspective largely informed by the majesty (*aiśvarya*) of the Lord, whereas his lovers operate within a perspective colored by sweetness (*mādhurya*).

"The particular typology of religious experience Rūpa presents in the *Bhaktirasāmṛtasindhu* utilizes all the aesthetic components of the classical tradition. The chief elements of this, however, are the varying object (*viṣaya*), shifting vessels (*āśraya*), and the resulting different religious experiences (*bhāvas*). Rūpa begins his presentation and analysis of the Primary *rasas* with an examination of the Peaceful *rasa* (*śānta-bhakti-rasa*). The particular form (*viṣaya-ālambana-vibhāva*) in which Kṛṣṇa is encountered in the Peaceful *rasa* is one appropriate to yogic meditation, the four-armed Viṣṇu (3.1.7-28), which is described as being appropriate for yogic meditation in texts such as the *Bhāgavata Purāṇa* (e.g., 22.8-14). The vessels of this *rasa* are the peaceful (*śānta*) devotees, defined as those who have achieved tranquility and then go on to experience a love for Kṛṣṇa. Examples given are the four mind-born ascetic sons of Brahmā: Sanaka, Sananda, Sanātana, and Sanatkumāra (3.1.12). Enhancing Excitants include listening to the principal Upaniṣads and residing in isolated places (3.1.18-19).

"Rūpa represents the resulting emotional experience (*bhāva*) as being somewhat similar to the joy of the *yogīs* (3.1.5). Jīva glosses the joy of the *yogīs* as an experience of the unqualified Absolute Reality (*nirviśeṣa-brahman*). However, the object of the *yogis*' quest is said to be the Self (*ātman*), whereas the object (*viṣaya*) of this *rasa* is the Lord (*īśa*). This is what makes the Peaceful *rasa* a devotional *rasa* for Rūpa; it is still a form of love (*rati*) directed toward Kṛṣṇa. Rūpa identifies the Foundational Emotion of rhis *rasa* as Peaceful Love (*śānti-rati,* 3.1.35). The classical understanding of the Peaceful *rasa* is that it is the absence of all emotions; it is the still ocean in which all waves of passion have been eliminated. This, however, would not be a true *rasa* according to Rūpa, who defines the experience of *rasa* as involving some type of love (3.1.4 and 46). All of his illustrations (3.1.36-45) involve a tranquil *yogī* who moves beyond the realization of the undifferentiated Brahman and the meditative state of objectless consciousness to an encounter with some form of Kṛṣṇa as the object of an astonishing love. A cornerstone of Vaiṣṇava philosophy is the tenet that the Lord (Bhagavān or Puruṣottama) represents a higher form of reality than that which is encountered as the undifferentiated Brahman. The peaceful devotees may reside in a calm ocean, but finally it must be an ocean stirred up to some degree by the surges of love which indicate an awareness of divine form. And the more motion in the ocean, the more intense the waves of emotions, the higher it is ranked on the hierarchical scale. Rūpa, therefore declares the joy of the *yogīs* to be limited or incomplete, whereas that joy related to the Lord is unlimited or complete (3.1.5). The Peaceful *rasa* is also placed lowest on the hierarchical scale because it involves only an encounter with the essential form (*svarūpa*) of the Lord, and is not connected in any way with his charming *līlās* or divine play (3.1.6).

"Moving up the hierarchical ladder, the next type of religious experience, or devotional *rasa*, is the Respectful *rasa* (*prīta-* or *dāya-bhakti-rasa*). This *rasa* is divided into two subtypes: Politely Respectful and Relationally Respectful. In the first, Kṛṣṇa (as the *viṣata-ālambana-vibhāva*) appears as the awesome master and highest object of worship (3.2.11-15) and the devotees (as the *āśraya-ālambana-vibhāva*) take the forms of his servants (3.2.6; four types are presented in 3.2.18-56). It may be of interest to note that the gods, such as Brahmā,

Śiva, and Indra are included in this latter category (3.2.19). In the second, Kṛṣṇa appears as a superior and protective elder (3.2.148) and the devotees take on the forms of his sons and other younger relatives (3.2.149). Kṛṣṇa's son Pradyumna is singled out as best among this type of 'vessel' or devotee (3.2.152). Dust from the feet of Kṛṣṇa is listed as an Enhancing Excitant of the first t ype, whereas his affectionate smile is listed as an example of an Enhancing Excitant for the second. Adhering scrupulously to one's assigned task (the example given is fanning Kṛṣṇa) is an Indication of the Politely Respectful *rasa*, and occupying a seat lower than Kṛṣṇa's is an indication of the Relationally Respectful *rasa*. All the remaining aesthetic components are likewise employed to nurture the particular Foundational Emotion of this *rasa* to a 'reliable' level. The resulting religio-emotional experience is connected with a relationship in which Kṛṣṇa as the supreme Lord is encountered as the worshiper's own caretaker (3.2.167-168). Since the intensity of this ty pe of relationship is compromised by a differential in power, it is surpassed by the following types.

"The third type of devotional *rasa* is that of Companionship (*preyo-bhakti-rasa*, also known as *sākhya-* or *maitrī-maya-rasa*. Here Kṛṣṇa appears as the devotee's friend, and the devotee assumes the position of Kṛṣṇa's friend, equal to Kṛṣṇa in form, dress, and qualities (3.3.8). The devotees who experience this *rasa* are completely unrestrained and enjoy confident familiarity with Kṛṣṇa. Here we begin to see the positive effects of the increasing presence of the 'sweetness' (*mādhurya*) and 'myness' (*mamatā*) perspectives referred to above, and the concomitant fading of the 'majestic' (*aiśvarya*) perspective that was dominant in the previous *rasa*. The friends are divided between those found in the city of Dvāraka and those found in the higher realm of Vraja. Arjuna is named as the best of the friends of the city (3.3.13). The higher group of Kṛṣṇa's friends in Vraja are further divided into four types: the 'allies' are slightly older than Kṛṣṇa, and therefore possess some parental affection for him; Kṛṣṇa's elder brother Balarāma is the chief example here (3.3.33). The 'dear friends' are the same age as Kṛṣṇa, and are therefore his equals; Kṛṣṇa's good friend Śrīdāma is singled out as the best this category of friend (3.3.40). The highest type of friends are the 'dear playful friends', since they are Kṛṣṇa's confidants in his secret matters of love affairs. Subala and Ujjvala are mentioned as the best of this type (3.3.45). The Indications of this *rasa* include such sports as wrestling, playing with balls, gambling, carrying one another on the shoulders, and play-fighting with sticks, as well as other activities such as sitting and sleeping with Kṛṣṇa on his bed, telling him entertaining jokes, playing in ponds, and dancing and singing with him (3.3.86-88). The unique feature of this *rasa* is its Foundational Emotion of 'love called "friendship" (*sakhya*) which exists between two persons of approximately equal status; it consists of confident familiarity and lacks any sense of awesome respect' (3.3.105. Because of the more equal power relationship, intimate friendship is possible, making this *rasa* much more intense than the previous two. It is also this feature that distinguishes the *rasa* of Companionship from both the Respectful *rasa* and the *rasa* of Parental Affection. Rūpa writes: 'Since there is the sweetness of identical emotional states in both Kṛṣṇa and his friends in the *rasa* of Companionship, it produces a special sense of wonder in the mind. In the *rasas* of Respectfulness and Parental Affection, however, the emotional states of Kṛṣṇa and his devotees are different and unequal. For this reason, connoisseurs whose hearts are filled with friendship recognize a special quality in the *rasa* of companionship that makes it unique among the *rasas*" (3.3.134-136).

"The second most intense *rasa* according to Rūpa is the *rasa* of Parental Affection (*vatsala-bhakti-rasa*). Here Kṛṣṇa (as the *viṣaya*) appears as a child in need of nurturing protection and the devotee (as the *āśraya*) assumes the position of an elder who cares for young Kṛṣṇa. These are opposite to the conditions of the Respectful *rasa*. Moreover, Rūpa states that since Kṛṣṇa is here the recipient of kindness and protection his majestic power is not manifest (2.3.4). Again, the absence of any sense of Kṛṣṇa's majestic power and the presence of a sense of his sweetness is the measure of the intensity and value of a *rasa*. Kṛṣṇa's foster parents Yaśodā and Nanda are ranked the highest among this type of devotee (2.3.10-16). The Enhancing Excitants are the sweet, charming, and mischievous ways of the child Kṛṣṇa. The Indications include such acts on the part of Kṛṣṇa's parents as smelling his head and giving him baths. A ninth and unique Response is added to the standard list of eight Responses for women in this *rasa*, the flowing of breast milk (3.3.45). The Foundational Emotion of this *rasa* is defined as Parental Affection (*vātsalya*), which 'consists of a love that is devoid of deferential respect and belongs to one who shows kindness to Kṛṣṇa as a needy recipient of kindness' (3.4.52). This *rasa* too has a unique feature: it will not diminish when not reciprocated (3.4.79). When mutual friendship is not returned it disappears, whereas there is no expectation of mutual friendship from a tiny baby. Rūpa, therefore, recognizes a unique strength in this kind of love.

"The most supreme devotional *rasa* and the highest tpe of religious experience possible is the Amorous *rasa* (*madhurā-bhakti-rasa*). Since he has written another book devoted entirely to this single *rasa*, the *Ujjvalanīlamaṇi*, Rūpa spends little time illustrating it here. Nonetheless, it is clearly the highest *rasa* for him and he presents it in the familiar terms of the classical *rasa* theory. The erotically charming Kṛṣṇa represented in the *Gītagovinda* is the object (*viṣaya*) of this *rasa* (3.5.5) and the *gopīs* of Vraja are its vessels (*āśraya*, 3.5.6). The most exalted of all the women–of all vessels or devotees for that matter–is Rādhā, daughter of Vṛṣabhānu (3.5.7). The Enhancing Excitants are exemplified by the sound of Kṛṣṇa's flute, and the Indications include such acts as smiles and sidelong glances. The Foundational Emotion of Amorous Love (*madhurā-rati*) is explained in terms of the various states of union and separation (3.3.24-35). The distinctive feature of this *rasa* is that it is not diminished by any circumstances (3.5.21). It is clear from his previous statements that this *rasa* encompasses the strengths of all the other forms of love, making it the *rasa par excellence.*

"In summary, Rūpa has created a typology of religious experience that ranks the various types of possible ultimate relationships in terms of intimacy with the divine and intensity of emotion. Within this typology Rūpa is able to place both the Peaceful (*śānta*) experience of the ascetic *yoga* tradition, which often define the ultimate state as the absence of all emotions, and the Amorous (*śṛṅgāra*) experience of passionate devotion, which seeks to utilize the power of all emotions to establish a solid connection with the divine as beloved. These two impulses represent polar tensions that have defined and enlivened much creative debate within Hindu philosophy, and Rūpa's representation provides yet another important way of viewing their relationship.

"This typology is not rigid, however, for Rūpa recognizes that the Primary *rasas* are frequently combined in various characters encountered in Vaiṣṇava scripture (3.4.80-84). In fact, to further nuance this typology, Rūpa maintains that from time to time one of the five previously described types of devotees experiences one of the seven Secondary *rasas*. (4.1.5). Discussion of the seven Secondary *rasas* comprises the final quadrant of the text, and a chapter is devoted to each. Again, the decisive factor is some form of love (*rati*) for Kṛṣṇa. For example, a devotee may experience humor (*hāsa*) but for this to be part of the experience of devotional *rasa* it has to be a form of humorous love toward Kṛṣṇa. Therefore, within Rūpa's system the Foundational Emotion of the Humorous *rasa* is Humorous Love (*hāsa-rati*, 4.1.6). Likewise, the traditional Foundational Emotion of amazement (*vismaya*) becomes

Amazed Love (*vismaya-rati*, 4.2.1). In a similar manner, Rūpa works into his system the remaining *rasas* of the classical theory. Rūpa makes it very clear, however, that Kṛṣṇa can never be the 'object' (*viṣaya*) for disgust (*jugupsā*, 2.5.41); Disgusted Love (*jugupsā-rati*) is associated with ascetics and usually takes the body as its object (4.7.1 and 8). The Secondary *rasas* serve to enhance the central love and give it variety, much like the Transitory Emotions.

"The *Bhaktirasāmṛtasindhu* ends with a discussion of the compatibility and incompatibility of the various *rasas*, and a brief presentation of false semblances of *rasas*. When compatible *rasas* interact, the result is an enhancement of the dominant *rasa* (4.8.16), whereas when incompatible *rasas* combine there is a diminishment of the dominant *rasa*, just as then salt is added to a sweet drink (4.6.53). Humor, for example, enhances the Amorous *rasa* (4.8.7), whereas a mixture of the Amorous *rasa* and the *rasa* of Parental Affection is highly damaging (4.8.60). A Semblance of a *rasa* (*rasābhāsa*) is defined as a defective *rasa*. Three types of defects are defined and illustrated; an *uparasa* has a defective Foundational Emotion, Excitant, or Indication (4.9.3), an *anurasa* has no connection with Kṛṣṇa (4.9.33), and an *aparasa* is located in some enemy of Kṛṣṇa (4.9.38). In all three cases, there is no true *rasa*.

"It is now time to summarize precisely how Rūpa represents the experience of *rasa*. In the beginning of the Southern Quadrant he states: 'Love for Kṛṣṇa is the Foundational Emotion that becomes the *rasa* of devotion (*bhakti-rasa*). It is raised by means of the Excitants, Indications, Responses, and Transitory Emotions to a relishable state in the heart of devotees engaged in such actions as listening to stories about the Lord' (2.1.5). It is clear here that although *rasa* becomes varied according to the capacities of its recipients, it is fundamentally one. The single Foundational Emotion of love for Kṛṣṇa is taken to be the unifying core of all true *rasas*, resulting in the simultaneously unified and multiple *bhakti rasa* or *rasa* of devotion. Moreover, the Foundational Emotion and *rasa* are not fundamentally different for Rūpa as they are, for example, for Abhinavagupta. In the previous verse Rūpa remarks that the Foundational Emotion of love (*rati*) becomes *rasa* when it is developed (*paripoṣa*) by the various aesthetic components just listed. His view on this subject is, therefore, much closer to that of Bhoja. The key element in Rūpa's entire system is the Foundational Emotion of love for Kṛṣṇa (*kṛṣṇa-rati*). Far from being based on ordinary *vāsanās*, as it is for most other theoreticians of *rasa* such as Abhinavagupta, here the Foundational Emotion is understood to be a very special manifestation of divine power. Once it has been established, all else follows. Rūpa makes it clear that this divine love is of such a nature that it naturally proceeds to the level of *rasa* with only the slightest exposure to the aesthetic components defined in the terms laid out in this book (2.5.106). It is also of importance to note in the verse quoted above that the location of *rasa* for Rūpa is the devotee. This includes both the original characters, such as Rādhā and Yaśodā, and the contemporary practitioner. The question of whether one is an original character, an actor, or a member of the audience is irrelevant according to Rūpa; the real issue is whether or not one's heart is imbued with the *bhāva* of love.

"Rūpa has something even more radical to say, however, in comparison with the classical *rasa* theory of Bharata. In his section on the Foundational Emotion, Rūpa asserts: 'This charming love makes Kṛṣṇa and related factors into an Excitant and other related aesthetic components, and then expands itself by means of these very components' (2.5.94). What he is saying here is that the Foundational Emotion of love makes objects into Excitants, or opportunities to experience love in intense ways. 'Ordinary' objects then become occasions for the expression or experience of love. An ordinary cloud, for example, may evoke the experience of love, but it is the *bhāva* or Foundational Emotion which makes the cloud into an object of love that determines the experience. This may be illustrated with an everyday example. Say one person is madly in love with another, but for some reason is separated from the beloved. If the beloved happened to leave a jacket behind, the sight of that jacket will be an occasion to experience the pangs of love. The jacket itself is not the foundational cause of the love, however, but is rather an object that evokes a preexisting love. Another person may very well walk past the jacket and experience nothing whatsoever, viewing it simply as an old piece of clothing. Again, the *bhāva* is the determining factor, and ths is what makes Rūpa's system quite different from Bharata's, wherein the dramatic objects function as Excitants to create a particular feeling. For Rūpa love is and remains foundational, or to repeat (and reverse) the common adage: 'Love is God". Once it has sprouted in the heart it expands and expresses itself by means of various aesthetic components. In this regard Rūpa writes: 'This process is just like the ocean which, having filled clouds with its own water, increases itself by means of this very rain water' (2.5.95). Besides suggesting the identity of love and Kṛṣṇa, this verse indicates more about the expanding nature of love; once established, it goes on increasing its own delight through its joyful play with various components, now seen as part of itself. This is the eternal play of love as understood by Rūpa and other Gauḍīya theologians.

"A grasp of Rūpa's views on the Foundational Emotion of love also helps us understand his great concern for spiritual practice (*sādhana*), for the main purpose of such practice is the generation of a *bhāva*, the love for Kṛṣṇa. He says: 'Diligent dedication to spiritual practices brings about desire (*ruci*) for Hari, then produces attachment (*āśakti*) for Him, and then causes the birth of love (*rati*) for Him" (1.3.8). Once this divine emotion of love has been generated, through its own playful nature it goes on and on to higher levels of intensity and enjoyment. This is the experience of *rasa*. Rūpa uses the word *prema,* which I have translated as "supreme love", as representative of the higher states of emotional experience. In the *Bhaktirasāmṛtasindhu* he identifies the higher states of *prema* or supreme love as *sneha* (tenderness) and *rāga* (passion) (e.g., 3.2.78). In the *Ujjvalanīlamāṇi*, however, he gives the more detailed list of the expansions of love as: *prema, sneha, māna, praṇaya, rāga, anurāga,* and finally *bhāva* (UN 14.60). The last of these, however is not to be confused with the *bhāva* that is the Foundational Emotion. Here the word *bhāva* mean *mahābhāva* ('great emotion'). This is the ultimate experience of love and the culmination of true *rasa*, which is associated with Rādhā, the most profound 'vessel' of divine emotion.

"The ultimate experience, then, for Rūpa is one continual and expansive religio-aesthetic experience of love. This involves playful interaction between the dynamically interconnected lover, beloved, and love itself. Once love has been established in the purified heart, the entire world becomes a divine state and an occasion for experiencing blissful love for Kṛṣṇa, who in fact (according to Gauḍīya theology)is not different from the world–not, at least, from the world seen with a clear mind and a soft heart characterized by the state of pure luminosity (*śuddha-sattva*)."

4.2 RŪPA GOSVĀMIN, *Ujjvālanīlamaṇi*

Neil Delmonico (Delmonico 1989, p. 326-327) indicates the state of the literature to that date on this important text, which remains largely unchanged till the present time of writing. "In spite of its great importance, no full-length study or translation into English has been made of the UN though it has been used and summarized by several scholars. The date of the text is not known, but it must have been written after 1541 which is the date of the completion of *Bhakrirasāmṛtasindhu.* Since the UN is quoted in the *Bṛhadvaiṣṇavatoṣaṇī* of Sanātana Gosvāmin which was completed in 1554, it must have been written before then.

"The text has been published many times with various commentaries. The first edition of the UN was the Baharampur edition published originally at the end of the nineteenth century with the commentaries of Jīva Gosvāmin (sixteenth centurt) and Viśvanātha Cakravartin (seventeenth century). This edition contained a translation into Bengali prose. Another edition of this text with the same commentaries was published by Nirṇaya Sāgara Press in Devanagari script in the Kāvya-mālā series (1913). The next was the semi-critical edition (1954) of Puri Gosvāmin with the same commentaries. It contained an unnamed verse translation of the text written in the seventeenth or eighteenth centuries. The most recent edition of the UN was that of Haridāsa Dāsa with the commentary, previously unpublished, of Viṣṇudāsa, a disciple of Kṛṣṇadāsa Kavirāja (sixteenth century). Though none of these was a critical edition and all contained mistakes and misprints, among them, the form of the text has become fairly well set."

In a subsequent piece by Delmonico, "The Blazing Sapphire (Ujjvala-nīlamaṇi)", Journal of Vaisnava Studies 5.1, 1996-97, pp. 21-52, we are promised a full-fledged edition and translation from the hand of Neil Delmonico, still to come as far as we know. However, the following summary of its contents is found in Delmonico 1997 (1), pp. 22, 36-38.

Summarized by Neil Delmonico

"The work is organized into fifteen chapters. The following brief description of the contents of the work will give some idea of the nature and richness of Rūpa's composition. It begins with a description of the hero of erotic devotion, Kṛṣṇa. His qualities are described and his various roles as husband and paramour are defined and illustrated. In the second chapter Rūpa describes Kṛṣṇa's five types of assistants, the Ceta (trusted servant), Viṭa (dependant companion), Vidūṣaka (joker), Pīṭharda (an equal attached to the hero by love), Priya-narmasakḥa (the most dear and confidential of friends), who help him in his love affairs in the eternal Vṛndāvana. In Chapter Three Rūpa takes up the subject of the objects of Kṛṣṇa's erotic love, his wives and extra-marital lovers. Citing the *Bhāgavata Puraṇa* (10.32.22), Rūpa gives the extra-marital lovers the greatest praise for they have overcome the most difficult obstacles to be with Kṛṣṇa, namely their ties to home and family. Of those lovers some have reached that greatness by spiritual discipline, some are goddesses within the universe, and some are his eternal loved ones. In Chapter Four, Rūpa focuses on the chief of Kṛṣṇa's beloved ladies, Rādhā, and her qualities are described and illustrated. She is described as the very essence of the 'great emotion' (*mahabhāva*), the highest form of divine love, and as the core. of the greatest of the powers, the pleasure-giving potency (*hlādinī-śakti*). The fifth chapter contains descriptions of the characteristics of heroines of erotic devotion, as embodied in various cowherd women Kṛṣṇa loves. Those are divided into three groups: the simple one (*magdhā*), young of age and new to love; the middle one (*madhyā*), a little older and equal in shyness and passion, and the bold one (*pragalbhā*), in the full bloom of youth and experience. It concludes with the eight states of conditions of the heroine.[1]

"Chapter Six contains a discussion of the leaders of the different groups of women inhabiting Vṛndāvana. They are divided according to the degree of their good fortune[1], into great, average, and less. Each category is then divided into

---

[1]These are the same as the eight states or conditions of the heroine discussed in Sanskrit literary critical texts. They are: desire for a tryst, preparation of self and place, anticipation of the lover's arrival, separation due to a failed tryst, anger due to betrayal, separation due to quarrel, absence of the lover (due to a journey), and complete control over the lover.

'saucy', soft, and in-between. The 'saucy' one is one whose statements are bold and whose words cannot be ignored. Rādhā belongs to the absolutely great category (as opposed to the 'relatively' great category) and is in between the 'saucy' and the soft. In Chapter Seven, the message-bearers and go-betweens that glue love relationships together are described and illustrated. The two major types of message-bearer are oneself (*svayam*) and a trusted one (*āpta*). If the message-bearer is oneself, the message may be passed verbally, physically, or by the eyes. The trusted one is one who would not beak faith even when faced with death and is of three types: she whose purpose is unknown[1], she who is entrusted with a task, and the letter bearer. In the eighth chapter cowherd girls are analyzed in terms of their friendships with each other. The same categories of great, average, and less with respect to good fortune are used along with 'saucy', soft, and in-between, but in this chapter the focus is on the cowherd girls' dealings with each other. The roles of heroine (that is, Kṛṣṇa's lovers) and the friends of the heroine are played against each other in the context of a hierarchy of five categories: absolutely great, relatively great, average, relatively less, and absolutely less. The absolutely great are the eternal heroines and the absolutely less are eternal friends. The others in between are sometimes heroines and sometimes the friends of the heroines. In the ninth chapter one finds the beauties of the Vṛndāvana analyzed by means of another aspect of their relationships with each other. There they are analyzed according to whether they belong to the same party, the party of a friend, the party of a friend of one's enemy, or the party of one's enemy .

"Up to this point in the text Rūpa has described what are technically known as the 'supporting evocators' (*ālambana-*

---

[1]This type of messenger notices by its symptoms the attraction between two would-be lovers and takes steps on her own to bring them together. See *Ujjvālamālamaṇi* [verse] 7.55.

vibhāva) of erotic love–that is, the persons who are either the objects of the possessors of that love. In Chapter Ten he describes the 'stimulating evocators' (*uddīpana-vibhāva*) or erotic love–those mental, verbal, and physical qualities, names, character traits, ornaments, and temporary moods of persons that stimulate or provide the conditions for reciprocal feelings of love. For instance, some of the mental qualities are gratitude, patience, and compassion. Chapter Eleven is devoted to the 'revealers' (*anubhāva*) of erotic love, the peculiar symptoms and actions that reveal to others the someone has love. The first of those is called *bhāva*, that special moment in the development of erotic love when the unmoved mind is first moved. [verse 11.6]. In the twelfth chapter, the psychosomatic revealers (*sātvvika-bhāva*) are described and illustrated. These are physical symptoms (like paralysis, perspiration, horripilation) that reveal the presence of intense erotic passion. Chapter Thirteen contains a discussion of the emotions that accompany and intensify erotic love (*sañcarin*), such as despondency, caused by being hurt or by separation or envy. The fourteenth chapter is dedicated to the discussion of the primary or enduring erotic emotion (*sthāyī-bhāva*), which is attraction for Kṛṣṇa (*kṛṣṇa-rati*), along with its various stages of development and intensification. In Chapter Five, the final chapter, are found descriptions of the various states of erotic love affairs, such as preliminary attraction (*pūrva-rāga*), love-in-separation (*vipralamba*), love-in-union (*sambhoga*), and so forth. As this summary can only hint, Rūpa's phenomenology is both a subtle and a thorough exploration of the Caitanya Vaiṣṇava version of eternal bliss. It has much to teach not only about religious rapture but also about human erotic love."

Delmonico provides translations of a few of the verses of this text (on pp. 34-47 of Delmonico 1997 (1)), as well a translation of the entire Chapter Four (in Delmonico 1997 (2)). We limit ourselves here to the first few verses, which will assist the reader in understanding the context of some passages of commentaries discussed in later sections of this work.

Translation by Neal Delmonico

I.1 "Victory to the Lord whose form is eternal, by whose name knowers of rapture are attracted, who always is thrilling Nanda by his character, who gives joy by his great beauty".[1]

["Victory to Sanātana's very self, the Master, arousing joy in the good by his acts, whose tongue was drawn to the holy name, who, through his own forms, spreads the sacrifice supreme."[2]

["Victory to my Master, Sanātana, inspiring joy in the saintly by his conduct, whose tongue was controlled by the holy name, who gives delight to me, his Rūpa."][3]

I.2 "That Sweet rapture, the monarch of sacred raptures, which was discussed briefly before among the major forms of rapture because of its confidential nature shall (now) be described separately in detail."

I.3 "Sweet attraction brought to state of relish by the evokers and [the] rest that will be described is said to be the sacred rapture called the Sweet One by the wise."

---

[1]"This verse has three possible and intended interpretations. I, therefore, have given separate translations for each interpretation. The first, represented by this translation, refers to Kṛṣṇa. The other two interpretations follow in brackets." (ND)

[2]"This interpretation refers to Caitanya, a.k.a. Kṛṣṇa Caitanya Mahaprabhu, the founder of the Caitanya Vaiṣṇava tradition,. Vīśvanātha Cakravartin provides this interpretation in his commentary." (ND)

[3]"This refers to Sanātana Gosvāmin, the elder brother and apparently teacher of the author."

94 1.4 "Kṛṣṇa and his beloved ladies are the supporting evokers of this [rapture]."

4.20 "The loveliness of her eyes forcefully swallows fresh water lilies, the radiance of her face surpasses forests of blossoming lotuses, and her body's glow puts gold to shame. How wonderfully this indescribable beauty of Rāḍhā shines!"

4.21 "Your hips have begun to glide swiftly [have become chariots], slim-waisted; your breasts have gradually rounded out [become discuses]; your eyebrows have attained the beauty of arches [the beauty of bows] and your two eyes now dart swiftly about [have become arrows]. The god of love has given you overlordship of his forces on earth and, arousing the lord of animals, who thinks himself victorious, has passed on to you the burden of his empire.

4.22 "Has lightning learned its quickness from your glance, moon-faced, or your glance from lightning? Surely here your glance is the master, Rādhā, since even my mind, quickest of the very quick, is beaten by it!"

4.23 "Friend, having spotted the line of the lips on your moon-face cleansed in the middle by the nectar of your smile, that quick Aghabhid (Kṛṣṇa), the best of the cakora, his mind thrilled by pleasure and intoxication, is rising up."

4.24 "Stealer of sin, be glad! See how the footprints, filled with markings of good fortune in the form of a crescent moon, a circle, a flower, a fine, and a coil, tell us clearly that Rādhā is hidden somewhere here."

4.3 RŪPA GOSVĀMIN, *Saṃkṣepabhāvatasandarbha/Saṃvādinī*

There are various editions. The following summary is taken from De 1961, pp. 238-253

Summary by Sushil Kumar De

"...(T)he author Rūpa himself informs us that his work really summarizes (*saṃkṣepeṇa*) what is said at great length by

Sanātana in his (*Bṛhad-)Bhagavatāmrta.* We are told that of all the adorable deities (*upāsya*) Kṛṣṇa is the chief. As one of the most fundamental doctrines of the Bengal school is that Kṛṣṇa as the supreme personal god of the faith is not an *avatāra* but the divine being himself in his essential character, Rūpa Gosvāmin begins his work by a discussion of the essential selfhood or *svarūpa* of Kṛṣṇa, which is one of the principal themes of his work; and in this connection he deals with the different manifestations and appearances of the supreme deity. Like its prototype, the work is divided into two parts, but the order in which the two aspects of the subject are discussed is reversed . Instead of dealing first with the *bhakta* as we have it in the original work, the *svarūpa* of Kṛṣṇa is propounded elaborately in the first part, while the second part, which is very short, determines the character and gradation of the *bhaktas*, who are represented as equally adorable. The two parts are, therefore, respectively named Kṛṣṇā and Bhaktāmṛta.

"At the outset the author records his intention to avoid the process of reasoning (*yukti-vistāra*), because he considers *śabda* or 'testimony' to be the chief *pramāṇa* or source of knowldge: and he thinks that this position is established in the *Vedāntasūtra* 1.1.3 and 2.1.11. As *tarka* is discarded, the method which follows is to make a dogmatic statement. which is often definitive, following it up by elaborate citations chiefly from the Vaiṣṇava *Purāṇas* or other Vaiṣṇava and Tantra texts. Sometimes the cited texts are further elucidated by means of explanatory *karikās*. The work is an epitome and convenient manual of the whole theological speculation of the school, but the most important part of its treatment is concerned with the doctrine of *avatāra* and its relation to the deity and the devotee.

"The *svarūpa* of Kṛṣṇa, which is dealt with in the first part of the work, is defined and classified into three aspects:

1. *Svayaṃ-rūpa*, which is not dependent on anything else (*ananyapekṣi*), that is, self-existent (*svataḥ-siddha*).

2. *Tadekātma-rūpa,* or hypostatic manifestation, which is identical in essence and existence with the *svayaṃ-rūpa,* but seems different by its appearance (*ākṛti*), attribute (*vaibhava*), etc. This manifestation may be either (a) *vilāsa,* which is of equal power with the *svayaṃ-rūpa* (*prāyeṇātma-samaṃ śaktyā*), e.g. Nārāyaṇa who is a *vilāsa* of the highest Vāsudeva (the later cult would regard Nityānanda as a *vilāsa in Gaurāṅga-līlā*), and (b) *svāṃśa,* which is inferior in power (*nyūna-śakti*), e.g. Saṃkarṣaṇa or the Matsya.
3. *Āveśa,* which consists of appearance in the 'possessed' forms of inspired men and prophets, into which the deity enters through *śakti, jñāna, bhakti,* etc. Śeṣa is cited as an example of *śakti-āveśa,* Sanaka of *jñāna-āveśa,* and Nārada of *bhakti-āveśa.*

"It must be noted that these forms are not *māyika* or produced by illusions, but that they are real and eternal (*nitya-rūpa*). The classification mentioned above may be represented thus in a tabular form:

The *Svarūpa* of Kṛṣṇa:

Svayaṃ-rūpa	*Tadekātma-rūpa*	*Āveśa*
	Vilāsa *Svāṃśa*	

Usually the *svāṃśa* and *āveśa* forms appear as *avatāras,* the *svayaṃ-rūpa* appearing only once in the *dvāpara* age as Kṛṣṇa. These appear as if in a new form (*apūrva iva*), either by themselves (*svayam,* e.g. in its self-manifestation as *tadekātma-rūpa*) or through some other means (*āvāntareṇa,* e.g. through a *bhakta* like Vāsudeva). The commentary explains that the phrase 'as if in a new form' implies that the deity exists at the same time in his essential eternal form. The *raison d'etre* of an *avatāra* is *viśva-kārya* or work of the world. The *avatāra* is thus a partial descent or appearance of the supreme deity in the world with the object of performing some action in the world, either through or without the medium of a phenomenal being. The term *viśva-kārya* is not explained by Rūpa Gosvāmin, but Baladeva Vidyābhūṣaṇa explains it as signifying cosmic action or action done in the world, which consists of (i) disturbance of the equilibrium of *prakṛti*, followed by the evolution of *mahat*, etc., (ii) increasing the delight of the gods and other beings by suppressing the wicked, and (iii) propagating the bliss of divine love among the expectant devotees and spreading pure *bhakti.*

"The *avatāras* may appear in various forms, but they are classified generally into three groups. The obvious object of this classification is to gather together all the *avatāras* who are spoken of in legends or pious texts as having appeared or will appear in the world, and unify them as Vaiṣṇava manifestations of the supreme Kṛṣṇa. These three general groups are

1. *Puruṣa-avatāras*. The first *avatāra* is *puruṣa*, who, though unconditioned, becomes the conditioned creator. This *puruṣa* appears in threefold aspect: (1) as the creator of the *mahat* (*mahataḥ śraṣṭṛ*), who is known as Saṃkarṣaṇa, the *kāraṇodakaśāyin,* (ii) as existing in the cosmic egg (*aṇḍa-saṃsthitaḥ*), who is named Pradyumna, the *guṇodaka-śāyin*, and (iii) as existing in all beings (*sarva-bhūta-sthita*), who is called Aniruddha, the *kṣīrodaka-śāyin*). This is really a modification of the older *vyūha*-doctrine of the Nārāyaṇīya, which doctrine however is referred to independently larer on.

2. *Guṇāvatāras*. These are *avatāras* according to the three *guṇas*, of which they are the respective presiding deities; viz. Brahmā as creator (*rajas*), Viṣṇu as protector (*sattva*) and Śiva as destroyer (*tamas*).

3. *Līlāvatāras*. The character of these *avatāras* is not defined, but these forms have been declared by the *Śrīmad-bhāgavata* 1.3. They are twenty-four in number as follows: (1) Catuḥsana, that is the four 'Sanas', who in four forms are really one, namely, Sanaka, Sanandana, Sanātana and Sanatkumāra,

who appeared as Brahmin ascetics to propagate *jñāna* and *bhakti*, (2) Nārada, the author of the *Sātvata Tantra*, (3) the Varāha, four-legged (*catuṣpād*), but also two-legged according to some (*dvipad*), (4) the Matsya, (5) Yajña, (6) Nara and Nārāyaṇa, (7) Kapila, (8) Dattātreya, (9) Hayaśīrṣa, (10) the Haṃsa, (11) Dhruva-priya or Pṛśnigarbha, (12) Ṛṣabha, (13) Pṛthu, (14) the Nṛsiṃha, (15) the Kūrma, (16) Dhanvantari, (17) the Mohinī, (18) the Vāmana, (19) Bhārgava (Paraśu-rāma), (20) Rāghava, (21) Vyāsam (22) Balarāma and Kṛṣṇa, (23) the Buddha, and (24) Kalkin. These are also the *kalpa-avatāras*, as they appear to each *kalpa*.

"The *Manvantara-avatāras*. At each of the fourteen *manvantara* there is an *avatāra* who destroys the enemies of Indra and becomes the friend of the gods. They are in their order (1) Yajña, (2) Vibhu, (3) Sayasena, (4) Hari, (5) Vaikuṇṭha, (6) Ajita, (7) the Vāmana, (8) Sārvabhauma, (9) Ṛṣabha, (10) Viśvakṣeṇa, (11) Dharasetu, (12), Sudhāman, (13) Yogeśvara and (14) Bṛhadbhānu. Of these Hari, Vaikuṇṭha, Ajita and the Vāmana are the chief (*pravara*).

"The *Yugāvatāras*. A *yugāvatāra* flourishes at each of the four *yugas*. They are according to their individual names (*nāman*) and color (*varṇa*): in Satya-yuga, Śukla (white), in Tretā, Rakta (red), in Dvāpara, Śyāma (dark) and in Kali, Kṛṣṇa (black).

"In each *kalpa* these *avatāras* become fourfold in accordance with the condition of *āveśa, prabhaba, vaibhava* and *paraiva*, which terms are now explained. The word *āveśa* literally means 'possession'. The *āveśa-avatāra* has already been mentioned; but this kind of *avatāra*, of which examples are the sages Sanaka, Sanandana etc., Kumāra, Nārada, and Pṛthu, is merely *aupacārika*; that is, they are not real *avatāras* but *avatāras* by analogy; because here the Lord enters into particular *jīvas* and thus exalts them into *avatāras*. Even Kalkin is supposed by some theologians (e.g. in *Viṣṇudharma*) as belonging to this order. The two terms '*prabhava*' and '*vaibhava*' practically mean the same thing, namely, power, but probably differ in the degree of the significance. This class of *avatāras* is identical in essence with the supreme deity (*svarūpa-rūpa*) and they are so-called according to the degree of their *śakti* or power (*śaktinām tāratamayena*), but they are inferior to the *parāvastha avatāra*. The *prabhava avatāra* may again be classified according as (i) their appearance does not endure for a long period of time, or (ii) their not having an extended reputation. The examples of the first kind are the Mohinī, Haṃsa and Śukla, who disappeared as soon as their work was finished; the examples of the second variety include such *śāstrakāra* (writing) ascetics as Dhanvantari, Ṛṣabha, Vyāsa and Kapila. The *vaibhava avatāras* are the Kūrma, the Matsya, Nārāyaṇa with Nara, the Varāha, Hayaśīrṣam Pṛśnigarbha, Balarāma, and the fourteen *manvantara-avatāras* beginning with Yajña...

"The *para-avastha* is described as possessed of the *para* or complete states (*sampūrṇāvasthā*), for these *avatāras* possess all the six *aiśvaryas* and are comparable to a lamp lighted from the original lamp. They are the Nṛsiṃha, Rāṃa and Kṛṣṇa.

"With regard to the Nṛsiṃha the author cites the authority of the *Bhāgavata, Padmapurāṇa* and Śrīdhara (who is known to have been a worshiper of Nṛsiṃha), and notes that the *māhātmya* or greatness of the Nṛsiṃha *avaṭāra* is described in full in the *Nṛsiṃhatāpanī Upaniṣad.* The Nṛsiṃha lives in Jana-loka, but also in Viṣṇu-loka. Rāma lives in Ayodhyā and in Mahāvaikuṇṭha. Some (e.g., *Viṣṇudharmottara*) are of the opinion that the four *vyūhas* (Vāsudeva etc.) were incarnated in Rāma, Lakṣmaṇa etc.; but according to the *Padma-purāṇa* the process of incarnation was as follows: Rāma=Nārāyaṇa, Lakṣmaṇa = Śeṣa, Bharata = the disc Sudarśana of Nārāyaṇa and Śatrughna = the Pāñcajanya conch-shell of the deity. Kṛṣṇa, according to the *Purāṇa*, lives in four places, viz. Vraja, Mathurā, Dvāraka and Goloka.

"In this connection the author discusses the question whether Rāṃa and the Nṛsiṃha can be regarded as *parāvastha-*

avatāras of equal grade with Kṛṣṇa. A *Viṣṇupurāṇa* text is quoted to equalize Rāvaṇa, Hiraṇyakaśipu and Śiśupāla, who were hostile respectively to Rāma, the Nṛsiṃha and Kṛṣṇa, but it is shown that the first two of these (Rāvaṇa and Hiraṇyakaśipu) did not attain *sāyujya* emancipation because they lacked true *bhakti* for the deity. Texts are also cited to show that Kṛṣṇa is the deity himself (*bhagavān svayam*), and not an *avatāra*. Rāma and the Nṛsiṃha have, no doubt, equal character or *svabhāva* with Kṛṣṇa, but they do mot possess the distinctive qualification of bringing emancipation to the enemy that is slain (*hatāri-gati-dāyaka*); for while Śiśupāla was finally emancipated, Rāvaṇa and Hiraṇyakaśipu had to suffer rebirth. Although all these *avatāras* are perfect (*pūrṇa*), there is yet a difference in excellence according as all the *śaktis* or energies of the Lord find expression in them or not. An *aṃśa* is that *avatāra* in which the all-powerful expresses only a part of his infinite power, while a *pūrṇa avatāra* occurs where all the powers are fully manifested. Although the *śakti* is the same in the case of a lamp and a heap of fire for burning down a house, there is yet a difference in their respective virtue of bringing delight by the removal of cold, and so forth.

"Incidentally Rūpa Gosvāmin discusses how contradictory qualities, like unity (*ekatva*) and diversity (*pṛthaktva*), fullness (*aṃśitva*) and division (*aṃśatva*) can inhere in Kṛṣṇa. This is explained as being possible because the power of the godhead is incomprehensible (*acintya-śaktita*); and this position is supported by the citation of Purāṇa texts. The sixteen *kalās* (i.e., parts or digits), assumed by the supreme being for the creation of the world (*bhavanānāṃ sisṛkṣayā*), are spoken of in the Vaiṣṇava *bhakti-śāstras* as his sixteen *śaktis* or energies. They are enumerated as Śrī, Bhū, Kīrti, Ilā, Līlā, Kānti, Vidyā, Vimalā, Utkarṣaṇī, Jñānā, Kriyā, Yogā, Prahvī, Satyā, Īśānā and Anugraha; but their respective characteristics are not explained.

"A modification of the much older *vyūha* doctrine is next mentioned by our author. The four *vyūhas* in their order of emergence are given as:

Saṃkarśaṇa presiding over *ahaṃkāra*,
Vāsudeva presiding over *citta*,
Pradyumna presiding over *buddhi*,
Aniruddha presiding over *manas*.

The author refers to the fact that in the *Nārāyaṇīya*, Pradyumna is presented as presiding over *manas*, and Aniruddha over *ahaṃkāra*, but the above view, in his opinion, is supported by all Pañcarātra scriptures. The four arms of Hari are said to represent the four *vyūhas*. In some *Sātvata* Tantra, we are told, there is an enumeration of nine *vyuḥas*, viz. Nārāyaṇa, Nṛsiṃha, Hayagrīva, Mahāvarāha and Brahmā, in addition to the four mentioned above; but the four appear to be the original and generally accepted *vyūhas*. The *vyūha*-doctrine is accepted by our author from these older sources, but its exact bearing upon the theology of his own school is not clearly explained. It appears, however, that the school does not accept fully the older position that each of these *vyūhas* is a cosmic spiritual evolute or creative emergence in successive order, parallel to the order of cosmic material evolutes of *ahaṃkāra* etc.; but it would regard each of the *vyūhas* (Saṃkarṣaṇa etc.) as independent creative manifestation of the primal *pūrṇa-avatāra* of the supreme being, each having (as already explained) a distinctive character and habitation of his own, like ever other kind of *avatāra*. Nor can each of these, in the opinion of the Bengaḷ school, be regarded as corresponding to the series of cosmic material causation like *ahaṃkāra, manas* and *buddhi*, which are, in its theory, the result of the extraneous *māyā-śakti* of the Bhagavat and are therefore non-conscious (*jaḍa*) evolutes. In other words, these *vyūha* manifestations are aspects of the *puruṣa-avatāra* of the Bhagavat, who do not correspond but apparently have presiding functions over the creative evolutes of *ahaṃkāra, manas* etc.

"The author next attempts to remove the erroneous view sometimes propounded that Kṛṣṇa is Vāsudeva, the first of the four *vyūhas*. He maintains that Kṛṣṇa is not an *avatāra* but the deity himself, who is greater than Vāsudeva; for Vāsudeva is merely an aspect of the *puruṣa-avatāra* for creative purposes. Every other form or manifestation as declared by the *Śrīmad-bhāgavata* (I.3.28) is *aṃśa* and *kalā*, but Kṛṣṇa is the supreme Bhagavat himself. This position is supported by a series of *Purāṇa* texts, which establish that inasmuch as there is an excess of qualities, especially of the quality of *mādhurya*, Kṛṣṇa is superior in turn to Brahman, Puruṣa, Nārāyaṇa, and consequently to all other deities, *vyūhas* and *avatāras*. In this connection the *Gopālatāpanī Upaniṣad* is cited as one of the greatest authorities. It is noteworthy that the Bengal school admits the reality practically of all deities mentioned in the *śāstras*, as well as of all *vyūhas*, *avatāras* and other forms or manifestations testified to by the *Purāṇas*l but it denies their alleged superiority to Kṛṣṇa. Kṛṣṇa is *par excellence* the only supreme deity; the other deities are there, but they are inferior to Kṛṣṇa and even derive their existence from him. Jīva Gosvāmin, for instance, states in his *Śrīkṛṣṇa-saṃdarbha* that Brahmā is the first *bhakta* of Kṛṣṇa, but Śiva, being described in the scriptures as an ideal Vaiṣṇava, is greater than Brahmā, while Lakṣmī who is the foremost embodiment of the teaching of *bhakti*, is greater than Śiva, and is therefore admitted into the highest companionship (*parama-sakhya*).

"The question as to how the Unborn can be born is answered by the mystical dogma of incomprehensible power (*vaibhava*) and by the metaphor that although the fire remains hidden in the fuel, it comes into existence by friction. The cause of divine manifestation is found in the theory of grace or *prasāda*, which the deity vouchsafes to his faithful devotee as an aspect of his inherent divine *śakti*.

"Then the author proceeds to discuss the *līlā* or divine sport of Kṛṣṇa, which is a display of his inherent divine energy or *śakti*. This topic is further elaborated in the *Śrīkṛṣṇa-saṃdarbha* of Jīva Gosvāmin in its philosophical aspect; but here the dogma is barely stated and supported by authoritative texts. The *līlā*, as an aspect of divine *śakti* or energy, is real and eternal (*nitya*), whether it is manifest (*prakaṭa*) or unmanifest (*aprakaṭa*). Hence also are Kṛṣṇa's forms (*mūrti*) and *avatāras* real and eternal. His *prakaṭa avatāra-līlā*, that is, his manifest birth in its real and eternal character, is the result of his grace or *anugraha* in the world, and he shows himself in the way in which his faithful devotee wishes to see him. As the *līlā* is eternal, his true *bhakta* even today sees Kṛṣṇa sporting in Vṛndāvana. His qualities or *guṇas* are not *prākṛta* or phenomenal, because he is beyond the sphere of the three *prākṛta guṇas* of *sattva, rajas* and *tamas*. It is for this reason that he is sometimes called *nirguṇa* or attributeless, but his real attributes are non-natural or super-sensuous (*aprākṛta*), being an essence of his inherent self (*svarūpa-bhūta*). Hence his form (*rūpa*) and name (*nāman*), his greatness (*aiśvarya*) and his retinue (*pārṣadas*), etc, through his display of *līlā*, a super-sensuous reality, although in his essence he is formless (*arūpa*), nameless (*anāma*), etc.

"That the *Kṛṣṇa-līlā* is real and eternal is laid down in the *Śrīmad-bhāgavat* and other Vaiṣṇava scriptures. The *līlā*, which is a display of the divine *śakti* or energy, is of two kinds, namely, *prakaṭa* or manifest, and *aprakaṭa* or unmanifest; the one is cognizable in the external world (*prapañca-gocara*), the other is not. In the *prakaṭa-līlā* Kṛṣṇa seems to go to and fro from Vṛndāvana, Mathurā and Dvārakā, but in the *aprakaṭa-līlā* he stays eternally in Vṛndāvana which he never forsakes as his eternal habitation. Here hs sports with one *gopī* and appears as Dvibhuja, although elsewhere he is sometimes Caturbhuja. At Vṛndāvana he is Kṛṣṇa, but at Mathurā he becomes Vāsudeva, while at Dvārakā he manifests his Pradyumna and Aniruddha forms,–which theory is a curious mystical attempt to reconcile the old *vyūha* theory with the new Kṛṣṇa legend. His birth as the son of Devakī appears in his *prakaṭa-līlā*, but in his *aprakaṭa-līlā* he is the eternal son of Yaśodā. In the *prakaṭa-līlā* there is an apparent separation from Vṛndāvana but during all this time he is really in union with his beloved ones. This union is of two kinds, namely, *āvirbhāva* and *agati*. The *āvirbhāva* occurs when he appears to his dear ones who long for him during separation; e.g. at the time of Uddhava's message, Kṛṣṇa appeared in Vṛndāvana, although he lived apparently in Dvārakā. When to prove the genuineness of his promise and to show his love to his dear ones he comes in his chariot to Vṛndāvana, it is called *agati*, e.g. the advent as described in *Śrīmad-bhāgavatam*. 10.39.33 ff. Thus by means of his manifest and unmanifest *līlā* he remains at the same time in the three places, Vṛndāvana, Mathurā and Dvārakā. His habitation is in reality twofold, namely Vṛndāvana and Dvārakā, the former again being twofold, namely, Vṛndāvana and Mathurā. The *goloka* or the highest paradise of the deity is really a *vaibhava* or display of *śakti*, of Vṛndāvana itself. In all these places his *līlā* is *nitya*, but Vṛndāvana is the best because here he lives eternally in all his glory and sweetness. This sweetness or *mādhurya* consists of his power (*aiśvarya*), his sport (*krīḍā*), his flute (*veṇu*) and his personal appearance (*mūrti*), all of which exist in fullness in Vṛndāvana .

4.4 RŪPA GOSVĀMIN, *Upadeśāmṛta*

The following translation ("T") is found in Upadesamrta 1997.

Translation by Bhaktivedanta Narayana Maharaj

1 (T2) "A wise and self-composed person who can subdue the impetus to speak, the agitation of the mind, the onset of anger, the vehemence of the tongue, the urge of the belly and the agitation of the genitals can instruct the entire world. In

other words, all persons can become disciples of such a self-controlled person.

2 (T25) "*Bhakti* is destroyed by the following six kinds of faults: (1) eating too much or collecting more than necessary, (2) endeavors which are opposed to *bhakti,* (3) useless mundane talk, (4) failure to adopt essential regulations or fanatical adherence to regulations, (5) associations with persons who are opposed to *bhakti,* and (6) greed or the restlessness of the mind to adopt worthless opinions.

3 (T39) "Progress in *bhakti* may be obtained by the following six practices: (1) enthusiasm to carry out the rules which enhance *bhakti,* (2) firm faith in the statements of the *śāstra* and the *guru* whose words are fully in line with the *śāstra,* (3) fortitude in the practice of *bhakti,* even in the midst of obstacles, or patience during the practice stage of *bhakti,* even when there is delay in attaining one's desired goal, (4) following the limbs of *bhakti* such as hearing (*śravaṇa*) and changing (*kīrtana*) and giving up one's material sense enjoyment for the pleasure of Śrī Kṛṣṇa, (5) giving up illicit connection with women, the association of those who are overly attached to women and the association of *māyāvādis,* atheists and pseudo-religionists, and (6) adopting the good behavior and character of pure devotees.

4 (T48) "Offering pure devotees items in accordance with their requirements, accepting *prasādī* or remnant items given by pure devotees, revealing to devotees one's confidential realizations concerning *bhajana,* inquiring from them about their confidential realizations, eating with great love the *prasāda* remnants given by devotees, and lovingly feeding them *prasāda*–these are the six symptoms of loving association with devotees.

5 (T53) "One who takes *kṛṣṇa-nāma* just once by calling out 'O Kṛṣṇa' is a neophyte devotee (*kaniṣṭha-adhikārī*). One should consider him to be his family member and silently respect him. One who, fully understanding the principle of *dīkṣā,* has

accepted initiation from a qualified *guru* and performs *bhajana* of Bhagavān in accordance with the Vaiṣṇava conventions is an intermediate devotee (*madhyama-adhikārī*). One should respect such a devotee who is endowed with the correct understanding of reality and illusion by offering *pranāma* unto him and so forth. One who is conversant with the science of *bhajana* as described in the *Śrīmad-Bhāgavata* and other Vaiṣṇava scriptures and who performs exclusive *bhajana* of Śrī Kṛṣṇa is a *mahā-bhāgavata* devotee. Due to his undeviating absorption in Kṛṣṇa, the pure heart of such a devotee is free from faults such as the tendency to criticize others. He is expert in *bhajana*, meaning that he mentally renders service (*mānasa-sevā*) to Śri Rādhā-Kṛṣṇa's pastimes which take place during the eight segments of the day (*aṣṭa-kalīya-līlā*). Knowing him to be a topmost devotee whose heart is established in the particular mood of service to Śrī Rādhā-Kṛṣṇa for w hich one aspires and who is affectionately disposed towards oneself, one should honor him by offering *daṇḍavat-praṇāma (praṇipāta)*, making relevant inquiry (*pariprasba*) and rendering service (*sevā*) with great love.

6 (T64) "Devotees situated in the material world should not be viewed with material vision, in other words, one should not consider them to be ordinary conditioned souls. The imperfections visible in their natures, such as birth in a low caste, harshness, lethargy and so forth, and the imperfections visible in their bodies such as ugly features, disease, deformities and so forth, are precisely like the appearance of bubbles, foam and mud in the Ganges. Despite such apparent pollution in the water of the Ganges, she retains her nature as liquified transcendence. Similarly, the self-realized Vaiṣṇavas always exist in the transcendental place and one should not attribute material defects to them.

7 (T70) "Aho! Those whose tongues are afflicted by the jaundice of *avidyā* (or, in other words, those who are afflicted by the ignorance born of being indifferent to Śrī Kṛṣṇa from a

time without beginning) cannot relish the nectarine names, form, qualities and pastimes of Śrī Kṛṣṇa, which are compared to the sweetest sugar-candy. Instead, these attributes taste bitter to them. But if with great faith one regularly takes this sugar-candy of chanting and hearing the transcendental names, form, qualities and pastimes of Śrī Kṛṣṇa, it gradually becomes relishable to him and destroys at the root his disease, the jaundice of *avidyā* or indifference to Śrī Kṛṣṇa. In other words, he becomes spontaneously attached to Śrī Kṛṣṇa.

8 (T76) "While living in Vraja as a follower of the eternal residents of Vraja who possess inherent spontaneous love for Śrī Kṛṣṇa, one should utilize all his time by sequentially engaging the tongue and the mind in meticulous chanting and remembrance of Kṛṣṇas names, form, qualities and pastimes. This is the essence of all instruction.

9 (T98-88) "Due to Śrī Kṛṣṇa's having taken birth there, the abode of Mathurā is superior even to Vaikuṇṭha, the realm of spiritual opulence. Superior to Mathurā is the forest of Vṛndāvana because there the festival of the *rāsa* dance took place. Superior to Vṛndāvana forest is Govardhana Hill because Śrī Kṛṣṇa raised it with His lotus hand and performed many pastimes there with His devotees. Yet superior to Govardhana Hill is Śrī Rādhā-kuṇḍa because it immerses one in the nectar of Śrī Kṛṣṇa's divine love. What intelligent person would not desire to render service to this magnificent pond, which is splendidly situated at the base of Govardhana Hill?

10. (T94-95) "One who selflessly performs virtuous acts in accordance with the path of *karma yoga* is superior to those who merely seek to fulfil their selfish desires. The *brahma-jñānīs*, who by dint of their spiritual knowledge are transcendental to the three modes of material nature, are more dear to Śrī Kṛṣṇa than those pious followers of the *karman* path who are forever occupied in performing virtuous deeds. More dear to Śrī Kṛṣṇa than the *brahma-jñānīs* are His devotees like Sanaka, who have abandoned the pursuit of knowledge and

who consider *bhakti* alone to be the best path. In doing so, they have followed the statement in *Śrīmad-Bhāgavata* 10.14.3: *jñāne prayaśam udapāsya*--one should abandon the endeavor for knowledge. Pure devotees like Nārada, who are resolutely fixed in *prema* for Kṛṣṇa, are even more beloved to Him than all such loving (*premī*) devotees. Amongst all those beloved *gopīs*, Śrimatī Rādhikā is more dear to Śrī Kṛṣṇa than His own life; in precisely the same way, He clearly loves her pond, Śrī Rādhā-kuṇḍa. Therefore, what highly fortunate, spiritually intelligent person would not reside on the banks of Śrī Rādhā-koṇḍa in a state of transcendental consciousness..."

5 RAGHUNATHA BHAṬṬA (1505-1579)

De 1961, p. 125, writes: "Of Raghunāṭha Bhaṭṭa nothing much is known, and he does not appear to have left any work. Murāri (iv.1 15-17) tells us that Caitanya met his father Tapana Miśra at Banares, where Caitanya became his guest on is journey back from Vṛndāvana and revealed his grace to the boy Raghunātha. Later on Raghunātha came to Caitanya at Puri and stayed there for eight months. At Caitanya's direction he returned home; and after four years, on the death of his parents, he came again to Puri and stayed for eight months. He was then directed by Caitanya to join Rūpa and Sanātana at Vṛndāṿana, where heappears to have lived thereafter. Caitanya is said to have given him a Tulasī garland. Kṛṣṇadāsa Kaṿirāja tells us that the Bhaṭṭa was well read in the *Śrīmad- bhāgavata,* and Rūpa used to take delight in his reading of that scripture."

Rosen 1991 "(He) is, in many way, the most mysterious of the Six Goswamis...the only one to have not left any literary contributions..." Rosen goes on (pp. 170-187) to provide what are thought to be such information as has been passed down.

6 GOPĀḶA BHAṬṬA (1503-1578)

The account below is based on Rosen 1991 (passages quoted in what follows, pp. 70 ff.). Caitanya first met Gopāla Bhaṭṭa, the seven-year -old boy of Vyeṅkaṭa Bhaṭṭa, in Srirangam. Rosen goes on to explain (based on David Haberman's analysis) that "the Krishna conception was superior to that of Nārāyaṇa, and after becoming convinced" the young Gopāla Bhaṭṭa to become a Caitanyite Vaiṣṇava. After a pertinent dream Gopāla Bhaṭṭa went to Caitanya to serve him, but was directed by Caitanya to join Rūpa and Sanātana in Vṛndāvana.

"As he grew in years, Gopāla Bhaṭṭa accepted his uncle, Prabodhānanda Sarasvatī, as his spiritual master. From him Gopāla Bhaṭṭa learned poetry, rhetoric, Sanskrit grammar, and Vedanta...As his reputation reached unprecedented proportions, he decided that he was ready to fulfill the mandate given to him by Shri Chaitanya: he was ready to go to Vrndavan."

"He soon wrote a book entitled *Satkriyasāradīpikā*, a classic on the tenets of Gauḍīya Vaiṣṇavism. Then he edited the *Haribhaktivilāsa*, which was written by Sanātana Gosvāmi.. In addition, he wrote a scholarly introduction to Jīva Gosvāmin's *Ṣaṭsandarbha* and a commentary on Bilvamaṅgala Ṭhakur's *Kṛṣṇakarṇāmṛta*."[1]

6.1 GOPĀLA BHAṬṬA, *Haribhaktivilāsa*

Rosen 1991, p. 73, tries to clear up a problem about the authorship of this work. "Of course, his most important work, the *Haribhaktivilāsa*, is generally attributed to Sanātana Gosvāmī, at least in its original form. It is said that Gopāla Bhaṭṭa later produced a shortened version and added to it the *Digdarśinīṭīkā*, which is the commentary of Sanātana Gosvāmī. Some say that the original plan for the *Haribhaktivilāsa* came

---

[1]See Dhruva Maharaj Das, *Vrindavan Dham Ki Kai!* (Saṇ Francisco, Entourage Publications, 1988), p. 51.

from Gopāla Bhaṭṭa, but was started by Sanātana Gosvāmī anyway. Because of the confusion, actual authorship is controversial. Nonetheless, the mammoth work is inevitably associated with both their names.[1]

"The historical evidence in regard to authorship is admittedly confused. On Shri Gopāla Bhaṭṭa's side, the *Haribhaktivilāsa* itself states that he wrote it for the satisfaction of Raghunāth Dās, Rūpa and Sanātana. But in the writings of Jīva Gosvāmin and Kṛṣṇadāsa Kavirāj, authorship is unequivocally given to Sanātana. Narahari Chakravarti writes in his *Bhaktiratnākara* that Sanātana actually wrote the *Haribhaktīvilāsa* but attributed the work to hiṣ younger contemporary. Nonetheless, Gopāla Bhaṭṭa Gosvāmī's name in the text itself cannot be ignored."

For a summary of the text see 3.3 on pp. 93-94 above.

7 JĪVA GOSVĀMIN (1513-1598)

The following account of Jiva's personal data is found in Elkman 1986, pp. 21-23: "Jīva's dates are not definitely known. Jadunath Sarkar places his date of birth at 1511 (Sarkar 1932, p. 3), and on the basis of our knowledge of Jīva's father's early death, we may assume that this date is more or less correct. Jīva's father, Anupama (also known as Vallabha), was the younger brother of Rūpa and Sanātana, and also a devout follower of Caitanya. Anupama first met Caitanya in his village of Rāmkeli when Caitanya stopped there on his aborted trip to Vṛndāvana in 1513, and left home shortly thereafter in the company of Rūpa. The two brothers met Caitanya again in

---

[1]For the most exhaustive treatment of this controversy please note the debate between S.K. De and Amarnath Ray in Indian Culture (Volume V, July 1938, pp. 57-71, and October 1938, pp. 199-206).

Prayāga, and later, as they were on their way to Puri to meet Caitanya again, Anupama died. This means that Jīva could not have been born later than 1514, and if the accounts of the *Bhaktiratnākara* are correct, that Jīva was already a young boy when Caitanya passed through his village, then the date of Jīva's birth must be pushed back another few years at least. At any rate, the placing of his birth 'between 1530 and 1540', as Mahanama Brahmachari has done (Mahanama 1974), is certainly not tenable.

"With his father dead and his two uncles now settled in Vṛndāvana, Jīva reportedly lost all interest in worldly pursuits, hoping only to join his two uncles in Vṛndāvana one day. By the time he had reached the age of twenty, his mother was also dead, and he resolved to lead the life of a Vaiṣṇava recluse in the company of Rūpa and Sanātana.

"Before heading to Vṛndāvana, Jīva first visited the town of Navadvīpa, where he was met by Nityānanda and taken to all of the places associated with Caitanya's youth. At the bidding of Nityānanda, Jīva proceeded to Benares to complete his studies in Sanskrit learning. There Jīva studied with a scholar by the name of Madhusūdana Vācaspati who, according to S. K. De, was 'an accomplished grammarian, Smārta and Vedāntist' (De 1961, p. 150), not to be confused with the Madhusūdana Sarasvatī of *Advaitasiddhi* fame. A. K. Majumdar disagrees. He writes, 'Jīva Gosvāmin studied under a Madhusūdana Sarasvati at Vārāṇasī, and it is quite likely that this teacher was none other than this great *advaita* scholar (Majumdar 1969, p. 89)..."'

"After completing his studies, Jīva joined the Gosvāmins in Vṛndāvana, where he took initiation with Rūpa and engaged himself in the study of the *Bhāgavata* and other Vaiṣṇava scriptures with Sanātana and the other Gosvāmins. Very little is known of Jīva's life in Vṛndāvana, with the exception of a single incident regarding a debate which took place between him and one Vallabha Bhaṭṭa.

"It seems that Vallabha had earlier challenged Rūpa to a debate, and that Rūpa had refused, conceding victory by default. Jīva, pained at this slight to his *guru*, sought out Vallabha and soundly defeated him in argument, only to be chastized by Rūpa and expelled from the Vaiṣṇava community on the grounds that he had succumbed to pride, one of the cardinal sins for a Vaiṣṇava. Ultimately, Rūpa forgave his nephew at the intercession of Sanātana, and Jīva was readmitted to the community.'" [It is not clear whether this Vallabha is the same as the famous founder of the Śuddhādvaita tradition. A footnote at this point provides Elkman's views on the matter.]

"As the last surviving member of the six Gosvāmins, the responsibility for the organzation of the movement fell squarely on Jīva's shoulders. S. K. De writes, 'Jīva became the highest court of appeal in doctrinal matters as long as he lived.' (De 1961, p. 130). It was also due to Jīva that the theology of Vṛndāvana made its way into Bengal and Orissa, spread by his three eminent proteges, Śrīnivāsam Barittanam and Śyāmānanda. Jīva was likewise a major force in making Vṛndāvana an important center of learning and religion, devoting his time and efforts to the construction of new temples as well as a library of Sanskrit religious literature. Jīva is said to have lived beyond eighty, and Jadunath Sarkar places his date of death at 1596 (Sarkar 1932, p. 3)."

For updated information on certain aspects of Jīva Gosvāmin life and works consult Brzezinski 2007. Notably, Brzezinski's information and argument on the dates of Jīva's birth and death supersede previous estimates of those dates, and we use them here.

7.1 JĪVA GOSVĀMIN, *Tattvasandarbha/Saṃvādinī*

Stuart Elkman, on pages 57-60 of Elkman 1986, provides the following summary of the contents of this, the first of the six sections of the *Bhagavatsandarbha* or *Ṣaṭsandarbha.*"ET" refers to Stuart Elkman's edition and translation, Delhi 1986, from which we have put together the appropriate page references.

A lengthier summary of this work is to be found in De 1961, pp. 257-272. For the fairly copious further literature cf. Bib 3, #1011.11.

Summary by Stuart Elkman

"Jīva's *Tattvasandarbha* forms the first volume of his six-part *Bhāgavatasandarbha* or *Ṣaṭsandarbha*. As the title of the work suggests, the *Bhāgavatasandarbha* is a compilation (literally, a 'stringing together') of carefully selected verses from the *Bhāgavata Purāṇa*, arranged and interpreted in such a fashion as to constitute a comprehensive philosophical system. As the first volume of this work, the *Tattvasandarbha* serves as an introduction to the work as a whole, and also contains a brief summary of the doctrines found in the other five volumes.

"The *Tattvasandarbha* may be broken down into two main segments: a *pramāṇakhaṇḍa*, in which Jīva ascertains the standards of knowledge to be used in the text; and a *prameyakhaṇḍa*, in which these standards are employed to determine the philosophical questions under discussion.

Jīva opens the work with a series of *maṅgala* verses to Caitanya, Rūpa, and Sanātana, and then explains the circumstances which led to the writing of the *Bhāgavata-sandarbha*. Jīva writes that the original version of these *sandarbhas* had been composed earlier by "a certain Bhaṭṭa from South India", presumably Gopāla Bhaṭṭa, one of the six Gosvāmins, and that Rūpa and Sanātana had urged Jīva to make some revisions and additions to the original text. Since Jīva acknowledges his debt to Gopāla Bhaṭṭa at the commencement of each of the six *sandarbhas*, it is likely that an earlier version, or at least outline, of the text did exist, although it is almost certain that Jīva, out of a sense of humility, has significantly de-emphasized his role in the authorship of this work. Jīva also makes the first of several statements here acknowledging his debt to the earlier Vaiṣṇava *ācāryas*, whom he identifies in *Sarvasaṃvādinī* as Rāmānuja, Madhva, Śrīdhara, and others.

Section 9 of the text is composed of what appears to be a simple *maṅgala* verse dedicated to Kṛṣṇa, but which, as Jīva himself notes, represents a concise statement of the essence of the *Bhāgavatasandarbha*. The verse is based on the famous lines from the *Bhāgavata* (1.2.11): 'That non-dual consciousness which the knowers of truth (*tattva*) consider truth is designated *brahman, paramātman,* and *bhagavat*.' The *tattva* which forms the subject of this first *sandarbha* and after which it takes its name is none other than the non-dual consciousness mentioned in the first line of this verse, and the following three *sandarbhas*, the *Bhāgavat, Paramātma*, and *Kṛṣṇa sandarbhas*, are all elucidations of this same *tattva* from different points of view.

"Section 9 contains a statement of the *anubandhas*, the preliminary questions which are considered necessary prerequisites for works or this kind; namely: (1) the subject matter of the text (the *sambandha*), which is the *tattva* mentioned above; (2) the purpose of the text (the *prayojana*), which is to instill love of God in the aspirant who reads it; and (3) the means of attaining this aim (the *abhidheya*), which is devotional practices as set forth in the *Bhāgavata*.[1] Thus, the first four *sandarbhas*, as previously mentioned, deal with the *sambandha*, the fifth, or *Bhaktisandarbha*, deals with the *abhidheya*, and the sixth, or *Prītisandarbha*, deals with the *prayojana*.

---

[1]The terms *abhidheya* and *prayojana* are used by Jīva in a special sense, corresponding to the notions of *sādhana* and *sādhya*, or means and ends. The same usage is also found in the *Caitanya Caritāmṛta* and seems to be peculiar to the Gauḍīya Vaiṣṇava school. (SE)

"Jīva then begins his investigation of the question of *pramāṇa* in order to discover the authority on which these questions may be determined. After first ruling out the possibility that sense-perception, inference, or related means of knowledge can be relied upon in deciding metaphysical questions, Jīva turns his attention to *śabdapramāṇa* (valid testimony or revelation). According to Jīva, the authority of the Vedas stems from the fact of their divine origin. Since, he maintains, the Purāṇas and Itihāsa are also divine in origin, their authority is to be considered equal to that of the Vedas. Jiva supports this proposition with numerous quotations, mostly from the Purāṇas themselves, but also from the Upaniṣads.

"Having established the authoritative nature of the Purāṇas and Itihāsa, Jīva proceeds to point out the advantages which they enjoy over the Vedas, namely that they are easier to comprehend, are available in their entirety, and are better suited to the present age. And of all the Purāṇas and Itihāsa, the *Bhāgavata Purāṇa*, Jīva claims, is best able to determine metaphysical or spiritual questions. JIva's arguments in favor of the pre-eminence of the *Bhāgavata* are based mainly on some unidentified verses from the *Garuḍa Purāṇa* which describe the *Bhāgavata* as representing a commentary on the *Brahmasūtra*, demonstrating the significance of the *Mahābhārata*, explaining the *Gāyatrī*, and representing (or fortifying) the Vedas. Jīva thus justifies his decision to rely on the *Bhāgavata* not only as his sole authority for this work, but also for its subject matter. As he explains in section 27, his own words are meant to introduce and explain the words of the *Bhāgavata*, just as the various *sūtras* of the *Brahmasūtra* serve the purpose of introducing the different Upaniṣadic verses indicated by them.

"Towards the end of the *pramāṇākhaṇḍa* (see 23-28), Jīva discusses the origin of the *Bhāgavata* commentary tradition and the procedures to be followed by him in his own interpretations of the *Bhāgavata* verses. According to sections 23 and 24, Śaṃkara knowingly expounded the false doctrine of Māyāvāda at the express command of Viṣṇu, so that beings would remain deluded and the present cycle of creation would continue. Śaṃkara, being an *avatāra* of Śiva and a devotee of Viṣṇu, could not, however, bring himself to apply the same distorted interpretation to the *Bhāgavata*, the most beloved text of Viṣṇu, and thus refrained from writing a commentary on it. Some of Śaṃkara's disciples, however, understood the doctrine of Māyāvāda to represent Śaṃkara's actual beliefs, and composed commentaries on the *Bhāgavata* from the Advaitic point of view. Madhva, characterized by Jīva as one of Śaṃkara's disciples, realized the mistake his fellow disciples had made, and wrote a commentary of his own representing the actual import of the *Bhāgavata* as understood by Śaṃkara.

"In addition to crediting Madhva with originating an authentic commentary tradition on the *Bhāgavata*, Jīva also claims to have cited certain scriptural verses from the writings of Madhva which he was unable to see in their original form. However, when it comes time to acknowledge the earlier philosophers who have influenced Jīva, only the names of Śrīdhara and Rāmānuja are explicitly stated. Jīva writes in section 27 that he will follow the *Bhāgavata* commentary of Śrīdhara, but only when it represents the purely 'Vaiṣṇava' point of view. Otherwise, he claims to follow the view of Rāmānuja or, if necessary, to give new interpretations based on the natural sense of the *Bhāgavata*.

"After completing the introductory portions, Jīva opens the text proper with a handful of verses from the *Bhāgavata* describing the origin of that Purāṇa. According to *Bhagavata Purāṇa* 1.7.4-11, Vyāsa, while seated for meditation one day, attained the state of perfect concentration of mind known as *samādhi*, and had the vision of the supreme *puruṣa* and *māyā*. He also realized that the individual, suffering because of the deluding power of *māyā*, can put an end to his misery by developing devotion for Kṛṣṇa. Vyāsa then composed the *Bhāgavata* in order to teach this truth to mankind. Later, he taught the *Bhāgavata* to his all-renouncing son, Śuka, who thereafter studied it daily.

"Jīva discusses these eight *Bhāgavata* verses in sections 29-49, in terms of the categories, *sambandha, abhidheya,* and *prayojana.* In the course of this discussion, Jīva offers refutations of the Advaitic doctrines of *pratibimbavaḍa* and *paricchedavāda*, and states his own position of Acintyabhedābhedavāda which attempts to reconcile both the dualistic and non-dualistic standpoints. This section also represents a brief summary of the ideas found in the remaining *sandarbhas*.

"Jīva then begins his treatment of the *tattva*, or philosophical principle, which is the actual subject matter of this first *sandarbha*. The *sattva,* described in section 51 as non-dual consciousness, is first considered from the individual, or *vyaṣṭi*, point of view as representing the essential nature of the individual soul, and then from the aggregate, or *samaṣṭi*, point of view as representing the ground of the universe (the *āśraya*).

"Since the *āśraya* principle is described in the *Bhāgavata* as the tenth and final characteristic of a Mahāpurāṇa, Jīva next discusses all ten topics one after the other, in order to show that the first nine ultimately serve the purpose of clarifying the meaning of the tenth, which represents the true import of the *Bhāgavata*. Finally, Jīva returns to the individual point of view to show that the same *āśraya* principle which constitutes the ground for the universe is also the ground for the individual souls, dwelling within all begins as the inner controller."

7.2 JĪVA GOSVĀMIN, *Bhagavatsandarbha/Saṃvādinī*

The following summary is to be found in De 1961, pp. 272-297. The text is edited by Chinmayi Chatterjee in Chatterjee 1972, which also contains a summary of the text on pp. xv-xxx. For further editions see the citations at Bib 3, #1011.1

Summarized by Sushil Kumar De

"The principal object of this *Sandarbha* is to establish and explain the concept of the Bhagavat. Having explained the concept of the Absolute as implied by the phrase *advaya-jñāna-sattva* in verse I.2.11 [of the *Bhagavata Purāṇa*], Jīva Gosvāmin now turns to an interpretation of the second line of the same verse, which further amplifies that concept. The line signifies that although the Absolute is one and indivisible, it has three aspects according to the particular capacity of realization of the devotee (*upāsaka-yogyatā-viśiṣṭyena*). The same ultimate reality, therefore, can be viewed respectively as Brahman, Paramātman and Bhagavat, although it is never, as Jīva Gosvmin carefully notes, designated by the term '*jīva*'. Our author now proceeds in this *Sandarbha* to explain these three concepts of the Absolute, which he takes as three stadiums or gradations of one and the same Reality. Here he deals principally with the concept of Bhagavat as the highest and most perfect manifestation of the *advaya-jñāna-tattva*. It is not perfectly clear if this peculiar doctrine of graded Trinity is actually and consistently implied in the *Bhāgavata*, but it is, at any rate, one of the fundamental postulates of the school which Jīva Gosvāmin represents. It is possible to find conflicting texts existing on the subject, but our author attempts to reconcile them, partly by rejecting those which go against the theory, partly by ingenuities of interpretation , and partly by presuming that the apparently contradictory terms or ideas are to be taken in different senses in different context, for instance by presuming that some apply to the concept of Brahman, some to that of Bhagavat.

"The concept of the Paramātman and its relation to *prakṛti* and *jīva* are dealt with in detail in the *Paramātmasandarbha*; the present *Sandarbha*, as its title implies, has for its principal theme the concept of the Bhagavat. There is no need for a *Brahmasandarbha*, for if the concept of the Bhagavat is clearly realized, that of Brahman will also be understood, and the latter concept has already been fairly fully explained by the school of Advaita philosophers. Brahman (neuter) is in fact the *nirviśeṣa* state of Bhagavat, and as the non-differentiated substance it corresponds to the Brahman of the school of Śaṃkara. But Bhagavat represents the highest being in the hierarchy of spiritual manifestations, the most perfect person in whom all the *viśeṣas* are most perfectly developed. In other words, Brahman is unqualified, but the Bhagavat is infinitely qualified by an infinity of blessed and perfect attributes. In the Bhagavat all the divine *śaktis* or energies eternally come into full play, but in Brahman they remain in a potential or non-discrete state. The essence of the *bhagavattā* or Lordship consists in this actualisation of the *śaktis*, the nature of which will be explained later on; and the Bhagavat, as the religious concrete, can be realized in the full display of his distinctive features, potencies, attributes, dwelling-places and associates. Brahman, on the other hand, is the philosophical Absolute, in which these attributes and powers remain undifferentiated; it is devoid of all *viśeṣas* and forms an absolutely homogeneous and indivisible substance. Thus, thought cannot be predicated as an attribute of Brahman, but thought forms its very essence; that is, Brahman is not a thinking being but the thought-substance itself: in the same way, Brahman cannot be said to exist but it is existence itself. The Bhagavat is regarded as the Lord in full manifestation (*pūrṇa āvirbhāva*), because the appearance in this case is accompanied by all the divine energies while Brahman, from this point of view, constitutes an imperfect or incomplete manifestation. The sacred texts, therefore, describe Brahman as the bodily luster (*tanubhā*) of the Bhagavat, and in the *[Bhagavad]Gītā* the Bhagavat describes himself as the *pratiṣṭhā* of Brahman. In other words, the realization of the Bhagavat, as taught by the theistic Vaiṣṇava school, indicates a state superior to the realization of the Brahman of the Advaitavādins; and we are told that Brahman is the object of realization of the Paramahamsas who are *jñānayogins*, but the Bhagavat reveals himself only to the *bhagavata-paramahaṃsas*, who are *bhaktiyogins*. Although the Bhagavat is one and indivisible reality, this distinction is possible because some *sādhakas* [seekers] do not possess the fullest capacity of realization; to them the highest reality therefore appears in the general or incomplete form of Brahman. Such *sādhakas* are the philosophers of the Advaita school, but the *bhaktas* proceed a stage further. There is, however, no absolute difference between the two forms; for the difference is one of degree only, and the limitation is in relation to the capacity and state of realization of the devotee.

"In order to elucidate the concept of the Bhagavat further, Jīva Goṣvāmin proceeds to discuss and analyze its attributes and explain its divine energies or *śaktis*. He begins by showing that these attributes reside really and eternally in the Bhagavat in intimate or inner relation, which is understood in philosophical terminology as the *samavāya* (perpetual co-inherence) relation, as opposed to the mere *saṃyoga* [contact] or separable relation. In other words, the *guṇas* and *śaktis* are not adventitious or *āropita*, but essential or *svarūpa-bhūta*. In this connection the author refers to the etymology or *nirukti* of the word '*bhagavat*' and shows, on the authority of the Purāṇas, that the various syllables indicate the various attributes and *śaktis* which go to make up the concept! ...

"But Jīva Gosvāmin takes pains to show that the three *prākṛta guṇas* (*sattva, rajas* and *tamas*) can be predicated only of the *jīva*, and not of the Bhagavat, who is beyond their sphere. We shall see later that these *guṇas* are due to the *māyā-śakti* of the Lord, but having eternally subjugated or transcended this *śakti*, which is extraneous to his essential self, the Lord himself is entirely unaffected by its influence. If therefore he has any *guṇa* it is *aprākṛta* or non-phenomenal. We are told that in the Vaikuṇṭha where he dwells, there is no *sattva, rajas* or *tamas;* but there is only a function of his *svarūpa-śakti* or intrinsic energy, namely, a pure existence of *śuddha sattva*, which is *prākṛtātīta* or beyond the sphere of the phenomenal world. It is called pure or *śuddha* because it is untouched by the influence of his extraneous *māyā-śakti*, to which are due the evolution of *prakṛti* and the *guṇas*. The absence of *rajas* indicates, we are further informed, that the Lord is incapable of being created (*asṛjyatva*), that of *tamas* implies that he is indestructible (*anāśatva*), and that of *sattva* signifies that he consists of pure existence (*sat*), pure consciousness (*cit*), and pure bliss (*ānanda*).

"In order to understand the concept of Brahman and the Bhagavat, as well as of the Paramātman, it would be necessary to understand the nature of *śakti* or divine energy, upon whose degree and quality of display the distinction really rests. Jīva Gosvāmin now turns to the peculiar theory of *śakti* which his theistic school teaches; but he points out at the outset that the *śaktis* possess the two characteristics of *acintyatva* and *svābhāvikatva*. By *acintyatva* is meant that the *śaktis* in themselves are inscrutable and beyond the reach of human thought and reason (*tarkāsaha*) or that they are capable of bringing about impossible effects (*durghataṭaghaṭakatva)*; but it also refers to the peculiar relation in which these *śaktis* stand to the *śaktimat*, the possessor of the *śakti*, and which consists of an inscrutable relation of difference-in-non-difference (*acintya-bhedābheda*). By *svābhāvikatva* is meant that the *śaktis* are natural to the Lord and constitute in their totality his very self or essence, although in his infinite power he actually transcends them. These ideas will be made clear as we proceed with a detailed consideration of the theory of *śakti*.

"The *śakti* or divine energy of the Bhagavat is viewed in three aspects and is accordingly grouped into three classes, namely *śakti* as *svarūpa*, *śakti* as *taṭasthā* and *śakti* as *bahiraṅga*. These are successively called *parā* or *svarīyaśakti*, *taṭasthā* or *jīvaśakti*, and *bahiraṅga* or *māyāśakti*. The division bases itself upon a text of the *Viṣṇupurāṇa* which styles them respectively as *parā, kṣetrajña* and *avidyā*. The present *Sandarbha*, which is concerned chiefly with the question of the *svarūpa* of the Bhagavat, deals naturally with the *svarupa śakti,* leaving the comsideratiom of the other two *śaktis* to the *Paramātmasandarbha* to which they are primarily relevant. The *svarūpa* or *parā śakti,* as the name itself implies, may be described as that energy which constitutes the intrinsic perfect selfhood of the Bhagavat and is therefore inseparable from him. This energy is thus *antaraṅga* or intrinsic, as opposed to the other *māyā-śakti* which is *bahiraṅga* or external and never affects his true self. This *māyā-śakti* causes the creation, sustenance and dissolution of the phenomenal world, and consists of an aspect of *bahiraṅga vaibhava* or extraneous power in the form of the material *prakṛti* or *pradhāna*. Although unconnected with the essential self, this energy is as real as the other, and not a power of illusion such as the Advaita-vādins presume; the resulting phenomanal world therefore is also relatively real. Through this *māyā-śakti, the Bhagavat* limits himself into his partial manifestation as the Paramātman, who is thus the godhead immanent in spirit (*jīva*) and nature (*prakṛti*). It must be admitted that a *śakti* cannot stand by itself, it must inhere in a body; in this sense the Bhagavat is much as the substratum of the *svarūpa-śakti* as of the *māyā-śakti* and in the form of the Paramātman the Bhagavat is a direct displayer of *māyā-śakti.* But this *śakti* is said to be extraneous to his essence or *svarūpa,* because this self-determined limitation does not exist in his highest form as the Bhagavat and is not the diverting influence of the *māyā-śakti* by the power of *bhakti*, which is an aspect of the display of the *svarūpa-śakti.* Thus, the highest form of the deity is uncontaminated by the *māyā-śakti*, and that highest uncontaminated form, therefore, can be attained only when the *jīva* is no longer under the bondage created by the *māyā-śakti.* The *taṭasthā* or *jīva-śakti* is, as the name itself implies, that form of the divine energy which, being distinct from both, does not fall under either of the above categories of *antaraṅga* and *bahiraṅga śaktis*, and which is yet related to both. The *jīva* or individual self is an aspect of this *śakti* which the Bhagavat displays in his role of Paramātman. Being subject to the *māyā-śakti*, the *jīva* cannot, until released, be connected with the *svarūpa-śakti*, which is beyond the affection of the *māyā-śakti*; but since the Bhagavat is the ultimate essential source of the *jīva*, who can in spite of deviation return to the Lord by shaking off the *māyā-śakti*, the *jīva* can yet be finally connected with the essential *svarūpa-śakti*. Hence to explain the nature and position of the *jīva* it is necessary to presume an intermediate *taṭasthā śakti* which is connected with, but distinct from, both the *antarāṅga (svarūpa)* and *bahiraṅga* (*māyā*) *śaktis*.

"Thus, in the highest form of the Bhagavat there is a direct and full display of his *svarūpa-śakti*, which goes to make up his *svarūpa* or perfect self.The other two *śaktis* are displayed indirectly through the medium of his partial form of Paramātman. In other words, these two *śaktis* have scope only when the *jīva* is in the earlier deluded (*vimohita*) stage, but when it attains the Bhagavat himself, the *jīva* is subject only to the *svarūpa-śakti* of the Lord, of which *bhakti* is a function. The highest form of the Bhagavat himself is indifferent to the work of the Paramātman or the other two *śaktis*, which give rise to creation, rebirth and bondage; but this indifference implies that the Bhagavat possesses the attribute of impartial benevolence to all. The delusion (*saṃmohana*) of the *jīva* produced by the *māyā-śakti* is not in itself pleasing to the Lord, and in his highest form of the Bhagavat he has nothing to do with it; but it is due to the *jīva's* natural averseness (*bahirmukhatā*) to the Bhagavat. This disinclination at a lower stage is due again to the deity's *taṭasthā jīva-śakti*, which is equally prone to his intrinsic *svarūpa-śakti* and to his extrinsic *māyā-śaktis*. But the question arises–why should the Bhagavat, who is merciful to the *jīva*, permit this act of delusion by the *māyā-śakti* which is a cause of suffering? The reply is that the *māyā*, as a *śakti*, having power over creation, is as such an eternal servant of the Lord, towards whom it is not possible for him to assume a hostile attitude; but as the Lord is at the same time full of mercy for the *jīva* he desires that the *jīva* should for fear of *māyā* take refuge in him and work for deliverance. As for the ultimate question of the reason for or necessity of such complicated display of three kinds of energy, the answer is that it is an aspect of his inscrutable (*acintya*) *līlā* or divine sport, and the existence and character of the threefold *śakti*, as explained above, are facts vouched for by the *Bhāgata* [*Purāṇa*] and other scriptures. If one objects to the absurdity of imagining two contradictory *śaktis* residing in the deity, the reply is that the Lord's power is inscrutable and even contradictions merge in him.

"The *svarūpa-śakti,* viewed in its different aspects, is classified, on the authority of the *Viṣṇupurāṇa,* into *saṃdhinī, saṃvit* and *hlādinī śaktis*, which correspond roughly to the *sat, cit* and *ānanda* of orthodox philosophy. The *saṃdhinī śakti* is the energy of existence of the self-existent being which also upholds the existence of the *jīva* and *prakṛti*. It is in relation to this *śakti* that the Bhagavat is described as the ultimate reality, and the world and the individual as relative reality. By the *saṃvit śakti,* the Bhagavat is both the knowledge and the knower, and makes others possessed of knowledge. The last, *hlādinī śakti* is the Bhagavat's energy of infinite bliss, by which he is bliss itself, becomes blissful and also causes in the devotee pure bliss. These *śaktis* exist infinitely in the Bhagavat; but since the *jīva* is only an *aṇu* or infinitesimal part of the Bhagavat, the smallest atom of the timeless divine existence, knowledge and bliss is capable of causing the existence knowledge and bliss of the *jīva.*

"All these aspects of the *svarūpa-śakti* are regarded as collateral attributes, existing inseparably and eternally in the Bhagavat; they are yet graded ina peculiar manner. Although in their totality they form the very self of the Bhagavat and therefore constitue an undifferentiated unity, yet of *saṃdhinī*, *saṃvit* and *hlādinī*, each succeeding *śakti* is supposed to include and supersede the preceding. The *hlādinī śakti*, therefore, is the most important, as it includes and transcends the other two. This prominence given to the *hlādinī śakti* explains the peculiar standpoint of Bengal Vaiṣṇavism which conceives that its deity is essentially composed of infinite bliss, which is his highest attribute and which necessarily involves the other attributes of knowledge and existence. By this *śakti* also he has the power of communicating atoms of this infinite bliss to his associates (*pārṣadas*) and his devotees (*bhaktas*). It must be noted in this connection that the *svarūpa-śakti* is supposed to take two forms, namely, (i) the *svarūpa*, which refers to the Lord himself, and (ii) *svarūpa-vaibhava*, which includes his associates, his residence, his devotees etc., which are thus parts or functions of himself. The theory which gives exclusive prominence to the *hlādinī śakti* may, therefore, be expressed in theological language by saying that this is the eternal *līlā* or divine sport of the Lord, which consists of pure and infinite bliss and which he enjoys with his associates and devotees; for they are merely aspects of his divine energy, and their very existence, consciousness and bliss are relative to the absolute existence, consciousness and bliss of the Lord. This brings us to the idea, to which we shall revert later on, of the Lord as *rasa* or *ānanda* which attribute is nothing but an aspect of the *hlādinī śakti*. This *rasa*, which constitutes the *svarūpa* of the Lord, must be taken ultimately to signify the highest and best *rasa* recognized by the Vaiṣṇava *bhaktiśāstra* of this school, namely, *mādhurya* or *madhura rasa,* which is another name of the religiously sublimated erotic sentiment. This attitude is a kind of erotic mysticism, which seeks to express religious ideas in the intimate language of earthly passion, for it conceives divine love as a reflex of the human emotion. The *śaktimat* in his infinite bliss sports with his own *śaktis*; in other words, the godhead realizes himself in his own bliss. The *śakti* is accordingly represented, in terms of human relationships considered in its emotional aspect, as his consorts or wives; and this devout yet sensuous attitude entirely humanizes the deity and his consorts and presents them in a lovable human relation to their associates and devotees. As the Lord is not only infinite bliss himself but he also makes others enjoy the bliss, the *bhakti* or ecstatic devotion, by means of which a taste of this infinite bliss is attained, is also an aspect or function of the *hlādinī śakti*. We shall see presently in the *Śrīkṛṣṇasandarbha* that as Kṛṣṇa is identified with the Bhagavat, Rādha, who is his eternal consort and greatest *bhakta* is represented as the highest form of his *hlādinī śakti*.

"This brings us to the question of the nature of the relation of the *śaktis* to the *śaktimat*. As the *jīva* is also an aspect of the divine *jīva-śakti*, the relation is the same as that between the *jīva* and *paramātman*; and the question accordingly assumes importance as one of the fundamental metaphysical questions regarding the relationship of the individual to the universal self. We shall have occasion to deal with the question from this point of view in connection with its treatment in the *Paramātma-sandarbha*; but we may briefly indicate here that the relation between the *śaktis* and the possessor of the *śaktis* is represented as an incomprehensible (*acintya*) relation of sameness and difference (*bhedābheda*). The whole theory thus receives the designation of Acintyabhedābhedavāda (incomprehensible dualistic monism), a peculiar point of view which distinguishes the Bengal school from other Vaiṣṇava schools by the qualifying word *acintya* which brings in a myštical attitude. It speaks of the inconceivable existence of distinction and non-distinction. The *śaktis* are non-different from the Bhagavat, inasmuch as they are parts or *aṃśas* of the diving being; but the very fact that they are part only makes the superlativeness of divine attributes inapplicable to them, and there is thus an inevitable difference. The *śaktis*, therefore, possess a reality which is indeed relative to that of the Lord but which is nevertheless absolute in itself. The respective character of the reality, however, of the three kinds of *śakti*, namely *anaraṅgā*, *bahiraṅgā* and *taṭasthā*, is not, as their names are designed to imply, entirely identical. This distinction has already been explained above, but it is also illustrated by an analogy. It is like the threefold aspect in which the sun manifests itself, namely, the solar disc (*maṇḍala*), the solar rays (*raśmi*) and the solar reflection or halo (*bimba*), *antaraṅgā* or *svarūpa-śakti* corresponding to the luminous disc or body of the sun itself, the *taṭasthā* or *jīva-śakti* to its rays scattered away but ultimately contained in the sun itself as their original source, and the *bahiraṅga* or the *māyā-śakti* being regarded as the reflection which is a real but dazzling emanation from the solar disc, obscuring it, but existing outside and not forming an integral part of the sun.

"Although this is the principal classification of the *śakti*s, they are said to be infinite in number, and all of them are presented as wives of the Lord. As such they are distinctive deities, having name, form and personality. The *antaraṅgā mahāśakti* of the Lord is Lakṣmī or Mahālakṣmī, who forms his *svarūpa* and, being the first manifestation, is the ground or *āśraya* of all other *śakti*s. The *bahiraṅhā śakti* is of course named *māyā*. Each othese again has many aspects and is named accordingly. The text mentions only some of the aspects of Mahālakṣmī as *svarūpa-śakti*; but each of them can also have an additional significance as aspects of the *bahiraṅga māyā-śakti*. Thus Śrī as an aspect of Mahālakṣmī signifies divine excellence or *bhagavat-sampad*; but Śrī as an aspect of *māyā* means worldly excellence or *jagat-sampad* " (More examples of such aspects are given.)

"This conception of inherent *śakti*s in the Lord naturally presents the idea of the Bhagavat as the perfect person, and conceives him not as a formless entity but as an embodied substance in which inhere infinite attributes and energies. Scriptural texts are cited in which the supreme being is described as *cid-ghana, ānanda-ghana, rasa-ghana* etc., and it is maintained that the word *ghana* (=compact or solid) implies the idea of *mūrti* or image, in accordance with the dictum *mūrtau ghanaḥ* of Pāṇini. The Lord is therefore not *amūrta* or unembodied, but possesses a blessed *mūrti* or form. It is, however, clearly explained that by this form or body of the Lord, his *mūrti* or *vigraha,* is not to be understood any gross or sensuous body like that of human beings. The limited limbs and senses of the *jīva* are due to the *jīva-śakti* only, and therefore they are phenomenal (*prākṛta*) and material (*jaḍa*); but the Lord in his *svarūpa-śakti* possesses a non-phenomenal and spiritual body. This body consists entirely of pure existence, knowledge and bliss, and he is therefore called *saccidānana-vigraha*. As there is no distinction of form and essence (*avagata-bheda*) in the Bhagavat, there is no differentiation between the different organs, so that existence, knowledge and bliss, which constitute his form, are eternally simultaneous and non-different from his essence. The divine person (*vigraha*) is therefore identical with the divine essence (*svarūpa*) in the supreme unity of the godhead. The attributes, like intelligence, bliss, etc., are merely terms or symbols to indicate aspects of his essence; and thus totality is called form or body because of its eternally self-manifest character (*vyūha*). His body, or what may be called his body, is his soul; it is eternal, supernatural and spiritual and has nothing gross, natural and material in it; but at the same time it is not *nirviśeṣa* or undifferentiated, it is something real and *saviśeṣa* possessing its own divine attributes. He is *vi-karaṇa* in the sense that he does not possess the human organs or senses, but he is also *sa-karaṇa* in the sense that he possesses divine or non-natural forms of these. The *śruti* texts establish that this body is like that of the human being, but the similarity is only in respect of form and not of the ingredients. The Lord is not subject to change (*vikāra-rahita*) or limitation, but by his *svarūpa-śakti* he can limit himself into a conditioned or unconditioned form. Hence it follows that Kṛṣṇa as the

Bhagavat never entered into a gross body like an ordinary *jīva*, but only appeared to do so. This divine form is no doubt unthinkable, but for purposes of meditation or devotion it is thinkable The scriptures describe the form sometimes as two-handed, sometimes as four-handed, or even six-handed or eight-handed, and as possessing head, eyes, feet etc. The assumption of these various forms does not imply impermanence or changefulness, for they are all real and eternal (*nitya*) and coexist in him, like the diverse forms of a *vaidurya-maṇi* (*lapis lazuli*), which make their appearance simultaneously. But Jīva Gosvāmin cites authorities to show that, although no particular divine form exists apart from his other forms, the two-handed form of the divinity, of which presumably man is the image, is the best and most beautiful for purposes of meditation and worship; for it exhibits his attributes to their best advantage.

"The Lordship of the Bhagavat which is described above is thus intrinsic to his selfhood; and the attributes and energies have no touch of gross quality in them, but inhere in his essential character (*svarūpa-bhūta*). The *vigraha* or the form of the Bhagavat is not someting different from his essence but is eternally identical with it (*pūrva-svarūpa-bhūta*) and therefore possessed of essential reality. It follows from this that when the Lordship of *vibhutva* is manifested in the sense of an *avatāra*, it is also intrinsic, real and eternal, even if the *avatāra* seemingly belongs to a past age. The Lord is unborn, but when we speak of his birth, only appearance or *prādurbhāva* is meant. Though the appearance occurs in the phenomenal world, it is itself not phenomenal but an expression at will of his essential divine *svarūpa*. Although the chief *vigraha*of the Bhagavat is one, he is capable of assuming simultaneously infinite forms. whether these forms be mere *prakāśas, āvirbhāvas* or *avatāras*; hence his attribute of *sarva-rūpa-svabhāvatva* or the capacity of assuming all kinds of forms and shapes. Even when the deity assumes phenomenal forms, he retains his non-phenomenal *svarūpa*.

But he appears to the devotee in the form or plane of realization which has been attained by the latter's devotion. it is, however, laid down that the deity always appears only in the form which is agreeable to his devotee. If he appeared in the disagreeable form of an ox to Rantideva, that form was illusory (*māyika*), for what is supersensuous cannot be horrible.

"Having established the general character of the Bhagavad-*vigraha*, Jīva Gosvāmin now proceeds to analyze in detail some of its special characteristics. These attributes are not something imposed from outside but they form invariable (*avyabhicāri*) aspects of the divine essence and therefore they are the deity's inherent attributes (*svābhāvika dharma*). These may be briefly summarized here as forming the constituent elements of the concept of Lordship: (1) The attribute of all-pervasiveness (*pūrva gatatva*), by means of which the Bhagavat cannot only pervade the universe, but, in spite of being one, he can appear as many at different places, not in a different but in the same form. This, we are told, is not *kāya-vyūha*, or mere illusory multiplication of the same form, all of which are in the same way in different places; for here, though the various forms are the same they can act in different ways. Each of these appearances thus is not illusory but real, and has the same divine characteristics and capacity of independent nature. In other words each appearance (*prakāśa-bheda*) has different egoism (*abhimāna-bheda*) and different series of act (*kriyā-bheda*), and this may occur simultaneously at the same or different places. (2) The attribute of self-luminosity or self-manifestation (*svaprakāśatva*). (3) The attribute of surpassing both the gross and the subtle (*sthūla-sūkṣmatiriktatva*), implying also the fact that the Lord is beyond mundane existence (*sat*) and non-essence (*asat*). (4) Non-liability to change or limitation (*avikāritva*). This attribute implies that the Lord is not subject to the six *vikāras* or forms of evolution, viz., *janman* (birth), *astitva* (existence), *vṛddhi* (growth), *parināma* (transformation), *kṣaya* (decay) and *vināśa* (destruction). He is also independent of the fourfold fruit of action (*caturvidha-kriyā-phala-rāhitya*), namely, *utpatti* (production), *prāpti* (acquisition), *vivṛti* (expansion) and *saṃskāra* (fruition or merit). (5) Possession of indwelling spirit-form (*pratyag-rūpatva*), not visible to the mortal eye. Hence he is the *antaryānin* or the inward ruler, and is called *adhokṣaja*, which term is explained as signifying that he exists beyond perception of the senses. He can be seen or perceived only in virtue of his own energy (*nija-śaktitaḥ*), and this energy comes into play only through his grace. (6) Non-liability to mundane (*prākṛta*) birth (*janman*), form (*rūpa*) and action (*karman*), but also the capacity of assuming all these in a vast and eternal character (*nitya*) by his *svarūpa-śakti.* We are told that such assumption of birth, though real and eternal in character (*nitya*), constitutes only an *āvirbhāva* and not actual mundane or human birth, but it either resembles mundane birth or is sometimes different from it. In other words, the appearance assume in the phenomenal world is really non-phenomenal, although in all respects it may appear as phenomenal. The deity is really *svayaṃ-rūpa*, that is, his form is identical with his essence; hence if he assumes the attributes of birth, childhood etc., these are not phenomenal, but attributes of his inherent divine nature. Of the same character is the form (e.g., *matsya*) which is assumed in an *avatāra*; and this form, as well as the exploits of an *avatāra*, he can assume or discard at will. In the same way, his *karman* or action is not guided by any motive, inasmuch as the Bhagavat is motiveless (*āpta-kāma*), but it is due to his *ānanda* or *hlādinī-śakti.* It is an aspect of his *līlā* or divine sport which is natural to his essence of bliss. As Baladeva Vidyābhūṣaṇa explains the idea in his *Govindabhāṣya*: that the most complete should proceed to the act of diversified creation is due to his *līlā*, which is not preceded by any desire of the fruits of action for himself. Jīva Gosvāmin further explains that this *līlā* arises from the awakening of the bliss intrinsic to the deity, and it has no reference to any particular motive of himself.

"In this way Jīva Gosvāmin proceeds to analyze the concept of Lordship or *bhagavatā* and discusses in detail the various divine attributes which constitute its principal features. One of the interesting points which he deals with as a fundamental creed of his school is the theory of the efficacy and diversity of the blessed name itself (*nāma-māhātmya*). The theory is based partly on the old doctrine of the eternity of sound; but the Bengal school goes a step further in maintaining the essential identity of the name and the possessor of the name (*nāma-nāminor abhedaḥ*). In other words, he believes that the name itself is the essence of the Lord, so that one who utters the name with devotion attains the Lord himself. Not only the name but even the syllable (*akṣara*) or its symbol (*saṃketa*); for instance, the syllable *om*) are enough to produce the same effect. Just like the *avatāras* of the Lord, this is a kind of *varṇa-avatāra*. The deity, however, is often called nameless or *anāman* in the scriptures, but this usage is on a par with the employment of terms like birthless (*ajanman*), formless (*arūpa*) or actionless (*akartṛ*). It does not mean that he has no name but that his name is *aprākṛta* or *aprasiddha*; that is, his name is not like the common names we have in the phenomenal world, but it possesses a spiritual significance and efficacy. It is for this reason that the name or names which have been established in the *śāstras* as bringing the Bhagavat himself instantaneously into consciousness are alone appropriate, and not those which are merely imaginary. In the same way Jīva Gosvāsmin speaks of the color which is appropriate to the deity, for the colored figuration of deities plays an important part in sectarian devotion in general. He informs us that the particular colors of the deity are not due to the presence of particular *guṇas*. The dark (*kṛṣṇa*) color of the Bhagavat does not indicate *tamoguṇa*, but it is a peculiar suggestion of his *svarūpa-śakti* (*svarūpa-śakti-vyañjitatvam*). The white color is often taken to signify *sattvaguṇa*, but the color of the Indian crane (*baka*), a bird which is proverbial for its cunning and its tendency to mischief, is white.

"Jīva Gosvāmin concludes this topic by summing up that all this assumption by the Lord of birth, form, action, name and color has no motive behind it, but they are to manifest his *svarūpa-śākti* and make his devotee enjoy its bliss; for the *bhakti* or devotional attitude itself is an aspect of his peculiarly wonderful nature which consists of the display of intrinsic bliss. If one argues that the Lord has no form, name, birth and color, this very argument would tend to put a limitation to his unlimited *śakti*. It is by *bhakti* alone, and not by Sāṃkhya and Yoga, that the true character of the Lord is attained. That the divine *vigraha* is the Bhagavat himself has been realized and testified to by great sages. This intuition of the great sages or *mahad-anubhava* is said to be the only true *pramāṇa* (*satya-pramāṇam*). For these great men are really *āveśa-avatāras* who, being inspired by the Lord, themselves partake of the nature of his *vigraha*. So also do his particular manifestations, his *aṃśas* or his *guṇāvatāras*; and their appearance possesses the same eternal, real and supernatural characteristics. But the Lord himself in his supreme form is far superior to all these.

"From the theory described above that the supreme deity is the perfect person, having a peculiar form and a characteristic set of attributes, it follows that he also has a transcendental dwelling place, distinctive color, decoration and association peculiar to himself as a personal god. Of his dark color we have spoken above. No doubt he dwells in the *jiva* or individual self and pervades the universe, but this is only in his partial aspect as the Paramātman. In his complete and perfect form as the Bhagavat he has a *dhāma* or residence far beyond the phenomenal world (*prapañcātīta*). His decorations are also transcendental and are a part of his divine essence. A symbolical meaning is therefore assigned to some of his ornaments; for instance, the *kaustubha* which the Lord bears on his breast is not a mundane precious stone, but typifies the *jīva-śakti.* Theses are thus manifestations of the deity's self assumed through his grace to his devotees, who alone have a beatific vision of them. All this is established by the vision of the great devotees, which is its only and true *pramāṇa,* In the same way the Vaikuṇṭha-loka (sometimes caled the Goloka or Mahā-vaikuṇṭha, to distinguish it from a lower Vaikuṇṭha,), which is his place of residence (*dhāma*), as well as his associates or attendants (*pārṣadas*), represents eternal and transcendental expression of his *svarūpa-śakti.* The word '*dhāma*' has also the sense of lustre, and is explained as the Lord's inherent power of manifestation; but as a personal god, the deity is represented as having a real, and not merely figurative, abode for the display of his *svarūpa*. This *loka,* which is conceived as the highest paradise of Bengal Vaiṣṇavism, cannot, on account of its being beyond phenomenal existence, be attained by *jñāna* or *karman.* Once attained there is no fall from it (*tato skhalanam*). Since it is beyond the phenomenal world, it follows that it cannot be attained by means of the three *guṇas*; it is therefore called *nirguṇa* or *guṇātīta*; for it is said in the *Bhāgavata [Purāṇa]* (xi.25.21) that by the *sattva-guṇa* men reach *svaraloka*, by the *rajoguṇa* the *naraloka* and by the *tamoguṇa naraka* or hell; but the *loka* of the Bhagavat is beyond the reach of these three *guṇas*. Hence it is eternal and beyond *prakṛti* (*prakṛteḥ param*) which is an effect of the *māyā-śakti*. It is consequently beyond the *māyā-śakti* itself, so that the *jīva* can never reach it as long as he is subject to that *śakti*. This *loka*, being an expression of the *svarūpa-śakti,* can be attained only by another aspect of the *svarūpa-śakti,* namely *bhakti*. Like the *vigraha* of the Bhagavat himself, his *loka,* which is thus really and eternally a part of himself, consists of the three attributes of *sat, cit* and *ānanda* (*saccidānana-rūpatva*). It is called by the Vedic name of Viṣṇupada, and it is higher than all other *lokas*, such as *svara-loka, śivaloka,* etc. Just as the form or *vigraha* of the Bhagavat makes its appearance in the world, so it is said that his *dhāma, pāda* or residence also sometimes makes its appearance. Although this appearance is real, it is usually not manifest (*aprakāśa*), but it becomes manifest only to the vision of the devotee who can always perceive the deity's eternal divine sport in his favorite earthly resorts like Dvāraka, Mathurā or Vṛndāvana.

"The above remarks apply also to the Pārṣadas or attendants and associates, who are the Lord's eternal retinue (*parikāra*) in his paradise, being parts of his own self (*sadaṅgabhūta*) and expressions of his intrinsic *ānanda* or *hlādinī śakti*. Thus, Śrī or Lakṣmī, his eternal consort, is, as we have already noticed, inseparable from his *svarūpa-śakti* (*svarūpānatiriktatvam*). The subject is treated in detail in the *Śrīkṛṣṇasandarbha;* but in the present connection Jīva Gosvāmin points out that to the deity's *pārṣadas* the bliss of worship (*bhajānanda*) is greater than the bliss they enjoy from their being merged in the divine self (*svarūpānanda*). The theory of this school is that release does not mean cessation from devotional activity; even these emancipated souls who are the deity's *pārṣadas* engage in an eternal worship of the Bhagavad-*vigraha*. They desire only a taste of his *mādhurya*, and not of his *brahmatva*, because it is the nature of the *vigraha* of the Bhagavat, which consists of bliss to make others enjoy that bliss (*sukhadatva*) as a *vilāsa* of his *svarūpa-śakti*.

"This last position Jīva Gosvāmin now attempts to establish by reverting to his original topic of the distinction between the two forms of the deity, namely Brahman and Bhagavat. The distinction is not a distinction of one into two, for the concept of ultimate reality is one and indivisible; nor is it a mere difference in designation according to difference of appearance. It is due to the deity's inherent power of *viśeṣa* or differentiation, by which there is a consciousness of difference even when there is no actual difference and by which the same substance appears as different. It must not, however, be supposed that the Lord's possession of *viśeṣa* necessarily makes him conditioned or qualified, for the possession of an infinity of attributes is the reason why he cannot be qualified or conditioned by any one of them. The relation of Brahman to Bhagavat is thus one of difference in non-difference. The distinction arises from the stage of degree of realization of the two kinds of devotee whose capacities are different and who follow different paths of *jñāna* and *bhakti* according to their respective capacity of worship. But the manifestation of the Bhagavat-form is said to be superior to that of the undifferentiated Brahma-form, because in the former state of realization the true self of the deity in its perfection is revealed through a complete display of his *svarūpa-śakti* or intrinsic energy. In the Brahma-form the full and special character of the deity is not reached; even the *prakāśa* of Brahman is not independent but due to the *śakti* of the Bhagavat. It must not be supposed that the vision of the one form is real and the other unreal, for the authority of the scriptures shows both to be real; nor should the one be regarded as a part of the other through the function of transformation or *vikāra*. The two forms in their essence are identical, but the apparent difference is due to a difference of vision based upon a difference of the mode of worship. In the one case, where the deity reveals himself in his undifferentiated state of Brahman, the vision is incomplete (*asampūrṇā dṛṣṭi*); in the other case, where the vision takes in the full *vigraha* of the Bhagavat, accompanied by all his *śakti*s which form his essence, it is perfect (*sampūrṇā*). For this full or proper vision (*saṃyag-darśarśaṇa*) we are told that *bhakti* is the only means, for *bhakti* is due to a display of the deity's *svarūpa-śakti* itself. This, therefore, establishes the superiority of the *bhakti* mode of worship to every other mode; for according as the deity reveals himself in his twofold aspect as Brahman and the Bhagavat, his *svarūpa-śakti* reveals itself correspondingly as *jñāna* and *bhakti*. The way of *jñāṇa* is indeed not wholly rejected, but since the Bhagavat is spoken of as the *aṅgin* (principal) and Brahman as *aṅga* (subordinate), the *brahmānubhava* or perception of Brahma is included (*antargata*) in the perception of the Bhagavat. But, at the same time, in the direct realization of the Bhagavata through *bhakti*, the realization of Brahman is not distinct (*na sphutaḥ*) and therefore superfluous. The bliss arising from the Brahmavāda is entirely merged in the superior bliss of Bhagavad-*darśana*. Hence it is maintained that devotional worship or *bhakti* for the Bhagavat is superior to the release or *mokṣa* consequent upon the knowledge or *jñāna* of Brahman. It is for this reason, as already noted above, that even the emancipated souls make light of mere *mokṣa* and delight in the continuous worship of the Bhagavat (*bhajanānanda*).

"Having established the superiority of *bhakti* to *jñāna*, Jīva Gosvāmin maintains that the scriptures which speak of *bhakti* are superior to the scriptures which speak of *jñāna*; that is, the devotional texts are superior to those which are merely philosophical. For, those scriptures which are inspired by *bhakti* lead to the Bhagavat, those which are actuated by *jñāna* lead to Brahman. It is true that Brahman being an appearance of the Bhagavat, scriptures like the Upaniṣads which lead to Brahman may also lead ultimately to the Bhagavat, yet, Brahman, being an imperfect appearance, the scriptures, which speak of Brahman, only dimly and incompletely perceive the true character of the Bhagavat. It follows from all th is that the *Śrīmad-bhagavat* is the greatest and the most authoritative of all scriptures because, apart from its other causes of greatness, it has for its exclusive theme the Bhagavat-*tattva* which is the greatest of the *tattvas*. It is superior to both the *jñāna-kāṇḍa* and the *upāsanā-kāṇḍa* of the Vedas, not only for the reason stated above, but also because its *ṛṣi*-author was an incarnation of the Bhagavat himself, than whom a greater author cannot be found (*parama-śreṣtha-kartṛtva*), and the direct beatific vision of the deity (*bhagavat-sākṣātjāra*) is described in the work itself. Hence all desirous of attaining the highest spiritual truth should constantly listen to it.

"In this connection Jīva Gosvāmin interprets the real purport of the four verses known as *Catuḥślokī* (vii.9.32-35), which speak of the Bhagavat, and form the keynote of the *Bhagavata(-Purāṇa)* itself. He explains that divine love is here called *rahasya* or secret (ii.9.30) because it consists of an indescribable blissful attitude which manifests by itself, and remains invariably inclined toward the *bhakta*. The Bhagavat as the ultimate reality is really indeterminable (*anirdeśya*), and even the Vedas cannot properly reveal him. But the secret is revealed by *sādgaba* (worship) and *preman* (love), which are phases of *bhakti*. Jīva Gosvāmin in this connection only briefly refers to the topics of *sādhana-bhakti* and *prema-bhakti*, which are dealt with more fully in his *Prītisandarbha*. The *sādhana-bhakti* is to be learnt from one's spiritual preceptor and from the injunctions of the *śāstras*, but *prema-bhakti* develops spontaneously through divine grace. By the *sādhana-bhakti brahmajñāna* is possible, but the Bhagavat is attainable by *prama-bhakti* alone. The meritorious acts prescribed by the Vedas, however, may lead one in the way of *sādhana-bhakti*, and in this manner he becomes better fitted for the highest *prema-bhakti*. The Bhagavat is thus the *samanvaya* or the synthesis of all *śāstras*, and he is in fact the supreme import of all the Vedas (*sarva-vedārthatva*). Hence, the sacred scriptures which give an account of the Bhagavat (*bhagavat-kathā*) have an efficacy the importance of which cannot be exaggerated."

7.3 JĪVA GOSVĀMIN, *Paramātmasandarbha/Saṃvādinī*

The following is found in De 1961, pp. 297-314. There is also a summary in Chatterjee 1972. For further material cf. Bib 3,#1011.8.

Summary by Sushil Kumar De

"The concept of the Paramātman, which is the main theme of this *sandarbha*, may be briefly described as the concept of the godhead in relation to nature (*prakṛti*) and spirit (*jīva*). In relation to the concept of Brahman, which implies the indiscrete and unconditioned (*nirviśeṣa*) absolute, the concept of the Paramātman indicates a particular conditioned (*saviśeṣa*) state; but in relation to the concept of the infinitely conditioned perfect person implied in the concept of the Bhagavat, the Paramātman is not a complete but a partial manifestation, having relation chiefly to the *māyā-śakti* and the *jīva-śakti*. In a passage in his *Kramasandarbha*, which is repeated in his *Bhaktisandarbha*, Jīva Gosvāmin concisely sums up the three concepts thus: 'By Brahman is termed pure consciousness which is other than that of the particular attributes characterized by the group of *śaktis*; the Paramātman indicates consciousness conditioned by (the *jīva-śakti* which is) a part of the abundant *cit-śakti*, and by the *māyā-śakti*, which consists of the function of inward regulation (in all beings); the Bhagavat is the consciousness conditioned by the complete and perfect manifestation of all the *śaktis*". It would follow from this that the Paramātman has two aspects, namely, *bhagavadaṅgatva* in relation to the *jīva*, and *jagadgatatva* in relation to *prakṛti* or *pradhāna*. In other words, the Paramātman is that phase of the godhead which is immanent, on the one hand, in the conscious *jīva*, and on the other in the non-conscious or material *prakṛti*.

"The necessity for postulating these concepts is not difficult to understand. For a theistic sectarian faith which believes in a personal god, the concept of the Bhagavat as a person is a philosophical necessity and justification; while the Advaitic concept of *nirviśeṣa* Brahman has to be recognized and reconciled, from its sectarian point of view, as a lower manifestation, vouchsafed to the religiously defective but intellectually keen seekers after spiritual truth. The reason for the third concept of the Paramātman is somewhat more complex. The idea of the *antaryāmin* as the inward ruler is Upaniṣadic and Deussen is probably right in thinking that from this idea developed the concept of a personal god in later theistic systems, in which the idea is, as here implicitly recognized. The term as well as the underlying idea of the Paramātman in relation to the *jīvātman,* in which is also absorbed the idea of the evolution of *prakṛti,* is a legacy of older philosophical systems. The difficulties, however, of the Advaita doctrine of *māyā* and of its highly monistic and idealistic interpretation of the relation of the *jīva* to Brahman made these theories unacceptable in their entirety to the dualistic school which Jīva Gosvāmin represents. As the school believed, somewhat in the Sāṃkhya manner, in the relative reality of the world, the Vedāntic theory of the unreality of the illusory world was not consistent with its dualistic position. To obviate these difficulties and to reconcile the traditional ideas mentioned above with its own view of a personal god, the deity in the lower form of the Paramātman had to be endowed with two real and eternal *śakti*s in relation to the *jiva* and *prakṛti,* the working of which, however, is supposed not to affect the essential selfhood of the god, just in the same way as the Advaita-vādin's *māyā* does not affect the personal and unconditioned Brahman

"The theme of the present *sandarbhas* is, therefore, the consideration of the relation of the *jīva* and *prakṛti* to the Paramātman and the corresponding functions of *jīva-śakti* and *māyā-śakti,* of which the Paramātman-form is, as it were, the presiding deity.

"We have alrerady see that the jīva is an expression of the *jīva-śakti* of the Bhagavat. This *śakti* is called *taṭasthā* or aloof, because it does not come under either of the categories of *svarūpa-śakti* and *māyā-śakti,* but is still closely connected with both. As the Bhagavat is the ground of the *jīva-śakti,* the *jīva* is indeed a part, albeit an influential part, of the Bhagavat; but as the *jīva* is liable to the influence of the *māyā-śakti* it cannot come directly under the *svarūpa-śakti* which is unaffected by this influence. But on account of its ultimate affinity with the Bhagavat, the *jīva* even in bondage has the inherent capacity of releasing itself; and when emancipated, it becomes a part of the *svarūpa-śakti* and is placed eternally beyond the influence of the *māyā-śakti.* This release, we have seen, comes through *bhakti,* which itself is an expression of the *hlādinī* or blissful aspect of the deity's *svarūpa-śakti;* but this topic will be dealt with in its proper place in the *Bhaktisandarbha.*

"This idea of the *jīva-śakti* will be clear from a consideration of the essential character of the *jīva.* In this connection Jīva Gosvṣmin quotes the authority of Jāmātmamuni who is said to have been a predecessor of Rāmānuja. This authority informs us that the *jīva* is neither a deity nor a man, nor a movable animal, nor an immovable plant; it is neither the body, nor the senses, nor the mind, nor life, nor intellect; it is neither an unconscious material object (*jaḍa*), nor liable to change nor yet consisting of mere consciousness; but, positively considered, a long list of distinguishing attributes can be predicated of it. It is self-luminous to itself (*svasmai svayaṃ-prakāśa*), uniform (*eka-rūpa*), possessing its own identity (*svarūpa-bhā*), conscious (*cetana*), having the attributes of pervading (*vyāpti-śīla*), consisting of *cit* and *ānanda* (*citānandātmaka*), subject of the consciousness of 'I' (*ahamartha*), different in different organisms (*pratikṣetraṃ bhinna*), atomic in size (*aṇu*), always pure (*nitya-nirmala*), possessing its own peculiar attributes of knowledge, action and enjoyment (*jñātṛtva-kartṛtva-bhoktṛtva-nīladharmaka*), and always possessing the natural tendency of resolving into a part of the Paramātman (*pramātmaika-śeṣa-svabhāva*).

"These terms will not be fully intelligible from the imperfect English rendering given above but will require some explanation to make them clear. From the negative characteristics described above the *jīva* appears to possesse two prominent attributes which are interrelated, namely, the attribute of unchangeableness and of retention of identity in the midst of difference. In other words, the *jīva* retains its identity in whatever individual existence it may lie, divine, human or otherwise. It is indeed an entity whose presence is brought about in the organic body by the *māyā-śakti,* but it is distinct from the several parts (the senses, the mind, body, etc.) of its receptacle. It is thus distinct from the body, and unlike the body it is not subject to change or decay; it is only through the *māyā-śakti* that the *jīva* in delusion identifies itself with the body. It is, however not a mere aggregate of (gross or phenomenal) consciousness *(jñānamātrātmaka na ca),* nor yet a production of material nature (*na jaḍa*). It is a single, permanent principle which manifests itself in and unifies a system of temporal and spatial states and activities, but is still different from this system and retains its identity through all these states and activities. This idealistic interpretation of the *jīva,* however, is not new, but its differentiation, by means of the *māyā-śakti,* as a subtle principle, which is neither mere consciousness nor mere unconsciousness, is presented in a way which is entirely peculiar to this dualistic school.

"Positively considered, the *jīva* possesses a large number of distinguishing characteristics, but since they are interconnected, they may be briefly explained under a few broad headings. One of the chief attributes of the *jīva* is that it is an entity which possesses consciousness (*cetana*). This must not be understood to mean that it is made up of a mass of gross consciousness alone, which view really resolves into a materialistic position, but that it is the underlying conscious principle itself. It follows from the acceptance of this attribute that the *jīva* is self-conscious, that is, it reveals itself to itself by its own consciousness; but it also has the capacity of revealing others. Its state of consciousness means that by its own consciousness it can stimulate the body, etc., into consciousness, like the light of a lamp which by revealing itself reveals others. This self-luminosity, however, cannot be in relation to the Paramātman, whose self-luminosity does not depend on anything else and from whom its ultimate illuminating power comes; but it is self-luminous in relation to material objects.

"But the *jīva* is atomic (*aṇu*), the word 'atom' meaning the smallest and finest indivisible entity conceivable. Hence the *jīva* is called 'a particle of atom of consciousness' (*cit-kaṇā* or *aṇu-cit*). And yet by virtue of its being a conscious principle it is capable of pervading the whole body (*vyāpana śīla*). In other words, it does not occupy space, yet pervades by consciousness the whole of the organism which it inhabits.

"This conscious principle is represented by the word 'I' and signifies the ego (*aham-artha*) but this *aham* is not the empirical ego (*prākṛta ahamkāra*), which is an act of material nature (*prakṛti*) upon the *jīva*. This consciousness, we have seen, is pure and indivisible, and is therefore to be distinguished from the ephemeral, diverse and impure consciousness given by the senses. This is what is meant by saying that the *jīva* is not a mere aggregate of consciousness given by the senses, but it is the essential conscious principle itself (*ipalabdhi-māntra* or *jñānaika-rūpa*). For, the *jīva* is beyond the reach of the body which is liable to change and decay (*vikāra* or *vyabhicāra*); it is the eternal witness as distinguished from the thing witnessed (*draṣṭṛ-dṛśya-bheda*). The true nature of this consciousness or the real ego can be realized in the state of dreamless sleep when the phenomenal consciousness (*ahaṃkāra*) is set at rest and the *jīva* remains as a self-conscious witness (*sākṣya-sākṣi-bheda*). This can also be inferred from the ordinary experience that the body is liable to suffering, but the *jīva* is always the object of divine love (*duḥkhi-premāspada-bheda*).

"It follows from the above characteristics of the *jīva* that it is always pure (*nitya-nirmala*), and this purity consists in the real ego, which is not affected by the impure effects of the *māyā-śakti*; for the *śuddha jīva* is said to be *māyātīta* or beyond the sphere of *māyā*. In relation to the body and the phenomenal world, however, its gross consciousness, which is the effect of the *māyā-śakti*, overpowers it and obscures its real nature even to itself. Even if the *jīva*, like the Bhagavat, consists of pure consciousness (*cid-rūpa*), it is yet inferior to as well as different, in this respect, from the Bhagavat, who is eternally superior to and unaffected by his own extraneous *māyā-śakti*. But in its essence it is a part or *aṃśa* of the Bhagavat. Its liability to *māyā* and bondage in *saṃsāra*, as well as its individual separate existence even after emancipation, makes it different from the Bhagavat, both in *svarūpa* and *sāmarthya*; but it is at the same time identical in its intrinsic affinity with the Bhagavat who is its ultimate source. This peculiar relation of identity in difference is also expressed by the postulate that the *jīva* is a part of the Bhagavat conceived not as the ground of *svarupa-śakti*, but as the ground of *jīva-śakti*, which latter being a *taṭasthā śakti*, is different and yet closely connected with both the *svarūpa-śakti* and the *māyā-śakti*.

"From this point of view all *jīvas* have been classified into two groups, viz. (i) those who are eternally inclined to the Bhagavat and naturally susceptible to his *svarūpa-śakti*, and (ii) those who are eternally adverse to him and therefore naturally prone to the *māyā-śakti*. The former are still *taṭastha* like the latter, and are *jīvas* who cannot be included in the category of *īśvara*, but they possess in a greater degree the capacity of releasing themselves. Possessing in a potential state the intrinsic attributes of consciousness and bliss, which are also divine attributes, they are easily disposed to the influence of the deity's highest *svarūpa-śakti*. Those coming under the second group become, on account of their hostile attitude, an easy prey to the *māyā-śakti* and its bondage, and are therefore overwhelmed into rebirth (*saṃsāra*), from which their only way of release is through *bhakti*; for *bhakti* brings them again under the influence of the *svarūpa-śakti* of the Bhāgavat.

"From the dualistic conclusion that the *jīva*, in spite of its essential identity, is yet different and has a separate existence as an eternal spiritual atom, which continues even after emancipation, it follows that the *jīva* is not one but many. Our author does not believe in the extreme monistic theory that the Paramātman is the only so-called *jīva* (*eka-jīva-vāda*), the apparent multitude of *jīvas* being no other than the Paramātman. On the other hand, he appears to agree with Rāmānuja's interpretation of *Vedānta-sūtra* ii.3.48 that although the *jīva* is a part or *aṃśa* of the Paramātman, and is essentially of the same character as an entity, it is yet actually separate and resides in a separate *kṣetra* or sphere (*pratikṣetraṃ bhinna*). But, even admitting a plurality of *jīvas*, this school does not accept the theory of actionless *puruṣa* who only looks on and experiences the consequences of the acts of *prakṛti*. A dualitic view such as this school upholds cannot make the *jīva* altogether independent of the fruits of action, even though its extreme theistic leanings make it present a somewhat modified dualism and make all actions subordinate to the will of the Lord. In its view, therefore the *jīva* is both a knower and an agent, and an enjoyer of the fruits of his own *karman*. This capacity for activity as an agent is a permanent and inherent capacity, but the activity is not independent of divine control, inasmuch as the *jīva* is an eternal servant of the Lord.

"This intrinsic connection of the *jīva* with the Paramātman is indicated by the qualifying epithet *svataḥ sarvadā paramātmaika-śeṣa-svabhāva*; that is, the *jīva* has always the natural tendency of ultimately resorting to the Paramātman alone as its ground. From this divine source it receives not only its attribute of consciousness but also its attribute of bliss (*cidānandātmaka*), of which more will be said hereafter.

"Although the *jīvas* are many and separate they are yet related to one another. There is a sameness in all *jīvas* (*eka-rūpa-bhāk*) because of the *jīva*'s essential divine characteristics. Differences, however, arise, in the first place, from a difference in the nature of acts done in this or previous births, and which make each suffer weal or woe accordingly and possess different character. Apparently, this occurs in the phenomenal world; but even when bereft of the gross body and freed from the bondage of the *māyā-śakti*, the different *jīvas* occupy different positions as the *parikāra* or attendant of the Bhagavat in the hierarchy of spiritual existence, according to the difference in their respective devotional attitude.

"This brings us now to the consideration of the character of the *māyā-śakti* in relation to the *jīva* and the Bhagavat. The Vaiṣṇava idea of *māyā* as a *śakti*, even if it is presented as a *bahiraṅga* or extraneous *śakti*, is not the same as the Śaṃkarite idea of *māyā* as a kind of illusion, from which however the original idea might have been borrowed and assimilated. Enough has already been said above which would give the general idea of this *māyā-śakti*, but one of the principal themes of this *sandarbha* is to expand this idea and consider in detail the functions of this *śakti*. It is called *bahiraṅga* (outer or external) because it does not form an ingredient of the real or intrinsic selfhood of the Lord. As a *śakti* or energy, however, it is real, and its effects are also real, but as it appertains to the deity in his partial or incomplete manifestation and not in his true nature, it is felt only at a lower plane of existence. In a verse quoted from the *Bhāgavata* ix. 33 in the *Bhāgavatasandarbha*, the *śakti* is defined as

ṛte 'rthaṃ yat pratīyeta na partīyeta cātmani/
tad vidvād ātmano māyām/

According to the interpretation given by Jīva Gosvāmin the verse may be translated thus: "What would be perceived outside the substance, i.e., outside the intrinsic selfhood of the Lord, and what would not be perceived irrespectively of it, is called the Lord's own *māyā*." If the Lord in his essence is perceived, the *māyā* is not perceived; that is, the *śakti* is perceived outside hs self. But the *śakti* cannot be perceived by itself without the Lord as the substratum that is, as an energy it presupposes the idea of an energizing substance or being, and cannot stand by itself.

"The *mayā* as a *śakti* has been classified into *jīva-māyā*, which is also called *nimitta-māyā*, and *guṇa-māyā*, which is also called *upādāna-māyā*. This classification is based upon the two functions of the principle of causality, namely efficient and material causation, ascribed to the *māyā-śakti*; and each of the aspects has a reference respectively to the *jīva* and *prakṛti*, the individual self and material nature. In the first aspect, *māyā-śakti* obscures the pure consciousness of the *jīva*, and in the second it brings about the material world as a balance of the three *guṇas* or sometimes causes change or evolution of forms by disturbing the equilibrium of the three *guṇas*. Hence, *māyā* is called *sṛṣṭi-sthityanta-kartā* or the *śakti* which causes the creation, support and dissolution of the world; and in the Upaniṣads *māyā* is represented figuratively as tri-colored (*trivarṇa*), which term has a reference to the three *guṇas*.

"The function of the *nimitta-* or *jīva-māyā* is two-fold, consisting of science (*vidyā*) and ignorance (*avidyā*), the first causing emancipation and the second bondage. The *jīva* in itself is eternally self-conscious of its true nature and is therefore as *śuddha jīva* eternally emancipated (*svato mukta eva*); sometimes this consciousness is explicit (as in the case of eternally emancipated souls), but more often it is implicit or obscured (as in the case of those who are subject to ignorance caused by *māyā*). *Vidyā* is the gateway for the ingress of this implicit consciousness. It may be objected that if *vidyā* leads to deliverance it should be an aspect of the *svarūpa-śakti* and cannot be counted as an expression of *māyā-śakti*. But *vidyāvṛtti*, as a *māyā-śakti*[1], must be taken to imply that it is not a form of the supreme consciousness itself but only a door or opening to the revelation of that consciousness which is an aspect of the *svarūpa-śakti*; and it cannot by itself make that

[1]The word is thus used in a sense somewhat different from what is understood in orthodox philosophy. *Vidyā* may be two-fold, being a function of both the *svarūpa-* and *māyā-śaktis*. (SKD)

revelation. *Avidyā* or ignorance has, again, a two-fold function, namely, (i) it acts as a covering which causes the concealment of the true nature of the *jīva* (*ācaraṇātmikā*), and (ii) it acts as a source of distraction (*vikṣepātmikā*), which overpowers the *jīva* by causing a conflicting consciousness in the form of the empirical experience of the body and the senses.

"The *jīva-māyā* or *nimitta-māyā*, as the source of efficient causation, involves the four concepts of *kāla, daiva, karman* and *svabhāva*, which terms are now briefly explained. *Kāla* is described as the *kṣobhaka* or source of provocation; and a verse from the *Bhāgavata [Purāṇa]* (iii.5.26) is quoted to show that by this function the Paramātman, in erotically figurative imagery, places the seed of creation in the *guṇamatī māyā*. It follows from this description that the *kāla* is not a substance but only a function or mode (*vṛtti*) of the Paramātman as the dispenser of the *māyā-śakti*, by which the equilibrium of the three *guṇas* in *prakṛti* is disturbed and effects are brought about. It thus regulates in a sense the process of creation but is in its turn regulated by the Paramātman; it has therefore no effect on the Bhagavat, who is eternally beyond *kāla*. *Karman* is described as the *nimitta* or efficient cause of the disturbance, and constitutes acts done not by the real ego but by the empirical ego in phenomenal existence, causing rebirth and bondage. Such acts, therefore, as devotional worship, which proceed from the real ego of the *jīva*, are not to be included in this category. The express proneness of *karman* for the production of consequences is called *daiva*. The *svabhāva* consists of impressions left by *karman* (*sat-saṃskāra*). The *jīva*, in its bondage to the *māyā-śakti*, is possessed of all these (*sadvān*).

"The *guṇa-māyā* or *upādāna-māyā*, as the source of material causation, consists of *dravya, kṣetras, prāna, ātman* and *vikāra*, which terms also require explanation. *Dravya* indicates the five elements in subtle states (*bhūtasūkṣmāni*); *kṣetra* is *prakṛti*; *prāṇa* means the vital principle, which is also called *vāyu*; the *ātman* is the gross consciousness or the *prākṛta ahaṃkāra* operated upon by the senses; and the *vikāra* consists of the five senses (*indriyāṇi*) and the five gross elements (*mahābhūtāni*), of which the *deha* or material body is a collective effect (*saṃghāta*), continuing in an uninterrupted stream like the sprout of seeds (*bīja-rohavat pravāha*). All these constitute in their totality the ingredients of material creation, which is the *upādāna* aspect of *māyā*, called *guṇa-māyā*. The *jīva* is related to it, as well as to the *jīva-māyā* described above. Primal matter is called indiscrete (*avyakta* or *avyākṛta*), because it is the equipoised condition of these constituents and of the *guṇas*. In itself it is unintelligent or unconscious, but creation proceeds only through the *īkṣaṇa* or look of the Lord, by which is perhaps meant this exercise of the *māyā-śakti* by the Paramātman. The state of equilibrium being thus disturbed, the three *guṇas* intermingle with one another and give rise to the manifold evolutes and effects ultimately producing the concrete and real world as a feat of the *māyā-śakti*. In spite of the professed adverse attitude of the school to the Sāṃkhya theory, the influence of Sāṃkhya ideas and the borrowing of its terminology are obvious. The school holds firmly to Sāṃkhya in regarding matter as a reality, and there is nothing specifically Vedāntic in its conception in this respect. *Māyā* is not matter itself as the Vedāntist believes, but it is a particular mode in which matter, which is a reality , is apprehended. But a theistic interpretation is given to this mode by regarding it as a cosmic effect of the Lord's energy or function which obscures the vision of the undevout to the ultimate reality. In relation to this ultimate reality, which is the Lord himself, matter must, however, be regarded not as an absolute reality, as Sāṃkhya maintains, but only a relative reality.

According to the views of the Bengal school, therefore, the creation of the world is not an instance of *vivarta* (illusory appearance) but an instance of *pariṇāma* (transformation). The theory of *vivarta*, which is a corollary from Śaṃkara's *māyā-vāda*, speaks of the illusory production of an effect (namely, the unreal world) from a real cause (namely Brahman), just as a serpent is a *vivarta* or illusory appearance of a rope. But the theistic Vaiṣṇava school believes in the reality and phenomenally separate existence of the world, relatively to the reality and absolute existence of the Bhagavat; and, therefore, it regards its creation as the result of *pariṇāma* or direct evolution, by which an effect of the same kind is produced in the material cause. There is a difference, no doubt, in the reality of the world and that of the Bhagavat, for the former is relative and non-eternal and the latter absolute and eternal. In a sense however, the world may be regarded as eternal, because even after dissolution it continues to exist in a subtle form in the Bhagavat, but it must still be regarded as non-eternal so far as it exists phenomenally and presents itself to our gross senses. But its being non-eternal or perishable does not mean that it is false or unreal, as some Vedāntists hold. The world as an effect has the same character of reality as its material cause (namely, the *māyā-śakti* of the Lord), although this reality may not be absolute reality. Since the deity, as the material and efficient cause of the world, evolves it out of himself by th *māyā-śakti*, he doers not su ffer any change or loss of essence inasmuch as this *śakti* cannot affect his true *svarūpa*. The deity is immutable even if he is the cause of the mutable world, and creation in this sense is a mystery. It is also further established that creation is spontaneous to the nature of the Lord. It does not proceed from any particular purpose or motive, in the sense in which the term is used with reference to human beings; for, the divine being in his perfection cannot be endowed with a particular purpose or motive.

The concept of the Paramātman, as a partial manifestation of the Bhagavat, has relation mainly to these energies of the Lord, namely the *jīva-śakti* and the *māyā-śakti*, and is, therefore postulated for this special purpose. The Paramātman is accordingly endowed with the powers of creation, sustenance and dissolution of the world, as well as of being the inward regulator of the individual self. The relation between the Bhagavat and the Paramātman is really one of gradation in the hierarchy of manifestations of one and the same reality. But since the two energies (*śaktis*) assigned to the Paramātman are regarded either as *taṭasthā* or *bahiraṅgā* (aloof or external) in relation to the intrinsic (*antaraṅgā*) divine energy, the function of the Paramātman operates only so long as the *jīva* is still. at a lower plane and is blind to the nature of true reality. Jīva Gosvāmin refers in this connection to [*Bhagavad]Gītā* texts (xiii.1.) relating to the *ksetra* and *kṣetra-jña,* and explains that the *kṣetra* ('field' or 'dwelling place') is matter or material body as the seat of the conditioned self, who as a conscious entity is technically styled *kṣetrajña*. But he rejects the Sāṃkhya interpretation of *kṣetrajña*, and maintains the theistic view that the *jīva* is *kṣetrajña* only relatively; for the Paramātman, as the inward ruler of the world and the individual self, is the only and real *kṣetrajña*. As the regulator of the individual self in its conditioned state, the Paramātman may again be the regulator either of the totality of individual *jīvas* (*samaṣṭi-jīvāntaryāmin*) or of each individual *jīva* (*vyaṣṭi-jīvāntaryāmin)*. In theological language we are told further that since the *avatāras* have relation to the phenomenal world, they all proceed from the Paramātman, and the Bhagavat is thus superior to all of them. One of the primal evolutes of the Paramātman in this respect is the *puruṣa*, who is regarded as the first (*ādya*) of the *avatāras*. This *puruṣa*, in its twofold aspect as the *garbhodaka-śāyin* and the *kṣīrodaka-śāyin,* is the presiding deity of the *jiva* in its singleness (*vyaṣṭi*) and totality (*samaṣṭi*) respectively. These two aspects of the *puruṣa*, again, are regarded as two subtle emanations of the *saṃkarṣaṇa-vyūha*, who is *kāraṇārṇavaśāyin* and who, according to the *varṇa*-doctrine, is supposed to preside over the *jīva*. Thus, as the immanent regulator of the individual *jīvas* and the phenomenal world, the *saṃkarṣaṇa* of the *vyūha*-theory is absorbed as being identical with the Paramātman, just as the much older conception of *puruṣa* is assimilated within the theological schisms of the Paramātman in relation to the *avatāras*.

"From what has been said above it will not be difficult to understand the theory which Jīva Gosvāmin propounds on the relation of the *jīva* to the Bhagavat. As the *jīva* is an aspect of the *taṭasthā jīva-śakti*, the relation is the same as between a *śakti* and the possessor of the *śakti*. The Bhagavat as the *śaktimat* is, no doubt, the ground or source of the *śakti* which cannot exist without him, but the *śakti* has also a capacity and existence of its own. The analogy of the sun and its scattered rays has already been cited above to illustrate the conception. The relation is thus one of non-difference as well as of difference (*bhedābheda*) in an inscrutable manner (*acintya*). The *jīva* is non-different from the Bhagavat because it is a part or *aṃśa*, even if an atomic part (*aṇu*), and possesses essentially the same characteristics of eternity, non-liability of change, etc., as well as the same attributes, in an infinitesimal amount, of *cit* and *ānanda*. If the Bhagavat is *pūrṇā cit* and *pūrṇā ānanda*, the *jīva* is *cit-kaṇā* and *ānanda-kaṇā*. But as the superlativeness of the attributes and characteristics belongs to the Bhagavat alone, and not to the *jīva*, there is an inevitable difference; and absolute identity can never be maintained. The *jīva* is also eternally subordinate to the Lord, for the common attributes in the case of the *jīva* are obscured and controlled by the *māyā-śakti*, while the Lord is never affected by this *śakti*, which indeed springs from him but which is yet external to him. The non-difference makes it possible for the *jīva* to approach him and be a part of his intrinsic *svarūpa-śakti*, but the difference keeps the *jīva* eternally separate and subordinate. Jīva Gosvāmin maintains this position not only by the citation of Purāṇa and other texts, but also by a peculiarly dualistic interpretation of *Vedānta-sūtra* i.2.12; ii.1.22 and ii.3.42-45. The Advaita texts, which speak of identity, should, in his opinion, be understood to affirm resemblance; for the *jīva*, being an *aṃśa*, naturally retains some of the divine character and becomes *like unto* the Bhagavat but it is never the same. It might be objected that if the *jīva* is a part of the Bhagavat, then all the imperfections of the *jīva* must also attach to the Bhagavat; but the reply to this furnished by the authority of *Vedāntasūtra* ii.3.45, which is interpreted to mean that the imperfections of the *jīva*, who is an expression of the Bhagavat's *taṭastha jīva-śakti* and not of his essential *svarūpa-śakti*, can never be ascribed to the highest being.

"In his *Tattvasandarbha* and elsewhere Jīva Gosvāmin takes some pains to refute the views of the Advaitavādins that the difference between the *jīva* and Brahman is not real but is due to *upādhi* (condition or limitation), by means of which the really unconditioned Brahman appears to condition himself (*pariccheda-vāda*) or limitedly reflects himself as *jīva* (*pratibimba-vāda*). The arguments against these Advaita theories are well known and need not be repeated in detail. Jīva Gosvāmin employs the usual arguments against the validity of the assumption of *upādhi* made by the Advaita-vādins. He argues that the *upādhi*, which according to the Advaita-vādins gives rise to a perception of difference which does not really exist, must be either real or unreal. If it is real (*vāstavat*), that is, if it is not imagined through *avidyā*, then how can Brahman, who is always unconditioned, be conditioned? Being without any attribute (*dharma*), he cannot have any limitation or *upādhi*; and being all-pervasive (*vyāpaka*) and without a form (*niravayava*), like *ākāśa*, he cannot be visible and reflect himself as *jīva*. The mere knowledge of the identity of the *jīva* and Brahman, again, can never get rid of the *upādhi* which, *ex hypothesi*, is real and therefore persists in spite of such knowledge. If, on the other hand, the *upādhi* is presumed to be unreal (*avāstava*), that is, due to *avidyā*, then how can it touch Brahman who is eternally free from any touch of *avidyā*? In such a case, Brahman, who is the sole reality, becomes unreal. It must be assumed, therefore, that those scriptural texts which have been often cited in support of identity, only speak of resemblance due to analogy and are, therefore, instances merely of that form of expression which is known as 'secondary application of a word based on resemblance' (*sādṛśya-lakṣaṇā*).It is not denied that the *jīva* resembles Brahman and is identical in some essential characteristics, but there is also a real distinction which cannot be transcended.

"This relation of non-identity is expressed by the supposition that the *jīva* is a part of the Bhagavat as the ground or substratum of the *taṭasthā jīva-śakti,* and not of the Bhagavat as the displayer of the *svarūpa-śakti.* But since the capacity for bliss is an inherent attribute of the *jīva* it finds a point of contact with the intrinsic *hlādinī śakti* or blissful energy of the Bhagavat through the mode of *bhakti*, which is nothing more than an aspect of this intrinsic divine entity. This natural capacity of the *jīva* restores his affinity or contiguity to the Bhagavat and counteracts its averseness, which springs from the effect of the external *māyā-śakti*. But the *jīva* is never an equal but a servant or *sevaka* to the Lord, who is the *sevya*, and its function is to carry out the Lord's will; even *bhakti*, however inherent in the *jīva* as an expression of the divine energy, can awaken only through divine grace (*prasāda* or *anugraha*). Even when freed from the bondage of the *māyā-śakti,* the *jīva* persists in its real and eternal character as an eternal spiritual atom worshiping the Lord. There are *śrutis* which affirm the distinction in the *jīva's* phenomenal existence and also in its state of release. The state of release, therefore, is only release from the earthly bondage of the *maya-śakti*, but not extinction on perception of identity, nor the merging of the *jīva* in the Bhagavat (*laya*). The emancipated self is in reality no longer the *jīva* or a part of the *jīva-śakti*, but becomes a part of the *svarūpa-śaktī* of the Bhagavat as his *parikāra* or attendant in his paradise. But since the relation of the *śakti* to the possessor of the *śakti* is, as we have seen, one of non-identity in identity, the relation naturally continues in the state of emancipation.

7.4 JĪVA GOSVĀMIN, *(Śrī)Kṛṣṇasandarbha/Saṃvādinī*

It has been edited several times, and summarized at last twice, once by Chinmayi Chatterjee (Jadavpur University Sanskrit Series, Jadavpur University, Calcutta, 1986, and earlier by S. K. De in De 1961, pp. 314-354. As De's summary is a bit long (and Chatterjee's is full of untranslated Sanskrit passages) what we provide in what follows is a set of excerpts from De's summary, identified by pages.

Summarized by Sushil Kumar De

"The interest of this *sandarbha* is more theological than philosophical. Its chief object is to apply the principles established in the three *sandarbhas* described above to the personality of Kṛṣṇa as depicted in the *Śrīmad-Bhāgavata,* and present him as the highest personal god of Bengal Vaiṣṇavism. Its theme is to maintain that Kṛṣṇa is not an *avatāra* or an incarnate being, but the deity himself, manifest in his perfect form as the Bhagavat. In other words, having established the concept of Bhagavat, Jīva Gosvāmin now proceeds to show in a definite way that Kṛṣṇa is the Bhagavat as the *advaya-jñāna-tattva* of its theology. From the point of view of the cult and sect, therefore, this is the most important and central *sandarbha*, the other three preceding *sandarbhas* being preliminary..." (p. 314)

"Jīva Gosvāmin attempts to establish that the *Bhāgavata* statement about Kṛṣṇa's absoluteness as the Bhagavat" [part of verse i.3.28 of the Bhāgavata reads 'Kṛṣṇa is the Bhagavat himself' (p. 317)] is a positive, unambiguous and emphatic *śruti* which must prevail over all other statements. It is therefore a definitive assertion of the *paribhāṣā* kind, which lays down an authoritative rule or proposition determining the sense of the whole work. A *paribhāṣā* is further described as that which is meant to bring certainty in the midst of uncertainty. As such, it occurs only once, and not repeatedly, as specifically defining a thing; but its singularity has the force of controlling and determining the sense of a plurality of other texts. It is thus a *mahāvākya* or a great proposition, like the phrase '*tat tvam asi*'; and the proper *śāstric* method would be to explain every other proposition, which appears inconsistent or contradictory, in the light of the significance of such a *mahāvākya*. It is also maintained that this *paribhāṣā* statement not only controls all other *Bhāgavata* texts but also conflicting texts in other Purāṇas, which must be interpreted in such a way as not to appear inconsistent with it...")(pp. 320-321)

"Jīva Gosvāmin next seeks, with a similar method, to establish the *bhagavattā* of Kṛṣṇa by showing that Kṛṣṇa is to be regarded as the source not only of the *puruṣa-avatāras* but of the *līlā-avatāras* who proceed from the *puruṣa*, but also of the *guṇa-avatāras*, namely, Brahmā, Viṣṇu and Śiva. He is thus superior to the recognized trinity of the Purāṇic mythology and religion. No doubt these *avatāras*, being aspects of Kṛṣṇa's manifestation, are each of them perfect (*pūrṇa*), but Kṛṣṇa is the most perfect (*pūrṇātama*)...Jīva Gosvāmin takes upon himself the task of marshaling a formidable army of Bhāgavata passages in support of the *mahāvākya*, which he designates as the king of all utterances, and attempts to show that Kṛṣṇa as the Bhagavat is not only the principal theme of the work [viz., the *Bhāgavata*] in more than half the number of verses comprised in it...(I)t is easy to explain that such deities as Nārāyaṇa and Vāsudeva, who are celebrated in the *Padma-purāṇa, Nārāyaṇa-Upaniṣad* and *Vāsudeva-Upaniṣad,* are merely henotheistically conceived as the supreme god, but they are really various aspects of Kṛṣṇa-Bhagavat..." (pp. 323-325)

"If there were any doubt regarding Kṛṣṇa's reality and eternity (*nitya-sthiti*) as the highest god, then the *śāstras*, which are worthy of the greatest confidence (*parāpṭa*), would not have given instructions regarding his worship and deliberately displayed the intention of deceiving (*vipralipsā*).

The Advaita-vādins, however, deny that there is an absolute reality called Kṛṣṇa; they say that this name and form have been imposed upon the unconditioned Brahman for the convenience of the dualistic ideas of worshipers. This, in Jīva Gosvāmin's opinion, is not correct; because imposition (*āropa*) can be imagined only on a thing which is conditioned in form and attribute, but not on a substance which is infinite in form and attribute. Jīva Gosvāmin repeats that the *nityatva* of Kṛṣṇa is established by *mahad-anubhava* or intuition of great sages, who are known to have received the direct vision of the deity and its desired effects...." (pp. 331-332)

"(T)he question of Kṛṣṇa's *dhāman* (abode) and *parikāra* (retinue) engages greater attention and occupies him [Jīva Gosvāmin] in the rest of the *sandarbha*." (p. 333)

"It has been said that Bhagavat-Kṛṣṇa eternally sports in his three *dhāmans* [abodes], namely, Dvāraka, Mathurā and Vṛndāvana, which are represented as three aspects of one and the same reality. If this is so, how is it that in the sacred texts the progression from Vṛndāvana to Mathurā, then to Dvāraka, and finally to Gokula is described? The answer to this puzzle is furnished by the supposition that all this is described only with reference to Kṛṣṇa's appearance in his *prakaṭa-līlā* in the phenomenal world; but the *aprakaṭa-līlā*, which is not revealed to the phenomenal world, eternally goes on these three *dhāmans*. This explanation necessitates an exposition of this theory of phenomenal and non-phenomenal appearances of the deity, or his *prakaṭa* and *aprakaṭa līlā*, to which Jīva Gosvāmin now turns his attention.

"...*Līlā* or beatific sport may be manifest or *prakaṭa* and unmanifest or *aprakaṭa* according as it can or cannot be apprehended directly by phenomenal beings. The testimony of the texts shows that both the *līlā*s are *nitya*, that is, real and eternal. As a matter of fact, one and the same eternal *līlā* appears in two fold ways on account of the limitations of the phenomenal *jīva*. As the real nature of the *jīva* is suppressed by the *māyā-śakti* and the *jīva* is thereby debarred from witnessing it, the *līlā* is unmanifest; but when the deity in his infinite grace and love to his devotees directly reveals himself in the phenomenal world, the self-same *līlā* becomes manifest. The *aprakaṭa* or unmanifest aspect of the *līlā*, therefore, is free from all contact of the phenomenal world and its objects, and the eternity of *līlā* is explained to mean that its characteristic flow is unimpeded, like time, and has no beginning, middle or end. It is also marked by the same incidents and characteristics...as also mark the *prakaṭa līlā*. The *prakaṭa līlā* also, in the same way, like the *vigraha* of the Bhagavat, is not subject to the limitations of time; but in it there is, through the intrinsic will-power of the *svarūpa-śakti* of the deity, a beginning and an end, as well as a mixture of phenomenal and non-phenomenal objects and an appearance of incidents like Kṛṣṇa's birth and death. Jīva Gosvāmin informs us that Kṛṣṇa's *prakaṭa līlā*, which was once witnessed by some eminently fortunate phenomenal beings, is even today revealed partially to men like himself." (pp. 343-344)

"The *aprakaṭa līlā,* again, is described as having two aspects. It may, in the first place, be what is realized in a limited way by the sacred *mantras* and *upāsanā*, or, secondly, it may be what is fully revealed by the flow of natural and inherent *rasa* or devotional sentiment (*svārasikī*). The former has a limit fixed by the particular time or place suitable to the particular *līlā* which forms the object of the *mantra*, and its character is also determined by such *svarūpa, dhāman* and *parikāra* of the deity as are prescribed for meditation by the particular *mantra.* In this respect, the infinitely varied *līlā* is restricted to a particular divine act or sport as given in a set formula or meditation-symbol; but this is necessary to the devotee in a preliminary stage when he is not yet accustomed to meditate upon and realize the endless forms of the *līlā*. The *svārasikī*, on the other hand, is not merely something which is record in the *mantra* or presented for meditation; the deity sometimes in his grace to the devotee actually reveals the *līlā* which is hidden from the vision of the ordinary mortal. In some cases, what is limited by the somewhat mechanical *mantra* and *upāsanā* becomes a living and natural realization. The *svārasikī* aspect of the *aprakāśa līlā* is not limited to particular divine acts or sport but it is varied at will according to the occasion. In its continuity and expansiveness as a stream of *līlā, the svārasikī* has been compared to the Ganges, while the *mantropāsanāmayī*, which is born out of it and is limited in its scope, has been compared to a lake or series of lakes circumscribed out of the stream." (pp. 344-345)

"Such simultaneous assumption of different divine forms at different places by the deity has already been explained in the *Bhagavat-sandarbha* as a natural result of the inherent divine power; but such manifestation or *prakāśa* is not like the reflection in the mirror (*pratibimba*) but like a halo (*bimba*) issuing out of the ultimate substance. The existence of reflection in the mirror is conditioned by the existence of the mirror; the reflection appears also in a reversed form and cannot be actually felt by such senses as touch; but the halo issuing out of a substance appears at will, by its inherent power, can be directly felt by touch and other senses, and does not differ in its essence from the substance. This analogy shows the reality of the different *prakāśas*, each of which partakes of the character of divine perfection. It follows that these *prakaśas* are not mere endless replicas of the same form, all having the self-same mode and sequence of acts; on the contrary, each has, by the unthinkable power of the deity, a separate reality and existence, as well as the capacity for independent action. The proof of all this lies in the fact that varied *prakāśas* of this character have been described in the *Bhāgavata*; and if they were not true, they could not have caused delight to learned people." (pp. 345-346)

"In different *prakāśas*, therefore, there are varied acts; and the effect of this is to produce a variety in the nature of the bliss (*rasa*) in each case. To support the peculiar *rasa* in each *prakāśa*, therefore, there are in each a difference of conceit (*abhimāna-bheda*) and a mutually exclusive knowledge of each other (*parasparam ananusaṃdhāna*), along with a difference in the mode of action (*kriyā-bheda*). In other words, the actors in one *prakāśa* are unaware of what is happening in the other, even if they themselves appear in both; and in each *prakāśa* they are possessed of the conceit that they are appearing only in that particular *prakāśa* in that particular manner. This theory of the exclusive individuality of each *prakāśa* makes it possible to understand that what appears as Kṛṣṇa's separation from his beloved in one *līlā* may be union in another. Thus, in the *prakāśa* at Vṛndāvana, at the termination of Kṛṣṇa's *prakaṭa līlā* at that place, it appears as if a separation occurs between Kṛṣṇa and the *gopagopīs*, but it is really not so; for even if Kṛṣṇa appears to be separated from his *parikaras* in the *prakaṭa līlā*, he is ever united with them there in the *aprakaṭa līlā* into which he enters simultaneously. In other words, union is an eternal fact in Kṛṣṇa's eternal *aprakaṭa līlā*, which goes on in all the three *dhāmans*; but since it is sometimes manifested and sometimes hidden from the view of phenomenal beings, there are apparent separations in the *prakaṭa līlā*. Thus, both the manifest and the unmanifest *līlās* can go on in the same *dhāmans*; and when the deity is not manifestly present in the *prakaṭa līlā*, he is to be regarded as present in unmanifest form in the *aprakaṭa līlā*. It can be shown from the sacred texts that, in the same place and at the same time, the *gopīs*, in their double capacity in the *prakaṭa* and the *aprakaṭa līlās*, have felt the bliss of union and sorrow of separation. All this may appear inconceivable to phenomenal beings, but all contradictions like union and separation have no essential validity in the *līlā* of the inconceivably perfect being. This theory enables our author to reconcile and explain such contradictions in manifestation as are sometimes found recorded in the sacred texts; for instance, separation from the *gopīs* at the end of the *prakaṭa līlā* at

Vṛndāvana, as well as from the Yādavas at the end of the *prakaṭa līlā* at Dvāraka. ..(" (pp. 646-647)

7.5 JĪVA GOSVĀMIN, *Bhaktisandarbha(Saṃvādinī)*

The work is summarized in De 1961, pp. 354-380. More recently, a three-volume edition and translation has been published from Vrndavana (Dasa 2005). For more complete account of the literature cf. Bi b 3, #1011.3.

Summarized by Bruce Martin

"The book as a whole is divided into three parts. The first part discusses the criteria for a complete methodology, and how *bhakti* alone meets that criterion. In this part, Jīva minutely analyzes the nature of devotion that defines its totality and absoluteness. The second part discusses the preeminence of the Lord's devotees. Amongst awakened sages, those whose hearts are saturated with devotion, being immersed in the intoxication of love, experience a consummate relation with the Absolute, in which God himself comes under the control of the devotee's love. By showing the completeness of the devotee's realization, the preeminence of devotion is indirectly established. In this part, the sages who are awakened to devotion are said to be the cause of *bhakti* flowing to living beings asleep to their original nature.

"In the final part of the book, Jīva discusses the actual practice of devotion. He begins by defining the intrinsic nature of pure devotion to distinguish it from its partial or impure manifestations. *Svarūpa-siddhi bhakti*, or devotion inherently constituted of divine potency, is said to be the actual methodology. This unalloyed devotion has two further divisions: *vaidhi*, devotion impelled by injunctions; and *rāgānugā,* devotion impelled by spontaneous attraction. These two topics make up the final subdivisions of the third part...

"In the first section of Chapter (*anuccheda*) I.1-9)[1], Jīva begins by discussing the need for a methodology. Because living beings are subject to ignorance, their attention is drawn to wards matter, towards the external and the superficial. For one whose heart is receptive due to having contacted sages in a previous life, hearing of the Absolute is sufficient to awaken his or her taste for transcendence.

"Those who have no such preparation of the heart, however, require a methodology to attain the Absolute. Jīva clarifies from the very outset that the methodology is not that of any sectarian religion. Rather, he defines it in the most concise and universal terms as *sāmukhya*, the simple act of turning one's face away from the temporal to encounter the Absolute. So, any process that enables this shift in awareness can be said to fulfill the condition of methodology.

"All over the world there have been basically two currents in the stream of religion: the path of pious works dedicated to God, which leads to heaven; and the path of meditation, silent prayer, and direct awareness, leading to liberation. Jīva adds a third, the path of ecstacy and spontaneous love, leading to a consummate relation with the divine that unfolds ceaselessly, in infinite variety, shape, quality and taste.

"Jīva acknowledges that there are different methods to create the shift in awareness, yet he is interested specifically in that which offers optimum completion of the individual being. Thus, in the first chapter of the book he discusses the criteria for a complete methodology. For this, a universal referent is first required, defining the fundamental nature of the Absolute.

"In *anuccheda* 6 Jīva Gosvāmin quotes *Bhāgavata Purāṇa* 1.2.11, in which it is said that all those who have witnessed the truth, regardless of their path, have realized it as non-dual

[1]In ET the *Bhaktisandarbha* is divided into 178 *anucchedas* or sections.

awareness. Yet the one non-dual awareness has been referred to as Brahman, Paramātman and Bhagavān in accordance with individual taste. Thus the common ground of being is non-dual awareness, realized by all those who have seen.

"In its Brahman feature, this refers to inscrutable awareness, devoid of characteristics like shape, quality, name and action. So, although Brahman is *nirguṇa*, or beyond the contamination of matter, it has no distinguishing characteristics of its own. Thus awareness of Brahman entails pure awareness, bereft of content. The path of *jñāna* aims at this type of awareness.

"Paramātmā refers to an expansion of an expansion of the Lord, immanent within the cosmos and the individual living beings. It is due to the animating principle of Paramātmā that primordial nature takes shape as the manifest cosmos. The living beings, who are parts of Paramātmā and thus conscious by nature, are impregnated into the cosmos in accordance with previous *karman* and desire. Paramātmā, residing in the sky of the heart, guides the living beings on their sojourn through existence, as a witness.

"The *yogins* realize this feature of the one non-dual being, as endowed with awareness and specific attributes such as form and quality, yet whose sphere of influence is limited to preservation of the cosmos. Thus in relation to Brahman, Paramātmā has specific attributes that make it more complete, yet lacking higher completion. Hence *yoga*, the path aiming at Paramātmā realization, can be said to be more complete than *jñāna*, leading merely to the generic awareness of Brahman.

"Bhagavān, implying that which encompasses all opulence and power to infinite degree, refers to the complete whole. Parmātmā is understood to be but an expansion of Bhagavān, whereas Brahman is but his bodily effulgence. Where effulgence is least dense we encounter the blinding light of indistingishable being. Where effulgence is dense, it takes shape as the entity of highest love, inviting his own parts to drop the unreal and join in the eternal play of love. Bhagavān, endowed with infinite attributes and predominating the transcendent realm, is the highest for of completion of the Absolute.

"*Bhakti* is a unique conscious aspect of divine power, stemming from Bhagavān himself. By its own will, flowing through the current of awakened sages, *bhakti* takes up residence in the receptive heart and enraptures the soul into the union of love with its sources. Because *bhakti* is a direct flow of the internal potency as well as the methodology to realize the Absolute in its feature of highest completion, it is the most complete process. This is the basic premise on which Jīva proceeds.

"In the remaining eight sections of the first chapter, Jīva examines the fact that *bhakti* meets the criteria of a complete methodology from various points of consideration. For a methodology to be complete, it should first of all be practical, which means that it should be easy for everyone to perform without any special requirements. Thus in section two (*anucchedas* 10-17) Jīva discusses the ease of devotion, stressing that it begins simply by hearing. This shows that the basic requirement of devotion is innocence–receptivity of the heart.

"For a methodology to be complete, it should also be directed towards the complete whole and not towards any partial manifestation of the whole. The fact that devotion is intended for the complete whole, Śrī Kṛṣṇa, and not towards the *devas* is discussed in section three (*anucchedas* 18-32).

"In section four (33-40) Jīva makes use of *vyatireka* or negative concomitance to establish the completeness of devotion. *Vyatireka* is a logical proposition employed throughout the text to indirectly establish the validity of an assertion by showing the defect of failing to apply the principle enunciated in that assertion. When a methodology is complete and hence pervasive, its non-performance will be seen as a gap.

Hence in this section Jīva points out the meaninglessness of life without devotion.

"In *Tattva Sandarbha*, the first book of the anthology, Jīva discussed epistemology and established *Śrīmad Bhāgavata* as his primary source of authority. Thus in section five (*anucchedas* 41-94) Jīva asserts that *bhakti* is the methodology by showing that it is advocated in every discussion between teacher and student in the *Bhagavata*.

"In section six (95-105) Jīva confirms the completeness of devotion by showing that it is the culmination of all methods. Again for a methodology to be complete, it should include all other methods, yet stand independent of all methods. Furthermore, all partial methods necessarily depend on the whole of which they are but parts. In this section Jīva shows that devotion meets the criteria of inclusiveness and authority.

"In addition, a methodology can be said to be complete when the result it fosters is complete. Thus in concluding this section (104), Jīva points out that the result of devotion is not mere oneness, but a state of affairs in which the whole comes under the subjugation of an infinitesimal part. The inconceivable reality is possible only through love.

"In section seven (106-107) Jīva returns to the discussion that a complete methodology should be directed towards ther complete whole, but from a different angle of vision. In section three the emphasis was on defining the character of the entity of highest completion, Śrī Kṛṣṇa. Now in this section Jīva discusses the expansiveness of the vision of an individual who has taken shelter of the complete. Such a person naturally honors all beings and all manifestations of the divine, such as the *devas*, while being simultaneously fixed in exclusive devotion to the whole.

"In section eight (108-113) Jīva brings out the point that for a methodology to be truly complete, it must be unavoidable, otherwise its non-performance would not be a defect, and hence it could not be the whole. Thus in this section he shows that devotion is the intrinsic duty for all, extending beyond even liberation. Jīva concludes this section (113), by hinting at the fact that devotion is the natural state of living beings, implying its comprehensive nature. This topic he will explore at length in 178, as a conclusion to the volume.

In the final section of the first chapter (114-120) Jīva reaches the culmination of his analysis of *bhakti* as complete methodology. In the first section he had defined methodology in the most concise possible terms, as *saṃmukhya*, the shift in awareness. Now (in 115) he will define the shift of awareness in specific terms, while preserving its universal quality.

"Quoting the fourth of the seed verses of the *Bhāgavata*, he reveals that a complete methodology is that which applies for all conditions of space and time, all performers, and is realized both directly and indirectly. As with *sāṃmukhya*, this definition does not entail any sectarian religion. Rather, it establishes the criteria by which methodology can be gauged. In a general sense, any process that creates a shift in focus towards the Absolute is the methodology. But that process which embodies these specific traits is absolute methodology. Jīva shows that *bhakti* meets the criteria.

"After establishing *bhakti* as the complete methodology in the first chapter, Jīva describes the nature of *bhakti* in chapter two (*anucchedas* 121-164). The first section (121-130) discusses *bhakti*'s power to purify. It removes inauspiciousness, obstacles and fear, and destroys sins to the extent of nullifying the inherent defect in reactions that have already taken effect (*prārabdha*). Furthermore, *bhakti* purifies the heart of desire and dispels ignorance, the cause of bondage. Section two (131-132) is a brief description of *bhakti*'s nourishing power–it enables the soul to blossom into complete awareness, virtue and bliss.

"Section three (133-138) discusses *bhakti's* quality of being *nirguṇa* or beyond the influence of the constituent qualities of material nature. Jīva points out that when knowledge and action are manifest in relation to the *nirguṇa* entity, they are naturally beyond the *guṇas*. All faculties, used in relation to the transcendent entity, promote *nirguṇa*. In 134 Jīva takes the discussion a step further, demonstrating that *bhakti* is *parama-nirguṇa*, beyond even the *nirguṇa* state of liberation. Again this emphasizes *bhakti* as a complete methodology because it aims at that which includes and transcends *nirguṇa* Brahman. Jīva also points out that the abode of the transcendent is *nirguṇa*, and even the faith that impels *nirguṇa bhakti* is called *nirguṇa*.

"Section four (139-144), embedded topically in the center of the first volume, discloses the very essence of *bhakti*, as a unique aspect of the internal potency (*svarūpa-śakti*). Being a conscious, self-manifest potency of the diverse, inherently constituted of bliss, it magnifies Bhagavān's own delight and bestows love of God. It is clear from Jīva's description that *bhakti* is a descent of the internal potency and not something generated through practice. Thus what Jīva implies by complete methodology is not any sort of device to awaken the consciousness, but rather a direct descent of the divine in the form of the conscious potency of devotion that infuses the individual consciousness with its own intrinsic nature.

"Section five (145-148) discusses some of the inconceivable results bestowed through devotion. Jīva's description follows a gradation. First devotion bestows full realization of God, then it enables one to attain the Lord directly, as well as bestowing other subsidiary results that far exceed the imagination. Finally, *bhakti* brings the Lord himself under control through the power of love.

"In the final section of chapter two (149-164) Jivā discusses an essential concept that once again specifies *bhakti* as complete methodology. For a methodology to be complete, it should be effective immediately, through a single participation. Jīva points out that not only does *bhakti* have this power but even a semblance of devotion can transport one to the abode of God. The only thing that can obstruct this unique power of devotion are offences. Thus in this section Jīva also discusses offences and their five primary effects. He concludes that the power of a single act of devotion bears fruit in a the offenceless heart.

"In the final chapter of the first volume (165-178) Jīva summarizes and refines the conclusions he has presented thus far. In section one (165-169) he offers five reasons why direct devotion is complete methodology, including the fact that *bhakti* is independent of all other processes and that it awards the supreme destination even by slight contact.

"Jiva then specifies the exclusive nature of the *bhakti* he is talking about by describing it as *ananya*, literally 'not having any other'. By implication, *ananya* means 'the whole', because only the totality can have no other. Devotion is complete because it stems from, resides in, and is directed towards the whole, not any other. By definition therefore, *ananya-bhakti* is also bereft of all desire, other than the consummation of love with the divine. The bulk of this section deals with the fact that both the Lord and the devotees are desireless and that devotion tainted with desire is mere show.

"In concluding this section, Jīva further qualifies *anantya-bhakti* as consisting of the nine primary limbs of devotion, such as hearing, singing and meditating on the names, forms, qualities and pastimes of the Lord. These acts are directly constituted of intrinsic potency, as will be pointed out in 234 (found in chapter two of the third volume).

"In section two (170-176) Jīva initiates a separate discussion to disclose the supremacy of devotion from a unique perspective, namely the basis of eligibility for the path. The sources of eligibility for *karman, jñāna* and *bhakti* are respectively desire for the fruit of action, freedom from such desire, and faith. *Karman* has no transformative power of its own, but can lead one to the transcendent paths of *jñāna* and *bhakti*. When through purification of *karman* desire is dropped, it leads to *jñāna*. When performance of *karman* brings one into the contact of sages absorbed in devotion, faith is awakened, opening the gateway to *bhakti.*

"*Jñāna* is thus understood to be dependent on detachment, whereas *bhakti* has no such prerequisite. As pointed out already in 137, the faith that impels devotion is itself *nirguṇa*. Thus faith, which is an attribute of the performer, is in essence a disposition of heart born of contact with those who embody truth. Since even the source of eligibility for *bhakti* is transcendent by nature, *bhakti* is complete methodology. Furthermore, *bhakti* continues even bey ond liberation, whereas *jñāna* desists at the same point.

"Jīva goes a step further to point out how general devotion is independent even of faith. For development of a specific *bhāva* in devotion, however, faith is an essential requirement. Jīva makes it clear that faith is not mere sentiment, but a deep conviction rooted in surrender. He also specifies the difference between true faith and conventional faith. In 176 Jīva returns to his original premise, that *bhakti* is complete because it awards realization of the complete, Bhagavān Śrī Kṛṣṇa. He discusses *jñāna, bhakti* towards Paramātman and *bhakti* towards Bhagavān and the respective realizations awarded by these three paths.

"In the final section of chapter three (177-178), which is the concluding portion of the final volume, Jīva discloses what he has been leading up from the very outset, that the true methodology is spontaneous attraction to the complete Absolute, replete with transcendent quality. By its nature the attraction is complete, being as the movement of water to and from its own source. By its nature it also transcends methodology, because practice cannot bring about this attraction."

7.6 JĪVA GOSVĀMIN, *Prītisandarbha/Saṃvādinī*

Sushil Kumar De summarizes the work in De 1961, 380-412. We provide here a portion (pp. v-xix) of the "Preparatory Note" provided by Chimayi Chatterjee as an introduction to her edition found in Chatterjee 1980. "E" refers to that edition.

For added references to the literature on this work consult Bib 3, #1011.9.

Summary by Chinmayi Chatterjee

"Final emancipation, *apavarga* or *mukti*, of the *jīva* for Śrī Jīva Gosvāmin is not total absorption of the *jīva* in Brahman, as the Advaitins hold, through the cognition of identity or oneness between them. In the *Paramātmasandarbha* Śrī Jīva Gosvāmin declares that identity or oneness should not be the relation of the *jīva* with Brahman. In the *Prītisandarbha* he describes the *jīva* as a part (*aṃśa*) of Brahman as the ray is part of the sun (E2). In release the part attains the whole. This attainment of release or *mukti* is of two types according to the nature of the object to be attained and the means to be applied for it. Thus, either the *jīva* attains the impersonal Brahman through the cognition of its essential state on the cessation of the function of the *māyāśakti*, also known as *avidyā*, or the *jīva* attains the Lord in His fullest and truest self in His own abode, Vaikuṇṭha, where the *jīva* is brought in contact with Him by His own inconceivable power. This release can be attained during lifetime or after the dissolution of the gross and subtle bodies in death (E23). Of these two types of release the latter consisting of the direct vision or *sākṣātkāra* of the proper form of the Lord is endowed with attributes and energies is far superior to the former consisting of the realization of the indistinct and attributeless form of Brahman (E3).

"Indeed, true release or *mukti* comes from divine revelation only (E10). Again, the vision of the Lord as endowed with the special attribute of belovedness is the best of all revelations of His divine self bearing other attributes. Such vision is caused by *prīti* which brings the highest happiness and the consequent cessation of misery (E3). So all beings should take resort to *prīti* only for reaching the ultimate goal (E4).

"The *mukti* occurring after death is of five types (E16). These are *sālokya*–attainment of the same place of divine habitation with the deity, *sārṣṭi*–attainment of the same divine condition, *sārūpya*–attainment of the same divine form, *sāmīpya*–attainment of nearness to the Lord, and *sāyujya* or absorption in the divine self. All these five types of *mukti* are unaffected by *guṇas* and one who attains these never returns to this phenomenal world. The *sāmīpyamukti* causes outward vision of the Lord while the other four lead to His inward vision. These are far better than the *kaivalyamukti* causing the absorption of the *jīva* in the impersonal Brahman since these *muktis* are marked by eternal revelation of the divine self of the Lord (E19).

"*Kaivalyamukti* or *brahmasāyujya* is different from the *sāyujyamukti* in which the *jīva* being immersed in the bliss of absorption in divine self loses the capacity of having a realization of the Lord as endowed with all energies. But if the Lord desires He brings the *jīva* attaining *sāyujyamukti* out of His own self and makes him His *pārṣada* or attendant capable of enjoying His supersensuous sports–*līlās*.(E18-19). Following the teachings of the *Bhāgavata Purāṇa* (3.20.13) Śrī Jīva Gosvāmin declares the superiority of *prīti* or *bhagavadbhakti* to all these five tpes of *mukti* which have no attraction for a Vaiṣṇava *bhakta* as in them there is hardly any scope for service to the Lord (E13). If there is any, that is welcome to him (E31). In this connection Śrī Jīva Gosvāmin classifies *ekāntibhakta* (who desires to attain the Lord only and nothing else) into two categories–(1) one in whom *prīti* has not yet emerged (*ajātaprīti*) and (2) one in whom it has already emerged (*jātaprīti*). The former regards *prīti* as the highest desired end (E30). The latter, again, embraces three types, viz. (1) one, the *śāntabhakta,* the one who yearns only for a realization of the divine self of the Lord, (2) one who with the conceit of a particular attendant wants to have the joy of seeing and serving the Lord, and (3) one who is His attendant. The *śāntabhakta* may, sometimes, desire to have a vision of the Lord, but never desires to serve Him. The second type of *bhakta* with the keen desire for having *prīti* may like to get favored with proximity so that he can better serve the Lord. All his intentions are manifestation of *prīti* only (E30-31)...

"...Śrī Jīva produces the *svarūpalakṣaṇa* (definition indicating the essential nature of the object to be defined) and the *taṭastha-lakṣaṇa* (definition indicating a property which is distinct from the essential nature of the object, yet by which the object to be defined is known) of *prīti.* The word '*prīti*' stands for *sukha* and *priyatā*. *Sukha* which is synonymous with *mud* (delight), *pramada* (extreme pleasure), *harṣa* (rapture) and *ānanda* (joy) is a particular consciousness consisting of merriness which belongs to some person. *Priyatā* identical with *bhāva* (affection), *hārda* (cordiality) and *sauhṛda* (friendliness) is also a particular consciousness consisting of merriness which involves agreeableness towards the object of love, and which emerges from the feeling of longing for the beloved rising from his agreeable disposition. *Sukha,* being of the nature of pleasure, only belongs to a self as its *āśraya* (locus or resting place) and has no *viṣaya* (object) to which it may be directed. But *priyatā* being a longing for an agreeable object has both *āśraya* and *viṣaya.* These two, *sukha* and *priyatā*, constitute the essential nature of *prīti* (E34). It is also called *bhakti* as it is directed to the Lord (E35). It is unmotivated and does not aim at any desired end. It rises spontaneously from the experience of the object (i.e. the Lord) and cannot be forcefully acquired. Pure *bhakti* or devotion when mingled with *prīti* becomes a natural emotion. It is superior to any kind of emancipation (E36). It represents the very nature of the *hlādiniśakti*, the bliss-yielding energy of the Lord which is placed eternally by Him in the devotees and by which He enjoys excessive joy in them (E38).

"The *taṭastha-lakṣaṇa* of *prīti* is based on a verse of the *Bhāgavata Purāṇa* [9.3.31] which states that devotees remembering the Lord or reminding others of Him with *bhakti* (love) caused by *bhakti* (consciousness or *jñānalakṣanā*) have their bodies thrilled with joy. *Prīti* causes the meeting of mind, horripilation, etc., which however fail to rouse devotion if there is no purity of the soul (*ālaya*). The purity of the soul is attained by the relinquishment of everything else except *prīti* (E39). Though *prīti* is one and indivisible (*akhaṇḍa*), it manifests itself by degrees according to the stages of the revelation of the divine self of the Lord who is its *viṣaya* or *ālambana*, i.e. object. As Kṛṣṇa is Bhāgavan Himself, so it is in relation to Kṛṣṇa only and in no other deity that the display of *prīti* becomes more perfect (E43).

"There may also be degrees in the manifestation of *prīti* according to the degree of excellence of other qualities of the devotee. Such qualities either prepare the mind of the devotee in specific ways for the rise of different devotional feeling or they may rouse particular types of conceit in the mind of the devotee (E45). Thus, *prīti* appears as *rati* when it gladdens the mind of the devotee; it is *prema* when it generates a feeling in which the Lord appears as one's own; by causing confidence it becomes *pranāta*; it develops into *māna* when it produces diversity of feeling for the Lord who is the most beloved one; when it causes the melting of the mind it is *sneha; sneha* becomes *rāga* when an excess of eager longing for the Lord is generated. In this state even a moment's separation from the Lord becomes unbearable to the devotee and the worst sorrow felt by hm during union with the Lord becomes the greatest happiness. *Rāga* becomes *anurāga* when it is felt as ever new and the deity also appears as ever new. *Anurāga* by causing maddening effect through unparalleled joy is turned into *mahābhāva* (E45).

"*Prīti* generates various conceits in the devotee also, such as friendship, parental affection, servitude or love in accordance with manifold revelations of the divine self of the Lord as friend, son, master or beloved husband to the devotee. Thus, the devotee considers himself as a friend of the deity, as one who favors Him or is favored by him or as the beloved wife of the deity (E46). As these conceits arise along with *prīti,* these are regarded as forms of *prīti* (E53). The favor (*anugraha*) of the deity which the devotee enjoys is either of the nature of compassion or of furtherance. Each of these two types may or may not be associated with an intimate feeling of affectionate regard (*mamatā*) of the devotee for the Lord. One who is without such feeling considers the Lord as *paramātmā* or *parabrahma* and is known as *jñāni-bhakta.* Like the moon gladdening the indifferent onlooker, the vision of the Lord gladdens the heart of such a devotee, though he is without a feeling of attachment for Him. The *prīti* of such a devotee is termed *jñāna-bhakti* which in Vaiṣṇava *śāstra* is known as *śānta-raśī* as it is marked by quietude or absence of passion (E46).

"The devotees who are gifted with the feeling of attachment for the Lord are classed into three types in accordance with three types of relationship conceived between them and the Lord, viz. as between the subject (*pālya*) and the protector (*pālaka*), servant (*dāsa)* and the master (*prabhu*), and inferior (who is caressed) (*lālya*) and superior (who caresses) *lālaka*) and their devotion also takes three forms viz. as dependence of the subject, servitude of the servant and respect for the inferior (E47). The *prīti* of the devotees who are endowed with the conceit of friendship, parental affection and love is known as *maitrya* (which again is of two types *sakhya,* intimacy, and *sahṛda,* fondness, *vātsalya* and *kāntāprema* respectively). The *kāntāprema* being marked by longing and desire for giving pleasure to the deity only is distinguished from *kāma* or sensuous desire aiming at one's own pleasure (E47).

The love of Kubja for Kṛṣṇa being associated with the desire of self-satisfaction is of the *kāma* type though it is *aprākṛta* (supermundane) having Kṛṣṇa as the object. The love of the damsels of Vraja being free from any such selfish motive is *kāntāprema*. *Prīti* thus embraces five types–*jñāna-bhakti, bhakti* (or *dāsya*), *vaiśalya, maitrya* and *kāntā-premam* of which the last is the best of all (E48). There may be admixture of two types of *prīti* in a single *bhakta*. For example, in Bhīṣma *jñāna-bhakti* is mixed with *dāsya-bhakti* (or *āśraya-bhakti*); in Yudhiṣṭhara the *dāsya-bhakti* and *vātsalya-bhakti* are mixed with *sakhya-bhakti* (E48). *Prīti* without any distinctive characteristic is *sāmānya* or general. A *bhakta* having such *sāmānya-* and *śānta-prīti* iknown as *taṭastha* and his *prīti* is called *taṭasthā* as it is not marked by the feeling of intimate personal attachment or *mamatā* (EE49).

"Other *bhaktas* are *parikara* (attendants) of Lord Kṛṣṇa and their *prīti* bearing an abundance of the feeling of attachment is called *mamatā-prīti* (E49). The *parikaras*, again, fall into two classes according as their preference to the experience of the supreme excellence of the divine *aiśvarya* or of divine *mādhurya* with which the Lord reveals himself to them. *Aiśvarya* indicates the mastery of the Lord while *mādhurya* means the loveliness of conduct, gravity, beauty, youth and sports as well as of the specific relationship with His devotees (E55). The Lord is best revealed in His *mādhurya* aspect (E56). So the experience of the devotee of the Lord in this aspect is the supreme consciousness which one aspires to attain (E58). The experience of the Lord in His *aiśvarya* aspect remains so long as *prīti* is not prominently felt. As soon as *prīti* gains prominence the *aiśvarya-jñāna* becomes subdued by it (E58).

"*Prīti* which manifests in five different forms as *śānta* or *jñāna-bhakti, dāsya, vātsalya sakhya* or *maitrī*, and *kānta-prema* is known as *sthāyī bhāva* (permanent mood) since it can reach the state of reliable sentiment (*rasa*) in association with appropriate cause *vibhāva*), effect (*anubhāva*), and auxiliary sentiments (*vyabhicāribhāva*) like *rati*, etc., of classical literature (E65). Though in orthodox rhetorical treatises *bhakti* or love for the deity (*bhagavad-viṣayā rati*) has been denied the status of *rasa* and has been reduced to an inferior position as *bhāva*, Śrī Jīva Gosvāmin establishes the validity of the concept of the *bhakti-rasa* through sound arguments and gives detailed analysis of this concept (E65). He restricts the objection of the orthodox rhetoricians to the love or *rati* directed to ordinary deities and not to the supreme Lord, Kṛṣṇa (E65). Śrī Jīva Gosvāmi's argument in this respect is that the ingredients which are necessary for the transformation of a *sthāyī-bhāva* into *rasa* are the intrinsic propriety of the *sthāyī-bhāva* itself for such transformation (*svarūpayogyatā*), the propriety of the cause (*vibhāva*) and the effect (*anubhava*) of the *sthāyī-bhāva* for causing such transformation (*parikarayogyatā*), and the propriety of the subject of the sentiment for the relish of such transformation (*puruṣayogyatā*). These three ingredients are present in *kṛṣṇarati* to the fullest extent. The propriety of *kṛṣṇarati* for being a *sthāyī-bhāva* cannot be negated since it cannot be obstructed by any feeling contradictory to or consistent with it and since it can produce joy greater than that of the realization of Brahman. The propriety of the cause and the effect of *kṛṣṇa-rati* should be admitted as these being presented by clever poets as related with divine objects are turned *alaukika* or super-mundane. The propriety of the subject is established by the fitness of the devotees like Prahlāda, etc., for the relish of *kṛṣṇa-rati*.(E65). So, even from the standpoint of orthodox rhetoricians *bhaktirasa* should be admitted (E66).

"According to the orthodox works on dramaturgy the locus of *rasa* may be (1) the original hero and heroine (*anukārya*) who are imitated by the actor, (2) the actor (*anukartā*) who imitates the role of the original hero and heroine, (3) the audience who is gifted with the capacity of relishing *rasa* and therefore is a man of taste (*sahṛdaya sāmajika*) and (4) if the actor possesses that capacity then both the actor and the audience. Śrī Jīva Gosvāmi admits this view and he points out that *rasa* consisting of *bhagavat-prīti* rises spontaneously in the *anukārya*, the *bhagavat-parikara* (attendants of Lord Kṛṣṇa), and is transferred to the *anukartā* (the actor or imitator) and the *sāmājika* (spectators) who are also devotees (*bhagavad-bhakta*). A literary composition hardly has any role to play in the emergence of *prīti* in them as of *rati*, etc., in secular poetry (E68). *Prīti* being associated with proper *vibhāva, anubhāva* and *vyabhicāribhāva* is transformed into *rasa* (E71). The *vibhāva* is of two types–the *ālambana* (the supporting cause) and the *uddīpana* (the exciting cause). Kṛṣṇa, who assumes the role of four types of hero as Dhīradatta, Dhīrapraśānta, Dhīroddhata and Dhīralalita, is the *ālambana vibhava* of *prīti* being its object and His beloved ones are also the *ālambanavibhāva* being the ground of that feeling (E71). The *uddīpana vibhāvas* are *guṇa* (quality), *jāti* (class), *kriyā* (action), *dravya* (individual substance) and *kāla* (time) which, being related with Kṛṣṇa, help to excite the *kṛṣṇa-rati* or *prīti* of the devotees (E73). The *anubhāva* of *kriyārati* or *prīti* which indicates the outward expression of that feeling is of two types–(1) *udbhāsvara* and (2) *sāttvika*. The former originates from the inward feeling and gets expressed through external acts while the latter comes out from *sattva* or the mind enriched by that feeling. There are eight *sāttvika-bhāvas* (e.g., *stambha, sveda* etc.) which are the same as those mentioned in orthodox works on dramaturgy (E87).

"The *vyabhicāribhāvas* or *sañcarībhāvas* (the auxiliary feelings) of *kṛṣṇa-rati* are thirty-three in number and these are also the same as are enumerated in orthodox *rasaśāstra* with this exception that these are always related with *kṛṣṇarati* (E87-88).

"The five types of *prīti* viz. *jñānabhakti, dāsya, vātsalya, maitrya* and *kāntabhāva*, in association with proper *vibhāvas* (both *ālambana* and *uddīpana*), *anubhāvas* (both *udbhāsvara* and *sāttvika*) and *vyabhicāri-(sañcari)bhāvas* become five types of *bhaktirasa*, e.g. *jñāna* or *śānta, bhaktimaya (dātya), vātsalya, sakhya* and *ujjvala* respectively. These are primary or *mukhya bhaktirasas* (E88). There are seven types of secondary or *gauṇa bhaktirasa,* viz. *hāsya, karaṇa, raudra, vīra, bhayāmaka, vībhaisa* and *adbhūta*)(E88-115). These are so-called because these attain this status only when their corresponding *sthāyī bhāvas* come to be related with *kṛṣṇa-priti* (134). These seven *gauṇa-bhakti-rasas* may be consistent with the *mukhya-bhakti-rasa* or contradictory to them or neither consistent nor contradictory, i.e., indifferent (E141). If in poetry concerned with Kṛṣṇa the relish of a *sthāyībhāva,* primary or secondary, is obstructed by the association of the relish of an incongruous *sthāyībhāva* then that is a case of *rasābhāsa* (E93) or if any *gauṇa-sthāyī-bhāva* is associated with another improper or incongruous *gauṇa-sthāyībhāva* (E95).

"Of the twelve tpes of *bhaktirasa* (five primary (*mukhya*) and seven secondary (*gauna*)) the *ujjvala rasa* is the best and sweetest of all. The *kāntābhāva,* the *sthāyībhāva* of this *rasa* has its origin either in the nature of Kṛṣṇa or in the nature of a particular girl (E13).

"This *rasa* is of two types–*vipralambha* and *sambhoga,* corresponding to the estrangement and union of Kṛṣṇa with his beloved, the damsels of Vraja. The *vipralambha* heightens the sweetness of *sambhoga* and it falls into four classes–*pūrvarāga, māna, premavaicitya* and *pravāsa* (E140). The *pūrvarāga* consists of *rati* which rises in the lover and the beloved before union by seeing each other or by hearing each other's qualities. It is displayed by ten types of amorous attitude (*kāmadaśa*) (E143). *Māna* indicates resentment as a bar to the realization of each other's love. It culminates in *praṇaya* and may or may not have any cause (E145). *Premavaicitya* (E147) is the attainment of *rati* marked by a feeling of separation even when the lover and the beloved are united. *Pravāsa* is the feeling of separation caused by the absence of the hero gone abroad (E141).

"In *sambhoga* the lovers enjoy each other's company as united together and it also is classified into four types corresponding to four types of *vipralambha* after which it occurs (E141).

"Śrī Jīva Gosvāmi strongly opposes the general trend of Vaiṣṇava tradition in which the *prīti* or love of the Gopīs for Kṛṣṇa is characterized as extra-marital-*parakīyā* or the illegitimate love of another man's wife for her paramour (*jāra* or *upapati*), since the Gopīs are married to the cowherds of Vṛndāvana. The reason advanced by the supporters of this tradition is this, that impediments and obstacles caused by the violation of social and ethical laws which hinder the easy flow of love of each couple tend to intensify that sentiment and hinder the easy flow of love of such couples [that] tends to intensify that sentiment and make its realization perfect. Such intensity and perfection can hardly be attained in the legitimate or marital (*svakīyā*) love of a woman for her husband (*pati*) which is not beset with impediments and obstacles. Śrī Jīva Gosvāmi regards the Gopīs as *svākiyā* or wives of Kṛṣṇa though they appear as *parakīyā* or another man's wife (i.e. wives of the Gopas) in the *prakaṭalīlā*. In the *Śrīkṛṣṇasandarbha* they have been conceived as embodying the *svarūpaśakti* of Kṛṣṇa. Here in the *Prītisandarbha* Śrī Jīva Goswaṃi emphatically declares that the Gopas are not real husbands of the Gopīs.. They only appear as such and their relation with the Gopīs is only an illusion (*pratyābhāsa*). The love of the Gopīs for Kṛṣṇa being itself self-established and of the highest class does not require adventitious support or strengthening of any kind (E121). By overcoming all obstacles, the strength of the sentiment, like that of a mad elephant, is only manifested; but it is not meant that the obstacles intensify that sentiment. Even if *aupapatya* (the state of being *upapatti*–paramount) be conceived of Kṛṣṇa for the Gopīs, as some want to hold, still that does not belittle the greatness of *kṛṣṇa-rati*. Indeed, the amorous love for another man's wife is to be blamed or deprecated only in the case of an ordinary hero, but not of Kṛṣṇa who appears on earth only to relish the quintessence of love of mankind."

7.7 JĪVA GOSVĀMIN, *Sukhabodhinī* on the *Gopālatāpanīyopaniṣad*
Manuscript citations at NCat VI, 139; VII, 285.

7.8 JĪVA GOSVĀMIN, *Brahmasaṃhitā-Sukhabodhinī.*

Sir John Woodroffe, going under the pseudonym "Arthur Avalon", provides in Avalon 1985, pp. 2-12 the following analysis of this work. We are not informed as to the original date of the first publication of this work.

Summarized by Arthur Avalon (Sir John Woodroffe)

"The *Brahmasaṃhitā* is according to Jīva Gosvāmi composed of one hundred chapters. The fifth chapter according to him contains the essence of the entire book as maxims or in *sūtra* form. It is on this account that he wrote the commentary to the fifth chapter alone. The book itself was brought by Caitanya Deva from the temple of Ādi Keśava in Mallāra in the Deccan. The *Caitanyacaritāmṛta* (Madhya Līlā chapter X) describers how delighted he was when he discovered this book. It also says that it contains the essence of all Vaiṣṇava *śāstras*. Śrī Caitanya evidently goes only to the fifth chapter and there is no trace of the remaining 99 chapters. Part of the *Nārada Pañcarātra* published by the Anandashrama Press of Poona is also called *Brahmasaṃhitā* and though that also is a Vaiṣṇava work and does not conflict with the teachings of the book here published it is entirely distinct. The commentary was written by Jīva at the request of his *guru* Caitanya Deva.

"The first verse of the book which has been commented upon at considerable length says that Krishna is but another name for the Supreme Brahman. He is the Lord (*īśvara*).. He is united with all the great *śaktis* (*parama*). He is *sat-cid-ānanda.*

He is without beginning (*anādi*). He is the Source (*ādi*), and is the cause of all causes (*sarvakāraṇakāraṇa*). The commentator draws his materials in support of the interpretation as above from the *Śrīmadbhāgavata,* the *Upaniṣads*, and the *Gītā*. He also quotes from the grammatical construction of the word and tradition.

"The second verse speaks of the Lotus of a thousand petals as Gokula...

"Verses 3 and 4 say that the *yantra* wherein is the *mantra* of eighteen letters is in the pericarp of the lotus. Jīva in his commentary to these verses quotes two verses from the *Gautamīya Tantra* one of which says that the *devatā* of the *mantra* is Kṛṣṇa, but the *adhiṣṭhātṛ devatā* (controlling divinity) is Durgā. He further quotes a text to show that Durgā is Mahāviṣṇu. The other verse says that Krishna is Durgā and Durgā is Krishna and he who makes a distinction between the two is never liberated from *saṃsāra.* He also quotes the *Sammohana Tantra* which says the same thing.

"Verse 5 says that in the filaments of the lotus abides the *āvāraṇa ḍevātā* of Kṛṣṇa and on the petals ṭhe *śaktiṣ*. Here Jīva quotes the Bṛhaḍ-Gautamīya Tantra,the *Matsyapūrāṇa*, the *Ṛkpārīśīṣṭa* and a text whose source is not traceable. This last mentioned authority quoted speaks of the *sahasrāra* lotus, on the petals whereof are the *devīs* (*śaktis*) and the Gopālas and in the middle of it the adorable Supreme Puruṣa (*śrīparamaḥ puruṣa*).

"Verses 6 to 9 describes the precincts of Gokula which is square in shape and is called *Śvetadvīpa.* '*Śvetadvīpa*' literally means 'white island' but here, as is explained later on, *śveta* (white) means 'pure, uncontaminated by anything worldly' and *dvīpa* is used in the sense of anything detached, not connected with *saṃsāra*. It is the abode of the four manifestations (*mūrti*), viz. Vāsudeva, Saṃkarṣaṇa, Pradyumna and Aniruddha and it is divided into four sections. The four aims of human existence, viz. *dharma, artha, kāma* and *mokṣa* are there as also the four Vedas (*Sama* and others) whereby the same can be attained...

"Verse 10 says that the Supreme *Deva* who is *sat* and *ānanda* is Light itself and *ātmārāma* and has no intercourse (*samāgama*) with *prakṛti* or *māyā*. *Ātmārāma* is defined as he who enjoys the Eternal Bliss which is within his own self.

"The Supreme *Deva*, it is said in verse 11, who is in a state of enjoyment with *māyā* (*māyayā ramamānaḥ*) is inseparable from Her...and enjoys with Her who is within Himself. This union, it is said in the same verse, is because of their desire to create.

"Another name for *māyā* is Ramā and Ramā is another name for *niyati* (v. 12) and *niyati*, the commentator says, is the imperishable *śakti* of Hari. The commentator in support of the statement that the *devī* is imperishable quotes texts from *Viṣnupurāṇa* which reads like a text from any *śākta tantra*.

"Verse 13 says that creation is the outcome of the union of *liṅga* and *yoni*.

"Verse 14 says that *puruṣa* is *śaktimān* and *maheśvara* is *liṅgarūpī*. This is followed by a paraphrase of the *Puruṣasūkta*:–'That *puruṣa* is thousand-headed, thousand-eyed, thousand-footed' and so forth and this *puruṣa*, it is further said, (v.16) is Nārāyaṇa. Nārāyaṇa is defined to be He who pervades humanity and in support of this the commentator quotes a text from *Manusaṃhitā* which says 'Nāra' means the waters and 'Nāra' and the waters are the offspring of man. He who abides in or pervades them is Nārāyaṇa.

"Verse 19 says that from the left side of *puruṣa* originated Viṣṇu and from his right Prajāpati (Brahmā) and from the space between the eyebrows of *puruṣa* emanated *śambhu* who is the luminous *liṅga*. The space between the eyebrows is the *ājñācakra*'. The *ājñācakra* of Nārāyaṇa is the place of Śambhu. This tallies with the Śākta conception of the *ājñācakra* where it is said that the *liṅga* which is in that *cakra* is *itara* which is lustrous like chains of lightning.

"Verse 29 speaks of the universe as the product of *ahaṃkāra*...

"Verse 20 gives the *mantra* of eighteen letters of Kṛṣṇa.

"Verses 32 and 33 declare the union in the lotus of a thousand petals of *prakṛti* with the ever-existing and luminous *citānanda*.

"Verse 34 says that the melody of Kṛṣṇa's flute is *śabdabrahman*.

"Verses 38 to 64 contain a hymn to Krishna under the name of Govinda. The hymn speaks of the Lakṣmīs or Śaktis by whom Govinda or Krishna is surrounded, of the way He protects and nourishes the worlds by His luminous form consisting of *satcidānanda*, of His non-duality or inseparateness (*advaita*) from creation of His perennial youth, of the ease with which He can be attained along the path of *bhakti*. At the same time, it is said, that it is difficult to reach Him by mere *jñāna*..

"Verse 43 says that the mind of man moves along millions of ways, but the minds of the Great Munis always tend towards Him.

"In verse 46, it is said that He abides in Gokula surrounded by countless *kalās* or *śaktis* who are but His reflections.

"In verse 50, it is said that it His *māyā* which brings forth the hundreds of worlds...

'In the commentary to verse 52 is quoted a long passage from Ch. IV of the *Gautamīya Tantra* describing Vrindāvana. It reads somewhat like the description of Kailāsa as in the *Mahānirvāṇa* and non-Vaiṣnava *tantras*.

"Verse 53 speaks of Durgā as His shadow (*chāyā*) and says that it is She who creates, maintains and destroys...

"...(I)t is said (v. 57) that the Lords of the various worlds live during the duration of one outgoing breath of Govinda. The hymn goes on to say that all *devīs* and *devas* bow to Govinda as he is the Supreme Lord over all.

"In verse 67 Govinda is spoken of as Mahāviṣṇu. This book clearly shows that Kṛṣṇa, Govinda, Mahāviṣṇu, Śiva, Brahman are but different names, looked at in different ways, of the One Supreme Spirit."

7.9 JĪVA GOSVĀMIN, *Bhaktirasāmṛtasindhu-Durghatasamāsagamaṇi*
Edited and translated by David Haberman.

7.10 JIVA GOSVAMIN, *Locanaracinī* on Rūpa Gosvāmin's *Ujjvalanīlamaṇi*

Edited several times; cf. Bib 3, #1011.12. Neal Delmonico has provided (in Delmonico 1997 (1), pp. 34-47) translations of a few sections of this work, whose title he translates as "Pleasing to the Eyes". Delmonico points out (p. 31ff) "that within fifty years of the text's [viz., the *Ujjvalanīlamaṇi*'s] circa 1554 C. E. composition, a controversy grew up among various factions of the Caitanya Vaiṣṇava tradition concerning the nature of the love relationship between Rādhā and Kṛṣṇa. The Bhāgavata Purāṇa depicts the relationship between Kṛṣṇa and the cowherd girls as extra-marital. Most of the girls were already married to others when they were drawn into the forest by the sound of Kṛṣṇa's flute one autumnal night to dance with him...and give themselves to him...The extra-marital, extra-legal nature of that relationship thus became an essential part of the Caitanya tradition's paradigm for how humans should passionately love God.

"The adultery of the cowherd girls and Kṛṣṇa's praise of it, however, have understandably enough troubled numerous members of the tradition. Rūpa Gosvāmin] confirms the extra-marital nature of some of Kṛṣṇa's relationships in his Sapphire [i.e., the *Ujjvalanīlamaṇi*] and defends it, saying that although such behavior is condemned for ordinary men, it is not for the divine Kṛṣṇa...On the other hand, from the perspective of the theology of the tradition, Rādhā is Kṛṣṇa's own pleasure-giving potency and thus it is eternally connected with him. How then can she be regarded as his paramour? In this question we see a conflict between moral-theological and mytho-poetic understandings.

"The most eloquent representatives of the moral-theological and the mytho-poetic sides of the debate are...Jīva Gosvāmin and Viśvanātha Cakravartin. One of the most important questions is that of the relationship of a religious movement to the society in which it arises and to that society's moral standards. Do religious movements normally re-affirm and strengthen the moral rules of their society as a way of stabilizing societies in turmoil? Or do they challenge and transgress those rules as a way of helping a static and possibly decaying social structure to grow?"

"One can hardly find better representatives for each side of the debate. Jīva Gosvāmin, who became the leader of the Vṛndāvana group after the deaths of his uncles, directed his genius and erudition to establishing a structure strong enough to support the movement's transition into a tradition...It is understandable, therefore, that he argued for the eternal marriage of Rādhā and Kṛṣṇa and laid the appearance of their illicit affair at the feet of the illusory power of Kṛṣṇa (*yogamāyā*), which operates only for the variegation and enhancement of his sport. Jīva even wrote a play, the *Mādhavamahotsava*, in which he described the marriage of Rādhā with Kṛṣṇa."

Since the work is presently untranslated, except for the few passages rendered by Delmonico–which unfortunately do not address directly the problem just raised–we shall delay further discussion of this debate until we reach the other disputant, Viśvanātha Cakravartin.

8 NĀROTTAMA DĀSA (16th century)

Isvaradasa, the editor and publisher of PBC, provides in his Introduction, p. 3, the following information about this author:

"Śrī Narottama dāsa Ṭhākura Mahāśaya was a disciple of Lokanātha Gosvāmī, a principal follower of Lord Caitanya. Lord Caitanya Mahāprabhu ordered Lokanātha Gosvāmī to go to Vṛndāvana and excavate lost places of Kṛṣṇa's pastimes. He foretold the appearance of Nārottama Dāsa to Lokanātha Gosvāmī, saying he would have a disciple who will manifest a unique style of *kīrtana* that will captivate all human beings.

"Ṭrīla Narottama dāsa Ṭhākura studied along with Śrīnivāsa Ācārya and Śyāmānanda Prabhu under Śrīla Jīva Gosvāmī. Thereafter, the famous trio were ordered to broadcast the writings of the Gosvāmīs in Bengal."

8.1 NĀROTTAMA DĀSA, *Premabhakticandrikā*

PBC continues: "Being an empowered Ācārya who teaches according to time, place and circumstance, Śrīla Narottama dāsa Ṭhākura composed *Prema Bhakti-candrikā* in a simple style of Bengali language..."

We have selected the portions of the text that have philosophic content. In order to give an idea of the plan of the work, at least as it appears in PBC, we have also provided the titles given in that work for the nine chapters in which it is arranged.

The following consists of selections from PBC.

Translation by Isvaradasa

1 GLORIES OF THE SPIRITUAL MASTER

2 THE PROCESS OF FIXED DEVOTIONAL SERVICE

1 The topmost process of devotional service is to worship the Lord with body and mind, giving up desires for fruitive

activities and mental speculation. One should serve Lord Kṛṣṇa in the association of devotees without worshiping any demigods.

2 The essence of *sādhana bhakti* is to carefully consider and follow the path displayed by the previous and the present *mahājanas* (great personalities). One should not neglect the practice of remembering the pastimes of the Lord, for devotional service should be performed with the mind as well as the body.

3 O my dear brothers, always give up the bad association of the *karmīs* and *jñānīs* from a distance, and give up the attachment for singing songs not related to Kṛṣṇa. Associate only with the devotions and merge in topics of the loving pastimes of Kṛṣṇa in Braja.

4 Please give up the association of the *yogīs, sannyasīs, karmīs, jñānīs,* meditators, and the worshipers of the demigods. Also abandon attachment for all varieties of fruitive activities, religious duties, distresses, lamentations and material objects. Just worship Kṛṣṇa, the lifter of Govardhana Hill.

5 Traveling to the holy places is a waste of energy and born from illusion, for the lotus feet of Śrī Govinda are the perfection of one's life. Therefore, one should give up pride and envy and with firm determination in the heart, one should always worship the Lord without deviation.

6 The best process of devotional service is to hear, chant, worship, glorify and meditate with faith on the names, forms, qualities and pastimes of Kṛṣṇa in the association of the devotees of Kṛṣṇa through the nine forms of *bhakti*.

7 I will serve Govinda with all my senses and I will not worship demigods and goddesses. This is the highest principle of devotional service. All other processes are simply born of pride and I feel great pain in my heart by seeing them.

8 The six enemies: lust, anger, greed, illusion, pride and envy and the five senses of sight, sound, smell, taste, and touch reside in my body but I am unable to control them. Although I

hear and understand repeatedly that one should serve Kṛṣṇa with all his senses, still I cannot accept this fact with firm determination.

9 I will engage lust, anger, greed, illusion, envy and pride in their proper places. In this way, I will defeat the enemies and with ecstacy in my heart, I will worship Govinda without difficulty.

10 I will engage my lust in eagerness to serve Kṛṣṇa and I will use my anger against those who are envious of the devotees. I will be greedy to hear the topics of Hari in the association of the devotees. I will be illusioned if I fail to achieve my worshipable Lord and I will feel proud to chant the glories of Kṛṣṇa. In this way, I will engage them in their respective duties.

11 Otherwise, independent lusty desires, which are the source of all unwanted things will always disturb the path of devotional service. What harm can lusty desires and anger do to a practitioner of devotional service if he associates with devotees?...

3 SELF-SURRENDER

4 UNDIVIDED SERVICE TO THE DIVINE COUPLE

5 A GLIMPSE INTO THE PATH OF LOVING ATTACHMENT

1 Now, I will explain the process of worshiping the upreme Lord through the path of attachment (*rāgānugā bhakti*). These statements are the essence and in accordance with the Vedas and the pure devotees. One should serve the Lord in Braja following in the footsteps of the *sakhīs* with a suitable spiritual body. In this way one's soul will be cooled and satisfied....

9 Whatever I aspire as a practitioner, I will surely receive in my spiritual body. It is only a consideration of immaturity or maturity. In the immature state, it is called *sādhana-bhakti* or regulated devotional service. In the mature state, it is called *prama-bhakti* or loving devotional service. This is the essence and truth of pure devotional service.

6 TOPICS OF MEDITATION FOR AROUSING PREMA-BHAKTI

11 O my mind, you should now this for certain that the dualities of sin and piety are all temporary. Wealth and followers are all false. You do not know where you will go after death. You do not feel pain about this, and still you continue with your sinful activities.

12 The state and administration of a king is just like an act of a play. It gradually vanishes in due course of time. O my mind, it is He, the Supreme Lord who causes this by His illusory energy. Be always afraid of falling under its control.

13 O mind, do not indulge in sinful activities because sinners are most fallen. Give up bad association from a distance. Although piety is the abode of material happiness, do not strive for it, rather give up the desire for piety and liberation.

14 Loving devotional service is the ocean of nectar. Be always drowned in that ocean. Everything else is like an ocean of sun. If you follow this process, you will achieve eternal bliss and all your lamentations will go away.

15 Never associate with non-devotees. Be very careful about them. Chanting the names of Rādhā and Kṛṣṇa is the highest form of meditation. Do not accept any other process as the goal of life.

7 THE CHARACTERISTICS OF AN UNALLOYED DEVOTEE

8 FIXED LOVING DEVOTIONAL SERVICE

1 Śrī Vṛndāvana, the place of the pastimes of Rādhā and Kṛṣṇa, is indescribable. It is self-manifest and full of ecstatic love. Happiness is eternally present there. It is devoid of the miseries of old age and death. The pastimes of Kṛṣṇa are constantly performed there.

5 O my mind, service to Śrī Hari is rarely achieved. Why then do you not worship Him? You are simply suffering due to material bondage. Abandon all fruitive activities and religious

duties prescribed in the Vedas and serve the lotus feet of the Lord with devotion.

7 The result of material enjoyments are dangerous. Why do you not worship Śrī Nandanandana, the Lord of Braja and the abode of ecstatic bliss? Desires for heavenly planets, liberation and enjoying the material world are hellish. They ruin one's human form of life.

8 Do not put faith in this temporary material body, because Yamarāja, the lord of death, is waiting next to you. The flow of *karman* is just like the ocean of sorrow. Consider this properly and worship the lotus feet of Rādhā and Kṛṣṇa with attachment under the guidance of *sādhu* and *śāstra*.

9 THE ULTIMATE INSTRUCTIONS

1 I will neither indulge in useless mundane topics nor hear them. I will only engage in spiritual cultivation. I will always pray to eagerly discuss the topics of my worshipable Lord, because everything else is simply unwanted.

5 The most successful method of devotional service is to constantly remember the pastimes of Kṛṣṇa in the association of devotees. When one attains loving devotional service, then his mind will be fully purified and the distress of his heart will be vanquished.

6 Consider material sense objects as dangerous, and material life as a dream. The human form of life is most suitable for worshiping Kṛṣṇa. Always sing about the loving pastimes of Rādhā and Kṛṣṇa. All other topics cause distress to the heart.

9 NĀRĀYAṆA BHAṬṬA (1531-1575)

We find the following account in Leena Taneja, "Reclaiming a voice from the periphery: the forgotten story of Narayan Bhatt", Journal of Vaisnava Studies 15.2, 2007, pp. 35-50. Noting the curious inattention paid to this important saint and writer, Taneja goes on to provide the following by way of biography pp. 41-43):

"Janakiprasad Bhatt, Nārāyaṇa Bhaṭṭa's biographer, tells us that his subject was a Telugu Brahmin born in 1531 in Madurai, Tamil Nadu, in the town of Mathurā Pattana on the banks of the Godavari in South India. He was born on the day of Nṛsiṃha Caturdaśī. His father's name was Bhāskara and mother's was Yaśomatī. Bhāskara was a Bhṛguvaṃśī Dalaśinatya Brahmin and a follower of the Mādhva *sampradāya*. At a young age, he lived with his learned uncle Śri Śaṃkara, who looked after his education. Under him he became well-versed in *śāstra*.

"One day when Nārāyaṇa Bhaṭṭa was bathing in the river Godavari he had *darśana* of Rādhā and Kṛṣṇa. At this time, the Lord revealed Bhaṭṭa's spiritual identity as the sage Nārada Muni and ordered him to fulfil his life's work–to make external the holy places of Vraja that were hidden--and gave him a small *mūrti* of Bāla-Gopāla (the child Kṛṣṇa) named Laḍaleya Ji, who He said would reveal the secrets of Vraja-*līlā* to him, guiding him in his discovery of the *līlā-sthālis*. The Lord directed Nārāyaṇa Bhaṭṭa to take the image to Rādhā-kuṇḍa, where he would reveal himself once again in the form of Madana-mohāna, the one who enchants even the god of love.

"Without delay, Nārāyaṇa Bhaṭṭa set out on pilgrimage to Vraja with Laḍaleya Ji. His journey took two years to complete because of the pranks of his deity. We are told that during their journey, Laḍaleya would assume its ideal form to sport with Nārāyaṇa Bhaṭṭa, but would immediately turn back to stone when anyone else appeared. Just like a playful child, baby Kṛṣṇa would 'spring to life and jump mischievously into the trees; when he tired he would climb affectionately into his devotee's lap.'.

Nārāyaṇa Bhaṭṭa eventually arrived in Vraja in the year 1545. Upon arriving, he immediately took the deity to Rādhā-kuṇḍa, hoping to see the deity of Madana-mohāna, which had been established there by Sanātana Goswami, who had turned the service of the deity over to his disciple Kṛṣṇadāsa Brahmacarī. However, to his dismay, when he arrived the doors of the temple were shut; so he sat down in meditation. Suddenly, the doors opened by themselves to reveal the deity of Madana-mohāna. Beholding this glorious sight, Nārāyaṇa Bhaṭṭa lay prostrated before the deity. who spoke to him, reminding him once again of his special identity as th incarnation of Nārada who had taken form to recover the sites of Vraja"....(Taneja provides an alternative account from the literature that gives greater importance to Rūpa's and Sanātana's part in Nārāyaṇa Bhaṭṭa's initiation.)

"Several important manuscripts (seven to be exact) were completed during his time in Rādhā-kuṇḍa, including what is arguably his most important work, the *Vraja-Bhakti-Vilāsa,* which was finished in 1552, [and summarized later in this article, pp. 44-45). It is not a work on philosophy.] After this, we are told that Nārāyaṇa Bhaṭṭa moved to Unchagrama [or Lalita Village, about one mile northwest from Varsana]. This is where he married and had a son named Dāmodara. He lived in this district until the end of his manifest pastimes, and while there he wrote the remaining texts of his career, which were about fifty in number.

"His *samādhi* (tomb) is located in Unchagrama...near where today stands a Bālarāma temple. This temple is especially significant since it was built by Nārāyaṇa Bhaṭṭa himself, and the deity of Bālarāma was also installed by him...Nārāyaṇa Bhaṭṭa also founded a temple dedicated to Lariliji (Rādhā) in Varsana near Unchagrama and another to Rādhā-rāmaṇa in Sanket. After his death, the service of these deities was passed down to his son and a disciple of Nārāyaṇa Bhaṭṭa named Nārāyaṇadāsa Śrotrī, whose descendants are still in charge of these temples."

9.1 NĀRĀYAṆA BHAṬṬA, *Bhaktibhūṣaṇasandarbha*

Manuscripts are cited at NCat XV, 149. Apparently it has been edited, but the usual sources show no record of it.

9.2 NĀRĀYAṆA BHAṬṬA, *Bhaktirasāmṛtaraṅginī*

Known only from its title.

9.3 NĀRĀYAṆA BHAṬṬA, *Rasikahlādinī*

This is said to be partly edited.

10 VIṢṆUDĀSA GOSVĀMI (1670)

Neal Delmonico (Delmonico 1997 (1), p. 49, fn. 22) tells us: "Viṣṇudāsa's date is uncertain. As he was apparently a disciple of Kṛṣṇadāsa Kavirāja and possibly the author of a small messenger poem (*dūtakāvya*) called *Manodūta*, he probably lived at the end of the 16th cent. and first part of the 17th cent."

10.1 VIṢṆUDĀSA GOSVĀMI, *Ujjvalanīlamaṇi-Svātmapramodinī*

Edited by Haridasa Dasa in 1965 (though no longer listed as available). Delmonico 1997 (1), p. 28 remarks: "(T)his commentary, though of little or no theological value, is of great aesthetic and literary importance because it adds literary critical comments and cites numerous verses from other works of literature in support of modification of Rūpa's arguments."

11.1 VAṂŚĪDHARA (1680?), Commentary on the *Bhāgavatapurāṇa*

This is found edited by Krishnashankar Shastri (1916-) in *Maharsīvedavyāsapraṇītam Śrīmadbhāgavatamahāpurāṇam* (with nine commentaries, Hindi and Sanskrit), 1965-, in nine volumes.

12 VIŚVANĀTHA CAKRAVARTI (1720)

As part of the Introduction to BG2000, pp. 30-31 Bhaktivedanta Narayana Maharaj provides the following: "He appeared in a family of *brāhmaṇas* from the community of Rāḍhadeśa, in the district of Nadia, West Bengal, and was celebrated by the name Hari Vallabha. He had two older brothers named Rāmabhadra and Raghunātha. In his childhood, he first studied Sanskrit grammar in a village named Devagrāma, and afterwards went to a village named Śaiyadābāda in the district of Murśidābāda, where he studied the *bhakti-śāstras* at the home of his *guru*. While he was still undergoing his studies in Śaiyadābāda, he wrote three books: *Bhakti-rasāmṛta-sindhu-bindu, Ujjvala-nīla-maṇi-kiraṇa* and *Bhagavatāmṛta-kaṇā*. Shortly afterwards, he renounced his household life and went to Vṛndāvana, where he wrote many books and commentaries...

"When Śrīla Viśvanātha Cakravartī Ṭhakkura was very old, he spent most of the time in *antar-daśa* (fully internal state) and *ardha-bāhya* (semi-external consciousness), deeply absorbed in *bhajana*. At that time a debate broke out in the state of Jaipur, between the Gauḍīya Vaiṣṇavas and Vaiṣṇavas who supported the doctrine of *svakīyavāda* (marital love). The antagonistic Vaiṣṇavas led King Jai Singh II of Jaipur to believe that *śāstra* does not support the worship of Śrīmati Rādhikā as the consort of Śrī Govinda Deva. They contended that Śrīmati Rādhikā's name is not mentioned anywhere in *Śrīmad-Bhāgavatam* or in the *Viṣṇu Purāṇa*, and that she was never legally married to Kṛṣṇa according to Vedic rituals.

"Another objection was that the Gauḍīya Vaiṣṇavas did not belong to a recognized line of disciplic succession (*sampradāya*). There are only four lines of Vaiṣṇava *sampradāyas* which have descended from time immemorial: the Śrī Sampradāya, Brahma Sampradāya, Rudra Sampradāya, and Sanaka (Kumāra) Sampradāya. The principal *ācāryas* of these four *sampradāyas* in the age of Kalī are: Śrī Rāmānuja, Śrī

Madhva, Śrī Viṣṇusvāmī and Śrī Nimbāditya respectively. Since the Gauḍīya Vaiṣṇavas did not have their own commentary on the *Brahma-sūtra*, they could not be accepted as a bona fide Vaiṣṇava *sampradāya* with a pure lineage.

"Mahārāja Jai Singh knew that the prominent Gauḍīya Vaiṣṇava *ācāryas* were followers of Śrīla Rūpa Gosvāmī, and he summoned them to Jaipur to take up the challenge from the Vaiṣṇavas in the line of Śrī Rāmānuja. Since Śrī Cakravartī Ṭhākura was very old, and was immersed in the transcendental bliss of *bhajana*, he sent his student...Śrīpāda Baladeva Vidyābhūṣaṇa to Jaipur to address the assembly. He also sent his disciple Śrī Kṛṣṇadeva along with Śrīpāda Baladeva Vidyābhūṣaṇa." (The writer goes on to describe Baladeva's role, culmnating in that author's composition of his *Govindabhāṣya* (see below, under Baladeva Vidyābhūṣaṇa).

"When Śrīla Viśvanātha Cakravartī Ṭhākura was about one hundred years old, he entered into *aprakāṭa* (unmanifest) Vṛndāvana in Śrī Rādhā-Kuṇḍa while absorbed in his state of transcendence. This took place on the firth day of the light phase of the moon in the month of Mādha (January-February) in the year 1676 Sakābda. His *samādhi* can be found today just next to the temple of Śrī Gokulānanda in Śrī Dhāma Vṛndāvan."

12.1 VIŚVANĀTHA CAKRAVARTI, *Bhagavadgītā-Sārārthavarṣiṇī*

Edited many times. It is translated in BG2000 (too long to reproduce here).

12.2 VIŚVANĀTHA CAKRAVARTI, *Bhagavatapurāṇa-Sarārthadarśinī*

Translated BL1140.4.N436.

12.3 VIŚVANĀTHA CAKRAVARTI, *Bhaktirasāmṛtasindhu-Bindu*

Translated (ET) by Klaus Klostermaier in JAOS 94, 1974, 96-107, who says (p. 98) that "this work was written in 1704

A.D. at Vṛndāvana...In [it]...Viśvanātha Cakravartī has not only condensed Rūpa Goswāmi's *summa* of *bhakti*-theology by leaving out the numerous quotations from the scriptures (mainly the *Bhāgavatam* and other *Purāṇas*) without sacrificing anything essential but he has at several places also expressed his own opinions which seems to be at variance with Rūpa's."

It is also found edited and translated by Bhaktivedanta Narayana Maharaja, Vrndavana 2006.

12.4 VIŚVANĀTHA CAKRAVARTI, *Rāgavārtmacandrikā*

Translated by Joseph O'Connell in Corpus, pp. 185-209. We initially present O'Connell's helpful "Introductory remarks", found on pp. 185-189. Cf. under #12.6 below for an edition with a translation.

Translated by Joseph T.O'Connell

"1. Praise, praise to those who like *cakara* birds savor the nectarous word of Śri Ṛūpa, by the droplets of whose mercy I shall utter this 'Moonbeam on the Way of Passion'.

"2. Passionate devotion (*rāgānugābhakti*), mentioned in brief in the previously issued Drop (*bindu*) from the Blessed Ocean of Nectar of Devotion (*bhaktisudhāmbodhi)*, i.e., *Bhaktirasāmṛtasindhu*), is discussed herein at length.

"3. Let it be (defined as) ritualistic devotion (*vaidhibhakti*) if the stimulus (*pravarttaka*) to devotion is scripture (*śāstra*); let it be (defined as) passionate (*rāgānugā*) if indeed longing (*lobha*) is the stimulus to devotion.

"4. Let commitment (*pravṛtti*) to devotion be (defined as) very firm desire (*suniścayacikīrṣā*); let two kinds of persons qualified for that (devotion) (*tadadhikārinau*) be (defined as those desirous due to scripture and (those desirous) due to longing.

"5. In that context longing (*lobha*) is characterized (*laksita*) by the feet of Śrī Rūpa Gosvāmin himself: 'When the mind (*dhī*) pays heed (*apekṣate*) upon hearing of the sweetness of their (i.e. Kṛṣṇa's and his beloved's) feelings (*bhāva*), etc., and (does) not in this context (pay heed) to scripture nor to logical argument, that is characteristic of the onset of longing (*lobhotpattilakṣaṇa*).'

"6. And it (i.e., *lobha*) is two-fold: that caused by the mercy of Bhagvān and that caused by the mercy of a passionate devotee. Among them that due to the mercy of a devotee is twofold: antecedent and current. Antecedent (*prāktana*) is that arising from the mercy of such a devotee living in the past; contemporary (*ādhunika*) is that arising from the mercy of such a devotee living in this present lifetime. In the former case one takes refuge at the feet of such a *guru* subsequently to longing; in the latter case commitment to longing (*lobhapravṛtti*) comes subsequently to taking refuge at the feet of the *guru*. As is said: 'This passonate (*rāgānugā*) (devotion) which has as its sole cause longing (*lobha*) due simply to the compassion (*kāruṇya*) of Kṛṣṇa and his devotees is spoken of by some as the way of nourishment (*puṣṭimārga*).

"7. And then, when inquiry occurs as to the means for attaining those longed-for feelings, there should be heed for scripture and logical argument on the part of a devotee having such longing. This is so because they (i.e., such means) are made known in no other way than by the injunctions of scripture and by logical argument based upon scripture. Similarly, if there be longing for milk, etc., there should be heed for the word s of advice of a worthy person experienced in the matter once the question of the means for it–'How may I have milk?'–occurs. Then from words of advice such as, 'The gentleman must buy a cow', etc., he should learn the procedures for driving a cow, feeding it grass, milking it, etc., but not on his own. As is said in the eighth book (of the *Bhāgavata Purāṇa*): 'As humans through disciplined efforts attain the fire within wood, the milk in cows, food and water in the earth and sustenance in hard work, so do they attain you within the elements (*guṇeṣu*) by means of intellect; so say the wise.'

"8. And this longing becomes greater and greater every day in proportion to the purity of the mind (*antaḥkaraṇa*) due to devotion, beginning with the characteristic (*lakṣaṇa*) taking of refuge at the feet of a *guru* on the part of devotees faring on the way of passion, continuing up to the moment of gaining immediate contact (*sākṣātprāpti*) with one's most desired reality (*svābhīṣṭavastu*), as stated by Bhagavān 'The more the self is purified by meritorious recitation, hearing and talking about me the more it sees, like an eye treated with ointment, the subtler reality.'

"9. When such longing has arisen there should be enthusiastic and exceeding commitment to the scripturally enunciated means of attaining those respective feelings, which (means) in some cases are disclosed by the mouth of a *guru* and in some cases by the mouth of an experienced magnanimous passionate devotee and which in some cases are manifested spontaneously by the operations of a mind purified by devotion; as in the saying of Uddhava: 'In the form of teacher or of individual consciousness (*caitya*) he shows the way to himself'. It is similar with the means of attaining pleasure in the case of those whose objective is pleasure.

"10. And that scripture–which constitutes the essence of all Upaniṣads–is precisely the Śrī Bhāgavata, the great Purāṇa, the mine of collections of such sayings as: 'Of whom I am the beloved the self, or the son, the friend, the *guru*, the confidant, the deity, the desired one...' And similar are the Śrī *Bhaktirasāmṛtārṇava (Ocean of Nectar of the Mood of Devotion)*, etc.., which excel in elaborating upon the devotion presented in above. In that (*Bhaktirasāmṛtārṇava*) are these three verses:

(a) 'Remembering Kṛṣṇa and his folk, the beloved, desired for oneself (*nijasaṃhita*), and delighted by talk about them, that one should dwell always in Vraja.'

(b) 'In this context service in the form of an aspirant (*sādhakarūpeṇa*) as well as in an accomplished form (*siddharūpeṇa*) is to be done in emulation of the folk of Vraja by one desirous of their feelings (*udbhāvalipsunā*).'

(c) 'Hearing, chanting of praise, etc., spoken of as ritualistic devotion, are to be understood by the wise as constituent parts here (i.e., in passionate devotion).' In this context the three are to be explained from the standpoint of the emulation of amorous pleasure (*kāmānugāpakṣe*).

"11. 'Remembering Kṛṣṇa' is stated first. The priority accorded to remembering in passionate devotion is due to the mental nature (*manodharmatvāt*) of passion. The 'beloved' is Kṛṣṇa, the supreme lord of Vṛndāvana, who displays himself in sports (*līlāvilāsin*) appropriate to one's own feelings (*nija-bhāvocita*). And his, Kṛṣṇa's, folk, of what are they? 'Desired for oneself,' i.e., fit to be longed for by oneself (*svābhilaṣaṇīya*): the blessed queen of Vṛndāvana, Lalitā, Viśākha, Śrī Rūpamañjarī *et al.* Even though Kṛṣṇa is desired for oneself, his folk are even more to be desired for oneself because they are exclusively situated within amorous (*ujjvala*, lit., flaming) feelings. 'Dwell in Vraja'; if not possible (physically), then mentally. That such dwelling is to be done even while having the body of an aspirant is evident from the verse that follows.

"'In the form of an aspirant'; in whatever (ordinary) body one occupies (*yathāvasthitadehena*). 'In an accomplished form'; in a body suitable for serving face to face the most desired one meditated upon within. 'By one desirous of their feelings': by one desiring to attain that feeling called amorous (*ujjvala*) which has as its objects (*viṣaya*) Kṛṣṇa, who is one's own beloved, and as its subject (*āśraya*) the folk of Kṛṣṇa, who are desired for oneself. 'Service' (*sevā*): serving (*paricaryā*) that is to be done with proper materials, etc.., both those presented mentally and those presented face to face. He indicated there the manner: 'in emulation of the folk of Vraja'" in emulation of such Vraja folk as Śrī Rūpamañjarī and others who are to be imitated in an accomplished form and such Vraja folk as Śrī Rūpa Gosvāmin and others who are to be imitated in an aspirant's form. And also to be considered as Vraja folk to be imitated as far as possible in the form of an aspirant are those persons who have attatined a relationship with Kṛṣṇa (*prāptakṛḍṇasambandhin*), i.e., Candrakānti and others and the sages of the Daṇḍaka forest and the scriptures (*śrutayas*) known from the *Bṛhadvāmana Purāṇa*. 'In emulation of them': with an eye to their respective worshipful services (*tattadācāradṛṭyā*).

"Having spoken in two verses in this way about remembering and dwelling at Vraja he then spoke of hearing etc.: 'Hearing, chanting of praises, etc...' Also included by implication (*ākṣepalabdhāni*) are taking refuge at the feet of the *guru*, etc. Without these (means) emulating the folk of Vraja, etc., would in no way be possible. Then 'by the wise': with wisdom, with discrimination; those (means) are to be done which are appropriate to one's own feelings, but not those which are obstructive of them.

"12. And among devotional practices these are not to be done even though enjoined in the *āgama* scriptures: self-worship (*ahaṃgrahopāsanā*), hand gestures (*mudrā*), installing gods in the body (*nyāsa*), meditating upon Dvāraka, worshiping Rukṃinī *et al.* and other (such practices). The reason is that in this way of devotion, it is heard, there is no fault even if there be omission of some of the constituent parts (*aṅgavaikalya*). As is said, 'Having established himself upon which, o king, a man never falters, as one running here does not stumble, does not fall, even though he blink his eyes.' There is fault, however, if there is omission of that which possesses the constituent parts (i.e., of passionate devotion as exercise, *rāgānugāsādhana-bhakti*), as in the statement 'Having taken refuge in which forms of Bhāgavata *dharma*–hearing, chanting praises, etc.-.. and according to the *smṛti* statement, 'Single minded devotion to Hari certainly would be tantamount to destruction if apart from the injunctions of '*śruti, smṛti, Purāṇa* and *Pañcarātra*.' If someone because of the idea that it is not right to neglect what is declared in scripture performs everything that is declared (including that) which is incompatible with one's own feelings even though the stimulus (*pravarttakatva*) is longing, then he attains the status of being a follower (*prajanatva*) of one of the queens in Dvārakā city. As is said: 'One who, experiencing intense desire for sexual union (*riraṃsāṃ suṣṭhu kurvan*), serves according to the entire (*kevalena*) way of injunctions attains the status of queen in the city.' 'Entire' (*kevala*): complete (*kṛtsna*), not omitting any constituent parts at all, not even those incompatible with one's own feelings, like worship of the queens, etc. '*Kevala*' is 'an adjective meaning unique or complete' (*evakṛtnayoḥ*) according to Amara.

"The interpretation (*vyākhyā*) does not follow that there is (attained) the status of a queen in the city (i.e., Dvārakā) via the entire way of injunctions and (some status) at Mathurā via a combined (*miśreṇa*) (way). What form is there at Mathurā analogous to the status of queen in the city of Dvārakā? If one should suggest being a follower of the hunchbacked woman then there would be an improper denigration of the results of combined enjoined devotion as compared with the results of entire enjoined devotion. If, on the strength of the text from the *Gopāla Tāpanī*–'The lord together with Rāma, Aniruddha, Pradyumna and Rukminī..'–it be concluded that the marriage with Rukmiṇī was at Mathurā and hence that there may be the status of attendant upon Rukmiṇī, such an (interpretation) would not be universally accepted. A second impropriety is: why should a worshiper of Rādhā or Kṛṣṇa attain either the hunchback or Rukmiṇī? In fact service in the way of injunctions (*vidhimārgeṇa*) (when) stimulated by longing is called the easy of passion (*rāgamārga*) and service in the way of injunctions (when) stimulated by injunctions is called the way of injunctions (*vidhimārga*, i.e., ritualistic devotion, *vaidhībhakti*). But service not related at all to injunctions is conducive to ruin according to the declarations of *śruti, smṛti* etc.

"13 Next there is addressed the concern over which of the acts of worship (*bhajanāni*)are constituent parts of passionate devotion, of what character they are (*kīdṛśīni*), what their essential forms (*svarūpāṇi*) are, how they are to be performed or not performed. Acts of worship of five kinds are seen in scripture: those composed of one's most desired feelings (*svābhīṣṭabhāvamayāni*), those having a relationship with one's most desired feeelings (*svābhiṣṭabhāvasambandhīni*), those harmonious with one's most desired feelings (*svābhiṣṭabhāvānukūlāni*), those not obstructive of one's most desired feelings (*svābhiṣṭabhāvāviruddhāni*), those obstructive of one's most desired feelings (*svābhiṣṭabhāvaviruddhāni*). Among them some have the form of accomplishing what is to be accomplished (*sādhyasāḍhanarūpāṇi*), some are material causes (*upādānakāraṇāni*) of that which is to be accomplished (*sādhya*), namely love (*preman*), some are instrumental causes (*nimittakāraṇāni*), some are signs of worship (*bhajanacihnāṇi*), some are helpful factors (*upakārakāṇi*), some are harmful factors (*apakārakāṇi*), some are neutral (*taṭasthāni*). These will be presented as classified.

"14. Among those the dutiful, the friendly, etc., are composed of one's most desired feelings, have the form of accomplishing what is to be accomplished; starting from taking refuge at the feet of a *guru*, (practices like) recitation of the *mantra*, meditation (*dhyāna*), etc., have a relationship with feelings because of being material causes of that which is to be accomplished; according to the statement, 'Let him recite continuously with an undisturbed mind,' they are regular and necessary acts (*nityakṛtyāni*); they have a relationship with feelings by being material causes since one notices recitation of the *mantra* even by those who are to be emulated in an accomplished form (*siddharūpeṇānugamyamānam*), as in the statement of the *Gaṇoddeśadīpikā:* 'The great prayer, the name of Kṛṣṇa, which is in contact with what one most desires (*svābhiṣṭasaṇsargi-*), is to be recited.' 'He, ruling all my senses, is the darling of the cowherd women.' The name of Kṛṣṇa, in contact with what one most desires, is indeed the great prayer, the best of all *mantras*. According to the sense it is the *mantra* of eighteen or of ten syllables that is spoken of. Thus is the meaning of the statement from the *Gaṇoddeśadīpikā* to be understood.

"Remembering, hearing about, etc., the sports, qualities, forms and names that are appropriate to one's own feelings (*svīyabhāvocita)* have relationship to feelings by virtue of being material causes. Accordingly: 'Let one wander about without attachment and without embarrassment singing the names and forms that refer to him (i.e., to Kṛṣṇa)'. According to such statements as 'Persons incessantly hear, sing, praise, remember and rejoice in what is beloved of you,' these are to be done incessantly (*abhīkṣṇakṛtyāni*). Here the subordination to changing of praise (*kīrtana*) even of remembering, the chief (constituent part) in passionate devotion, must be affirmed as certain because of the authority of chanting of praise in this (i.e., Kalī) age and because it is propounded (*pratripādanāta*) as the very best by all scriptures in all paths of devotion.

"The eleventh day fast, the eighth day birth festival and other observances (*vrata*) have the form of austerities (*taporūpāṇi*) because austerities are understood as cause of love according to the *śruti* texts being followed in the passage of the *Ujjvalanīlamaṇi* that goes: 'Having performed austerities with faith (*śraddhā*), full of love, they were born in Vraja.'; and because of the condemnation (*vigītatvāt*) of other austerity in this Kāli (age) (implicit) in the statement of Bhagavān: 'Whatever observance (*vrata*) is directed at me is austerity (*tapas*).' These are instrumental causes (*nimittakāraṇāni*); because it is heard that there is sin in their non-performance; they are regular and necessary (*nitya*). In that context there is relationship with feelings in the performance of the eleventh day fast and there is the contracting of sin against the (divine) names (*nāmāparādha*) in its omission, since one hears of the (sin of) killing the *guru*, etc., from statements of the *Skanda*, etc., such as 'Killing of a mother, killing of a father, and likewise killing of the *guru*...' and (one hears of) contracting an indestructible kind of sin from the statement of the *Viṣṇudharmottara*: 'Of the killer of a Brahmin, of the drinker of liquor, of the thief, or of one who violates his *guru's* wife...' In view of all this condemnation it is (seen to be) extremely compulsory. What is more, it is seen from statements of the *Skanda* that the eleventh day fast is the characteristic mark (*lakṣaṇa*) of a Vaiṣṇava: 'Of him who though having encountered the greatest peril or having arrived at the greatest bliss does not forgo the eleventh day fast is initiation (*dīkṣā*) (truly) Vaiṣṇavite'; 'He is truly called a Vaiṣṇava who has dedicated all his practices (*ācāra*) to Viṣṇu.' But in view of the prohibition for Vaiṣṇavas against food not offered to Bhagavān, the statement, 'If a Vaiṣṇava should eat on the eleventh day due to carelessness (*pramādataḥ*) is to be understood here as a prohibition even against food offered to Bhagavān.

"There is instrumental causality in the *kārttika* observance to the extent that it is austerity, material causality to the extent thatit is hearing, chanting of praise, etc. And especially from what is heard repeatedly in the remarks of Śrī Rūpa Gosvāmin 'Kārttikadevatā...Kārttikadevī...Ūrjjadevī......Ūrj-jeśvarī...' it may be understood to be capable of attaining the blessed queens of Vṛndāvana.

"According to the *smṛti* texts: 'O Ambarīṣa, always listen to the *Bhāgavata* recited by Śuka', it is declared that listening to the Śrī *Bhāgavata* is a regular and necessary duty. According to the statement in the twelfth book (of the *Bhāgavata*) which follows the word 'These remarks of the great ones have been spoken to you',–namely, 'One who much desires faultless devotion to Kṛṣṇa should always and incessantly listen to that fault-destroying recital of the virtues of the superlative one, which is recited always,'--hearing, etc., of the deeds of Kṛṣṇa, one's beloved, who is related to the tenth book (of the

Bhāgavata), are, as is applicable: required to be done always, required to be done incessantly, and related to feelings (of devotion).

"Such symbolic supports (*dhārsaṇāni*) as consecrated offerings (*nirmālya*), basil plant (*tulasī*), incense, sandal paste, garlands, clothing, etc., have a relationship to feelings. Symbolic supports such as garlands of *tulasī* wood, markings on the forehead with *gopīcandana* clay, etc., names, hand gestures, ritualistic insignia (*ācaraṇacihna*), etc., are harmonious (*anukulāni*) signs of being Vaiṣṇava. Service to, circumambulation about and prostrationbefore the basil plant also are harmonious.

"Acts of respect to cows, the sacred fig tree (*aśvattha*), the earth and Brāhmaṇas, etc., are not obstructive of that feeling are helpful factors. Service to Vaiṣṇavas is to be understood as having all the above mentioned characteristics. All these that have been enumerated are to be done.

"Just as on the part of the queen of Vraja (Yaśodā) there may be a higher priority of attention to the churned milk, curd, butter etc., which nourish him [than?] to Kṛṣṇa in person, the one to be nourished, as (is evident) from (her) having gone in order to bring the milk for him after having set him aside though hungry and sucking milk from her breast; so likewise on the part of devotees experienced in the mood (*rasa*) (of devotion) who are progressing on the way of passion it is not improper for thereto be greater attention paid to all those things which nourish than to the hearing, praising, etc., which are to be nourished.

"Self-worship, installing deities in the body, hand gestures, meditation upon Dvārakā, rituals for the queens (*mahīṣyarccana*) (of Dvārakā), etc., are harmful factors and are not to be done. Talk about, hearing of, etc., other *Purāṇas* are neutral.

"The (mention of) material cause, etc., in this context–even though there is no modification in devotion, its form being existence-consciousness-bliss–is due simply to the difficulty of analyzing (*durvitarkatvāt*). In devotional texts like 'In that context there are six feelings (*bhāva*), namely affectionate love (*sneha*), etc., which are expressions (*vilāsa*) of love (*preman*),' suggestion is effected (*vyañjitam*) by means of the word 'expression' (*vilāsa*), just as in treatises on mood (*rasaśāstra*) by means of words like 'stimulant' (*vibhāva*). Here indeed it is purely to facilitate understanding that words like 'material cause have been used. May this be pardoned by the virtuous!

II

"1. From this and other texts:–'He knows no loss, no exhaustion, no attachment to duties of his household, no cause for fear nor any anxiety at any time in any way; surrounded by fine bodied girls who have made of the god of love their confidant (*svāṅgīkṛtasuhṛaṅgābhir*), Hari sports far into the night loudly in the woods of Vṛndā,'–it may be objected that it is not possible for the blessed son of the village chief, charmed by expressions (*vilāsamugdha*) of love (*preman*) by the blessed queens of Vṛndāvana, to be attentive anywhere else. And if this be the case, then by whom is serving (*paricaryā*), etc., being done by countless passionate devotees in sundry regions, to be accepted? and by whom would entreaties, praises and recitations be heard? If it be proposed: by a portion of him, by the supreme self (*paramātman*), because of the unity of part and whole, such a resolution would be utter pain for such passionate devotees of Kṛṣṇa. So what is the solution? The statement of Śrī Uddhava is directly to the point (*sākṣāt*): 'O God, it indeed (*iva*) baffles my mind that you who always have self-awaremess (*sadātmabodha*) which is neither dulled nor incomplete (*akuṇṭhitākhaṇḍa*), the lord who is not inattentive should, as though simple, summons and inquires of me for advice.'

"The meaning is this: having definitely summoned me for advice, for deliberations undertaken with regard to going forth for the killing of Jarāsandha and the royal consecration, etc., that you should ask, 'Uddhava, you must tell me what is to be done here': 'you ask' (*pṛccheḥ*), i.e., you asked (*apṛcchaḥ*); 'not dulled', i.e. by time etc.; 'not incomplete', i.e. completely full; 'always' i.e. in every respect; just such awareness of self. He who possesses the all-knowing divine power (*samvicchakti*) asks as though simple, like any simple person. This is the meaning. This your simultaneous simplicity (*maugdhya*) and omniscience (*sarvajñya*) indeed (*eva*) baffles. Here the interpretation , 'you are as though simple, but are not really simple; it seems to baffle, but does not really', is not the right interpretation because it contains a lack of meaning (*saṅgatyabhāvāt*) that would call for a pointless classification of it with such meaningless statements as 'the works of one who is inactive,' 'the birth of the unborn', etc. And so, like simplicity amid the omniscience that prevails in the Dvāraka sport, omniscience amid the simplicity that prevails in the Vṛndāvana sport is to be understood as the accomplishment of his thought-transcending power. Thus it is described by Śrī Līlāśuka: 'In omniscience and in simplicity this great sovereignty...'

"2. In this context it is the imperceptive who say that omniscience is great majesty (*mahāiśvarya*), not sweetness (*mādhurya*); that the latter is the simplicity (*maugdhya*) of completely human sport, devoid of majesty.

"3. Sweetness, etc. are to be explained. Sweetness is the non-transgressing by great majesty of the limits of human sport both in its manifestation and in its non-manifestation. For example: (when manifested) the sport of a human child with characteristic of sucking at the breast, even during the killing of Pūtanā; the sport of a three month old child with very soft feet lying on his back, even while shattering a very hard wagon; the despondency due to fear of the mother, even as very long ropes were proving insufficient to bind him; the sport of tending cows, even while baffling Brahmā, Baladeva, *et al.*, even in the presence of omniscience. Likewise when majesty is present, but not manifested; the theft of milk and curds; naughtiness with wives of cowherds, etc. According to the statement that sweetness is the simplicity of ordinary human children boisterous at play would be sweetness; but it is not to be so understood.

"4. But majesty ((*aiśvarya*) becomes a display of dominance (*īśvaratvāviṣkāra*) when there is disregard for (the limits of) human sport, as was said in showing majesty to (his) mother and father: 'This form has been shown to you to mind former births; otherwise knowledge of my being does not arise for one in mortal form,' and as majesty was shown to Arjuna while in mortal form saying 'See this my majestic form'. And even in Vraja (by showing) more than a thousand four armed forms to Brahmā in the vision of 'Lovely greatness' (*mañjumshimā*).

"5. Awareness of majesty (*aiśvaryajñāna*) is that which provokes extreme slackening of one's own feelings due to heart-palpitating fear in the realization that this is the sovereign. Thus there is awareness of majesty lodged in a devotee, as indeed indicated by such statements of Vāsudeva as 'Your are not our sons, (but) the two primordial sovereign persons face to face', and the statement of Arjuna 'Whatever was said rashly with the idea that this is a friend...'

"Awareness of sweetness (*mādhuryajñāna*) is that which promotes greater firmness of one's own feelings due to the absence of even a trace of heart-palpitating fear even amid the discovery that this one is the sovereign. As, for instance, we learn of the absence of any slacking of the feeling of friendship (*sakhyabhāva*) on the part of Śrīdāma, Subala, *et al.*, even at the sight of Brahmā, Indra, Nārada *et al.*, saluting Kṛṣṇa's feet, with praises, singing, instrumental music, worship, offering of presents at the time for leading the cattle toward the cow pen, according to the words of the *Yugalagītā*: 'Which godlings, saluting with song, music and offerings, surrounded him..' and 'with feet being worshiped by the venerable on the road.' Likewise there is not even a trace of slackening of parental devotion (*vātsalya*) by the queen of Vraja on account of the words of consolation from the lord of Vraja; on the contrary, there is amid heartfelt rejoicing a firming up of feelings for the son: 'Fortunate am I that this my son is the supreme sovereign'! Similarly the affection of an ordinary (*prākṛta*) mother for her son grows ever more brilliant when her son becomes the sovereign of the earth. Thus there is to be understood a firming of the respective feelings of friends and of lovers: 'Fortunate are we whose very friend is the supreme sovereign;...whose beloved is the supreme sovereign.'

"However, awareness of majesty doers not shine so fully when there is union (between friends, lovers, etc.), because of the cooling quality of union, which maybe compared with moonlight; but in separation the awareness of majesty shines fully because of the heating effect of separation, which is comparable to sunlight.

"Because of the absence of heart-palpitating fear, respect, etc., there is no awareness of majesty in this statement: 'Enough of friendships with this black fellow who, though hunting was not his *dharma*, killed the monkey king like a hunter, though docile before his own wife, mutilated a lusting woman, (who) like a crow ensnared Bali and ate the offerings; it is hard to put aside the import of his tales.' Here there was no awareness on the part of the residents of Vraja prior to the lifting of Govardhana (hill) that Kṛṣṇa is sovereign. But even with the realization that this Kṛṣṇa is the sovereign, after the lifting of Govardhana and the journey to the realm of Varuṇa, it is pure awareness of sweetness, in the sense spoken of, that is full. And one does not hear on the part of the lord of Vraja (Nanda) even when he was aware–thanks to the statements of Varuṇa and Uddhava–that the sovereign was immediately present, even slightly, even in the heart, any statement like 'Kṛṣṇa is not my son', which would be comparable to Vāsudeva's statement "You two are not our sons.' Thus it is that for those situated at Vraja it is in all respects pure awareness of sweetness that is full: for those situated in the city (Dvāraka) it is awareness of sweetness mixed with awareness of majesty that is full.

"6. But, it may be objected, is it the case that Kṛṣṇa the son of Nanda in Vraj is aware of himself as sovereign, or not, in the way that Kṛṣṇa the son of Vāsudeva in city, even within human sport, is aware: 'I am the sovereign'? If he is aware (the objection continues), then during the sport of tying with ropes, etc., weeping due to fear of the mother, etc., should not occur. To say that this and like behavior is simply pretending would be an explanation of the dim witted, not of experienced devotees. If the experienced were to agree to such an interpretation then according to the statement 'If amazes me, this condition of you, whom fear itself fears, paralyzed by fear and worry, your face hidden, with eyes having mascara mixed with tears, when the cowherd woman placed ropes upon you who had been naughty', certainly awareness of majesty is attested to here by Kuntī and the authenticity of the fear, as is 'paralyzed by fear and worry,' is also certainly affirmed by her. If she knew that it was only pretending then amazement on her part would not occur; this is how it is to be understood.

"If, however, he is not aware of his own sovereignty, then how is the eternal knowledge of him who is full of eternal knowledge and bliss covered over? To this it is said that just as ignorance (*avidyā*), an operation of illusory power (*māyāvṛtti*), covers over the knowledge of living souls (*jīva*) in order to cause them to experience suffering after having cast them into the bondage of rebirths; and just as providential illusion (*yogamāyā*), an operation of the conscious power (*cicchaktivṛtti*), covers over even the knowledge of Śrī Krsna's retinue, the queen of Vraja *et al.*, who are beyond the material elements (*guṇātīta*), in order to enable them to experience the joys of the most sweet sports of Śrī Kṛṣṇa; so likewise to enable

Śrī Kṛṣṇa, even though his essential form is bliss, to experience even more bliss the essential operation of the conscious power (*cicchaktisāravṛtti*), i.e., love (*preman*), covers over his knowledge. There is no failing in its (i.e., Kṛṣṇa's knowledge's) omnipresence (*vyāpti*) since love pertains to his essential power (*tatsvarūpaśaktitvāt*). Similarly ignorance binds the living soul by its own operation, egoness (*māmatā*), in order to make it suffer; similarly the binding of the body of a blameworthy person is by means of ropes, chains, etc., and the binding of the body of an honorable person is with articles of worship (*argha*), scents, fine clothes, turban, etc. In sum, the living soul under the influence of ignorance is sorrowful; Kṛṣṇa under the influence of love is most happy. Kṛṣṇa's love-enveloped form is to be understood as a special enjoyment of pleasure (*sukhaviśeṣabhoga*) as is the form of a honey bee enveloped by the corolla of a lotus. Thus it is said, 'O Lord, do not depart from the lotus heart of our people', and 'Lotus foot (*aṅghripadma*) held by the cords of love..'

"Moreover, just as there is ordained a five-fold gradation of pain on the part of a living soul corresponding to the gradation of coverings of knowledge due to ignorance's own gradation (*tāratamya*), so likewise there is ordained an unlimited gradation of pleasure for one's object (*viṣaya*) and subject (*āśraya*) (i.e., Kṛṣṇa and the *gopīs*) according to the gradations of coverings of knowledge, majesty, etc., by love with its gradations. In that sense love combined with knowledge and majesty situated in Devaki, *et al*., does not give joy so exceedingly as does complete love situated in Śrī Yaśodā et al. which covers over knowledge and majesty and, binding by the courses of mineness its object and subject, renders each under the influence of the other. Therefore, Śrī Kṛṣṇa in the presence of the queen of Vraja *et al*., charmed by their parental and other love, is not even aware of his own sovereignty.

"That omniscience of his, however, that is seen at the time of arrival of various demons, forest fires and such calamities is to be understood as manifested precisely by that power of sport (*līlāśakti*) which does what is needed for protecting the various loving followers. But even at times of simplicity omniscience in respect of accepting worshipful service, etc., of aspiring devotees is accomplished through thought-transcending power (*acintyaśaktisiddha*); this has been explained before. Thus indeed have the distinction between the way of ritual and the way of passion, he distinction between majesty and sweetness, and the distinction between awareness of majesty and awareness of sweetness been made clear. And even the distinction between love of one's own (*svakīya*), i.e., marital love) and love of another's (*parakīya*, i.e., extra-marital love) has been elaborated in the explanations of the *Ujjvalanīlamaṇi*. In that context one attains awareness of majesty and the undifferentiated feelings of love of one's own and love of another's in Goloka in the great Vaikuṇṭha (heaven) through worship of Rādha and Kṛṣṇa in the way of rituals (*vidhimārga*). When there is longing for the sweet feelings (*madhurabhāvalobhitva*) one attains awareness of sweetness mixed with awareness of majesty and the feelings of love of one's own by virtue of being a follower of Satyabhāmā–due to the identity of Śrī Rādhā and Satyabhāma–in the realm of Dvāraka through worship in the way of injunctions (rituals). One attains pure awareness of sweetness and the feelings of love of another's by virtue of being a follower of Śrī Rādhā (*śrīrādhāparikaratva*) in the realm of Vraja through worshiping in the way of passion.

"Even though Śrī Rādhā is the joy-giving power (*hlādinīśakti*) born of the essential form (*svarūpabhūtā*) of Śrī Kṛṣṇa, and Śrī Kṛṣṇa is her very own (husband), still they are to be worshiped in conjunction with sport (*līlāsahita*) and not apart from sport; but nowhere in scripture composed by the seers (*ārṣaśāstra*) has there been mentioned any marriage for them in the realm of Vraja. Rādhā indeed is another's (wife) in both unveiled and veiled manifestations (*prakaṭāprakaṭaprakāśa*); this in brief is the conclusion of all exegesis.

"7. Next is presented the procedure for attaining face to face what is most desired by a person of passionate devotion who has ascended to the stage of love (*preman*) after (having reached) aversion from the worthless (*anarthanivṛtti*), devotedness (*niṣṭhā*), relish (*ruci*), and attachment (*āsakti*). As is said in the *Ujjvalanīlamaṇi*: 'Those persons who are passionately bound by that feeling are attentive in spiritual exercises (*sādhana*); having acquired through eagerness an intensity of passion adequate for it, they were born from time to time alone or in two's or threes's in Vraja. ' 'Intensity of passion' (*anurāghauga*) (means) eagerness for passionate worship (*rāgānugā-bhajanautkaṇṭhya*), not the permanent emotion (*sthāyin*) of constant passion (*anurāga*), because it is impossible that constant passion should arise in the body of an aspirant. 'They were born in Vraja' means that just as at the time of a descent (of Kṛṣṇa) the eternally beloved ones *et al.* take birth, so likewise those who exercises have achieved accomplishment take birth in the wombs of cowherd women. And then, thanks to the greatness of association with the eternally accomplished and other cowherd women who possess the great feeling ('essential love of Rādhā', Klostermaier) (*mahābhāva*) and by means of seeing, hearing, chanting of praise, etc., there are produced in that body of a cowherd woman even affectionate love (*sneha*), jealous love (*māna*), unhesitating love (*praṇaya*), passion (*rāga*), constant passion (*anurāga*) and the great feeling (*mahābhāva*); this is because it is impossible for these to arise in the body of an aspirant in a prior birth.

"Then there are the unusual characteristics (*lakṣaṇa*) of Kṛṣṇa's beloved ones in Vraja, as is said: 'There was extreme delight at the sight of Govinda, for the cowherd women, for whom a moment without whom (Kṛṣṇa) was like an eon,' and 'Absence becomes an eon for those not seeing you.' Considering a moment to be as long as a hundred eons is a characteristic of the great feeling (*mahābhāva*). It may be objected: in a veiled manifestation one may attain the feelings of affectionate love, etc., from association with eternally accomplished cowherd women upon attaining the body of a cowherd woman even without being born from the womb of a cowherd woman after the dissolution of the body of an aspirant who has ascended to the plane of love; what do you say? is this so or not? (Response) Not at all. Without birth from the womb of a cowherd woman there would be no customary relationships (*vyavahāra*) of human sport defined in such terms as: whose daughter is this female friend? whose daughter-in-law? whose wife? If it be stressed that the birth is in a veiled manifestation? By no means. Because it (i.e., a veiled manifestation of Vṛndāvana) is a realm exclusively for the accomplished (*kevalasiddhabhūmi*)–as is known from there being seen no entry by aspirants and materialistic persons (*prapañcikaloka*) into any manifestationof Vṛndāvana which is invisible to the material world (*prapañcikaloka*), there being seen entrance only by the accomplished–affectionate love (*sneha*), etc., feelings do not come to fruition there quickly by one's respective exercises (*svasvasādhana*). Therefore devotees in whom love has taken birth are brought by providential illusion (*yogamāyā*) into a manifestation of Vṛndāvana that is visible to the material world at the time of a descent of Śrī Kṛṣṇa for the sake of bringing to accomplishment those feelings after birth there, but before making contact with the limbs of Śrī Kṛṣṇa. From the sight of entrance therein by aspiring devotees, by persons caught up in work, etc. (*karmiprabhṛti),* and also by accomplished devotees it may be realized that it has the qualities of a realm for aspirants and of a realm for the accomplished.

"It may be objected: then where would extremely eager devotees stay for so long a time? To this it may be said: at the time of dissolving of the aspirant body there is at once (*sakṛt*) granted by the mercy of Bhagavān to that loving devotee, who is greatly eager with the long held desire for face to face service, a view of himself with his retinue and that desirable service, even though he has not attained affectionate love (*sneha*) and the other levels of love; as, for instance, (was granted) to Nārada. And a body of a cowherdess, made of consciousness and bliss, is given. And that very body is born by the agency of providential illusion (*yogamāyā*) from the womb of a cowherd woman in an unveiled manifestation of Vṛndāvana at the time of appearance of Kṛṣṇa's entourage. There is not a trace of delay in this because there is not interruption even of unveiled sport. Thus there is always an appearing of Śrī Kṛṣṇa and his entourage, even at the time of dissolution of the body of an aspiring loving devotee, in the respective Vraja realm in whatever universe (*brahmāṇḍa*) there is the unveiling of Vṛndāvana sports at that time.

"Hail, hail, greatly impassioned eager devotees! do not fear! be steadfast! it is well with you.

"8. 'O delighter in sport, O bee lusting after the buds of devotion, O treasure house of simplicity and omniscience, O darling of the cattle village, obeisance to thee.' You said, O Lord, 'I give that mental discipline (*buddhiyoga*) by means of which they come to me.' Thus I ask for this: 'O son of the chief of the cowherds, give me the mental discipline whereby there may be servitude to you who are adorned with the breasts of cowherd women.'

"Those who say that passionate devotion is in all respects and at all times beyond the injunctions of scripture are worthy of reproach and repeatedly are experiencing, have experienced and will experience disaster, according to such statements from the *Gītā* as 'Those who having rejected the injunctions of scripture make sacrifices with faith...' and without injunction, unoffered food...' Enough of this over-elaboration.

"Ah! may devotees of clear intellect discover by means of this Moonbeam the way of passion which is difficult even for the gods to see.

"Thus is completed the 'Moonbeam on the Way of Passion' (*Rāgavartmacandrikā*) by the great scholar, the gentlemen, Śrī Viśvanātha Cakravartin."

12.5 VIŚVANĀTHA CAKRAVARTI, *Ujjvalanīlamāṇi-Kirtanā*

Edited at least twice, one by Durga Prasad and Vasudeva Laksmana Sastri Pansikar, Delhi 1932, 1985, and again by Bhaktivedanta Narayana, Delhi 1993. See above under Jīva Gosvāmin's commentary for Neal Delmonico's account of what he calls the debate with Jīva Gosvāmin over the moral aspects of Kṛṣṇa's affair with the cowherd girls. He says (p. 33): "Writing a hundred and fifty years after the death of Caitanya, at a time when much of the magic and power of Caitanya's ecstatic experiences had been tamed into orthodoxy, he [i.e., Viśvanātha Cakravarti] sought to revive the tradition and bring back some of the spontaneity and intensity that it had had. It is therefore understandable that the extra-marital passion between Kṛṣṇa and the cowherd women–a passion whose intensity is at the core of the way humans should approach their deity–had a great appeal for him. He agrees with Jīva that theologically speaking Rādhā can never 'belong' to anyone else but Kṛṣṇa, and thus insists that ultimately there can be no illicit affair between them. Still, Viśvanātha insists, the illicit relationship is the essence of their relationship in their divine sport (*līlā*), and it is as they are in their sport that they are to be worshiped, not as they are apart from their sport. As he says in one place [in his commentary on I.21]

> 'Now, Rādhā is Kṛṣṇa's essential pleasure-energy (*hlādinī-śakti*). Therefore, she, in actuality, belongs only to him (*nityatva*); her belonging to another (*parakīyatva*, i.e. being married to another) cannot be.

This is true, but we worship Rādhā and Kṛṣṇa possessed of *līlā*, not without *līlā*.' Thus, Jīva in his concern for creating stability for the tradition finds a socially acceptable and theologically satisfying position, while Viśvanātha, with his concern for reviving the intense religious experience of the tradition, takes a position that emphasizes the experiential and passionate elements of divine love."

Delmonico translates Viśvanātha's commentary on the first few of Rūpa's text in the passages that are rendered in Delmonico 1997 (1) on pp. 34-45.

12.6 VIŚVANĀTHA CAKRAVARTI, *Bhagavatāmṛta-Kaṇa*

According to "Gaudiya History", a biography of Viśvānātha Cakravarti Thakura, an article that appeared in the monthly Bengali magazine *Gauḍīya*, 18th volume, number 218, 1922, under the editorship of Bhaktisiddhanta Sarasvati Thakura, this is "(A speck of Śṛī Rūpa Gosvāmin's Book *Laghubhagavatāmṛta*) 15 Sanskrit notes that sum up the information presented in Śrī Rūpa's book, which describes Śrī Krishna's various incarnations and plenary portions.""

The work has been edited and translated, with Viśvānātha Cakravarti's *Rāgavārtmacandrikā* (cf. under 12.4, above) and *Madhuryakadamvanī*, in *The Bhakti Trilogy: Delineations in the Esoterics of Pure Devotion,* Vrndavan 2007, as well as by Bhaktivedanta Narayana, Mathura 1993.

12.7 VIŚVANĀTHA CAKRAVARTI, Commentary on the *Gopālatapanīyopaniṣad*

The work is translated by Bhumipati dasa and edited by Mahanidhi Swami, published by Rasbihari Lal & Sons, Loi Bazar, Vrindaban-281121 (U.P.), India. There is also a summary of the Upanisād (pp. 9-17).

12.8 VIŚVANĀTHA CAKRAVARTI, *Madhuryakādambinī*

The "Gauḍīya" reference (see under 12.6 above) mentions several other works by Viśvanātha Cakravarti, with brief descriptions of some them. For this work we find: "(A Row of Clouds of Sweetness) 8 "showers of nectar' (chapters) of Sanskrit prose which scientifically analyzes the various stages of advancement that one ascends while on the devotional path."

See above under 12.6 for an edition and translation.

12.9 VIŚVANĀTHA CAKRAVARTI, *Aiśvaryakādambinī*

Again, the "Gauḍīya" reference says: "(A Row of Clouds of Majesty), a work mentioned by Viśvanātha in the second chapter of his *Madhuryakādambinī*. It is different from the work by Śrī Baladeva Vidyābhūṣaṇa of the same name. The book by Viśvanātha discusses the philosophy of "Dvaitādvaitavāda"; however, no copy of this work has ever been found."

13. RĀDHĀ DĀMODARA (1760)

In *Vedāntasyamantaka* Umesh Chandra Bhattacharjee tells us "In the colophon [of his book] he gives his name as Rādhādāmodara and incidentally tells us that he was a Brahmin; and from the fact that he makes a gift of this jewel (*syamantaka*) of Vedānta to Rādhikā, it is not difficult to infer that he was a Vaiṣṇava."

13.1 RĀDHĀ DĀMODARA, *Vedāntasyamantaka*

"In his *Siddhāntaratna* [viii.34], Baladeva tells us that Rādhādāmodara was his teacher. Commenting on this, he further tells us that Rādhādāmodara was a Kānyakubja Brahmin."

The work is edited by Umesh Chandra Bhattacharjee in Vedanta-syamantaka. The following summary ('The Philosophy of the Author') is found on pp. viii-xxvi of that work.

Summary by Umesh Chandra Bhattacharjee

"His book is divided into six chapters called '*kiraṇas*' (or rays) and the book as a whole is called '*syamantaka*' after a bright jewel of that name famous in the Purāṇas. The six chapters deal with (i) *pramāṇa*, (ii) *īśvara*, (iii) *jīva*, (iv) *prakṛti*, (v) *kāla* and (vi) *karman* respectively. The last five are the *prameyas* or subjects to be proved as distinguished from *pramāṇa* or proof, which latter is dealt with in the first chapter. The primary division of the book is, therefore, into two main sections, viz , *pramāṇa* and *prameya*, and this last, *prameya*, involves five topics.

"(i) Theory of *Pramāṇa*. Rādhādāmodara's theory of *pramāṇa* is very simple and he arrives at his conclusions without much ado. *Pramāṇas*, we are told, are variously enumerated; but the maximum number that need be considered is eight, viz., *pratyakṣa, anumāna, śabda, upamāna, arthāpatti, anupalabdhi, sambhāva* and *aitihya*. Of these, some admit only the first, some the first two, some an intermediate number and some again the whole list. But Rādhādāmodara will admit only the first three. The rest, so far as they can be accepted as *pramāṇas* at all, are included in one or the other of these three. For instance, *upamāna* is a combination of *śabda* and *pratyakṣa*. *Aitihya* or tradition is either inadmissible as proof when, for instance, we know nothing about he persons who make the statement, or it is only *śabda* or *āgama* when we know that the statement is made by a reliable person. And so on. Our author's brief analysis of the *pramāṇas* easily leads him to the conclusion that only three *pramāṇas* are valid.

"Of these three again, the first two, viz., *pratyakṣa* and *anumāna*, are often found unreliable and misleading. Examples can be easily found as to how sense-perception and inference give false information. Thus, a drop of water may be perceived as a drop, but then it falls into a mass of water, it is no longer perceptible. This shows the limitations of perception. Besides, errors in perception are also common. In the same way, inference, too, can be shown to be liable to error. Thus, the inference of the existence of fire in a place from which smoke is issuing is not always correct; for smoke may also be there when the first is just extinguished.

"The defects of perception and inference show that the only unerring source of knowledge is *śabda*. *Śabda*, again produces knowledge in different ways; sometimes it acts independently of perception and inference, i.e. gives knowledge which neither of these could give; sometimes it acts in conjunction with them, i.e., confirms and is confirmed by them; sometimes it acts in contravention of these two, i.e., gives knowledge apparently opposed to a perception or inference. And so on. But the chief thing about *śabda* is the capacity to produce knowledge that is constant and unvarying, and hence it is unerring. As a source of knowledge *śabda* is the most authentic and the most reliable.

"So far Rādhādāmodara is in perfect agreement with Jīva [Gosvāmin] and Vijñānabhkṣu. As a matter of fact, it is part of the fundamental position of Vedānta as a whole. In *Vedāntasāra* ii.1.11 we are told that *tarka* or mere discursive reasoning cannot lead to any definite conclusion; faith in *śruti*, therefore is the only way by which ultimate truth can be attained.

"But this general position-viz., faith in *śabda*–has been twisted by the different schools in different ways just to suit their purposes. The original position of Vedānta was undoubtedly a faith not in *śabda* in general but in *śruti*: it was the Vedas and pre-eminently the Upaniṣads which were regarded by the earlier Vedāntists as the exclusive source of knowledge or ultimate truth But when we come to the later schools, we find that *śabda* is used in such a sense as to include–as etymologically it undoubtedly did include–other kinds of scriptures also; and, on the strength of statements contained in these very latter scriptures themselves which belonged to a much later time, the conclusion is pressed upon us that they are of equal value with the *śrutis*: nay, more–and this is very important–they are the only kind of *śabda* that is accessible to men of our age. We cannot fathom the meaning of earlier *śrutis*–they are so obscure. But their meaning is made clear to us in the later scriptures, viz., the *Purāṇas* and other *smṛtis*; these, therefore, are the only form of *śabda* that we can use to a purpose.

"Jīva Gosvāmin is a prominent example of this attitude. In his *Tattvasandarbha* he takes considerable pains to establish this position with the aid of heaps of quotations from the *Purāṇas* themselves. In the first place, he tries to prove that for us mortals of the present decadent age, the *Purāṇas* are the only available form of *śabda:*

> *Tatra ca veda-śabdasya duspāratvād*
> *duradhigamāryatvācca tadarthamorṃāyakānāṃ*
> *munītāmapi purasyaravirodhād vedarūpo*
> *vedārthanirṇāyakaśvetikāsa-purāṇātmakaḥ*
> *śabda eva vicāraṇīyaḥ.*

"In the second place, Jīva attempts to prove that of the *itihāsas* and *Purāṇas*, the *Bhāgavata[purāṇa]* is the only one that contains the quintessence of them all.

Sarvapramāṇānām cakrvarttibhūtakam asmadabhibhmataṃ.
Again:

Tadevam pāramaniḥśeyasaniścayāya paurvāparyāvirodhensa vicaryate.

"Jīva accordingly proceeds to develop his philosophy by an explanation of the *Bhāgavata.*

"Vijñānabhikṣu does not lay much exclusive stress on the *Bhāgavata*; but he, too, considers the *Purāṇas* and the *Mahābhārata* as important for the knowledge of truth as the Vedas (Vide his introduction to the *Vedāntabhāṣya*).

"These writers, though differing in some other respects, agree in this important matter that for them the *Purāṇas* are as authoritative sources of knowledge as *śruti* itself; and, owing to our limited acquaintance with *śruti*, they are in practice more valuable for us.

"But Raḍhādāmodara would not openly adopt this position; rather he has declared himself opposed to this view. He categorically affirms that the knowledge of ultimate truth must be derived from *śruti* and *śruti* alone. The *ṛṣis*, by whom he obviously means the later *ṛṣis*, i.e. the authors of the *Purāṇas,* etc., are often found holding conflicting views; they cannot, therefore, be accepted as the source of ultimate knowledge...

"How far Rādhādāmodara follows this dictum in practice is a different question. For, we find him quoting the *Purāṇas* as frequently as he quotes the Vedas; and, curiously enough, for conclusions which he cannot support by *śruti* texts, e.g. that about the form (*vigraha*) of Viṣṇu, he depends exclusively on texts which are not even included in the usual list of the *Purāṇas* such as '*Viśvaksena-saṃhitā*', '*Ānandasaṃhitā*', '*Saṃkarṣaṇa-saṃhitā*' and so forth. But still in theory his declared adherence to the older Vedānta view of *śruti* as the only authentic *pramāṇa* marks him out from other writers of the same school, e.g. Jīva, Baladeva, and others. If he could stick to this position throughout, he would perhaps have developed a different philosophy altogether. But unfortunately it was hardly anything more than lip loyalty to *śruti*. For, in the very next chapter of his book, in complete self-oblivion, he proceeds to discuss the relative value of the different *Purāṇas* (p. 10 *et seq.*) and adopts exactly the same conclusion about them as Jīva Gosvāmin, viz., that the different *Purāṇas* appeared at different epochs of time and were suitable for the period in which they appeared but taking all of them together, it is only the *sāttvika Purāṇas* that should be accepted. This is equivalent to saying that we should accept only those which speak of Viṣṇu.

"It is a contradiction in his system, but the contradiction is more apparent than real. For, like other thinkers of the school, he apparently held that the *Purāṇas* of his school alone gave the entire truth that was to be found in the Vedas; the other *Purāṇas* misunderstood and, therefore, misinterpreted *śruti*.

And hence those who had faith in the Vedas might look to the *sāttvika Purāṇas* for help and guidance but not to the other *Purāṇas*. And he quotes (p. 11) Manu in support of this contention. Ultimately, therefore, his position with regard to *pramāṇa* is not materially different form that of Jīva and Baladeva. Between him and Baladeva the similarity almost verges on identity of examples and expressions (cf. Baladeva's commentary on Jīva's *Tattvasandarbha* with Chapter 1 of this book). Jīva in his *Sarvasaṃvādinī* (commentary on his own *Sandarbha*) discusses the question of *pramaṇa*. He gives a list of ten, i.e. two more in addition to our author's list of eight. But apart from this, there is little other difference between him and our author. We find a large number of identical expressions and illustrations. But for the fact that these expressions and illustrations occur in all the above three writers, a suspicion might arise in our mind that any of them was a pseudonym for either of the other two. This, however, is not possible in view of the fact that we find them in as many as *three* writers; we should rather conclude from this that these were a sort of stock expressions and examples of the school.

"(2) *Prameya*–The second part of Rādhādāmodara's book discusses the *prameyas* and falls into five chapters according to the number of these *prameyas*. These are: *īśvara, jīva, prakṛti, kāla* and *karman*. The *pramāṇas* having been discussed in the first chapter, the second begins with a list of *prameyas* and discusses the first of them, viz., *īśvara*. The following points are important in the theory of *īśvara:*

(a) *Īśvara* is the highest personal Being (*puruṣottama*) possessing attributes such as knowledge and joy (*ānanda*).

(b) He has no beginning and no end and is the ruler (*svāmī*) of all.

(c) We sometimes hear or him as being born; but that only means that he *appears* (*āvirbhāvamānna*) without loss of any of his natural attributes (*ahīnatvarūpasvabhāvatva*).

(d) And salvation can be attained by a knowledge of this divine personality.

"It is needless to say that our author bases this conclusion not so much upon reasoning as upon a compilation of texts, *śruti* as well as *smṛti*.

"An objection is anticipated that highest personality and rulership of the world have been attributed to several other deities as well, such as Rudra and Brahmā; can they also be regarded as the *highest* deity? The answer is obviously No, Viṣṇu or Hari and he alone is the highest Being. The other deities are all subordinate to him they are occasionally described in such a way as to convey the idea that they were the highest being, but this is very much like people paying homage to the servants of the king as if they were the king himself, although they received all honor on behalf of the king and as his representative. The other deities stood to Viṣṇu in the same relation as the servants of the king stood to the king; they derived all their honor and prestige from their master.

"This conclusion also, like the one preceding, is supported by a number of quotations from *śruti* and *smṛti*. It is interesting to note that of the various possible rivals of Viṣṇu for the highest position, Rudra or Śiva is considered the most formidable; for, his alleged claims are considered in greater detail and a more elaborate attempt is made to dispose of them. It is, no doubt, a fact that one of the appellations of Rudra, viz., *mahādeva*, itself signifies 'the highest deity"; but, we are told, the prefix *mahā* here has no special significance, just as it has none in the case of Indra; Indra and Mahendra (=Mahā + Indra) mean the same god; so does *mahā* in *mahādeva* mean nothing more than this that it is a proper name. We have plenty of texts where we are told that Rudra himself had on various occasions to implore the help of Viṣṇu and had to worship him for such aid. This proves beyond doubt that Viṣṇu is the highest deity. No doubt there are also books where Viṣṇu is said to have worshiped Rudra and sought his help–but that was only a *līlā* (*līlākhyameva bodhyam*) on the part of Viṣṇu–his condescending playfulness.

"The highest god, therefore, is Viṣṇu or Nārāyaṇa. He is the husband of Śrī and is the embodiment of *sattva*; Brahmā and Rudra represent *rajas* and *tamas* respectively. They are thus inferior to Viṣṇu. All this is proved by a carefully arranged selection of texts.

"The author is not forgetful of the fact that there are texts of a contrary implication also, specially among the *smṛtis*. But he boldly asserts that such *smṛtis* are to be rejected: for they contravene the *śrutis*, specially those that he has cited. Has not Manu said that *smṛtis* which contradict the Vedas are unacceptable? But he conveniently forgets that *all śrutis* may not justify his position either.

"One thing, however, is clear in his treatment of these deities and this deserves our careful attention: He does not deny the *reality* of these deities–not only of Brahmā and Rudra but of many others of whom the *śāstras* speak; he only denies their alleged superiority to Viṣṇu. According to him and his school, Viṣṇu is the highest deity; other deities also are there, but they are all inferior to him and even derive their very existence from him.

"We may note here in passing that in this attitude our author is only echoing the very apparent general tendency of all other sectarian interpreters of Vedānta. He, along with other Vaiṣṇava writers on Vedānta, identifies Brahma of Vedānta with Viṣṇu of their sect and places him at the top of the hierarchy of the gods. But following the same tendency, the Śaivas like Śrīkaṇṭha would identify Śiva with Brahma and place him at the top. But to proceed.

"This highest deity Viṣṇu has three attributes or powers (*śakti*), viz., *parā*, *kṣetrajñā*, and *māyā*. It is as endowed with this first power or attribute that he becomes the creator or efficient cause (*nimitta*) of the world. And as endowed with the other attributes, he is the material cause (*upādāna*) of the world. That is to say, the world is not different from him in essence. How far this idea is consistent with the conception of *prakṛti*, which also our author adopts, we shall see later. But here we must note that the world is not conceived as something altogether different in essence from its creator.

"In Hari or Viṣṇu, there is no such distinction as between body and soul–a distinction of which we are conscious in ourselves. In Viṣṇu the body is his soul: the essence of both is the same; that is to say, he has no doubt a form, but it is a form of the same essence of which consciousness is made. He is a spirit and has a spiritual form. His body, or what may be regarded as his body, has nothing gross or material about it; it is the same stuff of which the spirit also consists. Nevertheless, it would be incorrect to say that he has no form or *vigraha*. As before, this conclusion also is supported by a number of quotations from accepted authorities.

"Three attributes of Hari have been spoken of before; but in fact, he has an infinity of attributes and it is really for this reason that he cannot be qualified by any one of them. And this is why he is described as one without a second–an undifferentiated entity. Yet, owing to the presence of *viśeṣa* or differentiation of a peculiar kind, he can still be treated of as distinguishable from an other than himself. This *viśeṣa* is not exactly a difference but yet functions as a difference and produces the consciousness of a difference where there is no real distinction. Thus, we say 'Existence is', "Time *always* is'. 'Difference is different' (from the thing of which it is a difference), 'Space is *everywhere*', etc. If we analyze these judgments, it will be seen that the copula 'is' in the first example conveys the same meaning as 'existence', 'time' in the second example the same idea as is involved in 'always', and so on; yet the above judgments are possible: this is due to the existence of what is here called *viśeṣa*.

"This idea of *viśeṣa,* which is only touched upon by our author here, is more fully elaborated with the use of identical expressions in many places by Baladeva Vidyābhūṣaṇa, e.g. in his *Siddhāntaratna*. It was obviously the doctrine of the school which is described as that of 'unknowanble' (or indescribable) difference-non-difference (*acintyabhedābheda*).

"This highest being Hari is what is meant by the term 'ego' (*asmadartho bodhyaḥ*). The term 'ego' means the soul in its purest essence–the transcendental self, so to say. And hence it can dispel the illusion of those who approach it and is attainable only by the liberated. The 'I', in other words, means the highest and the most uncontaminated ego, which is the actor (*kartṛ*) as well as the enjoyer of the fruits of actions (*bhoktā*).

"It has been said before that the highest being or Viṣṇu is not altogether devoid of form–that he has a thinkable but at the same time highly spiritual form or *vigraha*. This form, we are now told, is sometimes two-handed, sometimes four-handed, and sometimes eight-handed. In fact, he has been described in all these three forms. This, however, does not imply change or impermanence in him. They are all eternal and co-present in him, and any may appear at any time, just as diverse form may make their appearance simultaneously in some precious stones (*vaidūryamaṇyau iva*). But still, the two-handed form, we are told, is more beautiful, exhibits his attributes better and may, therefore, be taken as the highest. Strictly speaking, however, no one form should be considered separate from the other two. What our author means perhaps is that the highest divinity has to be meditated and to that extent a form must be assigned to him; he can be meditated in various forms; but the best probably is the form or the image of man.–Has not the Bible also said that man was created by God in his own image? The image of man, therefore, is the best form in which divinity can be contemplated by us.

"This highest being not only bears the form of man but he is also the husband of Śrī. This is affirmed in several *śruti* texts. From the *śrutis* which speak of the absolute non-duality (*advaita*) of the godhead, it must not be imagined that there can be in the highest being no such differentiations that of Śrī as his consort. In fact, this differentiation is like the differentiation of fire and its heat–distinguishable from one another in thought yet inseparable. Viṣṇu's highest power is synonymous with Śrī and Sarasvatī. Of these two, again, the first is the higher, because it is the power of enjoyment (*hlādapradhāna*) which is superior to mere consciousness (*saṃcid*). But they should not be regarded as different from one another in any other sense than that in which different phases of consciousness are distinguishable from one another. And further, neither of the above two should be regarded as created: they are co-eternal with Hari himself.

"Like Hari, his consort also possesses infinite attributes. The power to bring salvation to mankind and the power to make Hari favorably disposed towards man, are among these attributes.

"Like Hari again, and with him, Lakṣmī also assumes different forms. Of these various manifestations of Lakṣmī, Rādhā is the highest and most perfect, just as of all the *avatāras* of Viṣṇu Kṛṣṇa is the highest and most perfect.

"(3) *Jiva*–The second of the *prameyas* is *jīva* or individual soul. *Jīva* is subtle and indivisible consciousness. In view of certain texts which our author quotes, he cannot accept the theory that Brahman is the only so-called *jīva* or conscious being and that there are no other conscious beings. On the contrary, he holds that there is a plurality of *jīvas*.

"Jīva is is eternal and has consciousness as its attribute. It is atomic (*aṇu*) and exceedingly fine, and yet by virtue of consciousness it pervades the whole body.

"The word 'I' also means the *jīva*, and its true nature can be appreciated in a state of dreamless sleep when gross self-consciousness *(ahaṃkāra)* is set at rest.

"The *jīva* or soul is different from the body and unlike the body it is not subject to change or decay. It is a part or *aṃśa* of the highest Being (*paramātmā*). And it is both an agent and an enjoyer of the fruits of its own *karman*.

"It should be recalled that our author has ascribed the same qualities of being an agent and enjoyer (*kartā* and *bhoktā*) to the Highest Being also. This obviously can be explained by the theory that the individual is but an *aṃśa* or part of the Infinite–a spoke in the wheel, as it were. The question certainly is not free from difficulty; but this difficulty is not peculiar to Rādhādāmodra's system.

"Rādhādāmodara cannot accept the theory that activity belongs to *prakṛti*, while *jīva* only looks on and experiences the consequences of these actions. In other words, although he adopts the Sāṃkhya concept of *prakṛti*, he is definitely against the inaction-theory of the *puruṣa*. According to him, consequences of action can belong only to the agent; so, since *puruṣa* or *jīva* has admittedly to bear the results of *karman* as he is responsible for the actions, the actions must be his, i.e., he must be credited with the capacity for activity also. And this capacity for action is a permanent attribute of the soul. But in this activity also, the individual is subordinate to the Infinite. In other words, the *jīva* is but a servant of the Lord and his function is to carry out His will.

"A question may arise here, viz., if *all* individual souls are but servants of the Lord, how can there be any differences among them and how can one instruct another? And if no instruction is possible, all philosophy becomes a vain endeavor. But this is not the fact. Just as fire contained in firewood is not kindled unless the wood is rubbed, so the stirring up of the soul by means of instruction is necessary in order that it may realize its true relation with the Lord. For this realization, one must approach a preceptor, and receive from him the inspiration of divine love (*bhakti*). This *bhakti*) is not possible without knowledge. Hence the need of instruction.

"The *jīvas* or individual souls continue to worship the Lord even when they are liberated. The distinction between the universal soul and the individual–between the infinite and the finite–between the *paramātman* and the *jīvātman*, is an eternal distinction and it continues even when the *jīva* is released from the bondage of earthly life. We have *śrutis* which affirm the distinction in earthly existence and also which affirm it in the *jīva*'s state of release.

"Some of the texts which seem to speak of the identity of the individual and Brahman should be understood as only affirming resemblance. Anything that is permeated by another thing imbibes the character of that other thing. So is *jīva* like unto Brahman. But there is a distinction between them which is never transcended.

"If Brahman could be characterized as mere consciousness and devoid of other attributes, such as greatness, subtlety, and so on, then his identity with the *jīva* might be suggested. But Brahman has these attributes also which mark him out as different from *jīva*.

"Nor can we describe Brahman as indescribable–as altogether unknown and unknowable. Though there are texts which say that words cannot express him, yet, after all, they only mean that he is never *fully* comprehensible and that words cannot expose him in his fulness. Partial knowledge of him and to that extent an expression of his attributes in words is certainly possible; otherwise, how can we reconcile with these the texts which say that the Vedas seek to *express* him? Brahman, therefore, must be understood as having more or less cognizable attributes which distinguish him from the individual.

"The theory that *jīva* is but an ephemeral reflection of Brahman in *avidyā* is untenable. The arguments against the *avidyā*-theory are well-known; and so far as he repeats them, the arguments of our author need not be reproduced here. But he advances one interesting objection against this theory which cannot but strike us as a logical quibble. If, he argues, it is contended that there is no distinction between Brahman and *jīva*, then a question will arise as to whether this non-difference (*abheḍa*) is different from Brahman or identical with him. It cannot be different, for obviously if there is something (in this case, *abheda*) other than Brahman, then that in itself disproves the absoluteness of Brahman and thereby the *abheda*-theory also. Nor can non-difference be identical with Brahman, for in that case the *śrutis* which affirm it would be guilty of redundancy by asserting what is self-evident. Underlying this second contention there is apparently the conviction that a *śruti* text must give us a real and synthetical proposition and not merely a verbal or analytical statement. A *śruti* cannot merely say 'A is A', 'Brahman is nothing but Brahman': for those propositions bring no real and new knowledge to the mind.

"Again, *abheda* cannot be taught, for where are the teachers of *abheda*? Does the pretending teacher know it? If so, he cannot think of the pupil as different from him and hence there can be no instruction. If he does not know *abheda*. surely he is not qualified to be a teacher; for, who can teach without knowing his subject? Obviously, therefore, there can be no teaching of *abheda*. So the theory of *abheda* or non-difference between Brahman and *jīva* is untenable. It will appear, however, that our author tries to demolish the *abheda* theory by assuming that if *abheda* be a fact, it must be a kind of attribute pertaining to Brahman. But is the absence of a difference to be understood as a positive quality like a differentium itself?

"This is also the way in which Rādhādāmodara attacks the *adhyāsa*-theory, viz., the theory that the world is an illusion brought about by *ajñāna* or ignorance. Is this ignorance true or untrue? Is it a fact or not a fact? If it be true, then it can never cease to be and an attempt to dispel it is in vain. If it is not true, then it cannot be believed in and there is no use discussing a thing which does not exist. Nor can it be something which is neither true nor untrue (*sadasadvilakṣaṇa*), for such a thing does not exist. Our author quietly forgets that whatever may be the fate of the world as an ultimate reality, ignorance in real life is a fact and it can be dispelled too. But to proceed.

"Rādhādāmodara concludes that the world is brought into existence by God with His *parā śakti* as its efficient cause and Himself again in His *pradhāna śakti* as the material cause; and the world is ultimately real.

"Incidentally our author develops a theory of error which deserves a passing notice. Error, he says, is possible in case of similarity, as when a post is taken for a man. If either of the two things be absolutely non-existent, then there can be no question of mistaking one for the other. We may not know things as they are, but there must be things in order that one of them may be mistaken for another, and error may be possible at all. Hence there is a real world; and hence again, there are finite selves or *jivas*,–eternally self-conscious like God and yet dependent on Him.

"(4) *Prakṛti*–Our author's views under this head are easily summed up: they are a replica of the Sāṃkhya theory of *prakṛti*, and need not detain us long. He, however, supports them with profuse quotations from *śruti* as well as *smṛti*. *Prakṛti* is of course the base of the three *guṇas* (*sattva, rajas, tamas*). The characteristics of these *guṇas* are well-known, as given in Īśvarakṛṣṇa and other Sāṃkhya writers, and also in the *Gītā*.

"Our author then proceeds to give an account of the evolution of the world out of *prakṛti*. If the three *guṇas* are equilibrated in *prakṛti*, then there is no world and we have what is called *pralaya* or dissolution. But when this equilibrium is disturbed and the *guṇas* intermingle with one another in different proportions, the world begins.

"First of all, there is *mahat*: this, again, is of three kinds according to the predominance of one or other of the *guṇas*, from *mahat* arises *ahaṃkāra* which again is of three kinds in the same way. *Sāttvika ahaṃkāra* gives the deities presiding over the senses and also over *manas*. *Rājasa ahaṃkāra* gives the external sense-organs both of cognition as well as of action–altogether ten in number. And *tāmasa ahaṃkāra* gives the five sense-objects, viz., space, etc., i.e. the *tanmātras* as well as the *mahābhūtas*–the subtle elements as well as the grosser elements. Out of these arises the universe consisting of the seven upper worlds and seven lower worlds and the fourfold life that inhabits it, viz., viviparous and oviparous and other animals and vegetables.

"Divisions of space (*dik*) are not counted independently, for they are but space itself viewed in relation to the movements of the sun. Similarly, the five *prāṇas* are not counted separately, for they are but modifications of *vāyu*.

"We have thus the twenty-four *tattvas* of Sāṃkhya, derived in an identical way. The conception of *liṅga śarīra* and *sthūla śarīra*–finer and grosser body–is also there but we need not dilate upon it.

"*Mahat* and its evolutes are all derived from *prakṛti*, and therefore, in the last analysis, should not be regarded as realities other than *prakṛti*, which is their common matrix. They are but modifications of *prakṛti* and are not essentially different from it, just as pots made of earth are not essentially different from the earth of which they are made.

"This explains the use of different names and numbers; in no other way can we explain our idea of an army or a wood or of any collection. A collection and the units constituting it are not fundamentally different. Between *prakṛti* and the evolutes the relation is more or less the same. Individually the evolutes are different from one another, together they make up *prakṛti*.

"This leads us to our author's conception of the causal relation. Cause and effect are but two states of the same thing; they are different each from the other, but are not different from the object of which they are states. The Nyāya school holds that the threads are different from the canvas; but this is wrong; for, we never perceive a canvas away from the threads. The Sāṃkhya school holds that they are different in identity ; but this is also wrong, for it is self-contradictory. Hence effect is identical with cause.

"So far as the evolution of *prakṛti* is concerned, the theory advanced here is in complete accord with that of the orthodox Sāṃkhya school. But as has been pointed out in a previous section, this *prakṛti* itself is one of the powers of the Divine Person. This marks our author off from the Sāṃkhya school as it is ordinarily interpreted and places him in the same line with Vijñānabhikṣu. But from Vijñānabhikṣu also he differs in his theory of the quintuple intermixture of subtle elements for the production of the grosser elements.

"(5) Time.–Time is something devoid of consciousness and is devoid also of the three *guṇas*. It is the cause of our conception of past, present and future, of simultaneity, of quickness, and also of creation and dissolution. It is described as revolving like a wheel from a moment to eternity.

"Time is eternal in the sense that it is never-ending and it is all-powerful. It existed even before creation. It regulates the processes of the world but is regulated, in its turn, by God. Time, therefore, has no effect upon God.

"(6) *Karman. Karman* is action brought about by effort and leading to other efforts; that is, action which is continuous and without a beginning, like the seed and the plant. It is a series without a beginning, but with an end.

(6) "*Karman* is of two kinds–good and bad. That which is forbidden by the Vedas and which leads to evil consequences is bad. And the opposite is good. Good actions, again, are of various kinds: obligatory (*nitya*), that is to say, one of which the non-performance is an evil; desirable (*kāmya*), i.e. that which is a means to an end and must be performed if a particular consequence is desired, e.g., if a man desires heaven, he must perform some *yajña*, which he need not perform otherwise; contingent (*naimittika*), i.e. an action which has to

be performed if something happens, e.g., when a son is born. If the contingency does not arise, the action also has not to be performed; but when the contingency occurs, the action is obligatory. Acts of atonement for wrongs done are another kind of good action. And so on.

"Of the various kinds of action, the *kāmya* actions like the prohibited actions are a hindrance to the attainment of *mukti*. And, therefore, they must be avoided. The other actions, viz. *nitya, naimittika*, and *prayaścitta*, should be performed, because they help to purify the soul. Actions done before the dawn of knowledge are, however, all destroyed by knowledge and those done after its appearance have no taint upon the knowing person.

"Thus it is by knowledge that the taint of *karman* is removed and it is by knowledge again that the Lord Hari may be attained. And there the soul resides in eternal bliss and has not to be born in flesh again.

"This knowledge is of two kinds–knowledge of the invisible (*parokṣa*) and knowledge of the non-invisible (*aparokṣa*).The first is derived from *śruti*; the second is what is expressed by the word '*bhakti*'. Of these, the first leads to Brahman in his *parā śakti* and the second leads to Brahman as directly manifested.

"Some say that pure *bhakti* alone, developed by association with devout men, can purify the soul and lead to the attainment of Hari. On the question suggested here, however, our author is not dogmatic. He is aware of the view that *bhakti* alone is enough; he would not say that it is wrong; but he seems to favor the other view that knowledge also is necessary and would explain *bhakti* itself as a form of knowledge. In this he differs from the more extreme section of the Vaiṣṇava philosophers.

"The five things thay one must care to know have been discussed. Let one know them, follow the discipline indicated herein, and he will find himself pure and capable of attaining Hari and eternal bliss will be his."

14 RŪPA KAVIRĀJ (1770?)

In his Introduction to SS, on pp. xi-xliv, Krishnagopal Gosvami discusses the authorship of the work listed as 14.1 below. He argues convincingly that it is not Jīva Gosvāmin, as was assumed by earlier writers, nor of Rūpa Gosvāmin as sometimes asserted. Nor is he a writer, a disciple of Hemalatā Ṭhākurāṇī, "the illustrious daughter of Śrīnivāsa Ācarya", who espoused the cult of *sahajiyā parakīyā*, pointing out that nowhere does the present author preach that cult. According to some he was prior to and perhaps the uncle of Viśvanātha Cakravartin. "The date of the work may be tentatively fixed to lie between the two limits of 1628 and 1672 A.D....One of the manuscripts of the *Sārasaṃgraha,* C, is dated as 1633 of the *śaka* era which is equivalent to 1711 A.D. If we presuppose a few years' antiquity we go back to a period lying broadly between 1628 and 1672 A.D. within which the treatise is likely to have been composed." These dates are evidently a bit suspect given the reasoning provided.

14.1 RŪPA KAVIRĀJ, *Sārasaṃgraha*

The following is excerpted from SS, pp. xx-xxxvi

Summary by Krishnagopal Goswami

"The present treatise elucidates the mysteries and significance chiefly of *mādhurya*. The treatment takes stock of all its implications connected with *rati* (love), *līlās* (ecstatic sports), *dhāmans* (sites of the ecstatic sports) and *sādhanas* (means of realization of *bhakti*). The whole dissertation is illustrated by appropriate quotations from the authoritative texts and commentaries...

"The entire subject is distributed under seven different heads, called *prakāśana* (exposition), *vailakṣaṇya* (difference), *nirasana* (repudiation), *sādhana* (means of realization), *virodhakhaṇḍana* (refutation of adverse views), *samarthotkarṣa* (excellence of *samarthā* aspect of love) and *upasaṃhāra* (conclusion)...

"According to the scholastic analysis of the *Ujjvalanīlamaṇi* of Rūpa Gosvāmin, *madhura rati* (erotico-mystic love) is classified into three: *sādhāraṇī, samañjasā* and *samarthā*. It is *sādharaṇī* (common-place) when, as in the case of Kubjā, the erotic enjoyment of the love towards Śrikṛṣṇa is for the sake of her own person. The marital love of Rukmiṇī and other royal wives for Śrīkṛṣṇa at Dvāraka is called *samañjasā* (consonant with established principles), since it is the love of the wives for Kṛṣṇa as their spouse being confined within the established code and conventions of society. In the *samañjasā* the enjoyment, however, is partly for the beloved and partly for the wife herself. Next comes the most excellent, viz., *samarthā* (the capable one)–it being the most capable of transmuting itself to the transcendental height of *mahābhāva*, which is appropriate to the *gopīs* and especially to Rādhā. The enjoyment derived from this is entirely for the sake of the beloved Kṛṣṇa and not for the self. Here Śrīkṛṣṇa is loved with all-absorbing astounding passion, in which all conventions and trammels of social ties are utterly transcended and the highest self *qua* bliss is realized in full.

"The crucial test of distinction between *samañjusā* and *samarthā* is that the former is *svakīyā* (marital) love, while the latter is *parakīyā* (extra-marital). The infinite passion of love which the *gopīs* in the Vṛndāvana manifestation of *līlā* depict towards Kṛṣṇa is conceived as of the *parakīyā* type. *Samarthā* is the basis of the *parakīyā* mysticism which by its unparalleled all-absorbing passion makes the *gopīs* oblivious to all conventions of family and society. It is for this reason that the crimson love of the *gopīs*, and specially that of Rādhā, is more than a match for the supreme Bhagavat–Kṛṣṇa, whose divine omnipotence yields place in the pleasantest and most ineffable graces of divinity...

"(The) *samarthā* species of love is a product of intuition characteristic of the *gopīs*. It is a result of sentiment spontaneous in itself and hardly an achievement from without. The *samarthā* love has its root in *svarūpa* which is an innate sentiment as evinced by intuition. But the *samañjuṣā* category of love arises out of *nisarga*, a faculty of natural proneness or aptitude, which for its effective realization is based upon experience. For example, the sensuous apprehension of the beauty and quality of the beloved lends vigor to this sentiment to turn into *samañjusā*.

"When we next advert to *mahābhāva* all that we can say is that it is that state of ecstatic devotional love which stands far above the level which the ordinary human being can normally aspire to reach. In the light of interpretation of the Bengal school of Vaiṣṇavism, the highest *bonuṁ* consists in the joy of love (*pramānanda*), which, passing through successive states of greater intensity, reaches that sublimated beatific sentiment of love which is called *bhāva* or *mahābhāva*. These are gradually (i) *preman* (the germination of love), (ii) *sneha* (constant attachment and fondness), (iii) *māna* (affected repulse of endearment owing to excess of emotion), (iv) *praṇaya* (friendly confidence and fellowship), (v) *rāga* (erotic transmutation of sorrow into joy), (vi) *anurāga* (love growing fresh without break), and lastly (vii) *bhāva* or *mahābhāva* (the highest erotico-devotional sentiment), which is the supreme realization of love as revealed by the *gopīs* and especially Rādhā. In Rādhā the *mādana* (intoxicating) aspect of *mahābhāva* is a special attribute which makes her love so transcendental.

"The *samartha* ḷove is also called *kāmānagā* (following desire), it being the result of spontaneous flow of heart. The *samañjusā* love is neither spontaneous nor free. In the former, Kṛṣṇa-Bhagavat in the humanized form of Nandagopa's son is loved and fondled as an object of *mādhurya* and is realized as such, while in the latter, he is regarded with respectful consideration being himself a Lord–the repository of *aiśvarya* (almightiness). The *samartha* phase of divine love looks upon Kṛṣṇa as the supreme paramour for the sake of whom all shackles of worldly connections are torn asunder, and he is infinitely loved for the sole pleasure of himself. In the *samajusā* love, which is purely marital, the code and conventions are scrupulously attended to.

"The next section in our book brings out the fundamental distinctions (*vailakṣaṇya*) between two sets of things which otherwise appear to be identical. These are the distinctions (i) between Vraja and Goloka, (ii) between the aspects of love shown by the *parakīya* maidens and those borne by a group of maidens who participated in the worship of Kātyāyanī (a goddess), (iii) between the *līlās* of Kṛṣṇa and those of the Matsya, the Kūrma and other incarnates, etc., and lastly, (iv) between the two modes of rhe realization of *bhakti* called *sādhakarūpa* and *taṭastharūpa*).

"Vraja is the place which witnesses aesthetic sport of *mādhurya* to irs best, while Goloka is the place where only *aiśvarya* is displayed in its full grandeur. But *aiśvarya* which inspires only awe hardly lays any claims upon the admiration of the devotees who have relish for pure erotico-aesthetic bliss. In Vraja the highest divinity manifests itself as a personal god of perfect bliss to be loved with unparalleled emotion by all his associates. This leads to the realization of the highest ecstatic joy which forms the inherent best characteristic of the Divine Person.

"In Goloka the Lord appears as the most powerful Divine Being. He is loved there by his consorts, the Lakṣmīs, with a feeling mixed up of awe and reverence. The sentiment of non-conventional free love cannot thrive in the realm of Goloka due to the ready recognition of omnipotence in the object of love. There the love borne by the Lakṣmīs is evidently marital and confined within the limitations of conventions. The *gopīs* in Vraja on the other hand transcend all conventions in their infinite passion of non-marital love, which is displayed unto

Kṛṣṇa, the son of Nanda, who is solely endowed with ineffable charm of the highest degree. Vraja and Goloka are thus distinguished in point of their connection with two different aspects of love.

"It is to be noted that the *samañjasā* or marital aspect of love is three-fold: *gauṇī, mukhyā* and *samañjusāprāyā*. There is obvious gradation of excellence in the order of this enumeration. The love of the Lakṣmīs for the Lord Nārāyaṇa at Goloka is of the first kind. The love of Rukmiṇī and other royal wives of Kṛṣṇa at Dvārakā is an example of the second kind. The third and the last category of the *samañjasā* love is illustrated in the sentiment of the maidens who purported to bestow their love upon Kṛṣṇa at Vraja as their spouse and propitiated the deity Kātyāyanī with this object in mind. The fact of secret union only lends to it some excellence, but that does not account for its absorption into the *samarthā* or non-marital aspect of love. The real test of distinction lies in the attitude of the mind with which the love is conferred, viz., whether it is viewed as marital or non-marital.

"Now as to the case of pure *samarthā* two classes of *gopī*s are mentioned as illustrations. These are *sādhanasiddhā*s (successful with means) and *nityasiddhis* (ever successful). The Purāṇic legends tell us that even some gods and sages aspired for a rebirth in the form of *gopīs* at Vṛndāvana to participate in the much-coveted Vraj-*līlā*. Through courses of devotional practices and meditations when at last they succeeded in accomplishing their object, they came to be called *sādhana-siddhā gopī*s. But the *nityasiddhā gopī*s are those who are eternally participating in the ecstatic erotic sports of Kṛṣṇa-Bhagavat as His constant associates. The aspect of love as borne by these two classes of *gopī*s is purely *samarthā* (non-marital). The love of *nityasiddhā* is of supreme excellence; it reaches the most sublimated stage of the *mahābhāva* realization indicating its super-sensuous appeal and significance. This is what sums up the relevant phases of distinction between the different manifestations of love.

"Some words on incarnation are necessary to introduce the distinctions between the *līlās* of Śrīkṛṣṇa and of the Matsya, the Kūrma, etc. An incarnation is so-called when Kṛṣṇa-Bhagavat either Himself or in His partial manifests comes down to the phenomenal world to subserve some purposes of the world. These are purposive manifestations and, as such, are called *karaṇalīlā* (effectuated by definite cause), for example, the *līlās* of the Mātsya and Kūrma etc. But the *līlā*, which has no extraneous purpose of its own, but shows itself by an urge in itself, is called the *kāraṇātīta līlā* (without an extraneous cause).

"The *līlā* of Śrīkṛṣṇa is spontaneous and a cause-in-itself. The guiding force consists here in affording *premānanda* (joy of love) to his devotees, and this is but the natural outcome of his character as Kṛṣṇa-Bhagavat. But although his *līlā* does not emerge out of a cause foreign to itself, some extraneous beneficial objects of the world are realized as a matter of simultaneous gain. The act of killing the great enemy of the world, Kaṃsa, is an example of this kind of extraneous advantage. Such combine benefits accrue from the self-same *līlā* only because Kṛṣṇa possesses inscrutable powers. He is said to the most Almighty of all. We hear from the *Bhāgavatapurāṇa*:

> *ete cāṃśakalāḥ puṃsaḥ kṛṣṇas tu bhegavṣn svayam*[1]
>
> 'Krsṇa is not merely an *avatāra* (incarnation), but also the Ultimate Reality or Bhagavat Himself. The other incarnations like the Matsya, the Kūrma, etc., are His partial manifests and their *līlās* are connected with the fruition of some positive objects of the world.'

"Again, the *līlā* of Kṛṣṇa-Bhagavat affords beatific joy to all as an ultimate reward, no matter if anybody acted hostile to

---

[1]BP I.3.28

Him. Even Kaṃsa did not fail to attain emancipation by his death at the hands of Śrīkṛṣṇa. But such is not the case in the *līlās* of His particular manifestations...

"Now let us proceed to describe and distinguish between the two modes of religious experience which lead to the realization of *bhakti* (devotional love). One is called *sādhakarūpa* (accomplishing with means) in the attainment of high emotional love for Kṛṣṇa who in the humanized form as the son of Nanda typifies the highest ecstatic grace and is looked upon as the *dolche amore.* The thoughts and acts of his near and dear ones who participated in the various love-sports at Vṛndāvana are the fountain-spring of inspirations for the devotees. The constant meditations, imitations and pursuits of those thoughts and acts enable the devotees to play the role of the ardent lovers of Kṛṣṇa. The highest realization by this means consists in spiritual exaltation of the erotic sentiment, and Kṛṣṇa, as such, is conceived as the sole male by his devotees who regard themselves as the females in love.

"The other mode is called *taṭastharūpa* (standing aloof), by means of which Kṛṣṇa as the Almighty Lord is worshiped with all humility and submission. Here God is not conceived as the most beloved person to be profoundly loved by the devotees in a bond of personal relationship. On the other hand, the Almighty Lord is looked upon as endowed with unspeakable powers and adored by the devotees as such with all forms of reverential and prayerful devotion.

"The third section, called *nirasana,* is an attempt at a repudiation of the facts forming the basis of the *svakīyā* theory of love. Thus the author assails first (i) the grounds of distinction between the *prakaṭa* (manifest) and the *aprakaṭa* (unmanifest) Gokula and the *līlās* connected therewith, and then he repudiates the view that (ii) the sojourn of Kṛṣṇa to the land of Mathurā took place in the person of the Nandagopa's son. (iii) Next, in five successive and subsidiary dissertations are refuted the so-called conclusions, namely that (a) the manifestation of the *parakīyā līlā* under the instrumentality of Yogamāyā is a mere fiction, and not a valid testimony, that (b) Rādhā present at the scene of the *vastraharaṇalīlā,* which is an event connected with awakening of the first sentiment of love (*pūrvarāga*), was no more than a virgin girl, that (c) Rādhā had no marital relationship with anybody else other than Śrīkṛṣṇa while she was a Navavṛndāvana, or when (d) she was either at Kurukṣetra or (e) at Vraja where Kṛṣṇa returned after having killed the demon Dantavakta. (iv) Refutations of these serve as a prelude to the repudiation of the *svakīyā* aspect of love in connection with the *aprakaṭa līlā* as traced in the fourth sub-section."

"In presenting a breezy survey of these repudiations it should be stated at the outset that the *līlā* of Śrīkṛṣṇa with his associates is conceived as not fundamentally different whether it is *prakaṭa* or *aprakaṭa*. It is to be remembered that the one and the same *līlā* is going on incessantly irrespective of any spatio-temporal limitations. The position is the logical counterpart of the conception that Kṛṣṇa-Bhagavat as a Divine Person is an eternal Being of infinite bliss energy. If, on the other hand, Gokula as the seat of the unmanifest *līlā* is supposed to be different from Gokula of the manifest *līlā,* the eternal character of the *līlā* falls to the ground. The two *līlās*, therefore are not at variance with each other, and there is little fundamental difference between them. The two different names are in respect of the form only. The *prakaṭalīlā* is manifest and visible at a particular time whereas the *aprakaṭa līlā* stands for both the past and the future *līlās* which are for the time being hidden from view. In the *līlā* of Śrīkṛṣṇa the most recognized role is played by the sublimated divine love of Rādhā and her associate *gopīs* for Kṛṣṇa as their beloved. The *prakaṭa* and the *aprakaṭa līlā* make no difference in the aspect of this divine love which to all intents and purposes is that of *parakīyā.*

"In the analysis of Gauḍīya Vaiṣṇavism Kṛṣṇa as the son of Nanda is the embodiment of the highest erotico-mystic bliss, and, it is said, he never parts from his favorite haunt Vṛndāvana, nor does he leave the company of his associates. But while Śrīkṛṣṇa pays a short occasional visit to Mathurā and other places, he is no longer recognized as the son of Nanda, but as the son of Vāsudeva. This is so because in the light of *nityalīlā* Vṛndāvana cannot be contemplated as without the presence of Śrīkṛṣṇa as the Nandagopa's son who is the eternal archetype of *mādhurya*. The sojourn of Kṛṣṇa to Mathurā in the guise of the Nandagopa's son, therefore, is an antithesis of the doctrine of *nityalīlā* and can hardly be deemed admissible.

"Now as to the part played by Yogamāyā in the scheme of Kṛṣṇa-*līlā* it is to be observed that she is the embodied personality, constituted of the *antaraṅgā cicchakti* (eternal spiritual power) of the Bhagavat, whose purpose is to promote and subserve the interests of the beatific love-sports between Kṛṣṇa-Bhagavat and His associates. In contradistinction to *bahiraṅgā māyā* (external delusive energy) of the individual soul, the powers and privileges of Yogamāyā extend even to sphere of divine *līlās* and possess real abiding values. The *parakīyā* sentiment of love demonstrated by the *gopīs* toward Kṛṣṇa through the purposive instrumentality of Yogamāyā is nothing but real and genuine, and it is surely one of supreme significance.

"The *vastraharaṇalīlā* is an occurrence on the day on which a party of virgin girls observed a vow in worshiping the deity of Kātyāyanī to obtain Kṛṣṇa as their spouse. Rādhā and her associate *gopīs* were present on the scene, and it is believed by some that they were equally virgin girls. But such conjecture is at variance with the testimony of the *Bhāgavatapurāṇa*. This *Purāṇa* in the two consecutive chapters (21st and 22nd) of *skanda* 10 intends to delineate the sentiment of *pūrvarāga* for Śrīkṛṣṇa respectively of the females already married to others and unmarried. The celebration of the worship of Kātyāyanī and the *vastraharaṇalīlā* connected therewith are described in the latter chapter, while the former indicates that Rādhā, Candrāvalī and other *gopīs* were no virgin girls even prior to the incident of the *vastraharaṇalīlā*. Again the sentiment of *pūrvarāga* in Rādhā must be said to emerge out of her *parakīyā* characteristics. In the authoritative opinion of the *Ujjvala-nīlamaṇi* the *parakīyā* aspect of love is an inseparable constituent of the *mādana* element of *mahābhāva*, which is never wanting in Rādhā. This leads to the irresistible conclusion that Rādhā, though included in the party of the unmarried girls on the occasion of the *vastraharaṇalīlā*, cannot be conceived as unmarried." (The remainder of this section gives further arguments, concluding) "Thus the *gopīs* at Vraja with Rādhā as their chief are never wanting in the *parakīyā* attributes of love. This sums up the contents of the five-fold repudiations of the *svakīyā* love in connection with the manifest *līlā*."

"With the aforesaid prelude the *svakīyā* theory of love is refuted next with reference to the unmanifest *līlā*. The extra-marital love is the pride and privilege of the *gopīs* to reach the highest fervor of *mahābhāva*. The denial of this in respect of the unmanifest *līlā* negates the very glory and effulgence associated with it. So the all-absorbing *parakīyā* love remains the same as ever, no matter whether the *līlā* is manifest or unmanifest. Some of the legends and episodes too furnish an adequate testimony to the *parakīyā* aspect of love at the unmanifest *līlā*.

"Next in the section, *virodhakhaṇḍana*, the so-called adverse views are assailed by an array of facts. The contention that the delineation of extra-marital love between Kṛṣṇa and the *gopīs* is a mere fiction and a seeming gesture does not stand scrutiny. Had this been so, the question of imputation for the guilt of extra-marital love as raised against Kṛṣṇa could have been easily answered by saying that it was all untrue. But Śukadeva, on the contrary, employs various other arguments to absolve Kṛṣṇa of the charge. He says *inter alia* that Kṛṣṇa is an Almighty Lord and His conduct, howsoever opposed to the human standard of ethics and approved usage, does not stand tainted with guilt, chiefly because he is the Divine Person.

"Again, the contention that the *līlās* of Vraja and Dvārakā delineated respectively in the *Bhāgavatapurāṇa* and the *Lalitamādhava* belong to two different categories is thoroughly rebutted. The two sets of the love-s ports are the incidents of the self-same category with only this difference, that Vraj is the scene of the sport trough which the supreme phase of blissful divinity in Kṛṣṇa is manifested in its entirety while at Dvārakā it is manifested in its partial aspect.

"In the section dealing with excellence of *samarthā* love, it is stated that this aspect of love affords the best emotional *inflatus* for the realization of the all-blissful concept of the Bhagavat in the humanized form of Śrīkṛṣṇa. The infinite superhuman *mādhurya* receives its fullest expression in Kṛṣṇa of Vraja. Vraja is the place which witnesses ecstatic devotional love in its highest pitch. Here the all-absorbing *samarthā* love of Rādhā obliges the Almighty Hari to discard His divine omnipotence and to present Himself in the most graceful humanized form as the son of Nanda. The *samarthā* love is at the root of this heightened glory of Vraja over the other abodes of *līlā*, namely Goloka, Dvārakā and Mathurā.

"The last section closes with a few words of observation on the eternal nature of the *līlā, dhāman, parihara* and *vigraha* (physical frame) of Śrīkṛṣṇa. Throughout the course of external manifestation of the *līlā, mādhurya* is exhibited as the highest attribute of Śrīkṛṣṇa whose manifestation of *aiśvarya* is but a means to an end. *Mādhurya* throws *aiśvarya* to the background, and this constitutes the inexhaustible treasure of joy for the devotees. The *rāgānugā* or devotional faith of love based on emotion is the only effective means for realization of this joy."

14.2 RŪPA KAVIRĀJ, *Rāgānugavivṛti*

Although no reference is found to such a work in the usual sources, there is reason to believe it may have been edited from Radhakunde in 19169-70.

15 BALADEVA VIDYĀBHŪṢAṆA (1780)

Writing in The O, No.1 Orissa Historical Research Journal, Volume 13,1 of April 1965, Padmasri P. Acharya provides extensive information, based on various sources. We provide here some of this that seems authentic pertaining to his date and place of residence. "Baladeva Vidyabḥūṣaṇa was born in the 18th century A.D. in a village near Remuṇā of the Balasore district. No thing about his birth is known definitely. He wrote in *śaka* 1658 (1764 A.D.) a *ṭīkā on* Rūpa Gosvāmin's *Stavamālā*".

"Baladeva Vidyabhusana studied grammar, poetics, etc., from a famous Pandit on the other side of Chilka lake. Then he studied Nyāya and Veda and went to Mysore to study Vedānta. At this time he was initiated by the Tattvavādins and argued with many Pandits and came to stay at the Tattvavādin Maṭha at Puri. After some time he was initiated by Rādhā Dāmodara, a *praśiṣya* of Rasikānda Deva Gosvāmin and studied *Ṣaṭsandarbha.* He obtained the title of Vidyābhuṣaṇa at the Gāltā conference at Jaipur where he composed *Govindabhāṣya*. Others say that he learnt *Bhāgavata* from Viśvanātha Cakravarti. Afterwards Baladeva became *sannyāsin* and was known as Ekānti-Govinda Dāsa.". (Sundrananda Vidyavinoda *Śrīkṣetra* (in Bengali), 1950).

P.P. Acharya (op. cit., pp. 8-9) goes on to confirm these accounts from other sources dealing with this period. He clarifies the "Gāltā conference": "Jai Singh of Jaipur succeeded at Amber in 1699 A.D. He got the title of Sawai (One and one-fourth) from the Moghul Darbar and was known as Sawai Jai Singh II of Jaipur. He transferred the capital to Jaipur city in 1728 A.D. The hillock called Gāltā is situated within a short distance of Jaipur city which was chosen as the temple site of Govindiji...Sawai Jai Singh ruled up to 1743 A.D. So the date of the Gāltā Conference may be safely assigned to a period of 5 years from 1735-1740 A.D. when Baladeva Vidyabhusana was in the prime of youth, say around 35 years old. He composed the *Ṭīkā* of *Utkallika-Vallari* in 1765 A.D. Viśvambhārānanda Deva Gosvāmin wrote that in 1885 there were men who saw Baladeva. If we accept that age of the persons about 100, Baladeva was living a long life about 90 years from 1705 t9 1795 A.D."

More recently Dr. (Mrs.) Sudesh Narang has published *The Vaiṣṇava Philosophy (according to Baladeva Vidyābhuṣaṇa)* (Delhi: Nag Publishers, 1984), which we refer to in what follows as Narang 1984. She reports the information found above, and in the first Chapter provides some useful accounts of the author's works which we have utilized in some of the summaries that follow. Still another account is found in Michael Wright and Nancy Wright, "Baladeva Vidyabhūṣaṇa: the Gauḍīya Vedāntist", Journal of Vaisnava Studies 1.2, 1993, 158-184.

It is relevant to note that some scholars (e.g., B.N.K. Sharma, Sushil Kumar De, Edward C. Dimock, and Stuart Elkman, for example) believe that Baladeva was a Dvaita philosopher. For a refutation of this notion see Kyokazu Okita, "Mādhva or Gaudiya? The philosophy of Baladeva Vidyābhūṣaṇa's Prameyaratnāvalī", Journal of Vaishnava Studies 16.2, 2008, pp. 33-48.

15.1 BALADEVA VIDYĀBHŪṢAṆA, *Īśopaniṣadbhāṣya*

Edited and translated by Gosvami Siddhanta Vacaspati. Calcutta 1895. Narang 1984 cites two other editions. According to Narang, p. 17, Baladeva 'has written commentaries on ten of the principal Upaniṣads, but at present only' this commentary is available..."

15.2 BALADEVA VIDYĀBHŪṢAṆA, *Bhagavadgītā-(Vi)bhūṣaṇa*

Edited several times. See Bib 3, #1448.1. The following summary is to be found in Narang 1984, pp. 17-18.

Summary by Sudesh Narang

"Enthused with the love of the most blissful Kṛṣṇa, Baladeva begins to comment upon this divine document. It preaches the principle of self-surrender and uttermost devotion to the Lord. The Gauḍīya Vaiṣṇavas regard the *Gītā* as the 'worldly personification' of the Supreme Person Kṛṣṇa. Commenting upon the said treatise, Baladeva deals with the philosophical aspect hitherto not forgetting the devotional aspects as well."

15.3 BALADEVA VIDYĀBHŪṢAṆA, *Brahmasūtra-Govindabhāṣya*

Edited several times; see Bib 3, #1448.2. Translated long ago by B.D. Basu in *Sacred Books of the Hindus* Volume 5 (Allahabad: Panini Office, 1912). The following summary is to be found in Narang 1984, pp. 20-21.

Summary by Sudesh Narang

"Baladeva, in his *Govinda Bhāṣya*, deals with the main topics on philosophy. He divides those topics under four heads in four books of the *Bhāṣya*. The *Govindabhāṣya* is named as *Caturlakṣaṇī* because it possesses four characteristic marks treated succinctly as follows:

"(i) The Rightful Claimant: A person who is detached from worldly pleasures, who is of tranquil mind, who possesses quietude, is self-controlled, whose heart is infused with devotion and faith and thus purified by due performance of all duties, religious and secular with the last desire of fruit, who is ever engaged in good thoughts and associates himself with the knowers of truth, is the one competent or rightful claimant to understand and study the scriptures (here it denotes especially the *Brahmasūtra*).

"(ii) The Principles of Relationship: The scriptures (i.e., the *śāstra*) aim at describing Brahman which is a distinct object to achieve. Though the scriptures also cannot explain it completely, yet they show a path into the knowledge of Brahman. This is the relationship between Brahman and the scriptures.

"(iii) The Principle of Realization: Kṛṣṇa, the personal form of the Absolute Brahma, is the eternal theme of the scriptures. He, the Absolute Existence, Intelligence, and Bliss; Whose power is infinite and inconceivable; Who possesses innumerable attributes and Who is all pure, He is to be realized through devotion.

"(iv) The necessity of the scripture: The ultimate end and the Supreme bliss of life is the realization of the Supreme Lord. Here arises the necessity of the Scripture which depicts sources to know the Lord. There are mainly three sources of knowledge, viz. perception, inference and the scriptural testimony. The scriptures which are faultless superhuman compositions are the only right source of knowledge. These help in removing false notions that prevent the realization of the Supreme Self. These recommend that love for Kṛṣṇa is the summum bonum of our life.

'The scripture deals with different topics. Every topic consists of five parts, viz., (i) subject-matter, (ii) doubt, (iii) anti-thesis, (iv) synthesis and lastly (v) consistency of one topic with the other portions which precede or follow it."

Surendranath Dasgupta, in HIP 4, pp. 439-445, provides more detailed summation of portions of this text, which are indicated in parentheses.

Summary by Surendranath Dasgupta

"Though one in Himself, He appears in many places and in the forms of His diverse devotees. These are therefore but modes of his manifestation in self-dalliance, and this is possible on account of His supra-logical powers, which are identical with His own nature (III.2.11) This, however, should not lead us to suppose the correctness of the *bhedābheda* doctrine, of the simultaneous truth of the one and the many, or that of difference and unity; just as one actor, remaining one in himself, shows himself in diverse forms, so God also manifests himself in diverse forms, in accordance with diverse effects and also in accordance with the mental plane and the ways in which diverse devotees conceive of Him (III.2.13). On account of his supra-logical powers the laws of contradiction do not apply to Him; even contradictory qualities and conceptions may be safely associated in our notion of Him. So also His body is not different in nature from Him; He is thus identical with His body. The conception of a body distinct from Him is only in the minds of the devotees as an aid to the process of meditation; but, though this is imagination on their part, such a form is not false, but as a matter of fact is God Himself (*deha eva dehī* or *vigraha evātmā ātmaiva vigrahaḥ*). On account of the transcendent nature of God, in spite of His real nature in bodily form as pure consciousness and bliss He may have His real nature in bodily form as Kṛṣṇa. This form really arises in association with the mind of the devotee just as musical forms show themselves in association with the trained ears of a musician (III.2.17).

"In this connection it may be observed that according to Baladeva even dream-creations are not false, but real, produced by the will of God and disappearing in the waking stage through the will of God (III.2.1-5). These forms appearing in the minds of the devotees are therefore real forms, manifested by God through His will working in association with the minds of the devotees. In this connection it may also be pointed out that the *jīvas* are different from God. Even the imagined reflection of Brahman in *avidyā*, introduced by the extreme monists to explain *jīva* as being only a reflection of Brahman and as having no real existence outside it, is wrong; for the notion of similarity or reflection involves difference. The *jīvas* are atomic in nature, associated with the qualities of *prakṛti*, and absolutely dependent on God. Though Brahman is all-pervasive, yet He can be grasped by knowledge and devotion. A true realization of His nature and even a sensuous perception of Him is possible only through *sādhya-bhakti*, not through *sādhana-bhakti*. The consciousness and bliss of God may be regarded either as the substance of God as His attributes.

"This twofold way of reference to God is due to the admission of the category of *viśeṣa*, by which, even in the absence of difference between the substance and the quality, it is possible to predicate the latter of the former as if such a difference existed. *Viśeṣa* is spoken of as the representative of difference (*bheda-pratinidhi*); that is, where no difference exists, the concept of *viśeṣa* enables us to predicate a difference; yet this *viśeṣa* is no mere *vikalpa* or mere false verbal affirmation. The ocean can be spoken of as water and waves by means of this concept of *viśeṣa*. The concept of *viśeṣa* means that, though there is no difference between God and His qualities, or between His nature and his body, yet there is some specific peculiarity which makes it possible to affirm the latterof the former; and by virtue of this peculiarity the differential predication may regarded as true, though there may actually be no difference between the two. It is by virtue of this concept that such propositions as 'Being exists', 'Time always is', 'Space is everywhere' may be regarded as true; they are neither false nor mere verbal assumption; if they were false, there would be no justification for such mental states. There is obviously a difference between the two propositions 'Being exists" and 'Being does not exist'; the former is regarded as legitimate, the latter is false. This proves that though there is no difference between 'being' and 'existence' there is such a peculiarity in it that, while the predication of existence of being is legitimate, its denial is false. If it were merely a case of verbal assumption, then the latter denial would also have been equally possible and justifiable. This peculiarity is identical with the object and does not exist in it in any particular relation. For this reason a further chain of relations is not required, and the charge of a vicious infinite also becomes inadmissible. If the concept of *viśeṣa* is not admitted, then the notion of 'qualified' and 'quality' is inexplicable (III.2.31).

"The concept of *viśeṣa* in this sense was first introduced by Madhva; Baladeva borrowed the idea from him in interpreting the relation of God to His powers and qualities. This interpretation is entirely differrent frm the view of Jīva [Gosvāmin] and others who preceded Baladeva; we have already seen how Jīva interpreted the situation merely by the doctrine of the supra-logical nature of God's powers and the supra-logical nature of the difference and identity of power and the possessor of power, or of the quality and the substance. Baladeva, by introducing the concept of *viśeṣa*, tried to explain more clearly the exact nature of supra-logicality (*acintyatva*) in this case; this has been definitely pointed out in the *Sūkṣma* commentary [on III.2.31].)

"The bliss of God is different from the bliss of the *jivās*, both in nature and in quantity, and the nature of their knowledge is different. Brahman is thus different in nature both from the world and from the *jīvas*. All the unity texts of the Upaniṣads are to be explained merely as affirming that the world and the *jīvas* belong to God (*sarvatra tadīyatva-jñānārthaḥ*). Such a way of looking at the world will rouse the spirit of *bhakti*. The revelation of God's nature in those who follow the path of *vaidhī-bhakti* is different from that in those who follow the *ruci-bhakti;* in the former case He appears in all his majesty, in the latter He appears with all his sweetness. When God is worshiped in a limited form as Kṛṣṇa, He reveals himself in his limited form to the devotee, and such is the supra-logical nature of God that even in this form he remains as the All-pervasive. It is evident that the acceptance of *viśeṣa* does not help Baladeva here and he has to accept the supra-logical nature of God to explain other parts of his religious dogmas.

"God is regarded as being both the material cause of the world and as the supreme agent. He has three fundamental powers: the supreme power, *viṣṇu-śakti*, the power as *kṣetrajña*, the power as *avidyā*. In His first power Brahman remains in Himself as the unchangeable; His other two powers are transformed into the *jīvas* and the world. The Sāṃkhyist argues that, as the world is of a different nature from Brahman, Brahman cannot be regarded as its material cause. Even if it is urged that there are two subtle powers which may be regarded as the material cause of the world and the *jīvas*, their objection still holds good; for the development of the gross, which is different from the subtle, is not explained. To this the reply is that the effect need not necessarily be the same as or similar to the material cause. Brahman transforms Himself into the world, which is entirely different from Him. If there were absolute oneness between the material cause and the effect, then one could not be called the cause and the other the effect; the lumpy character of the mud is not seen in the jug, which is its effect; in all cases that may be reviewed the effect must necessarily be different from the material cause. Such a modification does not in any way change the nature of Brahman. The changes are effect in His powers, while He remains unchanged by the modification of His powers. To turn to an ordinary example as an illustration, it may be pointed out that 'a man with the stick' refers to none other than the man himself, though there is a difference between the man and the stick; so though the power of the Brahman is identical with Brahman in association with His powers, yet the existence of a difference between Brahman and his powers is not denied. (II.1.13).

"Moreover, there is always a difference between the material cause and the effect. The jug is different from the lump of clay, and the ornaments from the gold out of which they are made;

also they serve different purposes and exist in different times. If the effect existed before the causal operation began, the application of the causal operation would be unnecessary; also the effect would be eternal. If it is held that the effect is a manifestation of that which was already existent, then a further question arises, whether this manifestation, itself an effect, requires a further manifestation, and so on; thus a chain of manifestations would be necessary, and the result would be a vicious infinite.

"Still, Baladeva does not deny the *pariṇāma* or the *abhivyakti* theory; he denies the Sāṃkhya view that even before the causal operation the effect exists, or that a manifestation (*abhivyakti*) would require a chain of manifestations. He defines effect as an independent manifestation (*svatantrābhivyaktimattvam kīla kāryatvam*), and such an effect cannot exist before the action of the causal operatives. The manifestation of the world is through the manifestation of God, on whom it is dependent. Such a manifestation can only happen through the causal operation inherent in God and initiated by His will. Thus the world is manifested out of the energy of God, and in a limited sense the world is identical with God; but once it is separated out of Him as effect, it is different from Him. The world did not exist at any time before it was manifested in its present form; therefore it is wrong to suppose that the world was at any stage identical with God, though God may always be regarded as the material cause of the world (2.1.14).

"Thus after all these discussions it becomes evident that there is really no difference of any importance between Baladeva's views and the Sāṃkhya view. Baladeva also admits that the world exists in a subtle form in God as endowed with His energies. He only takes exception to the verbal expression of the *kārikā* that the effect exists in the cause before the action of the causal operatives; for the effect does not exist in the cause *as effect* but in a subtle state. This subtle state is enlarged and endowed with spatio-temporal qualities before it can manifest itself as effect. The Sāṃkhya, however, differs in overstressing the existence of the effect in the cause, and in asserting that the function of the causal operatives is only to manifest openly what already existed in a covered manner. Here, however, the causal operatives are regarded as making a real change and addition. This addition of new qualities and functions is due to the operation of the causal will of God; it is of a supra-logical nature in the sense that they were not present in the subtle causal state, and yet have come into being through the operation of God's will. But, so far as the subtle cause exists in God as associated with Him, the world is not distinct and independent of God even in its present form (II.1.20).

"The *jīvas* too have no independence in themselves; they are created by God, by His mere will, and having created the world and the *jīvas* He entered into them and remained as their inner controller. So the *jīvas* are as much under natural necessity as the objects of the physical world, and they have thus no freedom of action or of will (II.1.23). The natural necessity of the world is but a manifestation of God's will through it. The spontaneous desire and will that is found in man is also an expression of God's will operating through man; thus man is as much subject to necessity as the world, and there is no freedom in man. Thus, though the cow which gives milk may seem to us as if it were giving the milk by its own will, yet the vital powers of the cow produce the milk, not the cow; so, when a person is perceived as doing a particular action or behaving in a particular manner or willing something, it is not he who is the agent, but the supreme God, who is working through him (II.1.24).

"But the question may arise, if God is the sole cause of all human willing and human action, then why should God, who is impartial, make us will so differently? The answer will be that God determines our action and will in accordance with the nature of our past deeds, which are beginningless. A further objection may be made, that if God determines our will in accordance with out past deeds, then God is dependent in His own determining action on the nature of our *karmans*; which will be a serious challenge to His unobstructed freedom. Moreover, since different kinds of action lead to different kinds of pleasurable and painful effects God may be regarded as partial. The reply to these objections is that God determines the *jīvas* in accordance with their own individual nature; the individual *jīvas* are originally of a different nature, and in accordance with their original difference God determines their will and actions differently. Though God is capable of changing their nature He does not do so; but it is in the nature of God's own will that he reserves a preferential treatment for His devotee, to whom he extends his special grace (II.1.35). God's own actions are not determined by an objective end or motive, but flow spontaneously through His enjoyment of His own blissful nature. His special grace towards His devotees flows from His own essential nature; it is this special treatment offered to His devotees that endears Him to them and that rouses others to turn towards Him (II.1.36)."

15.4 BALADEVA VIDYĀBHŪṢAṆA, *Brahmasūtra-Sūkṣma*

This is Baladeva's commentary on his own 15.3 *Govinda-bhāṣya*. It is printed with some of the editions of that work, for example, the edition by Bhaktivedanta Baman, Nadia 1973. The catalogues are not very helpful on this work.

15.5 BALADEVA VIDYĀBHŪṢAṆA, Commentary on the *Bhagavatapurāṇa*

Published in Oriya script with a commentary titled *Kāntimālā* by Kṛṣṇadevavedāntavāgīśā, Pāramārthika priyā pustakābalī 10, Kataka 1976.

15.6 BALADEVA VIDYĀBHŪṢAṆA, Commentary on Jīva Gosvāmin's *Tattvasandarbha*

This has been edited at least thrice, once from Calcutta in 1919, from Murshidabad in 1956, and again from Vrndavan in 1984.

15.7 BALADEVA VIDYĀBHŪṢAṆA, *Siddhāntaratna*

Edited, parts translated (see Bib 3 #1448.6). Narang 1984, p. 12, reports on some doubts having been expressed as to this being Baladeva's work. The doubters include Surendranath Dasgupta (HIP Volume 4, p. 438). However, Mrs. Narang does not accept his view.

Summary by Sudesh Narang

"*Siddhāntaratna* is an original philosophical work as it embodies arguments which strengthen and justify the nine truths that have been expounded by Baladeva in his *Govinda Bhāṣya*. This seems to be a supplement to the *Govinda Bhāṣya*. That is a clue to the authenticity of its authorship by Baladeva. Baladeva says to that effect, 'May this golden couch of *Siddhāntaratna* be worthy to beseat the *Bhāṣya* of the Vedānta which glorifies Kṛṣṇa and elucidates nine truths' [*Siddhāntaratna* 8, 32]. In the introductory verses, the author pays his obeisance to Śyāma Sundara, Śrī Caitanya, Vyāsa, Rūpa and Sanātana. He compares the last two persons to the Sun and the Moon, arisen in the Vaiṣṇava firmament to dispel the darkness of the doctrine of illusion. Also, in the closing section of this work Baladeva sings in the glory of Govinda Deva and acknowledges that the seeds of the basic principles of his philosophy were diffused by Ānanda Tīrtha (Madhva) and were brought to blossom by Caitanya. [*Siddhāntaratna* 8, 36].

"The book consists of eight chapters (*pādas*) which are named after the weapons and the divine names of the Lord. These deal with the following topics chapter-wise as follows:

(i) The highest desideratum of the *jīvas*;
(ii_ The majesty of God;
(iii) The highest truth is Viṣṇu;
(iv) He is the object of all the Vedas;
(v and vi) Arguments refuting the undifferentiated or the Absolute Brahman;
(vii) Refutation of the realization of one absoluteness;
(viii) Arguments in favor of the highest desideratum, i.e., the grace of the Lord."

15.8 BALADEVA VIDYĀBHŪṢAṆA, *Siddhāntadarpaṇa*

Edited and translated, e.g., by Haridasa Dasa, Haribole Kutira, Navadvipa 1942. The summary below is found in Narang 1984, pp. 15-16

Summary by Sudesh Narang

"In this treatise Baladeva strives to stress the fact that the *itihāsa* and the *Purāṇas* are not different from the Vedas. He presents Vedāntic arguments in favor of his doctrine. He, no doubt, admits the eternity of the Vedas but regards the Purāṇic treatises as supplement to the Vedas. He opines thus that both the Vedic and the Purāṇic thinkers regarded some Supreme Power as Absolute Reality. To them that Power is an object whose indicative word is *praṇava (om)*.

"The book consists of seven *prabhās*. It deals with the following topics:

(i) Refutation of the atheistic systems.

(ii) Refutation of the view that the *Purāṇas* are human writings.

(iii) The *Bhāgavata* is one of the eighteen *Purāṇas*.

(iv) The *Bhāgavata* is exclusively different from the *Devī Bhāgavata* and the *Kālikā Purāṇa*.

(v) The *Bhāgavata* is a testimony par excellence.

(vi) Veda Vyāsa composed the *Bhāgavata* and none else.

(vii) Refutation of the *guṇa* theory of Pañcaśikha (a Sāṃkhya preceptor)."

In HIP 4, pp. 439 and pp. 445-448 Dasgupta provides an account of the contents of portions of this work:

"The eternal possession of bliss and the eternal cessation of sorrow is the ultimate end of man. This end can be achieved through the true knowledge of God in His essence (*svarūpataḥ*) and as associated with His qualities by one who knows also the nature of his own self (*sva-jñāna-pūrvakam*). The nature of God is pure consciousness and bliss. These two may also be regarded as the body of God (*na tu svarūpād vigrahasya atirekaḥ*). His spirit consists in knowledge, majesty and power." (pp. 1-13).

"*Bhakti* is also regarded as a species of knowledge (*bhaktir api jñāna-viśeṣo bhavati)* (p. 29). By *bhakti* one turns to God without any kind of objective end. *Bhakti* is also regarded as a power which can bind God to us (p. 35); this power is regarded as the essence of the *hlādinī* power of God as associated with consciousness. The consciousness here spoken of is identical with the *hlāda*, and its essence consists in a favorable outflow of natural inclination (p. 37). This is thus identical with God's essential nature as consciousness and bliss; yet it is not regarded as identical with Him, but as a power of Him. (p. 38). Though *bhakti* exists in God as His power, yet it qualifies the devotee also, it is pleasurable to them both, and they are both constituents of it (p. 39). It will be remembered that, of the three powers, *saṃvit* is superior to *sandhinī* and *hlādinī* is superior to *saṃvit.* God not only is, but He extends his being to everything else; *sandhinī* is the power by which God extends being to all. He is Himself of the nature of consciousness; *saṃvit* is the power by which His cognitive action is accomplished and by which he makes it possible for other people to know. Though He is of the nature of bliss, He experiences joy and makes it possible for others to have joyous experiences; the power by which He does this is called *hlādinī* (pp. 30-40)."

15.9 BALADEVA VIDYĀBHŪṢAṆA, *Prameyaratnāvalī*

Edited several times; cf. Bib 3, #1448.4. The summary that follows is found in Narang 1984, pp. 13-15.

Summary by Sudesh Narang

"Baladeva was greatly influenced by Madhva. He summarizes his nine truths as well as Caitanya's teachings in his *Prameyaratnāvalī.* Baladeva has developed and molded those truths according to his own faith. In this particular treatise he cites passages from the Kauthumī section of the Vedas, the (*Iśā, Kaṭha, Muṇḍaka, Śvetāśvatara* and *Chāndogya*) *Upaniṣads*, the *Mahābhārata* (inclding the *Gītā*), the *Bhāgavata,* the *Viṣṇu,* and the *Mahāvārāha Purāṇa,* the *Narada Pāñcarātra,* the *Gautama Tantra,* the *smṛti,* the *Brahmasūtras* and the *Brahmasaṃhitā,* in support of his belief. Verses from the *Padma Purāṇa* have also been cited in emphasizing the importance of the Gauḍīya sect as one of the recognized sects.

"In the beginning, the author glorifies the three main deities of the Gauḍīya sect, viz., Govinda, Gopūnātha and Madana Mohana. He invokes their blessings in order to be able to expound the subtle nine truths. Also, he seeks loving devotion of Śrī Caitanya, Nityānanda and Advaita. Further, he traces the origin of the Gauḍīya sect to Madhva's sect and enumerates the nine philosophical tenets before he proceeds to expound them in the nine propositions. As such those principles are as under:

(i) Viṣṇu is the highest reality.

(ii) Viṣṇu is knowable through the scriptures.

(iii) The universe is real.

(iv) The difference between the Lord and the individual souls is real.

(v) There exists a gradation of souls in accordance with their status when they are either free or in bondage.

(vi) The individual souls are real and servants of the Lord.

(vii) Salvation lies in attaining Viṣṇu's lotus-feet.

(viii) Undivided devotion is the means to that end, i.e. salvation.

(ix) Triple evidence of knowledge is valid, i.e. direct sense-perception, inference and scriptural testimony. The last evidence is the most authoritative and reliable."

15.10 BALADEVA VIDYĀBHŪṢAṆA, *Sāraṅgaraṅgadā* on Rūpa Gosvāmī's *Laghu-* or *Saṃkṣepa-Bhagavatāmṛta*

The following is found in Narang 1984, p. 23:

Summary by Sudesh Narang

"It is a compact discourse on the Bhāgavata and the Purāṇa literature on the whole...known as *Sāraṅga Raṅgadā* (to wit, the one that enchants even animals or birds)."

"The purpose of the treatise is to describe the essential nature of the worshiped and the worshiper. Both the author and the commentator have exuberantly cited from the Vedas, the Darśanas, the Epics, the Purāṇas and the Tantras.

"There are two divisions of the treatise. The first and longer portion is named as *Kṛṣṇāmṛta* and the second, quite small, is *Bhaktāmṛta*. The former portion glorifies Kṛṣṇa, His manifestations, abodes and sports, whereas the latter ascribes divinity to the Lord's retinue and even to His devotees."

15.11 BALADEVA VIDYĀBHŪṢAṆA, Commentary on the *Gopālatāpanīyopaniṣad*

Edited by Mahanidhi Swami, and translated by Bhumipati, Rasbihari Lal & Sons: Vrndaban 2004. Edited [earlier] by Haridasa, Haribole Kutīra, Navadvīpa, 1942, says Narang 1984, p. 17, who provides the following remarks:

Summary by Sudesh Narang

"This Upaniṣad belongs to the Pippalāda branch of the Atharvaveda. Baladeva wrote a commentary on it with a view to emphasize the most adorable Gopāla form of the Lord who is possessed of six divine faculties. He becomes accessible to all his devotees. This Upaniṣad is highly respected in the Vaiṣṇava circle of Caitanya's followers..."

15.12 BALADEVA VIDYĀBHŪṢAṆA, *Vedāntasyamantaka*

Edited Calcutta 1886; Nasik 1941, e.g. The following summary is to be found in Narang 1984, pp. 16-17.

Summary by Sudesh Narang

"This treatise also is an exposition of Vedāntic thought in the light of the Gauḍīya Vaiṣṇava faith. It is an inquiry into the propositions held in esteem by the author himself in his *Govinda Bhāṣya*.

"It is composed in six *kiraṇas*. In each *kiraṇa* the author has attempted to refute the fundamental philosophical views as held by Śaṃkara. It treats of five eternal principles as against Śaṃkara's theory of Brahman.

"The first *kiraṇa* establishes the scriptures as a valid source of knowledge. In the next five *kiraṇas*, Baladeva dilates upon the five objects of knowledge. He regards his Person God Śrī Kṛṣṇa to be the Supreme Person. The individual soul is different-non-different from the Supreme Consciousness and yet eternally His servant. The inert matter and time are under the sway of the Supreme Lord. Actions of various kinds yield various fruits but the knower of Brahman simply sails across the ocean of fruits by way of knowledge."

16 SAVAI JAYASIMHA (1795)

This author is apparently the same person as Savai Jayasimha II or Jay Singh, the well-known maharaja of Amber (1699-1743), who gathered an important collection of Sanskrit, Persian and Arabic astronomical MSS., as well as printed European books. The following works are ascribed to him, although we have been unable to find more details. Consultation of, e.g. Google, yields references to various bits of information about him.

16.1 SAVAI JAYASIṂHA, Commentary on Jīva Gosvāmin's *Kṛṣṇasandarbha*

16.2 SAVAI JAYASIṂHA, Commentary on a *Laghubhāgavatāmṛta*

16.3 SAVAI JAYASIṂHA, Commentary on the *Brahmasūtras*

17.1 BHAVANĪCARAṆA TARKABHŪṢAṆA (1828), *Jñānasārataraṅginī*

Edited Calcutta 1828 (?)

18.1 KṚṢṆĀDEVA SĀRVABHAUMA (1850), *Kaṇtimālā* on Baladeva Vidyābhūṣaṇa's *Prameyaratnāvalī*

Edited several times, between 1878 and 1981; cf. Bib 3, #1448.4, p. 724

19 VĪRACANDRA GOSVĀMIN (1878)

Sushil Kumar De, in his Introduction to *The Padyavali: An Anthology of Vaisnava Verses in Sanskrit compiled by Rūpa Gosvāmin* (New Delhi 1990), p. cxxxi-ii, gives the following information about Vīracandra Gosvāmin:

"(He) was the son of Kiśorimohana Gosvāmin and descendant of Nityānanda. He was a native of the village of Mādo, near Mānkar, in Burdwan; and the more well-known Raghunanadana Gosvāmin, author of the Bengali poems *Rāmarasāyana* and *Rādhāmādhavo-daya*, was his step-brother. Vīracandra was the author of several Vaiṣṇava works in Sanskrit and in Bengali..."

19.1 VĪRACANDRA GOSVĀMIN, *Rūpacintāmaṇi-Ṭīkā*

Edited from Calcutta in 1927.

20 RĀDHĀRAMAṆA DĀSA GOSVĀMI (1890)

We find the following on p. vi of Upadeśāmṛta: "Śrī Rādhāramaṇa Dāsa Gosvāmī composed a Sanskrit commentary on *Śrī Upadeśāmṛta,* which is brief, yet essential. He appeared in the dynasty of the Vṛndāvana *gosvāmīs* who serve the Rādhāramaṇa Deity, who was established and served by Śrī Gopālabhaṭṭa Gosvāmī. His father's name was Śrī Govardhanalāla Gosvāmī and his grandather's name was Śrī Jīvana-lāla Gosvāmī. Śrī Jīvana-lāla Gosvāmī was his initiating spiritual master (*dīkṣā-guru*) and also his instructing spiritual master. Rādha-ramaṇa Dāsa Gosvāmī was a great scholar, author and poet in Sanskrit and Hindi. His *Dīpikā dīpanī* commentary on *Śrīmad-Bhāgavatam* is highly respected amongst scholars. Similarly, his *Upadeśa-prakāśikā* commentary is highly revered in Vaiṣṇava society."

20.1. RĀDHĀRAMAṆA DĀSA GOSVĀMI, *Bhagavatapurāṇadīpikā-Dīpanī*

We believe this work has been edited, but cannot find the specifics in the usual sources.

20.2 RĀDHĀRAMAṆA DĀSA GOSVĀMI, *Brahmasūtra-Tilaka*

Again, we believe this is available in print, but cannot locate a reference.

20.3 RĀDHĀRAMAṆA DĀSA GOSVĀMI, *Prakāśa* on Rūpa Gosvāmin's *Upadeśāmṛta*

The following is taken from Upadesamrta, where the entire commentary is translated. Page numbering following 'T' is to that work.

Translated by Bhaktivedānta Nārāyaṇa Mahārāja

1 (Verse One) (T3-7) "Let there be all victory for Śrī Rādhā-ramaṇa. I offer prayers unto Śrī Caitanya Mahāprabhu, who is accompanied by the unfettered ascetic (*avadhuṭa*) Śrī Nityānanda Prabhu, the identical manifestation of Śrī Baladeva, by Śrī Advaita Ācārya, the incarnation of Mahā-Viṣṇu, by His potencies such as Śrī Gadādhara, and by His associates like Śrīnivāsa. I take shelter of the Mahāprabhu, who is the fountainhead of all potencies of the world. I offer prayers with great respect and effection unto Śrī Rūpa Gosvāmin, whose entire wealth is *śṛṅgāra-rasa*. This means that the sole purpose of his life is to describe *śṛṅgāra-rasa*, also known as *unnatojjvala prema-rasa*, the highest and most radiant divine love of Śrī Rādhā-Kṛṣṇa. He is always immersed in the service of the lotus feet of Śrī Rādhā-Govinda. He has purified all the living entities of this world by giving instruction on the methodology by which this type of *prema* maybe obtained. I offer *praṇāma* unto Śrī Gopāla-bhaṭṭa Gosvāmī, who is very merciful to the destitute and wretched living entities who are

enamoured with the external energy. I offer *praṇāma* once more unto the ocean of mercy Śrī Caitanya Mahāprabhu, the incarnation who sanctifies this Kali-yuga, who distributes *śrīharināma* and love of God (*bhagavat-prema*) and who delivers the souls (*jīvas*) of this earth. I offer prayers unto Śrī Gopīnātha dāsa, a disciple of Śrī Gopāla-bhaṭṭa and servant of Śrī Rādhā-ramaṇa,. who has benedicted innumerable living entities by bestowing Śrī-gaura *bhakti*. I offer *praṇāma* unto my *gurudeva*, Śrī Jīvanalāla, of whom I am the grandson and servant. Offering *praṇāṃa* unto all of them, I am beginning this brief explanation of the verses of *Śrī Upadeśāmṛta*, written by Śrī Rūpa Gosvāmi for the benefit of the *sādhakas*.

"In *Śrī Bhakti-rasāmṛta-sindhu* Śrī Rūpa Gosvāmi has defined *uttamabhakti* as the cultivation of activities for Śrī Kṛṣṇa, performed with a favorable mood which is devoid of all other desires and which is not covered by knowledge aiming at the oneness of the *jīvas* with the Lord (*jñāna*) or by fruitive activity (*karma*) which is not meant exclusively for the Lord's pleasure. How can such *uttamabhakti* manifest in persons whose hearts are filled with shortcomings such as lust and anger? In the *Padma Purāṇa* is it said: 'How can Śrī Mukunda ever be manifest to a person whose heart is invaded by lamentation, anger and other agitations?'

"The purport of this statement is that when contaminations such as lust, anger and greed arise within the mind, the six overwhelming passions mentioned in the original verse cause the mind to become thoroughly engrossed in fleeting objects of sensual gratification. The cultivation of unalloyed *bhakti* is never possible in such a contaminated heart. Therefore, the instruction is given here to subdue these passions which impede the development of *bhakti*. The *sādhaka* who can tolerate these passions can instruct the entire world. The conclusion is that a *sādhaka* who has conquered his senses and subdued these passions can purify all the *jīvas* of the world by his resolute and pure *uttamā-bhakti*. Everyone may become the disciple of such a great personality.

""My dear Uddhava! My devotee whose voice becomes choked up with *prema*, whose heart softens and begins to flow with spiritual emotion, who cannot cease from crying even for an instant, who sometimes bursts into laughter, sometimes begins to sing very loudly, abandoning all shyness, and sometimes dances, purifies not only himself but the entire world.'

"It is essential to note here that by subduing the six passions described already, what is obtained is merely the qualification to enter the realm of *bhakti*. These are not direct limbs of devotional practice (*pradhāna-bhakti*) but, rather, the doorway through which one may enter the realm of *bhakti*. Because *bhakti* is the self-manifest function of the Lord's internal potency (*svarūpa-śakti*), when it make its appearance there six passions automatically become pacified.

2 (Verse Two) (T25-28) "In the beginning stage of the practice of *bhakti* the material proclivity is prominent in the hearts of the *sadhakas*. Therefore, they are unable to subdue the six overwhelming passions described in the first verse. Consequently, in this condition, many tendencies develop in the heart of the *sādhakas* which are very harmful to *bhakti*. In this verse those injurious tendencies are being described for the benefit of the *sādhakas*. The word *atyāhāra* means to eat more than required or to accumulate material objects. The word *prayāsa* means to endeavor for worldly objects or to be engaged in activities which are opposed to *bhakti*. The word *prajalpa* means to uselessly criticize and gossip about others, which is a gross misuse of time. The word *niyamāgraha*, when broken into its constituent parts, has two meanings: (1) *niyama* + *āgraha*-over-zealous-ness in the following rules, and (2) *niyama* + *agraha*–failure to accept rules. When the first meaning is applied, it refers to enthusiasm for those rules which yield an inferior results, such as promotion to the heavenly planes,

leaving aside the endeavor for the superior attainment of the service of the Lord. When the second meaning is appled, it refers to indifference towards those rules which nourish *bhakti*. The words *jana-saṅga* mean to give up the association of pure devotees and keep company with others. In the conversation between Devahūti and Kardama Muni in the *Śrīmad-Bhāgavatam* (3.23.55), there is a very nice instruction about giving up worldly association: 'O Devī! Association is the cause of both material bondage and liberation from material existence. When due to ignorance one keeps company with worldly-minded persons who are diverted from the path of *bhakti*, that association brings about one's material entanglement. When, however, one keeps company with pure devotees of the Lord, that association liberates one from material existence and causes one to obtain the lotus feet of the Lord.'

"Furthermore, Bhagavān Kapiladeva gives the following instructions to Devahūta; 'Those who desire to obtain *kṛṣṇa-prema*, which is the ultimate fruit of *bhakti-yoga*, should never indulge in illicit association with women. Learned sages who know the absolute truth say that for those who desire liberation from material existence and attainment of the lotus feet of the Lord, illicit connection with women opens wide the door to hell.'

"'One should never associate with foolish, agitated, materialistic men who identify the body as the self, who are most deplorable, and who are dancing dogs in the hands of women.' (*Śrīmad Bhāgavatam* 3.1.34)

"Having pointed out the defects of material association, the revealed scriptures (*śāstra*) forbid it. The agitation of the mind for compatible objects and the unsteadiness of mind which results from association with persons of many different opinions is known as *laulya*. Such unsteadiness of the mind is like an unchaste woman wandering sometimes upon the path of action (*karman*), sometimes on the path of *yoga*, sometimes on the path of *jñāna* and sometimes upon the path of *bhakti*. By this the predilection for *bhakti* is destroyed.

3 (T40) "The word *utsāhā*, or enthusiasm, refers to eagerness to perform the limbs of *sādhana* which enhance *bhakti*. The word *niścaya*, or conviction, signifies firm faith. *Dhairya* means not slackening one's execution of the limbs of *bhakti*, even when there is delay in obtaining the desired goal. The meaning of *tat-tat-karma-pravartanāt* is to fully renounce one's material enjoyment while endeavoring exclusively for the attainment of Bhagavān. In the *Śrīmad-Bhāgavata*, (11.19.24) Bhagavān Śrī Kṛṣṇa says to Uddhava: 'Devotion which is saturated with love for Me arises in the hearts of those who offer their very souls unto Me and who follow the religious principles which are favorable for *bhakti*. What other object remains to be obtained for those who have attained My *bhakti*?'

4. (T48) "In this fourth verse, the extrinsic symptoms of loving exchanges with pure devotees are described. As the meaning of this verse is perfectly clear, it does not require elaboration.

5. (T55-58) "This verse gives instruction on *svarūpa-siddhā-bhakti*.[1] We should respectfully offer *praṇāma* to those who have accepted initiation from a qualified *guru*. In all ways we should lovingly serve those who perform exclusive *bhajana* of Śrī Kṛṣṇa by *mānasa-sevā* and who are expert in the procedure of worshiping Kṛṣṇa's *aṣṭa-kālīya-līlā*, knowing them to be the

---

[1]All favorable endeavors (*ceṣṭā*) such as *śravaṇa, kīrtana, smaraṇa* and so on, as well as the manifestation of the spiritual sentiments which occur beginning from the state of *bhāva*, which are completely devoid of all desires separate from Śrī Kṛṣṇa and which are freed from the coverings of *jñāna* and karma, are known as *svarūpa-siddhā-bhakti* . In other words, all endeavors of the body, words and mind which are related to Śrī Kṛṣṇa and which are performed exclusively and directly for His pleasure without any intervention are known as *svarūpa-siddhā-bhakti*.

most desirable association. The meaning of 'exclusive *bhajana*' is to be solely devoted to the worship of Śrī Rādhā-Kṛṣṇa in Vraja, without attachment for Lakṣmī-Nārāyaṇa or other incarnations of Bhagavān. It says in the *Bhakti-rasāmṛta-sindhu* that amongst the exclusive devotees of the many differrent incarnations of Bhagavān, those whose hearts have been stolen by Śrī Nandanandana are the best because even the favor of the master of Lakṣmī, Śrī Nārāyaṇa, cannot attract their minds. Because such exclusive devotees are forever alert to cultivate *bhakti* in the company of those topmost devotees who are expert in relishing devotional mellows (*rasika*), as well as being like-minded and affectionate, their hearts are always free from contaminations such as the tendency to criticize others. Knowing these topmost devotees to be the most desirable association, one should respect them mentally, offer *praṇāma* unto them and render service to them with great love.

"Another meaning of this verse can be given. One should respect within the mind those who have accepted initiation from a qualified *guru* and chant *kṛṣṇa-nāma*. One should respect those who have accepted initiation from a bona fide spiritual master (*sad guru*), who have developed an understanding of *sambandha-jñāna*[1] and who perform *bhajana* purely, by offering *praṇāma* to them and so forth. The best devotees are those who are devoid of the tendency to

---

[1]*Sambandha-jñāna* is knowledge regarding *sambandha-tattva,* the mutual relationship between the Lord, the living entities and the material energy. The word *sambandha* means connection, relationship and binding. The living entities are eternally and inseparably connected to the Supreme Lord. Therefore, he is the true object of relationship. The general relationship between the living entities and the Supreme Lord is one of servant and served. However, in the perfectional stage of *bhakti*, one becomes established in a specific relationship with the Lord either as a servant, friend, parent or lover.

blaspheme others and who, being exclusively devoted to Śrī Rādhā-Kṛṣṇa, are forever alert to render service mentally to their *aṣṭa-kālīya-līlā*. Knowing such devotees to be established in the particular mood of service to Śrī Rādhā-Kṛṣṇa for which one aspires, to be affectionately disposed towards oneself and to be the topmost association, one should honor them in all respects by offering *daṇḍava-praṇāma (praṇipāta),* making relevant inquiry (*paripraśna*) and rendering service (*sevā*) with great affection. One should understand the eminence of Vaiṣṇavas according to this gradation.

"In the original verse by Śrī Rūpa Gosvāmin, the word '*ādi*', meaning 'and so forth', has been used after word '*ninda*', which means to criticize. We should understand this to indicate envy, aggression and other faults which generally accompany the tendency to criticize others. In the *Śrīmad-Bhāgavatam* (3.25.24) Kapiladeva says: 'O Sādhvi (virtuous lady)! The only desirable association is that of pure-hearted *sādhus* who always remain aloof from all varieties of bad association. By the influence of their association, the contaminations accrued through bad association can be eradicated.'

6. (T65) "Due to their residing within the material world, pure devotees seem to have some apparent defects from the mundane perspective. Nevertheless, we should not consider such devotees to be material or, in other words, to be ordinary conditioned souls. If one notices imperfections in their natures, such as harshness, anger, greed and so forth, or imperfections in their bodies, such as lack of cleanliness, ugliness, aging and so forth, he should never assign mundane attributes to them. It is impossible for these mundane imperfections to exist with devotees' spiritually perfected bodies. Therefore, to perceive these mundane defects in elevated devotees is offensive. This point has been made clear by the example of Ganges water.

7 (T71) "When *sādhakas* are still affected by the obstacles which impede progress in devotional life (*anarthas*) their minds are restless and disturbed. For this reason, it is not easy

for them to develop a taste for Bhagavan's name and so forth. Still, they should not relent even a little in their determination to continue performing *nāma-bhajana*. Being indifferent to Śrī Kṛṣṇa since beginningless time is called *avidyā*, or ignorance. In this verse such *avidyā* is compared to the disease of jaundice. When one is afflicted with this disease, his tongue's sense of taste is warped. Although Śrī Kṛṣṇa's names, form, qualities and pastimes are like the sweetest sugar-candy, a person afflicted by ignorance does not find them tasteful. By regularly taking sugar-candy, one's jaundice is gradually mitigated and the candy also begins to become tasteful to him. Similarly, by daily cultivating in a regulated manner the limbs of *bhakti*, headed by performing *kīrtana* of Śrī Kṛṣṇa's names and hearing narrations of His pastimes, a *sādhaka's' anarthas*, beginning with the tendency to commit offences, are eradicated and natural love for *śrī-nāma* and *hafri-kathā* awakens within him.

8. (T76-77) "At this point, these questions may arise in the mind of a new *sādhaka*: 'Where should one reside to cultivate the devotional activities, headed by the changing of Śrī Kṛṣṇa's name, and how should one go about it?" This verse, which constitutes the essence of all instruction, has been composed to answer these questions. The conventional meaning of the name of Kṛṣṇa is drawn from the verbal root *kṛṣ*, which means to attract or draw towards oneself. Thus Kṛṣṇa is famed as the attractor of the hearts of all living entities in the entire world. In Vraja He is known also as Yaśodānandana, He who gives delight to Yaśodā. Therefore, all devotees should utilize the entirety of their time in engaging their tongues in performing *kīrtana* of Śrī Kṛṣṇa's name, form, qualities and pastimes and their minds in remembrance of Him. They should reside only in Śrī Vrajamaṇḍala and follow elevated devotees.

"How should one follow devotees? By two types of devotion: *vaidhī* (devotion performed in conjunction with the rules and regulations of the scriptures) and *rāgānugā* (spontaneous devotion). Accordingly, there are also two types of *sādhakas*–those who follow the path of *vaidhī* and those who follow the path of *rāgānugā*. Among these two, it is especially desirable to follow a *rāgānugā-bhakta*. The meaning of *tad-anurāgī jñānāgāmī* is to follow the intimate, eternal devotees of Śrī Kṛṣṇa's *vrajalīlā*. One should cultivate *kṛṣṇa-bhakti* under the guidance of those *rasika gurus* who are themselves followers of the intimate eternal devotees of Śrī Vrajendra-nandana, who enacts human-like pastimes.

9. (T88-89) "The previous verse instructed us to perform *bhajana* while residing in Vraja. This verse very clearly answers precisely where one should reside within Vraja. Due to Śrī Kṛṣṇa's having taken birth there, the abode of Mathurā is superior even to Vaikuṇṭha, the realm of great spiritual opulence. Superior even to the abode of Mathurā is the forest of Vṛndāvana because there the festival of the *rāsa* dance took place. Superior to the Vṛndāvana forest is Govardhana Hill because it playfully rested in Śrī Kṛṣṇa's lotus hand, and because there Kṛṣṇa freely enjoyed many pastimes with His devotees. Yet superior even to this Govardhana Hill is the super-excellent Śrī Rādhā-kuṇḍa because it immerses one in the nectarine divine love which Śrī Kṛṣṇa, the moon of Gokula, feels for Śrīmatī Rādhikā. The scriptures declare that Śrī Rādhā-kuṇḍa is as dear to Śrī Kṛṣṇa as the daughter of Vṛṣabhānu Mahārāja, Śrīmatī Rādhikā Herself.

"All the above-mentioned spiritual realms or locations where Śrī Kṛṣṇa performed pastimes are manifest from His internal potency (*svarūpa-śakti*) and are therefore purely spiritual. However, Śrī Rādhā-kuṇḍa is superior to them all because of having manifested the highest display of the inherent variegated pastimes of *svarūpa-śakti*.

10 (T95-96) "In this tenth verse, yet another reason for taking shelter of and worshiping Śrī Rādhā-kuṇḍa is being shown. A follower of the path of *karma-kāṇḍa* who is interested solely in enjoying the fruits of his actions is actually indifferent to Bhagavān. More dear to Bhagavān are *jñānīs* who are

inclined towards *nirviśeṣa-brahma*, His impersonal aspect, which is merely a nonspecific manifestation of indifferentiated spirit. More dear to Bhagavān than such *jñānīs* are his devotees such as the four Kumāras who are devoid of *nirviśeṣa-jñāna*, inclination towards His impersonal aspect, yet possess *aiśvarya-jñāna*, awareness of his supreme majesty. Devotees such as Śrī Nārada who possess *prema-niṣṭhā*, a resolute and exclusive fixation in love for Him, are even more dear to Śrī Hari than such *jñānī-bhaktas*. Superior to such loving devotees are the *vraja-gopīs* who, due to possessing an indescribable and unprecedented love for Śrī Kṛṣṇa, are exceedingly dear to Him.

'In the *Padma Purāṇa* it is said: 'Just as Śrīmatī Rādhikā is most dear to Śrī Kṛṣṇa, Her pond, Śrī Rādhā-kuṇḍa, is equally dear to Him. Among all the beloved *gopīs*, none are as dear as Śrmatī Rādhikā.'

"This verse, quoted as *Ujjvala-nīlamaṇi* (4.5), proves that, amongst all the *gopīs*, Śrīmatī Rādhikā alone is Śrī Kṛṣṇa's dearmost beloved. In precisely the same way, Śrī Rādhā-kuṇḍa, Her pond whichis actually nondifferent from Her, is exceedingly dear to Śrī Kṛṣṇa andis also the topmost place of residence for devotees. Therefore, what spiritually insightful person desirous of performing *bhajana* would not take shelterof that pond? Certainly any such person would take shelter of Śrī Rādhā-kuṇḍa.

11. (T101-102) "It is only natural at this point to become eager to learn what special commodity can be attained by taking exclusive shelter of the limitless glorious Śrī Rādhā-kuṇḍa. 'The fruit of such exclusive devotion is the topmost variety of *kṛṣṇa-prema*'--Śrī Rūpa Gosvāmin is concluding his composition by affirming this philosophical principle (*siddhānta*). The *prema* being spoken of here is extremely difficult to achieve even for such exalted and dear devotees of Bhagavān as Nārada. In other words, this most elevated, radiant divine love (*unnatojjvala-prema*) which the *vraja-gopīs* possess for Śrī Kṛṣṇa is not only difficult for such dear devotees

to attain, it is actually impossible. Śrī Rādhā-kuṇḍa bestows this very *prema* upon one who bathes in its waters with a mood of special love and devotion. Here, Śrī Rādhā-kuṇḍa is both the *syayaṃ-karttā*, or the one who directly bestows that *prema* upon the devotees, and also the *viṣaya*, or object of the devotees' love. Who would not take shelter of this Rādhā-kuṇḍa? In other words, any devotee, skilled in the art of performing *bhajana* and sincerely desirous of achieving the topmost *prema*, would certainly do so.

"Relying upon a particle of Śrī Caitanya Mahāprabhu's mercy, I have composed this commentary as far as my intelligence allows in order to increase the transcendental pleasure of his devotees. This servant of the Śrī Rādhā-ramaṇa Deity and son of Śrī Govardhana-lāla, named Rādhā-ramaṇa dāsa, hereby concludes his commentary named *Upadeśa-prakāśikā* on Śrī Rūpa Gosvāmī's *Śrī Upadeśāmṛta.*"

21 BHAKTIVINODA ṬHAKKURA (1900)

In the Preface to Upadesa 1997 Bhaktivedānta Nārāyaṇa provides the following information: "He (Bhaktivinoda Ṭakkura) appeared in an educated and cultured family on September 2, 1838, in the village of Viranagara, which is near the place of [Caitanya] Mahāprabhu's appearance, Śrī Dhāma Māyāpura, in West Bengal. His childhood name was Śrī Kedaranātha Datta. He was a scholarly and ingenious student. During his household life, he held a high position as a government official under the rule of the British Rāja. During that time he served the innermost desire of Śrī Gaurasundara by translating the Upaniṣads, the *Brahma-sūtra, Śrīmad-Bhāgavatam, Bhagavad-gītā*, the commentaries of the Gosvāmis, composing his own devotional books, and by publishing weekly and monthly spiritual journals. In addition, he established *nāma-hatta* programs for the distribution of *hari-nāma saṅkīrtana* and *hari-kathā* from village to village and town to town, and he revived many forgotten holy places.

"In the end he renounced his wealth and family and took up permanent residence at Śrī Svānanda-sukhadakuñja, a garden in Śrī Godruma which is situated on the banks of the divine Bhāgirathī River within the boundary of Śrī Dhāma Navadvīpa. There he remained possessionless and established the ideal of the system for practicing spontaneous devotional worship (*rāgānugā-bhajana*). If he had not appeared in this world, Mahāprabhu"s birthplace, the places where Mahāprabhu performed pastimes and Mahāprabhu's instructions would still be concealed...

"He composed approximately one hundred books in Sanskrit, Bengali, Hindi, English, Oriya and other languages... He disappeared from this world on June 23, 1914."

A complete account of Bhaktivinoda Ṭhakkura's life and works is provided in HEM. Here we have listed only those works that are to our knowledge published in English.

21.1 BHAKTIVINODA ṬHAKKURA, *Pīyūṣāvarṣiṇīvṛtti* on the *Upadeśāmṛta*

Translated in Upadesamrta 1997. We provide selections here as "T". Mainly, we have omitted the frequently-provided quotations from earlier textual sources. The title is translated as "Commentary in the form of a nectarine shower" by B. N. Maharaja in T, p. 7.

Translation by Bhaktivedanta Narayana Maharaja

1 (T7-13) ..."These six urges present various types of obstacles in the immature stage for the practitioner entering the path of *bhakti*. At that time the devotee, by taking shelter of the mood of exclusive *śaraṇāgati* and by avoiding the ten kinds of offences to the holy names (*nāmaparādha*) becomes first to

dispel these obstacles through the power of *harināma-kīrtana* and so on...

"The devotees are intent on practical renunciation (*yukta-vairāgya*) and thus they remain aloof from dry renunciation. Therefore, the regulation to abandon all contact with the sense-objects does not pertain to them. When the agitation of the mind is withdrawn or, in other words, when one is devoid of thirst for material enjoyment, the impetuosity of the eyes, the life air, the hearing propensity and all other drives become pacified.

"Therefore, persons who have gained victory over these six overwhelming passions can conquer the entire world. The instruction to tolerate these urges is given only for householder devotees, because before giving up householder life one must first have abandoned all types of urges.

2 (T29-30) "*Atyāhāra, prayāsa, prajalpa, niyamāgraha, jana-saṅga* and *laulya* are six faults which are direcly opposed to *bhakti*. (1) The word *atyāhāra* is a compound word formed by combination of the prefix *ati*, which means too much or excessively, with the word *āhāra*, which means to seize, grasp or consume for one's own enjoyment. Excessive enjoyment of sense objects through any one of the senses and the endeavor to accumulate an excess of one's requirements are known as *atyāhāra*. Devotees who have renounced householder life are forbidden to accumulate material goods. *Gṛhastha* Vaiṣṇavas must acquire goods sufficient for their maintenance, but if they accumulate beyond their needs it is known as *atyāhāra*. Those who are eager to perform *bhajana* should not accumulate worldly goods like materialistic sense enjoyers.. (2) The word *prayāsa* refers to activities which are opposed to *bhakti* or those which are performed for the enjoyment of the senses. (3) To waste time in useless, mundane talks is called *prajalpa*. (4) The word *niyamāgraha* has two meanings. When one has obtained a progressively higher qualification but remains over-zealous to adhere to the rules pertaining to a lower qualification, it is

known as *niyamāgraha*. Failure to observe the rules which nourish *bhakti* or, in other words, an absence of firm faith is known as *niyamāgraha*. (5) To associate with persons other than Bhagavan's devotees is known as *janasaṅga*.. (6) The word *laulya* means both unsteadiness and greediness. In the first sense it refers to the fickleness of the mind to accept many different kinds of false doctrines or uncertain conclusions. In the second sense it refers to attachment for worthless material sense enjoyment. By *prajalpa* one indulges in criticizing *sādhus*, and by *laulya* one awakens a taste for many different temporary, uncertain conclusions. Both of these lead to *nāmaparādha*. Therefore, one should very carefully give them up.

3 (T41-42) "Maintaining one's existence by appropriate means and cultivating *bhakti* are two essential activities for devotees. The first half of this verse indicates attitudes which are favorable for the cultivation of *bhakti* and the second half describes how a devotee should conduct his life. Enthusiasm, optimism, patience, executing activities which nourish *bhakti*, renouncing bad association and adopting the good behavior of devotees are the means of obtaining success in *bhakti*.

(1) *Utsāha*–eagerness to follow the rules and regulations of *bhakti* is called *utsāha*. Without this enthusiasm, one's *bhakti* will vanish. Following the limbs of *bhakti* with great respect is real *utsāha*.

(2) *Niścaya*–the meaning of *niścaya* is firm faith.

(3) *Dhairya*–not slackening one's execution of the limbs. of *bhakti*, even when there is delay in obtaining the desired goal, is called *dhairya*, or patience.

(4) *Bhakti-poṣaka-karma*–there are two types of activities which nourish *bhakti*: positive injunctions (*vidhi*) and negative injunctions (*niṣedha*). Performing the limbs of *bhakti*, headed by *śravaṇa* and *kīrtana*, is the prescribed *vidhi*. Renouncing one's personal enjoyment for the purpose of giving pleasure to Śrī Kṛṣṇa is the primary *niṣedha*.

(5) *Saṅga-tyāga*–one should renounce the association of one's non-devotees, women and those attached to women. 'Non-devotees' here means sense-enjoyers, *māyāvādīs* and those who make a pretentious display of *dharma*.

(6) *Sad-vṛtti*–one should adopt the virtuous conduct of pure devotees and thereby maintain one's life in a suitable manner. Renunciate devotees should beg alms, preferably by performing *madhukārī*. This is a process of begging where, like a *madhukāra* or bee taking nectar from many different flowers, they accept very little alms from many different households. Householder devotees should sustain their lives by means which are favorable to the regulations pertaining to the Vedic system of social order (*varṇāśrama*)–this is *sad-vṛtti*.

4 (T48-49) "Bad association is unfavorable to *bhakti*; therefore it is imperative to abandon such association. Those who are intent on progressing in *bhakti* should associate with pure devotees who possess the power to free one from the tendency to fall into bad association. A description of the loving exchanges shared between devotees which nourish one's *bhakti* is found in this fourth verse. Lovingly giving another devotee that which he requires and lovingly accepting those items which are mercifully given by other devotees, revealing one's confidential realizations to devotees and hearing descriptions of confidential tenets (*tattva*) from pure devotees, lovingly serving devotees *prasāda* and accepting *prasāda* offered by devotees–these six kinds of exchanges constitute association with saintly persons (*sādhu-saṅga*) in its pure form. These six activities are the symptoms of love. One should serve *sādhus* by the performance of these activities.

5 (T58-59) "According to the instruction given in this verse, as long as a *sādhaka* remains within the *madhyama-adhikārī* stage, he is obliged to render service to devotees. The topmost devotee (*uttama-bhakta*) sees all living entities with equal vision. Therefore, he doesn't discriminate between devotees and non-devotees. The intermediate devotee (*madhyama-bhakta*)

is one who sincerely endeavors to perform *bhajana*. This fifth verse indicates how *madhyama* devotees should behave towards the topmost class of devotees. If one remains aloof from the association of men who are attached to women, nondevotees and sense-enjoyers, their faults will not come within him. Still, understandng neophyte devotees (*kaniṣṭha-bhaktas*) to be ignorant due to their lack of knowledge of *sambandha-sattva*, the *madhyama* devotee should be merciful to them. Hearing such neophyte devotees uttering *lṛṣṇa-nāma*, a *madhyama* devotee will respect them within his mind. If a *kaniṣṭha* devotee accepts initiation and engages in *hari-bhajana*, a *madhyama* devotee will show him respect by offering *praṇāma* to him. Understanding the association of *mahā bhāgavata* Vaiṣṇavas who are free from the tendency to criticize others to be most beneficial, one should honor them by rendering service to them. This service alone is the root cause of all spiritual perfections.

6 (T65-66) "The instruction of this sixth verse is that it is improper to perceive mundane defects in pure devotees and to consider them to be mere conditioned souls. It is impossible for pure devotees to fall into bad association and to commit offences to the holy name. Perhaps there can be some imperfections in their bodies and in their natures. Lack of cleanliness, deformity, ugliness, old age and so forth are bodily imperfections. Birth in a low caste, harshness, lethargy and so forth are imperfections in one's character. The water of the Ganges is considered to be pure despite the natural appearance of bubbles, foam, mud and so on within it, and its natuture as liquified transcendence is not lost. Similarly Vaiṣṇavas wjho have realized their eternal identities are not contaminated by the natural transformation of the physical bodysuch as birth, aging, death and so on. Therefore, even upon observing imperfections in a pure Vaiṣṇava, one intent on performing *bhajana* should never disrespect him. By disrespecting such a personality, one becomes an offender (*aparādhi*).

7 (T72-73) "In the third verse of *Śrī Upadeśāmṛta*, qualities and activities which nourish *bhakti* were given. In addition to those qualities and activities, this verse describes te procedures for the cultivation of changing *kṛṣṇa-nāma* and so forth with *sambandha-jñāna*. The tongue afflicted with the jaundice of *avidyā* cannot narrate the Kṛṣṇa pastimes or chant His name. But regularly taking the sugar-candy of hearing and chanting Kèāṇa's *nāma, rūpa, guṇa* and *līlā* with great respect is capable of eradicating the disease of ignorance. Each and every *jīva*, lke a minute conscious particle within a ray of the complete conscious Kṛṣṇa sun, is by nature an eternal servant of Śrī Kṛṣṇa. When the *jīva* forgets this fact, he is seized by the disease of ignorance. Due to this, he is devoid of taste for devotional activities, headed by the chanting of Kṛṣṇa's name. But by taking good association and by the resultant mercy received from the *sādhu, guru* and Vaiṣṇava, he becomes capable of remembering Kṛṣṇa's names, form, qualities and pastimes and he gradually obtains realization of his eternal self. As realization of the his external nature gradually expands, his taste for devotional activities like chanting *kṛṣṇa-nāma* increases accordingly. Simultaneously his ignorance is dispelled step by step. Ths is the basis for the comparison to sugar-candy. The tongue of one afflicted with jaundice will not find sugar-candy tasteful. But by taking this candy regularly, his jaundice is gradually cured and that sugar-candy will begin to become tasteful to him. Therefore, with enthusiasm, firm faith and patience, one should always continue to hear and chant Kṛṣṇa's names, form, qualities and pastimes.

8 (T78) "This verse describes the method of *bhajaṇa* as well as the topmost place for performing *bhajana*. With the intention of incessantly executing the gradual process of *sādhana*, one should exercise every moment of his life by engagng the tongue in nicely performing *kīrtana* of Śrī Kṛṣṇa's names, form, qualities and pastimes and then the mind in *smaraṇa*, or remembrance, upon them. This process should be

executed while residing in Vraja and under the guidance of devotees who are immersed in *vraja rasa*. The performance of this *mānasa sevā* or service rendered within the mind, is dependent solely upon residing mentally in Vraja.

9 (T89-90) "This ninth verse informs us that Śrī Rādhā-kuṇḍa is the best amongst all worshipable places. Because Śrī Kṛṣṇa took birth in the city of Mathurā, it is superior to Vaikuṇṭha, the realm of immense opulence in the spiritual sky. Within the district of Mathurā, the Vṛndāvana forest is the best location. Govardhana Hill is the best place within the entire area of Vraja due to Udārapāṇi, Śrī Kṛṣṇa having performed various tastimes there. Śri Rāda-kuṇḍa is splendidly situated just near Śrī Govardhana. It is the best place of all due to being the special storehouse of Śrī Kṛṣṇa's nectarine divine love (*pramāmṛta*). Is there any person intent upon performing *bhajana* who would not desire to render service to Śrī Rādhā-kuṇḍa? In other words, the devotees of Bhagavān most certainly render service to Śrī Rādhā-kuṇḍa. Either in their material bodies or in their spiritually perfected forms, devotees should execute the aforementioned process of *bhajana* while constantly residing in Rādhāṣ-kuṇḍa.

10 (T97) "Among the many varieties of *sādhakas* found in this world, the devotee of Bhagavān who performs *bhajana* while residing on the banks of Śrī Rādhā-kuṇḍa is the best and the most dear to Śrī Kṛṣṇa. This is described in the tenth verse. More dear to Kṛṣṇa than the followers of the path of karma are the *jñānīs* who search after the impersonal aspect of the absolute truth. More dear to Kṛṣṇa than all the varieties of *jñanīs* is a pure devotee who has abandoned the attempt to understand the absolute truth through the cultivation of knowledge. Amongst all varieties of pure devotees, the *premībhakta,* or one who dearly loves Kṛṣṇa, is the most dear to Him. Amongst all varieties of such loving pure devotees, the *raja-gopīs*, Śrīmatī Rādhika is Kṛṣṇa's dearmost, and Her pond, Śrī Rādhā-kuṇḍa, is similarly dear to Him. Therefore, the

intelligent person who possesses sufficient accumulated devotional merit (*sukṛti*) will most certainly reside on the banks of Śrī Rādhā-kuṇḍa and within the mind render service to Śrī Kṛṣṇa's eight-fold daily pastimes."

21.2 BHAKTIVINODA ṬHAKKURA, *Vidvadrañjana* on Baladeva Vidyābhūṣaṇa's *Bhagavadgītābhūṣaṇa*

Edited at least twice. Cf. Bib 3, p. 724, #1448.1.

21.3 BHAKTIVINODA ṬHAKKURA, *Vedārkadīdhiti* on Baladeva Vidyābhūṣaṇa's *Īśopaniṣadbhāṣya*

This has been edited by Srirup Siddhanti, with the editor's subcommentary, Calcutta 1970.

21.4 BHAKTIVINODA ṬHAKKURA, *Vedāntatattvasudhā* on the *Bhagāvatapurāṇa*

Partly edited in Bengali?

21.5 BHAKTIVINODA ṬHAKKURA, *Tattvasūtra*

S.N. Dasa in HEM p. 290 informs us that this work, composed in 1893, consists of "fifty Sanskrit aphorisms divided into five chapters. Bhaktivinoda gives a Sanskrit commentary on each verse, plus an elaborate Bengali commentary. All the conclusions presented in this book are backed up with quotations from the *Upaniṣads,* the *Purāṇas*, *Bhagavad-gītā, Pañcarātra,* and other sources."

The work is translated by Narasimha Brahmachari in TVTSAS pp. 70-228.

21.6 BHAKTIVINODA ṬHAKKURA, *Tattvaviveka*

Shukavak Dasa (at HEM p. 293) briefly describes this work: "*Tattvaviveka* subtitled *Saccidānandānubhūtiḥ*. This work discusses the different precepts of the Vaiṣṇavas in relation to the ideas of prominent Oriental and Western philosophers such as Plato, Aristotle, Comte, Schopenhauer, Berkeley, and so on.

The work is composed in 48 Sanskrit verses with detailed Bengali commentary on each verse."

The work is epitomized in TVTSAS by Narasimha Brahmachari. Narasimha's treatment is too long to be reproduced here.

21.7 BHAKTIVINODA ṬHAKKURA, *Bhaktitattvaviveka*

"A collection of four essays he composed originally in Bengali on the deliberation of devotional principles. The first Hindi edition of this material was serialized in issues from the fourth and fifth years (1958-9) of *Śri Bhāgavata Patrika*, a spiritual magzine in Hindi published monthly from Śrī Keśavajī Gauḍīya Maṭha in Mathurā."

Premavilasa Dasa (p. 5), in his Introduction to BTV, remarks: "Quoting abundantly from Śrīla Rūpa Gosvāmin's *Bhaktirasāmṛtasindhu* and Śrīla Jīva Gosvāmi's *Bhaktisandarbha*, Bhaktivinoda Ṭhakura shows how to discriminate between genuine pure devotion to the lord and the many forms of adulterated devotion."

The titles of the four essays, respectively, are:

1. The Intrinsic Nature of *Bhakti*
2. An Analysis of the Semblance of *Bhakti*.
3. An Analysis of the Natural Attributes of *Bhakti*.
4. An Analysis of the Qualification for *Bhakti*.

21.8 BHAKTIVINODA ṬHAKKURA, *Jaiva-Dharma*

Originally written in Bengali, this lengthy work is published in 2002 from Gaudiya Vedanta Publications (location not given). The title page of this English translation reads: *Jaiva-Dharma. The Essential Function of the Soul*, and it is translated under the guidance of Tridaṇḍasvāmi Śrī Śrīmad Bhaktivedānta Nārāyaṇa Mahārāja, containing 1063 pages. We provide here the Table of Contents and pagination:

Chapter 1: The Eternal and Temporary *Dharmas* of the *Jīva* - 1
2: the *Nitya-Dharma* of the *Jīva* is Pure and Eternal - 17

21.9 BHAKTIVINODA ṬHAKKURA, *Āmnayasūtra*

Edited and translated from the Bengali original, together with the *Tattvaviveka* and *Tattvasūtra,* by Narasimha Brahmachari., Madras 1979 (abbrev. TVTTAS), our ET. (Another translation is by Kusakratha Dasa, edited by Purnaprajna Dasa (Vrndaban: Rasbihari Lal & Sons, 2006.) In a brief introduction the ẹditor tellls us that this work "is strictly an orthodox classical work completely based upon the revealed scriptures and presented in the traditional style in the form of one hundred and thirty aphorisms along with a short commentary of each aphorism in Sanskrit, quoted from the various ancient scriptures. It helps the aspirants in engaging their life in the devotional practices by imparting them an intrinsic knowledge of all the esoteric principles of reality which should be necessarily studied in the Bhajan life by all the inquisitive aspirants after Bhakti." It was written in 1890, according to Shukavak N. Dasa: according to him the work is "a Sanskrit composition based largely on the Upaniṣads, presented as 130 aphorisms, with a short commentary on each aphorism in Sanskrit comprising quotes from various scriptures. Included is a Bengali translation called the *Laghu-bhāṣya.*" (HEM, p. 288).

Summarized by Narasimha Brahmachari

1 (E231-232) "With obeisance at the lotus feet of supreme Lord Sri Krishna Chaitanya Chandra who descended as a world teacher, Thakur Srilal Bhakti Vinode has composed these one hundred and thirty numbers of aphorisms by the grace of Vaishnavas. These aphorisms are based upon the eight types of scriptural evidences (*pramāṇa*) and six type of signs (*liṅga*) accepted for the determination of the purport of the revealed Vedas and presented under the spiritual order. Let this be whole-heartedly learned by the devotees of the Lotus Feet of Lord Sri Chaitanya. Sense perception (*pratyakṣa*), inference (*anumāna*), analogy (*upamāna*), sound (*śabda*), tradition (*aitihya*), absence of acquirement (*abhāva* or *anupalabdhi*), presumption (*arthāpatti*) and probability (*sambhava*)–these are the eight types of evidence. Introduction (*upakrama*), termination (*upasaṃhāra*), practice (*abhyāsa*), product of originality (*apūrvatrāphala*), interpretation (*arthavāda*) and reason (*upapatti*)–these are the six signs used for the determination of the purport. Sound or the word is understood by its dual faculties known as *abhidhā* or the root-meaning and *lakṣaṇā* or the metaphorical meaning. The metaphorical meaning may be taken into consideration only when the root-meaning of the word becomes unintelligible.

"After thoroughly studying all the scriptures and knowing the self-revealed spiritual evidence of the Vedas to be the supreme among all others, we are presenting these aphorisms termed as 'Śrī Āmnāya Sūtra'."

2 (E232) "The Supreme Reality is the one without second."

3 (E232) "That Reality is eternally existent and also endowed with inconceivable infinite potency."

4 (E233) "The Reality is eternally endowed with transcendental qualifications."

5 (E233) "The Supreme Reality is simultaneously unqualified."

6 (E233) "Owing to the inconceivable potency of the Supreme, both the mutually opposite characters of qualifying

and non-qualifying natures are perfectly assimilated in the Supreme, beyond the scope of any controversy."

7 (E234) "Qualified phase of the Supreme Reality is the most prominent among the two, since the unqualified state is incomprehensible."

8 (E234) "That super-prominent qualified phase of the Supreme is eternally existent in the four-fold forms of *svarūpa* (divine form), *tadrūpa vaibhava* (divine variety), *jīva* (indivdual soul) and *pradhāna* (*māyā*, material cause of the phenomenal universe)."

9 (E235) "These four types of eternal revelations are simultaneously distinct and non-distinct from each other, which is a supra-logical fact."

10 (E235) *Hladinī, sandhinī* and *saṃvit*–these three are the dominating faculties of the one *pariśakti.*"

11 (E235-236) The same *pariśakti* acts as *antaraṅgā, bahiraṅgā* and *tatasthā.*"

12 (E236) "The *śakti* or the divine potency becomes activated by means of the glance of the qualified supreme principle."

13 (E236) The divine principle is realized in three different attributes."

14 (E237) "In the performance of gnosticism the divinity is realized as the unqualified transcendental Brahman."

15 (E237) "In the performance of *astānga yoga*, the divine principle is realized as the immanent *paramātman.*"

16 (E237) "Innumerable are the manifestations of the *paramātman.*"

17 (E238) "All the divine manifestations like *aṃśāvatāra, līlāvatāra, yugāvatāra,* etc., are the Supreme Lords endowed with the transcendental potency, viz. *citśakti.*"

18 (E238) "In the performance of *śuddhabhakti* or unalloyed devotion, the Supreme Realty is realized as Bhagavān, the fullest embodiment of divine personality."

19 (E238-239) "That Bhagavān is realized in three different forms called *aiśvarya* (majesty), *madhūrya* (sweetness), and *audārya* (magnificence)."

20 (E239) "Divine manifestations of Bhagavan descend to this mundane world, along with his transcendental abode, by the power of his own internal potency."

21 (E240) "Every divine manifestation is associated with the respective abode of the Supreme Reality."

22 "Divine effulgence is the abode of Brahman."

23 "Universe is the abode of *paramātman*."

24 (E241) "*Paravyoma vaikuntha* is the transcendental abode of Bhagawan."

25 (E241) "*Māyā* is the reflected image of the eternally manifested divine abode."

26 (E241-242) "*Māyā* is also denoted by the term *pradhāna*.

27 (E242) "*Sattvaguṇa, rajoguṇa* and *tamogūṇa* are the nature of *māyā*, by which it encovers the sentient spirits through gross and subtle bodies."

28 (E242) "Non-sentient beings like space, time, action (*karman*), etc., are constituted in that *māyā*.

29 (E242-243) "Phenomenal variety of the external *māyā* is the perverted reflection of its transcendental variedness."

30 (E243) "Individual souls are the atomic rays of *paramātman*–the spiritual sun."

31 (E244) "Because of their marginal character, the jīva-*souls* are capable of serving either in the transcendental abode of the Supreme Lord, or in the phenomenal universe of *māyā*.

32 (E244) "The essential nature of the *jīva*-souls is purely transcendental.

33 (E244) "Every *jīva*-soul is an atomic sentient principle endowed with individual ego.

34 (E245) "*Jīva*-souls are endowed with the nature of knowledge and the knower (by which it can know itself and the Supreme Reality).

35 (E245) "Because of their aversion to the Supreme Lord, the fallen *jīva*-souls are entangled in the ignorance of *māyā*.

36 (E245-246) "For this very reason they have undergone the illusion of self-oblivion."

37 (E246) "Therefore, also they have been entangled with the terrific bondage of the activities of desires."

38 (E246) "Although the *jīva*-souls are unalloyed sentience by their nature, the forgetfulness of the Supreme has put them in a miserable condition of suffering in this universe by identifying themselves with the subtle and gross coverings of mind and body."

39 (E247) "When the fallen *jīva*-soul turns towards the Supreme, then again he will become free from all the miseries and his natural character will be obtained."

40 (E247) "Transcendental realization is obtained in the vicinity of the Supreme Lord."

41 (E248) "The fallen *jīva*-souls undergo four types of worldly phases."

42 (E248) "Deluded *jīva*-souls enter the phase of elevationism (*karmadaśā*)."

43 (E248-249) "By the inductive knowledge of the self, the *jīva*-soul enters the phase of abnegation (*nirdvandva*)."

44 (E249) "Indifference to both of these phases is productive of an intermediary phase."

45 (E249) "At the appearance of *bhakti*, the *jīva*-soul enters the phase of transcendental sentiments."

46 (E250) "*Jīva*-souls inhabiting this universe are mostly involved in the phase of elevationism (*karman*).

47 (E250) "Scarcely ever these *jīva*-souls may beget discretion about the course of worldly life."

48 (E250) "The enquiry after means of securing release from the worldly bondage follows that discretion."

49 (E251) "That honest inquiry will be frustrated if the evil companies are eschewed."

50 (E251) "If the holy-company is availed, then the scriptural purport of means to the Supreme Reality will be interrogated."

51 (E252) "Those who profess *karmamarga* [the path of action] say that the routine religious activities prescribed by the scriptures of *karmamarga* are the means for securing the ultimate goal of life."

52 (E252) "Those others who say that the impersonal monistic knowledge of the self is the *abhidheya* or the means, are known as *jñānīs*."

53 (E253) "If the *karman* [action] is conducted for piety, that piety is productive of withdrawal from secondary objects and when that withdrawal favors the culture of transcendental bliss, in that case the *karman* may be accepted as a secondary means towards securing the ultimate goal of life."

54 (E253) "When the knowledge of the self favors the culture of transcendental bliss, then it may be accepted as a secondary means. *Karman* and *jñāna* (knowledge of the self) are never accepted as the primary means (*abhidheya*).

55 (E253-254) "Those who are fortunate among human beings know that the performance–which works in developing the realization of the transcendental variegatedness–it is the means."

56 (E254) "In the holy company the fortunate souls acquire firm faith in the unalloyed devotion to the Supreme Lord."

57 (E255) "That faith is a basic devotional faculty of the heart, which excludes the other secondary means like *karman* and *jñāna*."

58 (E255) "That faith is characterized by the sign of self-surrender."

59 (E255-256) "That faith leads an aspirant to take shelter at the holy feet of the spiritual preceptor."

60 (E256) "Shelter at the holy feet of the preceptor is followed by the nine-fold devotional performances."

61 (E256) 'Hearing about the divine name, divine form, divine attributes, divine sports etc. is an organ of *bhakti* known as *śravaṇa.*"

62 (E256-257) "Chanting and narrating about the divine name, form, attributes, sports, etc., are the stage of *bhakti* called '*kīrtana*'."

63 (E257) "Remembrance of the name, form, attributes sports etc. is the third organ of the nine-fold devotion, called '*smaraṇa*'."

64 (E257) "Serving the feet of the Supreme Lord or '*padasevana*' is the fourth organ of *bhakti.*"

65 (E258) "'*Ālocana*' or worshiping the Supreme Lord is the fifth organ of *bhakti.*

66 (E258-259) "Consecration of the articles, contemplating upon the Supreme Lord with sacred hymns, invocation, wearing the Vaishnavite signs and the flowers offered to the Lord, drinking the feet-wash, observing the austerities of *ekadaśī,* etc., are the organs of worship."

67 (E259) "'*Vandana*' or salutation is the sixth organ of *bhakti.*"

68. (E259-260) "*Dāsya*' or servitude is the seventh organ of *bhakti.*"

69 (E260) "*Sākhya*' or friendly attitude is the eighth organ of *bhakti.*"

70 (E260) "*Ātmanivedana* or self-surrender is the ninth organ of *bhakti.*"

71 (E261) "Ten types of evil propensities must be eschewed at the beginning of the devotional performances."

72 (261-262) "The ten types of evil propensities can be renounced only by the practice of humbleness, kindness and balanced withdrawal under the influence of *bhakti.* The fourfold performances of the monistic school or *yoga* and *karman* are not capable of relieving them."

73 (E262) "Along with the maturity of the devotional performances, all the evil obstacles disappear."

74 (E263) "Misidentification of the self, attachment to transitory objects, offences and weakness against temptations–these are the four types of evil acquaintances (*anartha*) inherent in the heart of the fallen souls."

75 (E263-264) "A skilful aspirant after *bhakti* gets away with these four-fold *anarthas* with the help of devotional performances and by the grace of the preceptor."

76 (D253) "Skill in the devotional services generates firm faith."

77 (E264-265) "Further increase in devotional skill generates a great relish in the heart of the aspirant."

78 (E265) "In due course of time the relish turns out to be firm attachment."

79 (E265-266) "The firm attachment in *bhakti* gradually turns into the state of transcendental sentiments (*bhāva*). Up to the acquiring of *bhāva* the performance is called '*sādhana bhakti*'."

80 (E266) "Since the mundane specialties like heaven etc. are the product of ignorance, they are not the goal to be coveted by the *jīva*-souls."

81 (E267) "Attaining the state of non-distinction also is not the *summum bonum* of life."

82 (E267) "States of phenomenal distinction and non-distinction have nothing to do with the spiritual matters, but occasionally they may serve as the means" (see 53-54 above).

83 (E268) "But they are not commendable in every case."

84 (E268) "Transcendental variety is the final attainment of the *jīva*-souls."

85 (E268-269) "Transcendental sentiment arisen in the heart is called '*rati*'."

86 (E269) "When the '*rati*' or sentiments become hilarious and unalloyed, then it is denoted as '*prīti*'.

87 (E269-270) "When the '*prīti*' is endowed with extreme affection it is termed '*prema*'."

88 (E270) "When the *prema* is associated with resolute confidence it is called '*praṇaya*'."

89 (E270) "When the *praṇaya*' is colored with the semblance of diplomacy, that sentimental diversity if known as '*māna*'."

90 (E270-271) "The *prema* associated with the extreme liquidity of heart is known as *sneha*."

91 (E271) "The nature of *sneha* when it becomes intensely covetous is called *rāga*."

92 (E271) "The *rāga* which perpetually generates ever new freshness between its object and the shelter is termed '*anurāga*'."

93 (E272) "The *anurāga* intoxicated with unprecedented excellence is called '*mahābhāva*'."

94 (E272) "When the permanent sentiment or *rati* is fortified with four types of *sāmagrī* or ingredients it becomes *rasa* or the transcendental mellowing deliciousness."

95 (E273) "Primary *rasas* are of five types and the secondary ones are of seven."

96 (E273) "The first primary *rasa* is known as *śānta rasa*."

97 (E273) "The second primary *rasa* is *dāsya rasa*'."

98 (E274) *Sākhya rasa* is the third primary *rasa*."

99 (E274) "*Vātsalya rasa* is the fourth primary *rasa*."

100 (E274-275) "*Madhura rasa* is the fifth primary *rasa*."

101 (E275) "These five primary *rasas* are successively superior to each other."

102 (E275-276) "The seven types of secondary *rasa* are *hāsya, anubhūta, vīra, karuṇā, raudra, bhayānaka* and *bibhatsa*."

103 (E276) "When secondary *rasas* are mixed together with the primary ones the ocean of *bhakti rasa* gets swollen."

104 (E276-277) "*Sāmagrī* in the transcendental sentiments is of four types."

105 (E277) "The first *sāmagrī* is known as *vibhava*, and it is of two types, viz., *ālambana* and *uddīpana*."

106 (E277) "The second *sāmagrī* is known as *anubhāva*. It is of thirteen types."

107 (E277) "*Sāttvika bhāva* is the third *sāmagrī*, and it is of eight types."

108 (E278) "The fourth *sāmagrī* is known as *sanchāri* or *vyabhicāri*, and it is of thirty-three types."

109 (E278) "*Bhaktirasa* is the transcendental distinctive principle pertaining to the Supreme Reality and it is entirely free from the unwholesomeness of *māyā*."

110 (E278-279) "All the *rasas* in their entirety are found only in the sports of Lord Krishna."

111 (E279) "Krishna-*līlā* should be sought after in the spontaneous spiritual service of the unalloyed devotion."

112 (E279-280) "It is the ighest attainment of the *jīva*-souls to enter the field of *kṛṣṇalīla*, after gaining one's own spiritual form."

113 (E280) "Spiritual service and bliss of devotion to Lord Krishna are manifested in the supra-mundane plane in the transcendental form."

114 (E280-281) "Various spiritual places mentioned above are attainable by the *jīva*-souls according to their individual spiritual merits."

·115 (E281) *Vaidhi bhakti*, as codified by the scriptures, is generated by the faith in the transcendental divinity."

116 (E281-282) "The origin of *rāgānuga bhakti* is the strongest inclination after following the spiritual services of Vṛndāvana."

117 (E282) "*Vaidhi bhakti* is associated or mixed with the majestic aspect of the Supreme Lord."

118 (E282) "*Rāgānuga bhakti* is absolutely unmixed and quite stronger than *vaidhi bhakti*."

119 (E282-283) "The performances of *sādhana bhakti* are extended only up to *asakti* or the firm attachment to the Supreme. It follows from *śrāddha, sādhusaṅga, bhajanakriyā, anarthanivṛtti, niṣṭha, rucī* and then *asakti*."

120 (E283) "*Bhakti* from *bhāva* up to *mahābhāva* is known as *siddha bhakti* or the 'absolutely transcendental principle' of devotion. This *siddha bhakti* is of the form of *saṃvit-śakti* incorporating the blissful essence of *hlādini*."

121 (E283-284) "When the phenomenal propensities of the *jīva*-soul are nullified, once again it attains the normal spiritual characters. This is called *mukti*."

122 (E284) *Mukti* is of two types, namely *svarūpasiddha* and *vastusiddha*."

123 (E284-285) "That *mukti* is the constant follower of *bhakti*."

124 (E285) "Sometimes *bhakti* may accept the services of *jñāna* and *vairāgya* (knowledge and withdrawal)."

125 (E285) "By nature, *bhakti* is absolute and it is independent of knowledge and withdrawal."

126 (E286) "That *bhakti* is the glory of the unalloyed character of the *jīva*-souls."

127 (E286) "Fallen souls may acquire that *bhakti* only in the holy association."

128 (E286-287) "At time this *bhakti* is directly acquired by the grace of Lord Krishna."

129 (E287) "This *bhakti* is spread in the world by the deductive way of Vedic and preceptorial succession."

130 (E288) "Human effort itself is the mother of destiny. Therefore, with all the efforts one should serve the holy persons and scriptures."

22.1 VṚNDĀVANA TARKĀLAMKĀRA (20th century), *Saṃkṣepabhagavatāmṛta-Rasikaraṅgadā*

Edited Murshidabad 1870; Calcutta 1934.

23 GAURAKIŚORA GOSVĀMI (1838-1915)

Wikipedia provides the following: "Gaurakiśora Dāsa Bābajī (1838-1915) is a well-known *ācārya* from the Gauḍīya Vaiṣṇava tradition of Hinduism, and is regarded as a *mahātmā* or saint by followers of his lineage. During his lifetime Gaurakiśora Dāsa Bābajī became famous for his teachings on the process of Bhakti Yoga and for his unorthodox *avadhūta*-like behavior as a *sādhu*, or *bābajī* in Vṛndavan.

"He was born on November 17, 1838 in a simple mercantile family in the village of Vagyana, near to 'Tepkhola' in the district of Faridpur, part of modern day Bangladesh. After the death of his wife when he was thirty years old, he accepted the life of a Bābajī in the Gauḍīya Vaiṣṇava tradition under the tutelage of Jagannātha Dāsa Bābajī, after meeting the latter's disciple, Bhagavat Dāsa Bābajī. He became a mendicant, staying in the holy cities of Vṛndavana and Navadvīpa, deeply absorbed in singing and chanting the sacred names of Rādhā and Kṛṣṇa (Bhajan).

"In 1900, Gaurakiṣora Dāsa Bābajī gave initiation (*dīkṣā*) to Bhaktisiddhānta Sarasvatī Ṭhakkura. The former gave the latter the name 'Varṣabhanavī devī dayitā Dāsa'. Gaurakiśora Dāsa Bābajī's legacy would live on in his only disciple Bhaktisiddhānta, as he would later go on to preach all over India with his Gauḍīya Maṭh. Bhaktisiddhānta in turn gave *dīkṣā* to A.C. Bhaktivedānta Svāmi Prabhupāda, who preached the philosophy and culture of the Gauḍīya Vaiṣṇava traditi onon a worldwide basis through his International Society for Krishna Consciousness."

23.1 GAURA KIŚORA GOSVĀMI, *Tattvasandarbha-Suvarnālaṭā*

Edited.

24.1 AKṢAYA KUMĀRA ŚĀSTRI (1927?), *Prameyaratnāvalī-Prabhā*

The author edited Baladeva's work, with Kṛṣṇadeva Vedāntavāgīśa's *Kāntimālā* and his own *Prabhā,* from Calcutta in 1927.

25.1 ANUPANARĀYAṆA TARKAŚIROMAṆI (20th cent.), Commentary on Jīva Gosvāmin's *Bhāgavatasandarbha*

Edited.

BIBLIOGRAPHY AND ABBREVIATIONS

Avalon 1985 = *Brahma Saṃhitā with Commentary by Jīva Goswāmī and Viṣṇu-sahasra-nāma with Commentary by Śaṃkarācārya*. Edited by Arthur Avalon. Delhi: Bharatiya Vidya Prakashan, reprinted March 91985

BG2000 = *Śrīmad Bhagavad-Gītā with the Bhāvānuvāda of the Sārārtha-Vsarṣiṇī Ṭīkā by the crest-jewel of spiritual preceptors and guardian of the Śrī Gauḍīya sampradāya Śrī Viśvanātha Cakravartī Ṭhākura and Sārārtha-Variṣiṇī Prakāśikā-Vṛtti by Tridaṇḍisvāmī Śrī Śrīmad Bhakti-vedānta Nārāyaṇa Mahārāja.* Gaudiya Vedanta Samiti: New Delhi, 2000

Bib 3 = *Bibliography. Encyclopedia of Indian Philosophies*, Volume I. Compiled by Karl H. Potter. Delhi: Motilal Banarsidass, 3rd revised edition 1995.
An updated on-line version can be found at http://faculty.washington.edu/kpotter

BP = *Bhāgavatapurāṇa*

Brzezinski 2007 = Jan Brzezinski, "Jīva Goswami: Biography and Bibliography", Journal of Vaishnava Studies 15.2, 2007, pp. 51-80

BTV = *Bhakti-Tattva-Viveka. Deliberation upon the True nature of Devotion*. Composed by Śrīla Bhaktivinoda Ṭhakura. Translated from the Hindi edition of Śrī Śrīmad Bhaktivedānta Nārāyaṇa Mahārāja. Vrndavan: Gaudiya Vedanta Publication, 1997, 2001, 2006

CC = *Caitanya Caritāmṛta* of Kṛṣṇadāsa Kavirāja

Chatterjee 1972 = *Bhagavatsandarbha by Śri Jīva Gosvāmin*. Edited by Chinmayi Chatterjee. Jadavpur University Sanskrit Series 2. Calcutta: Jadavpur University, 1972

Chatterjee 1980 = *Śrī-Prītisandarbha of Śrī Jīva Gosvāmi*. Edited by Dr. Chinmayi Chatterjee. Calcutta: Jadavpur University, 1988.

Corpus = *A Corpus of Indian Studies. Essaysin Honour of Professor Gaurinath Sastri*. Calcutta: Sanskrit pustak Bhandra, 1980

Dasa 2005 = *Śrī Bhakti-Sandarbha. The Fifth Book of the Śrī Bhagavata-Sandarbhaḥ also known as Śrī Ṣaṭ-Sandarbhaḥ by Aṣṭottara-śata Śrī-śata Śrī-Śrīmad Śrīla Jīva Gosvāmi Prabhu pāda*. Translated by Dr. Satya Nārāṇa Dāsa, with an Introduction by Bruce Martin. Three volumes. Vrndavana, Mathura, U.P.: Jīva Institute, 2005

De 1961 = Sushil Kumar De, *Early History of the Vaiṣṇava Faith and Movement in Bengal*. Second edition. Calcutta: Firma K. L. Mukhopadhyay, 1961

Delmonico 1989 = Neal Delmonico, "For that sacred taste: the *rasa* problem in the works of Rupā Gosvāmin", in N.N. Bhattacharyya, ed., *Medieval Bhakti Movements in India: Śrī Caitanya Quincentenary Commemoration Volume*. New Delhi: Munshiram Manoharlal Publishers Pvt. Ltd., 1989, pp. 325-336

Delmonico 1997 (1) = Neil Delmonico, "The Blazing Sappphire: a translation in progress of Rupa Gosvamin's Ujjvala-nīlamaṇi", Journal of Vaisnava Studies 5.1, 1997, 21-52

Delmonico 1997 (2) = Neil Delmonico, "Rādhā: the quintessential Gopī (The fourth chapter of Rūpa Gosvāmins' Ujjvala-nīlamāṇi)", Journal of Vaisnava Studies 5.4, 1997, pp. 111-137

Dimock 1999 = *Caitanya Caritaṃṛta of Kṛṣṇadāsa Kavirāja*. A Translation and Commentary by Edward C. Dimock jr., with an Introduction by Edward C. Dimock Jr. and Tony K. Stewart. Edited b Tony K. Stewart. Cambridge, Mass and London, Englan: Harvard University Press, 1999

Elkman 1986 - *Jīva Gosvāmin's Tattvasandarbha. A Study on the Philosophical and Sectarian development of the Gauḍoya Vaiṣṇava Movement.* Delhi: Motilal Banarsidass, 1985

Haberman 2003 = *The Bhaktirasāmṛtasindhu of Rūpa Gosvāmin*, translated with introduction and notes by David L. Haberman (Indira Gandhi National Centre for the Arts, New Delhi and Motilal Banarsidass Publisher Pvt. Ltd.), Delhi 2003

HEM = *Hindu Encounter with Modernity. Kedarnath Datta' Bhaktivinoda, Vaiṣṇava Theologian.* By Shukavak N. Dasa. Los Angeles: Sanskrit Religious Institute, 1999

HIP = Surendranath Dasgupta, *History of Indian Philosophy*, 5 volumes. Cambridge: Cambridge University Press, 1922. First Indian edition, Motilal Banarsidass, Delhi, 1975.

ISC = Amūlyacaṇdra Sena, *Itihāsera śrīcaitanya*. Calcutta: Kiraṇa Kumāra Rāya through Sārasvata Lāibreri, 1965

JAOS = Journal of the American Oriental Society (New Haven). 1 (1843) - 133.1 (2013) (PJ2.A62) [electronic]

JCM = *Caitanya Maṅgala* of Jayāṇaṇḍa Mīśra, ed. Bimenbehari Majumdar and Sukhamay Mukhopadhyay. Calcutta: The Asiatic Society, 1971

KCC = *Kṛṣṇacaitanyacaritāmṛta* of Murāri Gupta, ed. Mṛṇālakānti Ghoṣa, with Bengali trans. by Haridāsa Dāsa. 4th ed. Calcutta: by the editor, 459 GA [=1945 A.D.]

KCCM = *Kṛṣṇacaitanyacaritāmṛta Mahākāvya* of Kavikarṇapūra (Paramānanda Sena), ed. with intro. and Bengali trans. by Prāṇkiśora Gosvāmī. Calcutta: by the editor, n.d. [1377 BS]

Klostermaier 1974 = Klaus Klostermaier, "The *Bhakti-rasamṛtasindhubindu* of Viśvanātha Cakravartin", Journal of the American Oriental Society 94, 1974, pp. 96-107.

LCM = Caitanya Maṅgala of Locana Dāsa, ed. Mṛṇālakānti Ghoṣa, with the pdas of Locana Dāsa. Calcutta: 1354 BS

Mahanama = Mahanamabrata Brahmachari, *Vaiṣṇava Vedānta*. Calcutta: Das Gupta and Co. Ltd., 1974

Majumdar 1969 = A. K. Majumdar, *Caitanya: His Life and Doctrine*. Bombay: Bharatiya Vidya Bhavan, 1969

Narang 1984 = (Dr. (Mrs.) Sudesh Narang, *The Vaiṣṇava Philosophy (according to Baladeva Vidyābhuṣaṇa)*. Delhi: Nag Publishers, 1984

NCat = New Catalogus Catalogorum (V. Raghavan, K. Kunjunni Raja et al., eds.). Madras 1949-. In progress.

PBC = *Śṛī Prema Bhakti-candrikā. The Moonrays of Loving Devotion.* Srila Narottam dāsa Thākkura Mahāśaya. Bengali texts, roman transliterations, English translations by Visvanatha Cakravarti Thakura. Isvara dasa and Touchstone Media, Vndavana 2000

Rosen 1991 = Steven Rosen, *The Six Goswamis of Vrindavan.* Aylesbury, Bucks, Englaṇ: FOLK BOOKS, 1990; Revised edition published in 1991 in conjunction with Bhaktivedanta Book Trust Ltd. P.O. Box 324, Borehamwood, Herts, WD6 1NB, U. K.

Sarkar 1932 = Jadunath Sarkar, *Chaitanya's Life and Teaching.* Calcutta: B. C. Sarkar and Sons, 1932

SS = *Sarasaṅgrahaḥ (A Work on Gauḍīya Vaiṣṇavism) attributed to Rūpa Kavirāja.* Edited by Krishnagopal Goswami Astri. Asutosh Sanskrit Series Vol. III. Calcutta: University of Calcutta, 1949

TVTSAS = *Tattva Viveka, Tattva Sutra & Amnaya Sutra* by Bhakti Vinode Tnhakur. Englsh rendering from the Bengali origin by Sri Narasimha Brahmachari. Madras: Sree Gaudiya Math, 1979

Upadesamrta 1997 = *Śri Ūpadeśāmṛta. The Ambrosial Advice of Śrī Rūpa Gosvāmin.* With the commentaries of Śrī Rāma-ramaṇa dāsa Gosvāmi, Śrī Bhaktivinoda Ṭhakura and Ṭrī Bhaktisiddhānta Sarasvatī Gosvāmii 'Prabhupāda'. Translated from the Hindi editoin of Ṭrī Ṭrimad Bhaktivedānta Nārāyaṇa Mahārāj. Mathura: Gaudiya Vedanta Publications, 1997

Vedantasyamantaka = *Vedanta-Syamantaka (of Rādhādāmodara), being a Treatise on Bengal Vaiṣṇava Philosophy*. Edited with Introduction, Notes and Appendices by Umesh Chandra Bhattacharjee. Lahore: Moti Lal Banarsi Dass, 333

GLOSSARY-INDEX

activity (*pravṛtti*) - 59, 84, 116, 176, 179, 221-223, 263, 301-302, 312-314, 316, 325-326
, devotional - 169, 307
actor (*kartṛ; anukartā*) - 120, 194, 210-211, 261, 285
ādhunika, see contemporary
ādi, see beginning
adultery - 43, 218
advaita, see nonduality; inseparability
Advaita Vedānta - 81, 83, 106, 145, 150-151, 153-154, 156, 173-174, 186-187, 191, 204, 295
Advaita Ācārya (15th c.) - 18-19, 21, 24, 26, 33, 56
Advaitamataranda (Sārvabhauma) - 83
Advaitasiddhi (Madhusūdana Sarasvatī) - 145
adventitious (*āropita*) - 154
aesthetics (*rasaśāstra*) - 24, 30, 36-37, 45, 99-100, 211
affection (*bhāva; prema; priyatā*) - 112, 115-116, 140, 157, 206,208, 225, 243, 305-306, 329, 342
, parental - 99, 108, 110, 112, 116-117, 119, 207-208
āgama, see scripture
age (*yuga; dvāpara*) - 20, 24-25, 57, 80, 124, 130, 149, 163, 228, 237, 255
, old - 223, 282, 306, 315
agent (*kartṛ, kartā, karmin*) - 107, 179, 249, 262-263, 288, 290
aggression - 26, 306
agitation - 111, 138, 301, 303, 312
ahaṃkāra, see ego; consciousness, phenomenal; consciousness, self- or gross
aiśvarya, see majesty; greatness; power
12.9 *Aiśvaryakādambinī* (Viśvanātha Cakravarti) - **252**
Ajita - 132
akhaṇḍa, see indivisible
ākhḍā, see monastery
ākṛti, see appearance
24 Akṣaya Kumāra Śāstri (1927?) - **333**
Alaṃkārakaustubha (Kanapuri Kavi) - 67

, instrumental or efficient (*nimitta-*) - 182, 184, 236-238, 259, 265
, material (*upādaṇa-*) - 135, 181-182, 184, 236-240, 259, 265, 288-289, 323
celibate, celibacy - 38, 42, 44
ceṣṭā, see act(ion), physical
cetana, see consciousness
Chakravarti, Banu - Bāṇā - 50
Chakravarti, Janārdana - 56, 65
Chakravarti, Jāṇhavīkumāra - 47
Chakravarti, Narahari - 57, 144
Chakravarti, Ramakanta - 13-72
change (*vikāra*) - 108, 181, 184, 261-262, 290-291
-ful, subject to change (*-rahita*) - 162-163, 176-177, 186, 288
-less or inability to (*avikāritva*) - 164, 175, 288
changing (*kīrtana)* - 139, 237, 316
chanting - 97-98, 141, 223, 232, 234, 238, 247, 316, 332
character, manifest (*vyūha*) - 127, 129, 131, 135, 139, 161-164, 179-180, 192-193, 199, 235, 264, 288, 315, 323-325, 331
characteristic(s) (*lakṣaṇa*) - 32, 58-59, 76, 97, 99-100, 122, 124, 134, 150-151, 155, 164, 167, 179, 186, 188, 192, 197, 209, 223, 230-231, 238, 247, 264, 266, 271, 273, 278
Chatterjee, Bankimchandra (1900?) - 42, 67
Chatterjee, Chinmayi - 151, 189, 204-213
Chatterjee 1972 - 151, 172, 386
Chatterjee 1980 - 204, 386
Chatterjee,Suniti Kumar - 13, 46, 65, 71
Chattopadhyaya, Bankimchandra, see Chatterjee, Bankimchandra
Chattopadhyaya, Gita - 51, 69
Chaudhuri, Acyutaran - 51
Chaudhuri, Bāsantī - 69

jāti, see class; universal property
jaundice - 140-141, 307, 316
Jayadeva- 13-14, 17,, 46, 67, 70-71, 75
Jayānanda - 51, 53, 69, 80, 89-91, 338
jealousy - 31, 45, 111, 247
Jessore - 93
jewel (*syamantaka*)- 109, 252, 335
jīva, see (individual) self
7 Jīva Gosvāmin (1513-1598) - 21, 24-26, 56, 59-61, 66-67, 102, 105, 112, 123, 136-137, 143, **144-219**, 220, 250, 255-256, 267, 281-282, 298, 319, 333, 336-337
Jīvanalāla - 305
jñāna, see knowledge; awareness; consciousness
17.1 *Jñānasārataraṅginī* (Bhavanīcaraṇa Tarkabhūṣaṇa) - **298**
joker (*vidūṣaka*) - 123
joy (*ānanda*) - 30-32, 35, 38, 54, 58, 60, 86, 101-102, 107, 113-115, 121, 127, 139, 149, 167, 169, 175, 179, 205-208, 210, 212, 216, 223, 244-246, 257, 261-262, 271-273, 275, 280, 291, 294, 304, 308, 312-315
    , God's - 29, 159-160
jug, see pot
juggler - 43
jugupsā, see disgust
Kailāsa - 217
kāla, see time
Kālī - 60, 77
    , age of (*-yuga*), see *yuga, kāli*
Kālikā Purāṇa - 294
Kālindī (river) - 35
Kalkin - 132
kāma, see desire; libido
    -daśa, see attitude, amorous
Kamakala (Mulk Raj Anand) - 61
Kāmarūpa, see Assam
Kāmasūtras (Vātsyāyana) - 61

pervasion (*vyāpti*) - 175, 177, 216, 262
pervasive, all- (*vyāpaka-*) - 33, 164, 167, 187, 198, 286-287
phala, see act(ion), result/fruit of
phenomenal (*prākṛta*) - 30, 131, 137, 155-156, 162-163,, 165-168, 177, 179, 182, 184-185, 188, 191-192, 194, 205, 274, 323-324, 328, 331
piety - 94, 222-223, 326
pilgrim - 14, 22
-age - 22. 24. 81-82, 84-85, 87-88, 225
planet, heavenly- 223
Plato - 318
play (*līlā*) - 77, 104, 114, 122, 197, 242, 278, 308
(drama) - 42, 219, 223
, Kṛṣṇa's - 23, 34-35, 97, 116, 221, 225, 276-277
pleasure (*sukha*) - 30-32, 75, 124, 128, 139, 208, 218, 232, 245, 272, 310, 313
, amorous - 233
, extreme (*pramāda*) - 206
-energy - 250
, God's - 301, 304
, gradation of -245
, worldly (*bhukti*) - 101, 283
poem, poetry, poet - 14-17, 24, 30-31, 36, 39-41, 43, 45-46, 49, 65, 75-76, 86, 95, 143, 210-212, 218-219, 227 281, 299
poison- 34
pollution - 140
pond, see Rādhākuṇḍa
poor, poverty - 14, 25-26, 38, 42
possession (*āveśa*) - 132, 165, 169-170, 294, 311
potency, see power
power (*śakti; aiśvarya*) - 26. 32-33. 35. 59-60, 94, 103, 112, 115, 117-118, 133, 138, 150, 153, 155, 158, 184,192, 197, 200, 209, 219, 244, 250, 259, 262, 278, 287-288
, absolute; great (*mahā-*) - 59, 102, 134, 166, 293